Emerging Topics and Technologies in Information Systems

Miltiadis D. Lytras
Universisty of Patras, Greece

Patricia Ordóñez de Pablos
Universidad de Olviedo, Spain

INFORMATION SCIENCE REFERENCE

Hershey · New York

Director of Editorial Content: Kristin Klinger
Managing Editor: Jamie Snavely
Assistant Managing Editor: Carole Coulson
Typesetter: Larissa Vinci
Cover Design: Lisa Tosheff
Printed at: Yurchak Printing Inc.

Published in the United States of America by
    Information Science Reference (an imprint of IGI Global)
    701 E. Chocolate Avenue, Suite 200
    Hershey PA 17033
    Tel: 717-533-8845
    Fax: 717-533-8661
    E-mail: cust@igi-global.com
    Web site: http://www.igi-global.com

and in the United Kingdom by
    Information Science Reference (an imprint of IGI Global)
    3 Henrietta Street
    Covent Garden
    London WC2E 8LU
    Tel: 44 20 7240 0856
    Fax: 44 20 7379 0609
    Web site: http://www.eurospanbookstore.com

    Library of Congress Cataloging-in-Publication Data

Emerging topics and technologies in information sytems / Miltiadis D. Lytras and Patricia Ordonez de Pablos, editors.
    p. cm.
 Includes bibliographical references and index.
 Summary: "This book communicates the various challenges and great opportunities that information systems research produces"--Provided by publisher.
 ISBN 978-1-60566-222-0 (hardcover) -- ISBN 978-1-60566-223-7 (ebook)
 1. Management information systems. 2. Information technology--Technological innovations. 3. Information resources management. I. Lytras, Miltiadis D., 1973- II. Pablos, Patricia Ordonez de.
 HD30.213.E44 2009
 658.4'038011--dc22
                    2008033933

British Cataloguing in Publication Data

A Cataloguing in Publication record for this book is available from the British Library.

To Elvira and Joaquín, my parents
- Patricia

Table of Contents

Preface xiv

Chapter I
Measuring and Reporting Technological Capital in Companies 1
    Patricia Ordóñez de Pablos, University of Oviedo, Spain
    Miltiadis D. Lytras, Universisty of Patras, Greece

Chapter II
Revisiting Agility to Conceptualize Information Systems Agility 19
    Pankaj, Indiana University of Pennsylvania, USA
    Micki Hyde, Indiana University of Pennsylvania, USA
    Arkalgud Ramaprasad, University of Illinois at Chicago, USA
    Suresh K. Tadisina, Southern Illinois University Carbondale, USA

Chapter III
Global Understanding Environment: Applying Semantic and Agent Technologies to
Industrial Automation 55
    Vagan Terziyan, University of Jyväskylä, Finland
    Artem Katasonov, University of Jyväskylä, Finland

Chapter IV
Targeting E-Commerce to Chinese Audiences and Markets: Managing Cultural and Regional
Challenges 88
    Jeff Hsu, Fairleigh Dickinson University, USA

Chapter V
Enterprise Resource Planning System: Issues and Implementation 102
    Edward T. Chen, University of Massachusetts Lowell, USA

Chapter VI
A Secure Characteristics of Wireless Ad-Hoc Networks 115
    Sandip Vijay, I.I.T. Roorkee, India
    S. C. Sharma, I.I.T. Roorkee, India

Chapter VII

A Survey on Approaches to Adaptation on the Web.. 136
Jorge Marx Gómez, Oldenburg University, Germany
Thanh Tran, Karlsruhe University, Germany

Chapter VIII

A Personalized Portal on the Basis of Semantic Models and Rules.. 153
Jorge Marx Gómez, Oldenburg University, Germany
Tran Duc, Karlsruhe University, Germany

Chapter IX

British Consumers' Attitudes and Acceptance of Mobile Advertising 165
Sylvie Laforet, University of Sheffield, UK
Hannah Limahelu, University of Sheffield, UK

Chapter X

Determinants of ERP Implementations: An Empirical Study in Spanish Companies....................... 180
Javier de Andrés, University of Oviedo, Spain
Pedro Lorca, University of Oviedo, Spain
Jose Emilio Labra, University of Oviedo, Spain

Chapter XI

Emerging Topics and Technologies in Information Systems... 198
Jaakko Ikävalko, Helsinki University of Technology, Finland
Seppo J. Hänninen, Helsinki University of Technology, Finland
Ari Serkkola, Helsinki University of Technology, Finland
Ilkka Kauranen, Helsinki University of Technology, Finland

Chapter XII

Technology-Related Privacy Concerns: An Emerging Challenge... 208
Cliona McParland, Dublin City University, Ireland
Regina Connolly, Dublin City University, Ireland

Chapter XIII

Fear of Flying and Virtual Environments: An Introductory Review 221
Giovanni Vincenti, Gruppo Vincenti S.r.l, Italy

Chapter XIV

A Context-Based Approach for Supporting Knowledge Work with Semantic Portals...................... 231
Thomas Hädrich, Martin-Luther-University Halle-Wittenberg, Germany
Torsten Priebe, University of Regensburg, Germany

Chapter XV

A Survey of Web Service Discovery Systems 254

    Duy Ngan Le, Nanyang Technological University, Singapore

    Angela Goh, Nanyang Technological University, Singapore

    Cao Hoang Tru, Ho Chi Minh City University of Technology, Viet Nam

Chapter XVI

User Relevance Feedback in Semantic Information Retrieval 270

    Antonio Picariello, Università di Napoli Federico II, Italy

    Antonio M. Rinaldi, Università di Napoli Federico II, Italy

Chapter XVII

A Preliminary Study toward Wireless Integration of Patient Information System 282

    Abdul-Rahman Al-Ali, American University of Sharjah, UAE

    Tarik Ozkul, American University of Sharjah, UAE

    Taha Landolsi, American University of Sharjah, UAE

Compilation of References 297

About the Contributors 325

Index 331

Detailed Table of Contents

Preface xiv

Chapter I

Measuring and Reporting Technological Capital in Companies 1
Patricia Ordóñez de Pablos, University of Oviedo, Spain
Miltiadis D. Lytras, Universisty of Patras, Greece

The chapter addresses the importance of knowledge-based resources proposing indicators to measure and report technological capital in companies. The first part of the chapter develops a conceptual framework to analyze organizational learning and its outcomes. It focuses on the strategy perspective of organizational learning, addressing its ontology, contributions, and problematics. The second part is focused on a particular type of knowledge—the technological capital—that is institutionalized knowledge in the form of technologies. This section proposes a map for the different types of technological capital of companies: idiosyncratic, core, ancillary, and compulsory. The chapter shows the results of a case study with European firms measuring and reporting technological capital. Finally the chapter summarizes main conclusions for management.

Chapter II

Revisiting Agility to Conceptualize Information Systems Agility 19
Pankaj, Indiana University of Pennsylvania, USA
Micki Hyde, Indiana University of Pennsylvania, USA
Arkalgud Ramaprasad, University of Illinois at Chicago, USA
Suresh K. Tadisina, Southern Illinois University Carbondale, USA

There is no systematic study of Information Systems (IS) agility in academic and practitioner IS literature and the concept is not well defined. For rigorous academic studies of IS agility, a proper definition/conceptualization of IS agility is needed. To fulfill this objective, existing published work on agility is analyzed. The analysis demonstrates that the existing definitions may need improvement to aid in arriving at a definition of IS agility. A new definition of agility that captures its core properties is proposed. The advantages of this definition over existing definitions is demonstrated and it is used to define IS Agility. Salient features of an agile IS are discussed and the utility of the proposed definition in arriving at attributes of an agile IS is demonstrated. Efficacy and validity of the proposed definition is demonstrated through interviews with IS executives from a diverse set organization. Lastly, avenues for future research are proposed.

Chapter III

Global Understanding Environment: Applying Semantic and Agent Technologies to
Industrial Automation 55

Vagan Terziyan, University of Jyväskylä, Finland
Artem Katasonov, University of Jyväskylä, Finland

Industry pushes a new type of Internet characterized as the Internet of Things, which represents a fusion of the physical and digital worlds. The technology of the Internet of Things opens new horizons for industrial automation, that is, automated monitoring, control, maintenance planning, and so forth, of industrial resources and processes. Internet of Things definitely needs explicit semantics, even more than the traditional Web – for automatic discovery and interoperability among heterogeneous devices and also to facilitate the behavioral coordination of the components of complex physical-digital systems. In this chapter, the authors describe their work towards the Global Understanding Environment (GUN), a general middleware framework aimed at providing means for building complex industrial systems consisting of components of different nature, based on the semantic and the agent technologies. The authors present the general idea and some emergent issues of GUN and describe the current state of the GUN realization in the UBIWARE platform. As a specific concrete case, they use the domain of distributed power network maintenance. In collaboration with the ABB Company, we have developed a simple prototype and vision of potential add-value this domain could receive from introducing semantic and agent technologies, and GUN framework in particular.

Chapter IV

Targeting E-Commerce to Chinese Audiences and Markets: Managing Cultural and Regional
Challenges.. 88

Jeff Hsu, Fairleigh Dickinson University, USA

The market for e-commerce to Chinese audiences is one which has tremendous potential, given the fact that the number of potential users and customers is projected to exceed that of English-speaking Western users. However, managing the host of cultural issues that come up is an important need which must be met. This chapter examines the cultural issues which are relevant to sites targeted at China and Chinese-speaking audiences, including user and consumer behavior patterns, categorizing China using Hofstede's cultural dimensions, examining traditional and historical attitudes, and addressing business issues including trust, payment, and infrastructure challenges. In the chapter design principles based on these are proposed, as well as an examination of the differences between the cultures of China, Taiwan, Hong Kong, and Singapore.

Chapter V

Enterprise Resource Planning System: Issues and Implementation 102

Edward T. Chen, University of Massachusetts Lowell, USA

Enterprise Resource Planning (ERP) is the method of trying to unify all processes within an organization into one software system or database. Enterprise Resource Planning Projects should not be entered into lightly. Not only are ERP projects a new software program to learn, but they are a new way of thinking. This chapter provides a brief history of ERP; follows by the advantages and disadvantages of ERP for organizations considering the adoption of ERP. The next section introduces various strategies of ERP implementation with a list of ERP software vendors. ERP is a long-term IT investment. The total cost of ownership is analyzed and discussed with several cases of ERP implementation.

Chapter VI

A Secure Characteristics of Wireless Ad-Hoc Networks.. 115

Sandip Vijay, I.I.T. Roorkee, India

S. C. Sharma, I.I.T. Roorkee, India

This chapter reviews the secure characteristics of mobile devices that can use wireless networks (ad-hoc) almost any where and any time, by using one or more wireless network technologies. Currently, most computers communicate with each other by using wired networks. This approach is well suited for stationary computers, but it is not appropriate for mobile devices. These technologies enable the use of infrastructured networks (3GPP) and ad-hoc networks. Furthermore, the authors describe the gateway specification, requirement for implementation for ad-hoc networks. The minimum, essential, and additional functional requirements for effective functionality of gateway are presented in tabular form. At the end, the future functional requirement and the features of multiple ad-hoc networks are also described.

Chapter VII

A Survey on Approaches to Adaptation on the Web.. 136

Jorge Marx Gómez, Oldenburg University, Germany

Thanh Tran, Karlsruhe University, Germany

Approaches to adaptation have been proposed by many different research communities, Hypermedia System and Intelligent Tutoring in particular. The task of adaptation breaks down to a mediation of resource provision and resource demand. In doing so, it is necessary to obtain some representation of them, either directly or through intermediate models that can be further processed to arrive at this information. Correspondingly, major differences in adaptation approaches manifest themselves in the employed sources, the way they are represented and the techniques used to derive the user demand from them. Therefore, we like to structure this survey according to these model-related aspects.

Chapter VIII

A Personalized Portal on the Basis of Semantic Models and Rules... 153

Jorge Marx Gómez, Oldenburg University, Germany

Tran Duc, Karlsruhe University, Germany

A portal is a Web-based single point of access that delivers information and applications to a user on its own and by the integration of external services. With most portals, various users in the role of customer, supplier, employee, and so forth, can configure the available content and the functionalities in their own way and access them over multitude of devices – mobile phone, PDA, and PC to name a few (Priebe; Pernul, 2003). Whereas this type of portal can be seen as an adaptable system, adaptive portals shall adapt themselves to the individual user.

Chapter IX
British Consumers' Attitudes and Acceptance of Mobile Advertising 165
    Sylvie Laforet, University of Sheffield, UK
    Hannah Limahelu, University of Sheffield, UK

This wireless advertising is considered to be an important alternative advertising medium in the future, due to its numerous advantages over traditional media. However, little research has been conducted on consumer acceptance of this medium in particular, in the United Kingdom. This study explores consumers' attitudes towards and acceptance of mobile advertising, using focus group interviews. Results indicate that British consumers generally do not accept mobile advertising. Although mobile adverts are seen as interesting, eye catching, and motivating consumers to browse. Consumers who accept the technology do not see the need to have adverts on their mobiles. Those who dislike this medium are comfortable with using the Internet through their PCs as they do not see the benefits of mobile advertising, due to its small screen and speed limitation. Managerial considerations are also discussed.

Chapter X
Determinants of ERP Implementations: An Empirical Study in Spanish Companies........................ 180
    Javier de Andrés, University of Oviedo, Spain
    Pedro Lorca, University of Oviedo, Spain
    Jose Emilio Labra, University of Oviedo, Spain

This chapter aims to determine the factors influencing the decision of implementing an ERP system in a country where technology awareness and the technological development are not as high as those of some others. Firstly, the authors assume that adopters make rational choices but the authors also introduce an alternative innovation model based on the imitation perspective. A questionnaire was sent to the Spanish listed companies and the ERP; adopting firms were compared with a matched control group. The main results indicate that the only factors stemming from the rational-choice perspective, whose influence is relevant, are firm size and the ROI ratio. Also, the authprs found that the introduction of the euro and the Y2K issue had an influence in the ERP decision. The influence of the sectoral adscription was supported partially. These findings evidence a certain influence of the imitation effect. The results of this chapter could eventually be extrapolated to the countries whose national culture is similar to that of Spain.

Chapter XI
Emerging Topics and Technologies in Information Systems.. 198
    Jaakko Ikävalko, Helsinki University of Technology, Finland
    Seppo J. Hänninen, Helsinki University of Technology, Finland
    Ari Serkkola, Helsinki University of Technology, Finland
    Ilkka Kauranen, Helsinki University of Technology, Finland

Technology programs are a means to facilitate the development and commercialization process of new innovative technologies. They are forums for the exchange of information and for networking between companies and research institutes. The programs provide opportunities and financial support to carry out ambitious research and development projects and to build business expertise. The core of technology programs are joint research projects between companies and research institutes. The objective of the study is to increase understanding of how such joint research projects within technology programs evolve in practice. The emphasis is on identifying factors that enhance the commercialization of new technologies and on finding barriers of commercialization. Based on the findings, practical recommendations are given on how the concept of technology programs can be further developed to utilize the unused potential in such programs.

Chapter XII
Technology-Related Privacy Concerns: An Emerging Challenge... 208
    Cliona McParland, Dublin City University, Ireland
    Regina Connolly, Dublin City University, Ireland

While Internet-based technologies have the potential to empower users immensely, individuals are becoming increasingly aware of the ways in which those technologies can be employed to monitor their computer-based interactions. In the past, much attention has focused on the impact of technology-related privacy concerns from a transactional perspective. However, privacy concerns regarding communication monitoring are now emerging as a significant issue with the potential to negatively impact both productivity and morale within the computer-mediated work environment. This chapter outlines the evolution of technology-related privacy concerns. The lack of definitional consensus and the resulting conceptual and operational confusion that surrounds the privacy construct is described. Furthermore, the significant deficit of rigorous academic studies on this topic is highlighted. The current state of privacy legislation in Europe is addressed and some of the key challenges that face researchers who may wish to conduct research on this phenomenon are outlined.

Chapter XIII
Fear of Flying and Virtual Environments: An Introductory Review 221
    Giovanni Vincenti, Gruppo Vincenti S.r.l, Italy

Fear of flying is a common problem that many people have to face. As varied as the causes may be, all kinds of fears have many aspects in common. Much is known to us about fear, and the fields of psychology and psychiatry teach us that many times we can conquer fears simply by exposing the subject to the dreaded object. Human-Computer Interaction has branched even in this direction, including the treatment of phobias. With the help of Virtual Reality researchers around the world have recreated using a computer the way that psychologists and psychiatrists cure fears, adding a twist. Many times patients are supposed to go the extra mile and expose themselves, little by little, to what they are afraid of. Virtual Reality brings this type of exposure directly to the patient, with the comfort that such fear can be stopped at any time, since it is only a computer simulation. The most successful studies have been performed on arachnophobia, or the fear of spiders. There are also studies that deal with the fear of heights and the fear of public speaking. Some studies have also been performed on addressing the fear of flying using a virtual environment. This work is a review of such methods, and an explanation of the principles behind the motivation for these studies.

Chapter XIV

A Context-Based Approach for Supporting Knowledge Work with Semantic Portals...................... 231
Thomas Hädrich, Martin-Luther-University Halle-Wittenberg, Germany
Torsten Priebe, University of Regensburg, Germany

Knowledge work can be characterized by a high degree of variety and exceptions, strong communication needs, weakly structured processes, networks and communities, and as requiring a high level of skill and expertise as well as a number of specific practices. Process-oriented knowledge management suggests to focus on enhancing efficiency of knowledge work in the context of business processes. Portals are an enabling technology for knowledge management by providing users with a consolidated, personalized interface that allows accessing various types of structured and unstructured information. However, the design of portals still needs concepts and frameworks to guide their alignment with the context of persons consigned with knowledge-intensive tasks. In this context the concept of knowledge stance is a promising starting point. This paper discusses how knowledge stances can be applied and detailed to model knowledge work and support to support it with semantic context-based portals. We present the results from implementing a portal prototype that deploys Semantic Web technologies to integrate various information sources and applications on a semantic level and discuss extensions to this portal for the support of knowledge stances.

Chapter XV

A Survey of Web Service Discovery Systems 254
Duy Ngan Le, Nanyang Technological University, Singapore
Angela Goh, Nanyang Technological University, Singapore
Cao Hoang Tru, Ho Chi Minh City University of Technology, Viet Nam

Web services form the core of e-business and hence, have experienced a rapid development in the past few years. This has led to a demand for a discovery mechanism for web services. Discovery is the most important task in the web service model because web services are useless if they cannot be discovered. A large number of web service discovery systems have been developed. Universal Description, Discovery and Integration (UDDI) is a typical mechanism that stores indexes to web services but it does not support semantics. Semantic web service discovery systems that have been developed include systems that support matching web services using the same ontology, systems that support matching web services using different ontologies, and systems that support limitations of UDDI. This paper presents a survey of web service discovery systems, focusing on systems that support semantics. The paper also elaborates on open issues relating to such discovery systems.

Chapter XVI

User Relevance Feedback in Semantic Information Retrieval 270
Antonio Picariello, Università di Napoli Federico II, Italy
Antonio M. Rinaldi, Università di Napoli Federico II, Italy

The user dimension is a crucial component in the information retrieval process and for this reason it must be taken into account in planning and technique implementation in information retrieval systems. In this paper we present a technique based on relevance feedback to improve the accuracy in an ontology based information retrieval system. Our proposed method combines the semantic information in a general knowledge base with statistical information using relevance feedback. Several experiments and results are presented using a test set constituted of Web pages.

Chapter XVII

A Preliminary Study toward Wireless Integration of Patient Information System..........,...................... 282
Abdul-Rahman Al-Ali, American University of Sharjah, UAE
Tarik Ozkul, American University of Sharjah, UAE
Taha Landolsi, American University of Sharjah, UAE

This paper presents the results of a study toward generating a wireless environment to provide real-time mobile accessibility to patient information system. A trial system is set up where database, internet, and wireless personal digital assistants (PDAs) are integrated in such a way that the medical professionals like physicians, nurses and lab assistants can create, access and update medical records using wireless PDAs from any location in the hospital which is covered by wireless LAN. The same services which can be carried out via fixed terminals with internet connectivity can be carried out using wireless PDAs. The implementation has used and integrated many technologies like Active Server Pages (ASP), Visual Basic®, Structured Query Language (SQL) Server, ActiveSync®, IEEE802.11 Wireless Local Area Network (WLAN) technology and wireless security concepts. The paper details the architectural aspects of technology integration and the methodology used for setting up the end-to-end system. The proposed architecture, its performance data and the common implementation barriers are reported.

Compilation of References 297

About the Contributors 325

Index 331

Preface

In a world were traditional business practices are reconsidered, economic activity is performed in a global context, new areas of economic development are recognized as the key enablers of wealth and income production, and the quest for collaboration and exploitation of synergies is recognized as an Information Technologies Primer, this book brings together academics, researchers, entrepreneurs, policy makers, and government officers aiming to contribute to the debate on emerging topics and technologies in information systems.

In the context of the knowledge society, the focus of research in this area has been set on applications of technologies for user-centered learning, building on the concept of human learning and on sound pedagogical principles, with the key objectives to be:

- To increase the efficiency of learning for individuals and groups.
- To facilitate transfer and sharing of knowledge in organisations.
- To contribute to a deeper understanding of the learning process by exploring links between human learning, cognition, and technologies.
- To promote humanistic visions for a better world based on open learning for all.

Technology enhanced learning is the best term to describe the domain of knowledge society technologies as applied in the learning context: "Learning for anyone, at any time, at any place". With the shift towards the knowledge society, the change of working conditions and the high-speed evolution of information and communication technologies, peoples' knowledge and skills need continuous updating.

The book "Emerging Topics and Technologies in Information Systems" aims to become the reference edition for all those interested in knowing the current state of the art in technologies and trends in information systems field.

The special feature of this book is that it goes beyond the verbalism of wishful thinking and applies modern approaches through emerging technologies like knowledge portals, push/pull technologies, Web 2.0, Semantic Web, adaptive and personalized technologies, metadata and content standards, free and open source software, ubiquitous and pervasive technologies, intelligent agents, content/knowledge management systems and grid technologies, among others.

From the other hand, all the state-of-the-art themes are categorized and for the full list we develop strategies supported by emerging technologies. An important feature of the book we would like to highlight is the focus on real cases. For every strategy, supported by a key theoretical issue and a combination of technologies, the discussion is made in an organizational context. Real-world cases are used to show how theory supports practice and vice versa.

Additionally we also include further readings of a complimentary nature to the contents of the rest of our publication. As an added value to our readers, the further readings are to provide additional related data in support of the book's comprehensive concepts, principles, and results, as well as studies that build upon the appeal of this publication as a one-stop reference source.

Chapter I
Measuring and Reporting Technological Capital in Companies

Patricia Ordóñez de Pablos
University of Oviedo, Spain

Miltiadis D. Lytras
University of Patras, Greece

ABSTRACT

The chapter addresses the importance of knowledge-based resources proposing indicators to measure and report technological capital in companies. The first part of the chapter develops a conceptual framework to analyze organizational learning and its outcomes. It focuses on the strategy perspective of organizational learning, addressing its ontology, contributions, and problematics. The second part is focused on a particular type of knowledge—the technological capital—that is institutionalized knowledge in the form of technologies. This section proposes a map for the different types of technological capital of companies: idiosyncratic, core, ancillary, and compulsory. The chapter shows the results of a case study with European firms measuring and reporting technological capital. Finally the chapter summarizes main conclusions for management.

INTRODUCTION

Companies are aware that knowledge is their most valuable and strategic resource in the present business environment. Managers know they have to manage the process of learning and measure its outcomes, knowledge-based organizational resources, if they want to be competitive. However, most of the companies neither have knowledge management models nor measurement tools to help them manage better their learning outcomes, like skills, knowledge, expertise and competences. It is therefore important that they know how international pioneer learning organizations have managed and measured their organizational knowledge.

This chapters is structured into four sections. The first section proposes a conceptual framework to analyze organizational learning and its outcomes, such as knowledge at individual, group, organizational and interorganizational level, respectively. The second section is focused on knowledge embedded in organizational structures and processes: the structural capital. It studies the different forms of organizational structural capital of companies: idiosyncratic, core, ancillary and compulsory. Section three shows the results of a case study done in pioneer learning organizations in Europe regarding knowledge measuring and reporting. It analyzes the main indicators used for quantifying the knowledge embedded in the firm. Finally, the last section shows the main results and implications for the management of knowledge drawn from this paper.

THE LEARNING PROCESS IN THE COMPANY

Introduction

The Resource Based View of the Firm (RBV) will help us to explain how important knowledge-based intangible resources are to reach and maintain a sustainable competitive advantage. This view of the firm studies the way to employ and combine strategic organizational resources so that the competitive advantage becomes sustainable as well as the nature of income-generating resources and the origins of heterogeneity. Later we will move to the literature on Organizational Learning to tackle key issues arising out of the discipline today, such as how to transform knowledge at individual level into knowledge at organizational level as a result of the learning process in the firm.

Resource Based View of the Firm

Introduction

This section analyses the main strategic implications from the Resource Based View of the firm. This theory explains how and why companies reach a sustainable competitive advantage and are able to maintain it. The underlying idea is to consider the company as a cumulus of unique resources of different nature, and so move away from the traditional business perspective to analyze the companies according to their market activities (Barney, 1991, 2001; Grant, 1991, 1997; Hamel and Prahalad, 1994; Penrose, 1959; Peteraf, 1993; Teece, 1980, 1982; Wernerfelt, 1984).

The Competitive Advantage in the Company

It is necessary to own, identify and exploit strategic resources to be able to develop a strategy that makes competition possible on the basis of these resources. Companies are therefore very interested in identifying, getting to know and analyzing their resources and abilities to find out which of them are superior or different. They can carry out a unique activity or an activity that is superior to the one of their competitors and at the same time achieve better results (Barney, 1991).

Strategic resources can be studied from two perspectives: the first one points out that organizational knowledge drawn from the coordination of different skills and individual and specific resources are essential for the development of a strategy that can achieve a sustainable competitive advantage (Amit and Schoemaker, 1993; Grant, 1991; Reed and DeFillippi, 1990). The second perspective confirms the idea that the internally accumulated resources represent the strategic base for the development of a sustainable competitive advantage. In the process of resource gathering we can identify the following relevant characteristics: diseconomies when it comes to understanding the necessary time for its development, derived economies on the level of available resources and causal ambiguity. This perspective sees resources simply as stocks whereas the first perspective attributes a more dynamic and developmental nature to the resources (Dierickx and Cool, 1989).

From the resources' perspective, the conditions that bring about the competitive advantage are as follows: heterogeneity of resources, imperfect resource mobility, *ex ante* and *ex post* limits on the competition (Peteraf, 1993). These four conditions are not independent but related to each other. Out of these four, the heterogeneity is the most essential condition and at the same time indispensable for the competitive advantage.

1. *Ex ante* limits on the competition: these limits allow the firm to have a dominant position over a resource even before rival companies start competing for it. The control over a scarce and valuable resource only leads to financial income when the competitors were unable to recognize its *ex ante* value or cannot exploit it in a profitable way because they do not have the necessary additional resources.

2. *Ex post* limits on the competition: The firm should have resources that permit achieving and maintaining a competitive advantage in the long term. The *ex post* limits on the competition delay, increase the price of or prevent imitation or excelling the competitive

position of the more profitable companies by already existing competitors or potential rivals. These limits prevent the imitation of a company's competitive advantage. Overcoming the limits would make the imitators pay such a high price that no profit would be made in such an attempt.

3. Heterogeneity: according to the resource and capability theory, performance differences between companies in the same sector were caused by different efficiency levels achieved through the heterogeneous resources of the companies. Companies that have a better combination of resources and capabilities than others will also obtain much better results.

4. Imperfect mobility: i.e. resources cannot be bought or sold because there is either no clear definition of the property rights or they have a very high specific character that makes it impossible to exploit them outside the firm.

The way to reach this competitive advantage in the long term is a management process with the following phases:

- to identify strategically relevant resources
- to select those that are important for future market needs
- to measure these intangible resources, especially knowledge-based resources
- to implement programs that allow the development, extension, protection, storage and renewal of these resources

Organizational Learning and Isolating Mechanisms

Now the question *how can we maintain this competitive advantage in the long run?* arises. In other words, how can the company keep its competitive advantage free from damage through its competitors on the market?

The answer to this question can be found in Rumelt's (1984) concept of "isolation mechanisms", which protects the company against imitation and preserves its flow of income. These include the property rights of scarce resources and several so-called rights in the form of delays, information asymmetry and friction preventing imitating competition. Other isolating mechanisms include learning, costs to change suppliers as well as costs to look for buyers and scale economies when special assets become necessary. However, it is also difficult to show the causal ambiguity concept. This is basically the uncertainty that exists with regard to what causes the different efficiencies among companies. Moreover, this concept avoids that potential imitators know what they have to imitate to reach this competitive advantage or how to achieve it (Lippmann and Rumelt, 1982).

Dierickx and Cool (1989) believe these differences between resources are caused by factors that avoid the imitation of stock of valuable but not commercially exploitable assets. How far an asset can be imitated depends on the nature of its process. The characteristics that prevent imitation are as follows: diseconomies of time pressure, mass asset efficiency, interconnections of resource stocks, resource erosion and causal ambiguity.

There is no doubt that these resources make up the backbone of the resource-based company theory. Their main characteristics are as follows: 1) not commercially exploitable, developed and accumulated within the company, 2) strong tacit character and social complexity, 3) arise from abilities and organizational learning, 4) they are immobile and linked to the company, and 5) their development depends on the "path", that is, they are contingents in the learning levels, investment, asset stock and previously developed activities.

If we want to analyze a company's competitive potential we need to know the stock of all available resources and the way in which the company is able to combine and exploit the resources together. The latter determines the organizational capability. The capability concept has got a dynamic connotation which expresses the conjunction between the resources and the organizational tasks through which we manage to coordinate and encourage an adequate interrelation among technological and human resources to develop a function or a determined activity (Amit and Schoemaker, 1933).

Finally a strategy's competitive success depends on the company's intangible assets, but the dynamic of these intangible assets are also widely determined by the contents of this strategy. It is the strategy that determines the approach of the company's activity and provides action lines to coordinate activities in such a way as to enable the company to face and influence the changing environment.

A Framework for Organizational Learning

Introduction

Literature on the learning organization is largely different from literature on organizational learning. The learning organization literature, which is best characterized by Pedler, Boydell, and Burgoyne (1989, 1991) and Senge (1990), is action oriented and is geared toward creativity and to an ideal organization in which learning is maximized. On the other hand, the organizational learning literature is "analytic and concentrates on understanding learning processes within organizational settings, without necesarily trying to change those processes" (p. 1086).

The literature of organizational learning has grown very rapidly in the last 10 years. According to Easterby-Smith (1997) six major perspectives have made significant contributions to the understanding about organizational learning. They are sociology, psycology, cultural anthrophology, production management, management science and strategy. In this paper we will only focus on the strategy perspective of organizational learning, addressing its ontology, contributions and problematics. From this view, the literature on organizational learning focuses on competitions and learning is evaluated according to whether is gives one firm a competitive advantage over others. As Hamel and Prahalad (1993) state, "being a learning organization is not enough; a company must be capable of learning more efficiently than its competitors" (p. 80).

Let us continue with the concept of learning organization and later we will focus our paper on organizational learning. What is a learning organization? Surprisingly a clear definition of learning has proved to be elusive over the years. As as first step, we consider the following definition proposed by Garvin (1993):

"A learning organization is an organization skilled at creating, acquiring and transfering knowledge and at modifying its behaviour to reflect news knowledge and insights." (p. 80)

The examination of the activities required for an organization to learn, led us to the consideration of the following levels of analysis. At the core of the study of the learning process is the distinction between two levels of analysis: ontological and epistemological. On the one hand, the epistemological level proposes the existence of two major types of knowledge: tacit and explicit. Tacit knowledge is acquired through experience. It is a form of knowledge with which we are all intimately familiar. It appears as if it were acquired through "osmosis" when we enter into a new organization, or when we begin an activity that is different from what we are accustomed to (Polanyi, 1966). Explicit or codified knowledge is transmittable through formal, systematic language, and may adopt the form of computer programs, patents, diagrams, or similar. On the other, the ontological level differenciates among individual, group, organizational and interorganizational levels of knowledge stocks.

These epistemological and ontological levels are the start point of Nonaka and Takeuchi's (1995) spiral of knowledge creation. Through the interaction of tacit and explicit knowledge, four *knowledge conversion modes* are developed: socialization (from tacit knowledge to tacit knowledge), externalization (from tacit knowledge to explicit knowledge), combination (from explicit knowledge to explicit knowledge) and internalization (from explicit knowledge to tacit knowledge).

This spiral moves from individual level towards organizational or inter-organizational level, finalizing the first knowledge creation spiral by generating embedded knowledge, that is to say, structural knowledge.

Another learning model is described by the *4I framework* proposed by Crossan, Lane and White (1999). They conceive of organizational learning as a dynamic process of strategy renewal occurring across three levels of the organization: individual, group and organizational. These authors propose a 4I framework focused on the relationships between the three levels of learning and two learning flows. At individual level, the *intuiting* process takes place. At group level, the *interpreting* and *integrating* processes are developed. Finally, the *institutionalizing* process is the last stage in the organizational learning process. These modes of learning are linked both by social and psycological processes. This framework is operationalized as the strategic learning assessment map (SLAM) and analyzes simultaneously knowledge stocks and flows in the organization.

Another conceptualization of the levels of organizational learning is presented by Boisot (2002), who proposes a "social learning cycle". According to this author, social learning occurs "when changes in the stocks of knowledge held by one or more agents in a given population triggers coordinate changes in the stocks of knowledge that are held by other agents in the population" (p.70). Naturally these changes will not necessarily be all in the same direction for all agents. Thus the way the different agents "internalize incoming information through adjustments to their existing stocks of knowledge, and the different meaning and interpretations they attach to it, constitutes a source of further opportunities for generating new knowledge or disregarding old knowledge –that is, for learning" (p. 71). This social learning cycle is divided into six phases: scanning, problem solving, abstraction, diffusion, absorption, and impacting.

These models recognize that the key challenge for the firm is the transformation of learning across individual, group, organizational and inter-organizational levels, respectively. For example, how firms can convert employee's knowledge into organizational knowledge. This conversion process is called *institutionalization*. It involves embedding individual and group learning in non-human aspects of the organization –knowledge deposits- including systems, structures, strategy and processes. The conversion completes its process sucessfully if the individual learning feeds forward into group learning and learning at the organizational level in terms of changes to systems, structure, strategy, culture and procedure. In sum, learning at organizational level represents the translation of shared understanding into new products, processes, procedures, structures and strategy. It is the non-human artifacts of the organization that endure even though individuals may leave.

Companies Not Only Learn but Also Unlearn

Organizational learning begins with the development of new ideas at individual level. However, knowledge creation is a process that depends on actions and requires experience, experimentation and reflection (Nonaka, 1991; Senge, 1990). This idea is clearly reflected in the distinction between *single* and *double loop* learning (Argyris and Schon, 1978). Single loop learning consists

of comparing the consequences of actions with desired outcomes, and modifying behavior if deviations exist. This is an incremental process of action and reflection, focused on the continuous improvement of the existing system. Double loop learning, on the other hand, is a process that goes beyond the mere detection and correction of errors. It entails examining actions and outcomes, as well as the underlying assumptions on which they are based. In this vein, Levitt and March (1988) posit that without purposeful analysis of the underlying assumptions and systems, organizations may become victims of "competency traps" (i.e., inferior institutionalized procedures but nevertheless lead to acceptable performance).

Both single and double loop learning can contribute to the creation of value. However, single loop learning will lead to incremental improvements, while double loop learning tends to generate innovative or radical changes. However the dynamics of competition in today's business environment makes organizational knowledge obsolete in a short period of time. Thus the firm needs to get ride of this institutionalized knowledge in order to efficiently create or acquire and deploy strategic knowledge that serves a source of competitive advantage. Here the *organizational unlearning* process appears. It involves the process of reframing past success programs in order to fit them with changing enviromental conditions.

Hedberg (1981) states that firms operating in highly dynamic environments must have skills to "unlearn" if they wish to survive. Thus he continues saying that "knowledge grows and simultaneously becomes obsolete as the environment changes. Organizational survival depends both on learning and acquiring new knowledge as well as on disregarding obsolete knowledge that may contribute to error making". The activity of knowledge disregarding—"unlearning"- is as much as important as learning. However, firms find more difficult getting ride of this knowledge than creating new knowledge. In this sense, Easterby-Smith (1997) proposes two modes of organizational unlearning: a radical one, which questions values and procedures as well as the value of these elements for individuals; and an incremental one, where new knowledge is stored above the old knowledge, thus hindering the process of knowledge recover.

A FRAMEWORK FOR THE ANALYSIS OF KNOWLEDGE STOCKS IN COMPANIES: THE INTELLECTUAL CAPITAL APPROACH

Introduction

Knowledge-based organizational resources have become the source of the most important competitive advantage for the company. Within the field of strategic management researchers are more and more aware that from a theoretical perspective the most relevant variables are exactly those that are less identifiable and less quantifiable. There is no doubt that one of these variables is the intellectual capital of the organization.

In the mid 90's a new term starts to increasingly catch attention in the field of strategic management: the intellectual capital. We see intellectual capital as representing the "stock" of knowledge that exists in an organization at a particular point in time. It encompasses all those knowledge-based resources that create organizational value but are not included in the financial accounts. The intellectual capital concept in a wider term means knowledge, applied experience, organizational technology, relations to clients, suppliers, as well as professional capabilities that give a competitive advantage on the market. Thus, the intellectual capital represents the group of distinct basic capabilities: some are of technological origin where knowledge and the experience accumulated by the company are included. Others are of organizational origin and of an origin typical

of "action processes" in the organization. And others are of personal character concerning attitudes, aptitudes and capabilities of organization members (Edvinsson and Malone, 1997; Lytras and Ordóñez de Pablos, 2007, 2009).

Intellectual capital literature offers a static view of knowledge-based resources and aims to offer a map of firm's stocks of these resources through their measurement.

Components

The development of knowledge-based resource typologies has received great attention in the intellectual capital literature. These typologies vary as much in their terminology as in the degree they explicitly analyze the qualities of firms' knowledge-based resources. However, in spite of their differences we begin to see convergence among them. And now we will define each of the intellectual capital components: human capital, relational capital and structural capital.

The *human capital* is defined as the individual knowledge stock of the employees of an organization. Employees contribute to the intellectual capital creation by means of their competence, their attitude and their mental agility. The competence includes abilities and education, whereas attitude shows the employees' behavior towards their job. And finally, mental agility allows employees to modify organizational practices and develop innovative solutions for problems.

The *relational capital* is the second intellectual capital component. In a narrower sense, relational capital encompasses present knowledge in relations that are already established with environment. The base of relational capital is the knowledge that was accumulated by the different parties during exchanges with a third party. For that reason, this knowledge scope is external to the company and it is also external to the human capital that already exists within the company. Relational capital, however, can be measured as

Figure 1. Concept of intellectual capital

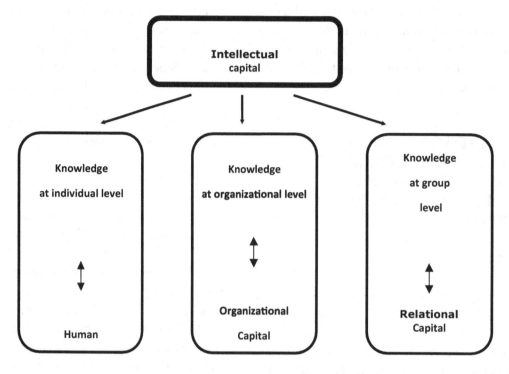

a longevity function. Therefore, this resource becomes more valuable as relations with customers, suppliers, shareholders etc. last longer. Finally, thanks to its external nature relational capital is the knowledge that is hardest to codify (Ordóñez de Pablos, 2004, 2005).

The last component of intellectual capital is *structural capital*. It is the knowledge that remains in the company when employees go home. Therefore, the company owns it. In addition Boisot (2002) states that structural capital is "where the value added by the nonlinearities of the knowledge creation process is assumed to reside" (p.69). Inputs to this process are provided by human capital, and the company, acting as residual claimant, captures the surplus. On the other hand, structural capital encompasses all forms of knowledge deposit which is not supported by the human being such as organizational routines,

strategies, process handbooks and databases, and many more (Walsh and Ungson, 1991).

Structural capital is subdivided into organizational and technological capital. Organizational capital includes all aspects that are related with the organization of the company and its decision-taking process, such as organizational culture, structural design, coordination mechanisms, organizational routines, planning and control systems, and many more. Technological capital includes all technical and industrial knowledge, like results from research and development and from process engineering.

Now that we have defined the three components of intellectual capital we will only concentrate on one component which we will study in the next sections of this paper: the structural capital. So far this component is the least studied element in the intellectual capital literature.

TECHNOLOGICAL CAPITAL IN COMPANIES

Introduction

Structural capital is knowledge at organizational level created through the institutionalization of both individual and group knowledge present in the firm during the learning process. If we assume that not all knowledge and capabilities that exist in the company are strategic, we first have to determine the types of structural capital that really exist and how we can turn them into a source of competitive advantage. According to the works of Snell, Lepak and Youndt (1999) and Ulrich and Lake (1991), we then have to analyze the strategic potential of the company's structural capital in relation to two dimensions: idiosyncratic value and uniqueness.

The resource based theory states that the high value of resources when they make organizations improve their effectiveness while making use of opportunities and neutralizing threats. How can we create value within the Strategic Management? Here value is created by increasing the share of profits for the customer in relation to the costs associated with achieving those profits. The structural capital of the company, therefore, can add value if it contributes to a cost reduction or to an improvement of services or characteristics of the products for the customers.

Figure 2. Technological capital matrix

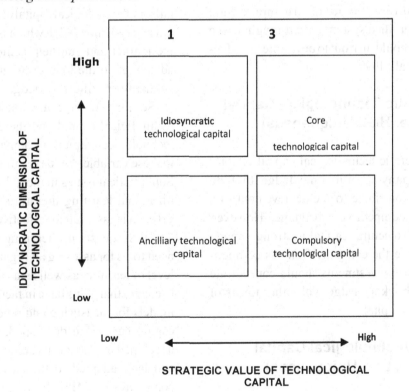

Source. Adapted from Snell, Lepak and Youndt (1999)

Collis and Montgomery (1995), however, point out that the importance of structural capital also grows as it contributes to the creation of a competitive differentiation. From an economic perspective, the cost transaction theory suggests that the companies get a competitive advantage when they have organization specific assets which cannot be copied by rivals (Williamson, 1975). As the uniqueness of structural capital increases, companies are encouraged to invest significant resources into its capital management to reduce risk and to capitalize on its productive potential.

Figure 2 shows the result of the juxtaposition of these analyzed dimensions. The result is a conceptual framework for mapping different forms of structural capital a company may have. With the help of this framework, we can study the ways to manage the different forms of technological capital in order to maximize their contribution to the organization. It is generally believed that we need different systems of human resources to manage the different types of structural capital and that one unified system used throughout the organization could turn out to be counter-productive (Snell et al., 1999).

Idiosyncratic Technological Capital (Low Value, High Uniqueness)

The idiosyncratic technological capital encompasses company-specific knowledge that do not directly contribute to the achievement of a long-lasting competitive advantage. However, this form of structural capital is strong enough to differentiate the company from its competitors. Therefore, investments should concentrate on relating this knowledge with other forms of technological capital.

Ancillary Technological Capital (Low Value, Low Uniqueness)

The ancillary technological capital is the knowledge that is neither especially useful to create value for the customer nor company-specific. In most of the cases this type of knowledge is a by-product of the company's own activity.

Core Technological Capital (High Value, High Uniqueness)

Companies should convert their employees' core knowledge and the consequences of their relations with other agents (shareholders, suppliers and customers, among others) into the companies' own knowledge to maintain their competitive position. The firm should transform its human and core relational capital into knowledge that is inside the structures and organizational processes, like technological capital.

Compulsory Technological Capital (High Value, Low Uniqueness)

Another form of technological capital is the compulsory technological capital of the company. This is a general knowledge which is widely spread on the market and can help achieve a competitive advantage in the long term, although it is not a company-specific knowledge.

So far we have analysed the concept of technoligical capital and the different forms of technological capital a company has according to these variables: value creation and uniqueness. Some critical issues in most discussions of organizational learning literature are left unsolved; yet each is essential for effective implementation. One is the question of learning measurement. We need tools for assesing an organization's rate and level of learning as well as its learning evolution to ensure that gains have in fact been made. Some models for measuring and reporting intellectual capital have been developed, as the 3R Model developed by Patricia Ordóñez de Pablos in 2004 and later adapted to the case of multinational companies by Miltiadis D. Lytras and Patricia Ordóñez de Pablos in 2008.

EMPIRICAL EVIDENCE OF TECHNOLOGICAL CAPITAL IN COMPANIES

Data

Once the conceptual framework to analyze technological capital is developed, now we discuss the results of the case study of this research[2]. The case study was designed to focus on European learning organizations and their ability to measure their learning outcomes. The objective of this paper is to study the indicators of technological capital as used by pioneer learning organizations in the measurement of knowledge-based resources and in the building of a new type of corporate report called Intellectual Capital Statement or Report.

Prior to the presentation of the case study, let's define the concept of intellectual capital report. In accordance to The Danish Agency for Trade and Industry (2000) the objective of an intellectual capital report is "to give an image of the organizational effort to build, develop and display resources and abilities in relation to the employees, customers, technology and processes. The intellectual capital accounts underline the development of a future value of the company and also its competitive advantage in the Knowledge Economy" (p.4). Moreover, this report shows an essential part of the Knowledge Management. According to The Danish Agency for Trade and Industry (2001), it "informs about organizational efforts to achieve, develop, share and institutionalize knowledge-based resources which are necessary to create value for the company by means of improving their growth, flexibility and innovation" (p. 13).

Table 1. Intellectual capital reports in pioneering firms

FIRM	SECTOR/ACTIVITY	INTELLECTUAL CAPITAL REPORT YEAR/S	COUNTRY
ARCS	Research organization	1999-2000-2001	Austria
Carl Bro	Consulting	1998-1999-2000-2001-2002	Denmark
Cowi	Engineering and related services	1999-2000-2001/2002	Denmark
Dieu	Course provider	2000/2001-2001/2002	Denmark
Systematic	Software development	1999-2000-2002	Denmark
DLR	Aerospace research center	2001	Germany
Intercos	Colour cosmetics	2002	Italy
Plastal	Injection-moulded plastic components	2002	Italy
Balrampur Chini Mills	Sugar producer	1996/97-1998/99/-1999/2000	India
Navneet	Publisher	1999/2000	India
Reliance	Various (finance, telecom, oil & gas, etc)	1997	India
Shree Cement Limited	Cement manufacturer	2000-2001	India
Bankinter	Banking	2000-2001	Spain
BBVA	Banking	1999-2002	Spain
BSCH	Banking	2000-2002	Spain
Caja Madrid	Banking	2002	Spain
Mekalki	Mechanized integral services	1998	Spain
Union Fenosa	Electricity	1999-2000-2001	Spain
Celemi	Learning Solutions	2000	Sweden
Skandia	Insurance	1994-1995-1996-1997-1998	Sweden
Telia	Telecom solutions	2001*	Sweden
EES Group	Provider of lighting and earthing	2002	UK

Table 2. Technological capital indicators in intellectual capital reports

INTELLECTUAL CAPITAL REPORT (III) TECHNOGICAL CAPITAL			
CATEGORY	SUB-CATEGORIES AND INDICATORS	YEAR	
		YEAR$_{T-1}$	YEAR$_T$
SC1 SC11 SC111 SC112 SC113 SC12 SC121 SC122 SC123 SC13 SC131 SC132 SC14 SC15 SC16 SC17 SC18	**A. INFRASTRUCTURE** **(Office, computer capacity, phone service)** I.Investment 1. Investment in premises and office equipment 2. Investment in computer equipment 3. IT expenses per employee II. Servers 1. No. of servers per worker 2. No. of hits on web-site per day 3. Average number of homepage hits per month III. Office 1. m² office space 2. PCs per office IV.No. of employees connected via email V.Reliability of hardware and software VI.Employees with the option of teleworking VII.Employees with corporate mobile phone VIII.Employees with corporate laptop		
SC2 SC21 SC22 SC23 SC24 SC25 SC26 SC27 SC28 SC29 SC20	**B. KNOWLEDGE-BASED INFRASTRUCTURE** I.No. of best practices on the intranet II.No. of employees with intranet access/total staff III.Shared documents on the intranet IV.% of updated knowledge documents on the intranet V.No. of databases to which the firm has access VI.No. of employees with Internet access/total staff VII.No. of shared knowledge databases VIII.No. of participants in best practices processes IX.No. of knowledge management projects X.Database searches		

SC3	C.ADMINISTRATIVE PROCESSES		
SC31	I.Average response time for calls to switchboards		
SC32	II.% of inquiries handled within the same day		
SC4	E.INNOVATION		
SC41	I.Innovation results		
SC411	1. No. of products/services		
SC412	2. No. of new products/services		
SC413	3. Volume of sells linked to new products/		
SC414	services introduced last year		
SC415	4. Total innovation		
SC416	5. % of group turnover		
	6. Average turnover project		
SC42	II. Innovation investment		
SC421	1. No. of shared ideas and experiences		
SC422	2. Average number of ideas per employee		
SC423	3. Investment in product development		
SC424	4. Investment in process improvement		
SC425	5. Investment in I+D+I projects		
SC426	6. Centers of Excellence		
SC427	7. Ongoing projects		

* C=Core, A=Ancilliary, CM=Compulsory and I=Idiosyncratic

The primary data collection method for the case study was the analysis of intellectual capital reports obtained from the companies. Thus in 2002, we contacted a group of 8 European learning organizations that measure knowledge-based resources and asked them for their collaboration in this research. We analyzed intellectual capital reports of companies operating in the service sector (mainly banking, insurance and consulting) in Austria, Denmark, Spain and Sweden.

The report of this firm that include the social dimension and actions taken to date in this area up to year 2001 is called "Telia's Relations 2001", not intellectual capital report. This firm also elaborates the annual report and another report called "Telia's Business 2001".

In addition, in some cases field interviews with senior managers involved in the measurement of knowledge were conducted. The interviews followed a semistructured format based on an interview guide. There were both an open endded sequence of questions and a focused set of questions designed to evaluate specific organizational attributtes and/or in some other cases we added a survey questionnaire.

Results of the Study

Here we will present the main conclusions from the case-studies of this international research. First, we will describe the structure of an intellectual capital report in detail. Roughly speaking, this report has got two clearly differentiated sections. The first section collects information about strategies and intellectual capital actions developed in the company. The second part gives information about the indicators for technological capital found in the analysed intellectual capital reports.

Firms tend to show intelellectual capital indicators in tables because they offer a comparative view in relation to preceding years. Similarly, these tables also include information about short- and long-term objectives in relation to these indicators.

As shown in Table 2, the indicators for this component of technological capital can be divided into the following sections: 1) general infra-structure, 2) knowledge-based infrastructure, 3) administrative processes and 4) innovation.

- General infrastructure: it shows the compa-ny's equipment indicator concerning offices, computer capacity and telephone services, among others.
- Knowledge infrastructure: it measures the intranet utility and the company's database. This category encompasses indicators like the number of best practices available in the company's intranet and the percentage of documents about knowledge available in the intranet, and many more.
- Administrative processes: they show the or-ganizational efficiency as regards customer service.
- Innovation: it collects information about investments in product and process devel-opment, number of services and/or new products, etc.

It is important to indicate what type of indicator the firm is measuring and reporting. There are four main forms of technological capital indicators: core, ancilliary, compulsory and idiosyncratic. The identification and categorization of each indicator helps to develop an appropriate policy to manage each particular form of knowledge.

MAIN CONCLUSION

Managers know that learning organizations are not built overnight and that "if you can't measure it, you can not manage it". Traditionally the solution has been "learning curves" and "manufacturing progress functions". However, for companies hoping to become learning organizations these measurements are incomplete as they focus on only single measure output and ignore that affects other firm variables, like new product/services introductions, improvements and quality. Thus

firms need to develop another measures to quatify knowledge-based resources and create strategic knowledge maps, which make conceptual entities more visible.

All over the world companies are aware of how important measuring and managing the output of their learning process, that is, knowledge. In 1994, the Swedish company Skandia measured its knowledge stocks and, moreover, produced its first intellectual capital report ever published in the world. Other companies, primarily in Denmark and Spain, followed in the footsteps of Skandia and carried out their intellectual capital measuring at the same time when they published Intellectual Capital Reports.

The companies measure their intangible re-sources because of the advantages they produce. The results of an international study (Ordóñez de Pablos, 2004) show that companies not only obtain internal benefits from intellectual capital measuring which results in a better internal management of the company but also external benefits. The latter can be found in the strategic positioning, acquisition of innovations developed by other companies, customer loyalty, cost reduc-tions and improved productivity.

One of the knowledge-based organizational resources least studied in literature is the structural capital. That is the reason why the objective of this paper was to analyze the concept of structural capital and the different ways it is present in the company. Structural capital is "organizational-level knowledge" present in the firm as a result of a learning metaprocess called *institution-alization*. This knowledge basically resides in organizational routines, processes, strategy and culture, which codify and preserve memories and knowledge. Furthermore, this paper shows the major implications of an international research among pioneer learning organizations in measur-ing and reporting their stocks of knowledge. It discusses main indicators found of organizational embedded knowledge -structural capital- present in these organizations and groups them into six categories: infrastructure, bureaucratic processes, customer support, innovation, knowledge-based quality and infrastructure improvement. In total 32 indicators are found.

We also observed that learning organizations not only measure the result of the learning process -their knowledge-based resources- but also tend to produce and publish an *intellectual capital report*. This report together with the traditional company annual report gives corporate information that helps to give a holistic image of this information and its resources.

Finally, we also have to reveal the urgent need for some norms which guide the making of intellectual capital reports in such a way as to guarantee the objectivity of the information and the comparability of reports given by other companies, nationally and internationally. We should point out the pioneer work done in Denmark by the Danish Agency for Development of Trade and Industry and in Spain by the Meritum Project, whose work resulted in the publication of some guidelines about how to produce the Intellectual Capital Report, respectively (Danish Agency for Development of Trade and Industry, 2000, 2001; Ordóñez de Pablos, 2004). These guidelines aim to armonize the indicators used as proxies for learning outcomes by pioneer organizations.

REFERENCES

Amit, R., & Schoemaker, P. J. (1993). Strategic assets and organizational rent. *Strategic Management Journal, 14*, 33-46.

Argyris, C. (1977). Double loop learning in organizations. *Harvard Business Review*, September-October.

Argyris, C. A., & Schön, D. (1978). *Organizational Learning: A Theory of Action Perspective*. Reading, MA: Addison-Wesley.

Argyris, C. (1992). *On Organizational Learning*. Cambridge MA: Blackwell.

Bandura, A. (1977). *Social Learning Theory*. Englewood Cliffs, NJ: Prentice-Hall.

Bankinter (2000). *Annual Report 2000*.

Barney, J. (1991). Firm resources and sustained competitive advantage. *Journal of Management, 17*(1), 99-120.

Barney, J. B. (1992). Integrating organizational behaviour and strategy formulation research: A resource-based analysis. In P. Shrivastava, A. Huff and J. Dutton (Eds.), *Advances in strategic management, 8*, 39-61.

Barney, J. B. (2001). Is the resource-based view a useful perspective for strategic management research? Yes. *Academy of Management Review, 26*(1), 41-56.

BBVA (1999). *Annual Report 1999*.

Boisot, M. (2002). The creation and sharing of knowledge. In C. W. Choo. and N. Bontis (Eds.), *The Strategic Management of Intellectual Capital and Organizational Learning*. Oxford University Press.

Bontis, N. (1999). Managing organizational knowledge by diagnosing intellectual capital: framing and advancing the state of the field. *International Journal of Technology Management, 18*, 433-462.

BSCH (2000). *Annual Report 2000*.

Collis, D. J., & Montgomery, C. A. (1995). Competing on resources: Strategy in the 1990s. *Harvard Business Review*, July-August, 118-128.

Cook, S. D. N., & Yanow, D. (1993). Culture and organizational learning. *Journal of Management Inquiry, 2*(4), 373-390.

COWI (1999). *Intellectual Capital Report 1999*.

Crossan, M., Lane, H., & White, R. (1999). An organizational learning framework: From intuition to institution. *Academy of Management Review, 24*(3), 522-537.

Crossan, M. M., Lane, H. W., White, R. E., & Djurfeldt, L. (1995). Organizational learning: Dimensions for a theory. *The International Journal of Organizational Analysis, 3*(4), (October), 337-360.

Daft, R. L., & Weick, K. E. (1984). Toward a model of organizations as interpretation systems. *Academy of Management Review, 9*, 284-295.

Danish Agency for Development of Trade and Industry (2000). *Intellectual Capital Statement-Towards a Guidelines.*

Danish Agency for Development of Trade and Industry (2001). *A Guideline for Intellectual Capital Statements: A Key to Knowledge Management.*

Dierickx, I., & Cool, K. (1989a). Assets stock accumulation and sustainability of competitive advantage. *Management Science, 35*(12), 1504-1511.

Dierickx, I., & Cool, K. (1989b). Assets stock accumulation and sustainability of competitive advantage: Reply. *Management Science, 35*(12), 1512-1513.

Dixon, N. M. (1992). Organizational learning: A review of the literature with implication for HRD professionals. *Human Resource Development Quarterly, 3*(1), 29-49.

Easterby-Smith, M. (1997). Disciplines of organizational learning: Contributions and critiques. *Human Relations, 50*(9).

Edvinsson, L., & Malone, M. S. (1997). *Intellectual Capital. Realizing Your Company's True Value by Finding its Hidden Brainpower*, Harper Collins Publishers, Inc., 1ª ed.

Galbraith, J. R. (1977). *Organization Design.* Reading, M.A: Addison-Wesley.

Garvin, D. A. (1993). Building a learning organization. *Harvard Business Review*, July—August, 78-91.

Gherardi, S., & Nicolini, D. (2002). The sociological foundations of organizational learning. in C. W. Choo and N. Bontis (eds.), *The Strategic Management of Intellectual Capital and Organizational Learning.* Oxford University Press.

Grant, R. (1991). A resource-based theory of competitive advantage: Implications for strategy formulation. *California Management Journal, 33*(3), 114-135.

Grant, R. (1996a). Toward a knowledge-based theory of the firm. *Strategic Management Journal, 17*(Winter special issue), 109-122.

Grant, R. (1996b). Prospering in dynamically competitive environments: Organizational capability as knowledge integration. *Organization Science, 7*(4), 375-388.

Grant, R. (1997). The knowledge-based view of the firm: implication for management practice. *Long Range Planning, 30*(3), 450-454.

Hamel, G., & Prahalad, C. K. (1993). Strategy as strech and leverage. *Harvard Business Review*, March-April, 75-84/

Hamel, G., & Prahalad, C. K. (1994). *Competing for the Future.* Boston: Harvard Business School Press.

Hedberg, B. (1981). How organizations learn and unlearn. In P. C. Nystrom and W. H. Starbuck (eds.), *Handbook of Organizational Design*, New York: Oxford University Press, (pp. 3-27).

Hedlund, G. (1994). A model of knowledge management and the N-form corporation. *Strategic Management Journal, 15*, 73-90.

Huff, A. S., & Jenkins, M. (2002). *Mapping Strategic Knowledge.* Sage Publications.

Levitt, D., & March, J. G. (1988). Organizational learning. *Annual Review of Sociology, 14*, 319-340.

Lippman, S., & Rumelt, R. P. (1982). Uncertain imitability: An analysis of interfirm differences in efficiency under competition. The *Bell Journal of Economics, 13*, 418-438.

Lyles, M. A. (N/D). Learning among joint venture sophisticated firms. *Management International Review, 28*(Special Issue): 85-98.

Lytras, M. D., & Ordóñez de Pablos, P. (2009). Managing, measuring and reporting knowledge-based resources in hospitals. *International Journal of Technology Management, forthcoming.*

Lytras, M. D., & Ordóñez de Pablos, P. (2007). The building of the intellectual capital statement in multinationals: challenges for the future. In K. O'Sullivan (Ed), *Strategic Knowledge Management in Multinational Organizations.* Idea Group Inc. (pp. 195-206).

Nelson, R., & Winter, S. (1982). *An Evolutionary Theory of Economic Change.* Harvard University Press.

Nicolini, D., & Meznar, M. B. (1995). The social construction of organizational learning. *Human Relations, 48*, 727-46.

Nonaka, I. (1991). The knowledge-creating company. *Harvard Business Review*, noviembre-diciembre, (pp. 96-104).

Nonaka, I., & Takeuchi, H. (1995). *The Knowledge Creating Company: How Japanese Companies Create the Dynamics of Innovation.* Oxford University Press.

Ordóñez de Pablos, P. (2004). A guideline for building the intellectual capital statement: the 3R Model. *International Journal of Learning and Intellectual Capital, 1*(1), 3-18.

Ordóñez de Pablos, P. (2005). Intellectual capital accounts: what pioneering firms from asia and europe are doing now. *International Journal of Knowledge and Learning, 1*(3), 249-268.

Ordóñez de Pablos, P., Edvinsson, L., & Lytras, M. D. (2008). The Intellectual Capital Statements: Evolution And How To Get Started. In M. Lytras, M. Russ, R. Maier, and A. Naeve, (Eds.), *Knowledge Management Strategies.* IGI, (pp. 64-91).

Pedler, M., Boydell, T., & Burgoyne, J. G. (1989). Towards the learning company. *Management Education and Development, 20*(1), 1-8.

Pedler, M., Boydell, T., & Burgoyne, J. (1991). *The Learning Company.* McGraw-Hill, Londres.

Penrose, E. T (1959). *The Theory of the Growth of the Firm.* New York: John Wiley & Sons.

Peteraf, M. A. (1993). The conerstones of competitive advantage: A resource-based view. *Strategic Management Journal, 14*, 179-191.

Polanyi, M. (1966). *The Tacit Dimension.* London: Routledge & Kegan Paul.

Priem, R. L., & Butler, J. E. (2001a). Is the resource-based "view" a useful perspective for strategic management research? *Academy of Management Review, 26*, 22-40.

Priem, R. L., & Butler, J. E. (2001b). Tautology in the resource-based view and the implications of externally determined resource value: Further comments. *Academy of Management Review, 26*, 57-66.

Reed, R., & Defillippi, R. (1990). Causal ambiguity, barriers to imitation and sustainable competitive advantage. *Academy of Management Review, 15*(1), 88-102.

Rumelt, R. P. (1984). Towards a strategic theory of the firm. In R. B. LAMB (ed.), *Competitive Strategic Management.* Englewood Cliffs, NJ: Prentice-Hall. (pp. 556-570).

Senge, P. M. (1990). *The Fifth Discipline: The Art and Practice of the Learning Organization.* New York: Doubleday Currency.

Shrivastava, P. (1983). A typology of organizational learning systems. Journal *of Management Studies, 20*(1), 7-28.

Skandia (1994). *Intellectual Capital Report, 1994.*

Skandia (1996). *Supplement to the Annual Report. Customer Value, 1996.*

Snell, S. A., Lepak, D. P., & Youndt, M. A. (1999). Managing the architecture of intellectual capital: Implications for strategic human resource management. In G. R. FERRIS (Ed.), *Research in Personnel and Human Resources Management, S4*, 175-193.

Spender, J-C (1996b). Making knowledge, collective practice and Penrose rents. *International Business Review, 3*, 4.

Spender, J-C. (1996a). Organizational knowledge, learning and memory: Three concepts in search of a theory. *Journal of Organizational Change Management, 9*, 63-79.

Systematic (1999). *Intellectual Capital Report 1999.*

Systematic (2000). *Intellectual Capital Report 2000.*

Teece, D. J. (1980). Economies of scope and the scope of the enterprise. *Journal of Economic Behaviour and Organization, 1*, 223-247.

Teece, D. J. (1982). Towards an economic theory of the multiproduct firm. *Journal of Economic Behaviour and Organization, 3*, 39-63.

Ulrich, D. (1991). Using human resources for competitive advantage. In R. Kilmann & Associates (Eds.), *Making Organizations Competitive*. San Francisco: Jossey-Bass. (pp. 129-155).

Ulrich, D., & Lake, D. (1991). Organizational capability: Creating competitive advantage. *Academy of Management Executive, 5*(1), 77-92.

Walsh, J. P., & Ungson, G. R. (1991). Organizational memory. *Academy of Management Review, 16*, 57-91.

Weick, K. E. (1979). *The Social Psycology of Organizing*. Reading, MA: Addison-Wesley.

Wernerfelt, B. (1984). A resource based view of the firm. *Strategic Management Journal, 5*, 171-180.

Williamson, O. E. (1975). *Markets and Hierarchies*. New York: Free Press.

Chapter II
Revisiting Agility to Conceptualize Information Systems Agility

Pankaj
Indiana University of Pennsylvania, USA

Micki Hyde
Indiana University of Pennsylvania, USA

Arkalgud Ramaprasad
University of Illinois at Chicago, USA

Suresh K. Tadisina
Southern Illinois University Carbondale, USA

ABSTRACT

There is no systematic study of Information Systems (IS) agility in academic and practitioner IS literature and the concept is not well defined. For rigorous academic studies of IS agility, a proper definition/conceptualization of IS agility is needed. To fulfill this objective, existing published work on agility is analyzed. The analysis demonstrates that the existing definitions may need improvement to aid in arriving at a definition of IS agility. A new definition of agility that captures its core properties is proposed. The advantages of this definition over existing definitions is demonstrated and it is used to define IS Agility. Salient features of an agile IS are discussed and the utility of the proposed definition in arriving at attributes of an agile IS is demonstrated. Efficacy and validity of the proposed definition is demonstrated through interviews with IS executives from a diverse organization set. Lastly, avenues for future research are proposed.

INTRODUCTION

Change is the rule of the game in the current business environment. The rate of change has been continuously increasing due to factors like globalization and the opportunities presented by the development and evolution of technologies. Not only are the changes occurring at an increasing rate, they are becoming increasingly unpredictable. This unpredictability can involve: when a known change will occur, what an unknown change will look like, or a combination of these. The rapid rate of change implies that an organization needs to become an expert at changing and morphing itself rapidly in response to a change. Retention of leadership position requires that an organization should be able to change at will in any direction, without significant cost and time, to counter a threat or to capitalize on an opportunity. Such an organization may be characterized as an agile organization. For most organizations the survival and/or retention of market share demands that it should be able to change faster than, or as fast as, new entrants and rivals.

Most high-level executives agree to the need for agility (Sullivan, 2005). CEO Peter Bonfield of ICL Plc (an IT company from the United Kingdom), observed as far back as 1995 that ICL's experience had taken it to the conclusion that companies do not have to become global players to survive in the global market, but they do need to be nimble enough to compete with these global players or they face the erosion of their domestic base (Bonfield, 1995). A survey of CEOs and human resources leaders in large corporations on the role of speed and agility in their organizational and HR strategy, revealed that 65% of the CEOs identified speed and agility as critical to their business plan, and 54% of the CEOs had set specific speed and performance measures in their business plan (Gandossy, 2003).

Need for Information Systems Agility

Information Systems (IS) pervade all aspects of organizational functioning. Effective and efficient information processing in today's information intensive-environment can only be achieved using computer-based IS. It can be argued that IS are a necessity for any modern organization that seeks to meet its performance expectations (Pankaj & Hyde, 2003). Information Systems embed the core of business processes in areas like ecommerce and service operations. As such, almost all changes in business processes sought by modern organizations require changes in IS. Agility of a modern organization is directly linked to the agility of its IS. If IS cannot change within the given time constraints then either the change cannot be implemented, or the efficiency and/or effectiveness of the changed business process may be compromised.

While there is a need for IS agility, changing IS in a timely fashion has traditionally been a difficult endeavor. Allen and Boynton indicated as early as 1991 that existing IS were anything but flexible[a] (Brandt R Allen & Andrew C Boynton, 1991). Legacy IS, most of which are difficult to change, are still operational today and have been characterized as a ticking time bomb since they constantly hinder business improvements due to their inability to change (Friedlos, 2006). These systems support up to 50% of the critical business processes in many organizations (Friedlos, 2006) and organizations relying on these legacy IS suffer from a lack of competitive flexibility when it comes to the effective use of IT (Reddy & Reddy, 2002). These organizations face the problem of how to adapt to, and adopt, new and emerging technologies while leveraging existing IS. Many organizations that have grown through mergers and acquisitions have gathered more variety in their IS thereby further aggravating the problem of change (Reddy & Reddy, 2002).

It has been quite difficult to achieve the desired changes to IS at a reasonable cost and, perhaps more importantly, within a reasonable time frame (Galal-Edeen, 2003). As such, the area is of significant concern to IS executives. The SIM Delphi study of top IS executives in 1996 found that building a technology infrastructure to respond to rapid changes in the competitive environment was a major concern (Brancheau, Janz, & Wetherbe, 1996). In the 2003 SIM survey, speed, and agility of IS ranked as one of the top 10 concerns of executives. Today the challenge for organizations is to structure or configure their current and future IS to meet a variety of changing requirements, many of which are not yet known as the IS are built. The IS must be agile to meet the continuous and rapid changing information-processing needs of the organization.

Problem Statement

Over the last three decades, the computer science and the software engineering disciplines have introduced several new technologies and processes for developing and designing systems that are easy to change. In the IS industry it includes initiatives/frameworks like "Utility Computing" from IBM, "Adaptive Infrastructure" from HP, Grid Computing, Service Oriented Architecture (SOA), etc. On a conceptual level, examples of initiatives/solutions include: increasing levels of abstraction where each layer is logically separated from others (e.g., storage virtualization, data independence and orthogonal persistence in databases, distribution transparency in distributed systems, write-once run-anywhere ability of programming languages like Java); better traceability of requirements through the system development life cycle; shorter development life cycles using evolutionary prototyping and eXtreme Programming (XP); etc.

However, conceptual cohesion amongst these evolving computing efforts has always been difficult and lacking (Michelis et al., 1998). The mainstream use of these evolving technologies in the design and development of IS can best be described as limited. For example SOA principles and technologies have been around at least since 2000 but started gaining some traction in 2005 (Meehan, 2005). In the systems development arena, though agile software development using methodologies like eXtreme Programming (XP) and SCRUM are gaining traction, their use is still restricted to small teams and to small projects. Most big IS have been, and are still, developed and deployed using the traditional waterfall methodology[b]. As offshore outsourcing (offsourcing) has gained popularity, the waterfall methodology is alive and well despite many of its shortcomings in constructing a changeable IS[c]. In summary, while organizations highly desire and seek IS agility, several challenges need to be overcome before IS can become agile

The fragmented nature of the initiatives and the lack of cohesion, provides no real answer to the question of how to make an IS agile in a systematic and integrative fashion. One can no doubt come up with an exhaustive list of features based on what is in existence but again without much integration and cohesion. This problem stems from the absence of formal theory in the area. *IS agility as a latent/formal construct has not been studied in the MIS academic literature.* There have been limited studies on the construct of IT/IS infrastructure flexibility (Brandt R. Allen & Andrew C. Boynton, 1991; Byrd & Turner, 2000; Duncan, 1995), but not on IS agility. Based on the review of the academic and practitioner literature in IS agility, theory development in the area of IS agility may best be characterized to be in a prescience stage (Melcher & Schwitter, 1967), where scores of models and theoretical models compete for attention and new paradigms are continually being formulated. The theories are loosely formulated with persuasive power but lack scientific precision. The study of IS agility needs to progress along the lines of a formal theory-building exercise. The first step in the study of

IS agility as per methodological guidelines for research (Melcher & Schwitter, 1967), would be to come up with a definition of IS agility. Though several conceptualizations have been put forward by numerous practitioners and consultants, they do not adequately define IS agility. Hence this very first step of defining IS agility is the primary aim of this study. Studies that just focus on definitions are often not exciting and questions about the utility in the real world are often raised. Hence the study also demonstrates how the new definition can lead to attributes of an agile IS in a cohesive and integrative fashion.

RESEARCH APPROACH

Defining a construct using rigor is an important aspect of theory building. Lack of rigor often leads to competing and fuzzy conceptualizations. Hence the research approach taken in this study aims to incorporate as much rigor as possible within the constraints of time and resources.

Some Criteria for Good Definition

A definition for agility and IS agility should adhere to the guidelines for a good definition. Classically, a good definition contains a genus (the type of thing defined) and differentia (what distinguishes it from others of the same genus). An ideal for which to aim, is to be able to begin with a minimal set of primitive terms and define more complex concepts reductively in terms of these (Markus, 2006). This study seeks a definition of agility as a set of primitives that capture the core properties. The definition can then be extended to specific organizational areas like IS and specific attributes that aid in empirical studies can be captured. Some other desirable properties of a good definition are: conceptual clarity and plausibility (make scientific sense); details of specific variables, elements, or components of the model/construct; explanatory value; and predic-

tive value (Rossi, 2006). A definition proposed in this research will be demonstrated to meet these criteria. Most existing definitions of agility and IS agility do not meet these criteria.

IS Agility as Specialization of Agility

IS agility should be treated as a specialization of the general concept of agility (similar to entity generalization and specialization in databases). It is important to call out this relationship at this stage in case it may appear that the research approach is focused more on agility and is restricted in its treatment of IS agility. IS agility should be congruent with the general construct of agility. Based on the criteria presented for good definition, the core primitives that define agility, if valid, should apply verbatim to IS agility. A definition that is entirely specific to IS agility may have tautological implications as opposed to one which captures the core primitives. For instance, a definition which defines an agile IS as modular, loosely coupled, and standards based, that results in effective and efficient change, is defining an agile IS in terms of the mechanisms that result in such agility and the desired results of these mechanisms. Such definition is process-oriented and tautological at the same time. While defining constructs, especially latent constructs, is inherently tautological (Borsboom, Mellenbergh, & Heerden, 2003), this work attempts to arrive at a definition independent of its manifestation and antecedents and focuses on the core structural properties. A desirable effect of this would be the absence of spurious correlations in empirical studies. The specificity of the definition for IS is manifested in the attributes that come into play when applying the core primitives to an IS. The specificity is an interplay between the core primitives that define agility and the attributes or characteristics of an IS which capture these primitives. This philosophy from generalization to specialization also guides the research approach.

Research Steps

Congruent to the discussions in the previous sections the starting point for arriving at a definition of IS agility was to attempt an inductive extension of the existing published definitions of agility to IS agility. Agility as a field of study has existed in the manufacturing area for more than a decade. An inductive extension of existing definitions would also provide a unifying theme across disciplines and time. Section 3 details the results of an extensive study of the agility literature that was conducted to review the definitions of agility based on the guidelines for a good definition and arrive at a definition of IS agility. Approximately 400 published articles from academic peer-reviewed journals, peer-reviewed conference proceedings, and practitioner publications, were examined for the core characteristics of agility[d]. The definitions were evaluated based on the criteria for a good definition and it was concluded that a better definition was needed. A deductive approach was adopted to come up with a definition of agility. This definition is presented in Section 4. This definition was extended to IS to define an agile IS. The definition as it applies to specific aspects of an IS is detailed in Section 5 and focuses on the interplay of the core primitives and specific characteristics of an IS. The researchers deemed the proposed definition to be very different from the existing definitions, and hence the definition was validated through interviews with IS executives. This was an initial validation and has been followed by an empirical study. Section 6 presents the results of this validation study. Finally, Section 7 discusses the implications for future research.

At this stage it is important to point out the distinction between the agility of IS itself versus IS support for organizational agility. IS are an important factor in enabling organizational agility through their support for timely and relevant information that may be needed at the time of a change. The role of IS in organizational agility has been considered important since the time agility gained foothold in the mainstream management literature (Devor, Graves, & Miles, 1997). Agility of IS itself is a different aspect and this study is aimed at the study of agility as a property of IS.

LITERATURE REVIEW AND ANALSYIS OF EXISTING DEFINITIONS OF AGILITY

The Dominant Agility Framework

The use of agility as a competitive strategy gained momentum as the result of a joint study in the 1980s by the federal government and US industry that resulted in a two-volume report from the Lee Iacocca Institute at Lehigh University titled *21st Century Manufacturing Enterprise Strategy Project* (Devor et al., 1997). In this report, the term "agile manufacturing" was used to characterize a different form of industrial competition. Subsequently, the focus was expanded from manufacturing agility to agility at the enterprise level by the "Agility Forum" at Lehigh University. The concept of enterprise agility entered mainstream management focus as a result of the 1995 book by Goldman, Nagel, and Preiss, "Agile Competitors and Virtual Organizations" (Goldman, Nagel, & Preiss, 1995). This work is considered one of the seminal works in the area of agility.

Goldman et al. framework is a systemic framework comprised of four dimensions: *Cooperating Resources; Customer Enrichment; Relentless Change; and Leveraging People, Information, and Knowledge.* Based on Goldman's framework one could define an agile organization (though Goldman et. al. have not given this definition) as one that uses *cooperating resources* and *leverages personnel, knowledge, and IT* to produce *products and services that enrich the customer* in a *relentlessly changing environment.* As per the criteria for a good definition, the definition derived from this framework does not provide a genus or a differentia and it is overly broad, expansive, and complex as opposed to being based on a set of primitives. Other definitions in the literature derived from this framework also appear to suffer from the same problems. Many of these and other definitions incorporate the antecedents and consequences, as well as specify agility as a process rather than a set of structural properties (Melcher & Schwitter, 1967). In addition, the definitions do not distinguish between the related concepts of adaptability and flexibility.

Analysis of Existing Definitions of Agility

Appendix 1 contains a compilation of some definitions of agility proposed in the existing academic and practitioner literature. Some of the key observations, for the purpose of arriving at a definition of agility that fulfills the criteria of a good definition and could be extended to IS, are outlined below:

1. Agility is needed due to unpredictable changes in environment, customer demand, technology, etc. All definitions point to a need for the existence of agility as a capability to cope with change. Unpredictable changes in the environment is an antecedent for agility, hence it may be excluded for the definition, since an argument can be made that agility may exist in absence of these antecedents. While the two are closely related, one may want to arrive at a definition that segregates the properties in the definition from the reason(s) why those properties are needed.

2. Most definitions use manufacturing terms to define agility. This is not surprising since agility concepts were first adopted and applied by the manufacturing sector. A definition of agility needs to focus on generic and core properties which apply to all aspects of the organization and are not based on properties specific to an area. An

organization can develop a set of capabilities at various levels and in different functional areas to be agile. Some parts, functional elements, and/or aspects of the organizations may show agility and some may not. A definition of agility that is based on the core properties would apply in all situations and at all levels and aspects of an organization in a similar fashion. Existing definitions do not fulfill this criterion adequately.

3. Time is an important element of agility and it is specified in different ways as an attribute of action/response: quick reaction (Bessant, Francis, Meredith, & Kalinsky, 2001; Bititci, Turner, & Ball, 1999; Brown & Agnew, 1982; James, 2005; McGaughey, 1999; Noaker, 1994; O'Connor, 1994; Richards, 1996; R. Shafer, 1999; Sieger, Badiru, & Milatovic, 2000); time-based competition or short lead times (Meredith & Francis, 2000; Narasimhan, 1999; Richards, 1996; Sahin, 2000; Sieger et al., 2000; Vasilash, 2001; Vastag, Kasarda, & Boone, 1994; Vokurka & Fliedner, 1997; Vokurka, Zank, & III, 2002); etc. As such, any definition of agility has to incorporate some element of time into the definition.

4. Most definitions define agility in terms of flexibility (Abdul-Nour, Drolet, & Lambert, 1999; Bessant et al., 2001; Devor et al., 1997; Hopp & Oyen, 2004; C.-C. Huang, 1999; C.-Y. Huang, Ceroni, & Nof, 2000; Long, 2000; Meredith & Francis, 2000; Narasimhan, 1999; Ota, 2001; Pfohl, 1997; Pullin, 2001; R. A. Shafer, Dyer, Kilty, Amos, & Ericksen, 2002; Sharifi & Zhang, 1999; Vasilash, 2001; Vernadat, 1999; Vokurka & Fliedner, 1997; Vokurka et al., 2002; Yusuf, Sarahadi, & Gunasekaran, 1999); and adaptability (Backhouse & Burns, 1999; Bessant et al., 2001; Bititci et al., 1999; W. Christian & Frederick, 1996; Dove, 1995a; Kassim & Zain, 2004; Meier, Humphreys, & Williams, 1998; Melarkode, From-Poulsen, &

Warnakulsuriya, 2004; Meredith & Francis, 2000; Pfohl, 1997; R. Shafer, 1999; R. A. Shafer et al., 2002). Flexibility and adaptability are concepts that are distinct from agility and defining agility in terms of these may violate the differentia criterion (what distinguishes agility from others of the same genus). There is some explicit mention in the published academic literature to the fact that agility is a different and possibly higher order concept as opposed to flexibility (Abdul-Nour et al., 1999; C.-Y. Huang et al., 2000; C.-Y. Huang & Nof, 1999; Langer & Alting, 2000; R. A. Shafer et al., 2002; Vokurka & Fliedner, 1997, 1998; Vokurka et al., 2002) and adaptability (R. Shafer, 1999; R. A. Shafer et al., 2002). While the relationship between these three concepts (agility, flexibility, and adaptability) is not an objective of this research, the published research does allude to the existence of agility, especially network agility in the absence of flexibility (C.-Y. Huang et al., 2000; C.-Y. Huang & Nof, 1999). In arriving at a definition of agility that is based on a set of primitives, the primitives may need to define properties of agility independent of the related concepts of flexibility and adaptability.

5. Most definitions do not define agility as a minimal set of primitive terms that can be used reductively to define more complex concepts and hence extending the existing definitions to define IS agility is a non-trivial task. As an example, the IS[e] is presented as a component of agility (P. H. Christian, Govande, Staehle, & Jr., 1999; Christopher, 2000; Devor et al., 1997; Hibbert, 1999; Hoek, 2000; Hopp & Oyen, 2004; Langer & Alting, 2000; Meredith & Francis, 2000; Yusuf et al., 1999) and so these definitions cannot aid in defining IS agility.

6. Agility is a set of dynamic capabilities/abilities/competencies (Bessant et al., 2001; Meredith & Francis, 2000; Vokurka

& Fliedner, 1997). These abilities are context-specific (Vokurka & Fliedner, 1997). The set of primitives used in a definition of agility should capture these abilities and should be invariant with respect to time and context so that the definition is valid in different contexts and at different times as it is. For instance, virtual organizations[f] and interorganizational collaboration are proposed as a core component of agility (Bessant et al., 2001; P. H. Christian et al., 1999; Christopher, 2000; Day, Forrester, & Burnett, 2000; Devor et al., 1997; Goldman et al., 1995; Hibbert, 1999; C.-Y. Huang et al., 2000; C.-Y. Huang & Nof, 1999; Langer & Alting, 2000; Meredith & Francis, 2000; Yusuf et al., 1999). However, this may not hold in all contexts and at all times, since in many cases a good supply chain may suffice instead of a virtual organization. Additionally virtual organizations may be considered as a mechanism to achieve agility rather than a component of agility.

7. Operationalizing the existing definitions of agility does not appear to be an easy task. Primary reasons for this have been specified before and include: broad and lack of focus on core properties; use of terminology from a specific area; use of antecedents and consequences; use of related concepts like flexibility and adaptability; etc. Many would qualify as a framework as opposed to being a definition. The literature reviewed had only two systematic attempts at operationalizing the construct of agility. These included defining a set of activities/business-processes needed for agility and setting a reference level for these activities (Bessant et al., 2001; Dove, 1996b; Meredith & Francis, 2000). These operationalizations, again, do not provide an easy way of either extending the definition of agility to organizational components like IS or arriving at a set of properties of an agile IS.

The review of the published academic literature demonstrates several deficiencies in the existing definitions of agility. The definitions are not extensible and applicable at various levels and to various aspects of an organization and so cannot be extended to IS to obtain a definition of IS agility. In the absence of a good definition, one cannot operationalize IS agility to a set of specific variables, elements, or components for use in empirical studies.

DEVELOPMENT OF A DEFINITION OF AGILITY

Towards a Definition of Agility

To search for underlying core properties/primitives that may be used to arrive at a definition of agility, the researchers looked at the origins of agility. Agility has its origins in the biological world. Agility in living beings is rooted in motion and is manifested when the living being is in motion. It is related to the quickness of motion:

1. Webster's dictionary defines agility as "quickness of motion".
2. The Oxford dictionary defines agility as "dexterity in motion".
3. On the Internet, the top search results on agility relate to agility games for dogs (e.g., www.agilitynet.com). These games test the quickness of motion of the dogs. A Google and other search engine alerts on agility consistently (as to the day of writing of this manuscript) return articles/pieces related to canine agility as a major theme.
4. The combat aircraft industry has been testing and measuring for agility of aircraft for many years. US Air Force experts characterize agility as the ability to change maneuver state (Richards, 1996). Maneuverability is referred to as the maximum turn rate. Agility

is described as how fast an aircraft can go from one direction to another.

One way to arrive at a definition of agility may be to disaggregate the quickness of motion into a set of structural properties and extend it to collective social bodies like an organization or an enterprise. To study the elements of quickness of motion one may examine the phenomenon in living beings from where the concept has originated. A living being exists in a context or environment and the first step in being agile is to sense a shift in this context or environment. In other words, a change has to be sensed and the stimuli that may indicate a change have to be registered. The second step in being agile is to diagnose what has been sensed, primarily to determine how the change will affect the living being. For example, for a lion chasing a gazelle, a change in the direction of the gazelle can mean the lion losing its meal. Once the diagnosis is made, then the living being needs to select a course of action and execute the action. For the lion it may mean that it changes its course to follow the gazelle or take an alternative course that will enable it to intercept the gazelle. While this may appear to be a normal decision-making cycle, it is not so. The reason it is not a normal decision-making cycle is that the activities of sensing a change, diagnosing the change, selecting an action, and executing the action, all happen in a time-span that is the same as the one in which the process of interest is happening. In this study, this aspect of time is branded as real-time. Real-time is the essence of agility. Sensing, diagnosis, selection of an action, and the execution of an action occurs in real-time so as to avoid a threat or to capitalize on an opportunity[g].

Definition of Agility

Based on the examination of the characteristics of the motion of living beings where agility entails acting to a sensed change in real-time, agility may be stated to be comprised of three abilities. These abilities are:

1. **Sense**: Ability to sense the stimuli for change in real-time.
2. **Diagnose**: Ability to interpret or analyze stimuli in real-time to determine the nature, cause, and impact of change.
3. **Respond:** Ability to respond to a change in real-time. Response is further disaggregated into *Select* and *Execute.*
   3.1. **Select**: Ability to select a response in real-time (very short planning time) to capitalize on the opportunity or counter the threat.
   3.2. **Execute**: Ability to execute the response in real-time.

All three abilities have to exist to result in a successful real-time response to a change. If the sensing is flawed, then the organization may sense a change where there is none and expend resources wastefully. It may also try to sense too much and waste resources. On the other hand, where there is a change and it is not sensed, the results may range from loss of market share and competitive advantage to more drastic ones like exiting a product line completely. At times the organization may not sense the correct, or needed, stimuli or may sense too few stimuli. Once a change has been sensed, it has to be diagnosed correctly. Accurate diagnosis enables the organization to filter out change signals from noise and determine the nature, cause, and impact of change. Once a change has been diagnosed, a response should be selected and executed in real-time. Executing the response completes what one would term as an agile maneuver. Response should meet the time constraints as the top priority and may compromise on facets like elegance of the solution. Many parallel and repeating cycles of sense, diagnose, select, and execute, occurring in real-time, exist at a given instance in an agile organization.

The definition of agility presented here has some similarity to existing definitions but it is unique and possibly complete in its use of real-time. Similar definitions have been used for describing an adaptive organization (Haeckel & Nolan, 1996) and agility of ecommerce sites (Canter, 2000). Canter capitalizes on the Air Force's observe, orient, decide, and act (OODA) loop as the agility mechanism while Haeckel and Nolan describe an adaptive organization as

Figure 1. Conceptualization of agility

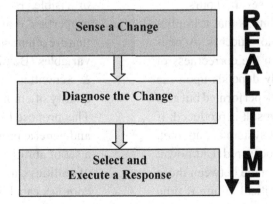

a sense-and-respond organization incorporating adaptive cycles of sense, interpret, decide, and act. Haeckel and Nolan's definition is essentially similar to what this study presents, except that they do not conceptualize it as agility and lack a pronounced stress on real-time. "Diagnose" and "Select" used here though different from the notions of "Interpret" and "Decide" used by Haeckel and Nolan, achieve the same effect.

Real-Time

This section elaborates further on real-time since the researchers encountered some confusion about the concept of real-time. It has become common to treat real-time as meaning something happening in an instant. Real-time does not necessarily mean milliseconds or microseconds or instantaneously. The measure of real-time will vary based on the context of change/process. Federal Standard 1037C (Telecommunications: Glossary of Telecommunication Terms) defines real-time as the time for performance of some task, during the actual time that the related physical process occurs. Congruent to this definition it is important to realize that the actual physical length of time for real-time, differs in strategic, tactical, and operational contexts since the related processes span different physical time lengths. The real-time in a strategic context may range from months to years, while the real-time in the operational context may range from a few minutes to several hours.

A second facet of real-time is that it implies time as a critical element for success. A real-time system is one in which the correctness of the task performed not only depends upon the logical correctness of the task performed but also upon the time at which the result is produced. If the timing constraints of the system are not met, system failure is said to have occurred (Unknown, 2002). A distinction can be made between those systems that will suffer a critical failure if time constraints are violated (hard or immediate real-time), and those that will not (soft real-time) and

can recover (Anonymous, 2006). For example, a car engine control system or a pace maker is a hard real-time system because a delayed signal to the engine or the heart may cause critical failure or damage. Typically, violation of constraints in a soft real-time system results in degraded quality, but the system can continue to operate. Hard real-time versus soft real-time does not necessarily relate to the length of time available for action (Anonymous, 2006). Any agile component within an organization including IS also meets this requirement of a real-time system. A hard or soft failure occurs if the time constraints for execution of a response are not met.

Strengths of the Proposed Definition

It needs to be demonstrated how the proposed definition addresses the deficiencies in the existing definitions and provides an improvement:

1. The proposed definition focuses on the core properties of agility. The core properties are defined in structural terms and not process terms and hence do not use any antecedents or consequences of agility as part of the definition. Thus agility as a property of an organization may exist when the conditions conducive to its use may not exist and agility may also be present even when its consequences may not be explicitly demonstrated or visible. By focusing on the structural properties, it avoids tautological problems that are often associated with defining latent variables (Borsboom et al., 2003; Melcher & Schwitter, 1967) and may improve the quality of empirical studies.

2. The proposed definition focuses on core and generic properties. It defines agility as a set of abilities (primitive terms). This set of abilities can then be used to define more complex capabilities and abilities within an organization at various levels of analysis. The definition is not based on properties

specific to an area and stays the same when applied at different organizational levels or to different functional areas or when applied to a specific component of an organization like the IS. This will be demonstrated when the definition is extended to define IS agility.

3. It was stated that time is an important element of agility. The proposed definition ties agility to real-time. Only one existing definition uses real-time (the emphasis is not as pronounced as in the current definition) to define an agile manufacturing system by characterizing it as follows: "A system that shifts quickly among product models or between product lines ideally in real-time to meet customer demand" (Yusuf et al., 1999). The focus on real-time in the proposed definition captures the essence of agility.

4. The proposed definition of agility is unique and distinct with respect to the similar constructs of flexibility and adaptability. Though there are several differences that may be outlined, the primary difference is manifested here with stress on real-time which is not an element of either flexibility or adaptability. Furthermore agility is not defined using either flexibility or adaptability.

5. Agility is a set of dynamic capabilities/abilities/competencies. The proposed definition of agility requires ability in four areas. These four areas are invariant with respect to time and context. For instance, in different contexts and over a period of time, specific attributes that allow sensing or diagnosis in real-time may be different but they will still add up to the overall ability of sensing or diagnosing in real-time.

6. Operationalizing the definition or arriving at a set of attributes that enable sensing, diagnosing, selecting a response, and executing a response in real-time is easier due to focus on specific core properties as opposed to the

existing definitions which are overly broad (IS agility has been operationalized in a follow-up study using these core properties).

Weaknesses of the Proposed Definition

One could consider some weaknesses in the definition. The first one being that because this definition is based on the core properties and is generic, its extension to IS may be considered to lack specificity to IS. The benefits of this has been discussed in Section 2 and the specificity is demonstrated during operationalization when the interplay between the attributes of an IS and the definition comes into play. Still the definition may lack enough buzz to invoke immediate interest of practitioners. Some researchers may consider the extension to IS agility as a trivial exercise given the perceived lack of specificity of the extended definition to IS.

Another issue may arise from the use of real-time. When considering agility in an organizational context, the unit of analysis moves up from physical bodies to collective social bodies/constructs. One may argue that in the context of such complex social constructs, it may be impossible to do anything in real-time and hence question the use of real-time. Given the several constraints (including those of technology) that organizations face, especially where humans are involved, achieving real-time may be elusive. It is also quite possible that true agility and responsiveness may need to be founded on complete automation to overcome the cognitive limitations of human beings. Still the researchers believe that this does not imply that the definition itself needs modification for its use of real-time. Absence of real-time makes agility a non-unique construct and blends the construct into several related terms in area of effective decision-making. Real-time is what the organizations should strive for when starting on a pursuit of agility. Over a period of time, IS and other mechanisms may enable true real-time sensing, diagnosis, selection, and execution, if the focus on real-time is maintained.

AGILE INFORMATION SYSTEMS / INFORMATION SYSTEMS AGILITY

The definition of agility presented in this study may be extended to define IS agility. An agile IS may be defined as one that can sense a change in real-time, diagnose the change in real-time, select a response in real-time, and execute the response in real-time. This definition fits well with the various current IS agility initiatives like utility computing, grid computing, adaptive data centers, service-oriented architecture (SOA), etc. These initiatives are oriented towards real-time response as specified in the proposed definition. For example, adaptive data centers are aimed at scaling server/processing capacity up or down in real-time as the peak load requirements change.

An agile IS can continuously shift states in real-time from one *stable state* to another in response to changes. The difference in these states may be small or big depending upon the nature of the change. The stability of the resulting states is an important requirement because modern IS are fairly complex and modification to one part of the system can have inadvertent effect(s) on some other part(s) causing an outage which can, in turn, lead to disruption of business processes that these IS support.

Next the specific characteristics of an agile IS are discussed. For the purpose of discussion IS is conceptualized as a combination of human and IT components operating within an organizational context (Byrd & Turner, 2000). The IT component includes hardware, software, storage, and networking and the human component includes the IS personnel/staff responsible for planning, development, operation, and maintenance of the human and IT components. One may conceptualize IS in many other elaborate ways spanning various levels and aspects of the organization,

the conceptualization adopted here is more apt for treating IS as an artifact with well defined boundaries incorporating both technical and human components.

Sensing a Change in Agile Information Systems

Sensing means that relevant signals/stimuli are received and that the information on the level/measure (both objective and subjective) of parameter(s) with which the stimulus is concerned, is recorded. The ability to correctly sense the relevant parameters is a prerequisite to recognizing a shift in them. For example, ensuring the Quality of Service (QoS) on a network requires accurate sensing of the traffic of different priorities so that if a burst of high priority traffic occurs, bandwidth may be immediately allocated to that traffic. Accurate and timely sensing is especially important in cases where the state/position of the IS has to shift constantly to meet the stated performance goals. This is illustrated in the case of network management where bandwidth has to be continuously allocated between network traffic of different priorities.

Signals come from everywhere (Quinn, 1980). The ability to receive signals is contingent upon several factors. Physical limitations of the receiver (human or machine) may limit what signals are received (Haeckel & Nolan, 1996). The perceptual limitations of the IS personnel (individual and groups) may pose additional limitations (Billings, Milburn, & Schaalman, 1980; Quinn, 1980). As such, an IS should employ a wide variety of sensors that include machines, personnel, and social entities (groups and teams) to sense the stimuli. An agile IS should be able to sense stimuli from internal, organizational, and environmental changes. Internal changes originate from within the IS, e.g. increase in disk access during database operations; organizational changes arise due to factors outside the IS function but within the organization, e.g. selection of additional suppliers; and environmental changes arise due to factors external to the organization and may effect IS directly or through the mediating effect of organizational factors, e.g. end of support for a software product.

Some example attributes that may enable an IS to sense a change in real-time are as follows: All IS staff with basic knowledge of business and its operations; Some staff with in depth knowledge of business and its operations; Good interpersonal skills in IS staff; Ability of the IS staff to work in cross-functional teams; Involvement of IS staff in all business level planning; Periodic and/or ad-hoc assessment of the skills of the IS staff either internally or externally; etc. Additional attributes related to the technology components and personnel would be included.

Diagnosing the Change in Agile Information Systems

Recognizing whether a change has happened or is going to happen is a non-trivial task. Intel chairman Andy Grove stated that this is perhaps one of the most difficult tasks that an organization faces (Grove, 1999). In cases of IS, accurate and timely diagnosis has become ever more difficult due to the increasing complexity and distributed nature of IS. An important objective of the diagnosis is to distinguish signal from noise[h]. Stimuli need to be analyzed to sense a change. Since all real world processes have some variance associated with them, a stimulus may not always signify a change. At times, a stimulus may be small enough to be ignored as noise individually, but collectively with other stimuli, it may indicate a significant change. Hence stimuli may need to be combined to sense a change.

An accurate and timely diagnosis provides answers to questions like what is the change, where is it occurring, when has it occurred or will occur, who are affected by the change, what is the cause of the change, and what is the effect of the change. Additional stimuli may be examined after

an initial diagnosis due to the high complexity and distributed nature of modern IS. Complexity may often make it difficult to infer the linkages between cause and effect and inference of cause is necessary to arrive at a effective response to the change.

Diagnosis may be objective and algorithmic, and/or subjective. Subjective diagnosis involving IS personnel would involve psychological limitations like aspiration level triggers (where what is sensed is compared against internal performance levels or aspiration criterion), recency effects (Kiesler & Sproull, 1982), etc. Sensitivity to the limitations of social and individual cognition that may be amplified in a real-time scenario and mechanisms to compensate these limitations may be required.

Some example attributes that may enable an IS to diagnose a change in real-time are as follows: High levels of analytical skills in the IS staff; Multi-skilled IS staff (multiple areas of technology as well as business skills); Availability of software applications for manipulation of data from stimuli (spreadsheets, reporting applications, OLAP, aggregating transactional data, etc.); Availability of software applications for partial or complete diagnosis of stimuli (data mining, text mining, case based reasoning, Artificial Intelligence applications); Knowledge of the organization's business and its operation by the IS staff; etc. Additional attributes related to the technology components and personnel would be included.

Selecting a Response in Agile Information Systems

Once a change has been diagnosed, a response is selected. This may range from taking no action to a complete reengineering of some aspects of IS. The primary criterion selecting a action in an agile IS is to meet the time constraints. For this reason, an exceptionally effective and sound rational response that is late may be regarded as a failure when compared to a quick patch job that meets the time constraints. Additional criteria for a response are cost of the response, scope of the response, and robustness of the response (Dove, 1994). These additional constraints may be used if several responses satisfy the time constraints. Ideally an agile IS chooses a response that can be executed within the given time constraint (in real-time), with minimum cost, maximum scope, and maximum robustness. These four constraints constitute a comprehensive set of constraints that can be used to select a response. For instance, constraints on time and cost will help in choosing between outsourcing versus in-house development since outsourcing may result in a faster response (especially in cases where there is a lack of in-house skills) and constraints on robustness will help in choosing between new technologies (with higher probability of instability and bugs) versus trusted old technologies.

Some example attributes that may enable an IS to select a response in real-time are as follows: Project Managers with an accurate knowledge of controllable, partially controllable, and uncontrollable factors; Scientific and formal estimation methods that can estimate the time, cost, robustness, and scope of a response; Experienced and knowledgea ble IS staff for estimating the time, cost, robustness, and scope of a response; Access to knowledge bases (e.g., sizing guidelines) of vendors of IT components to aid in estimation; etc. Additional attributes related to the technology components and personnel would be included.

Executing the Response in an Agile Information System

Execution is perhaps the most important part of agility since most failures occur at this stage. Executing the response in real-time is contingent on resources available. Possible lack of elaborate planning due to real-time requirements, and the complexity and distributed nature of modern IS is likely to make the execution a challenging exercise. For real-time execution, most contingencies

have to be handled on-the-fly through reallocation of resources or by having alternatives. Existing knowledge areas in operations management and software engineering like "Resource-Constrained Project Scheduling Problem (RCPSP)", that involves scheduling of non-preemptable project activities subject to precedence and resource constraints in order to minimize the project duration (Demeulemeester, Reyck, & Herroelen, 2000), can be employed to arrive at response execution strategies in an agile IS. Response execution may also incorporate alternatives for a chosen response/action. This would be done during response selection. For example, if an application development is behind schedule then it may be outsourced to meet the time constraints or off-the-shelf/hosted applications may be used along with modification of the existing business processes (this may involve more elaborate manual procedures). In selected cases where the physical real-time is substantially larger than the physical cognitive time associated with the actor (human or machine), impending execution failures or problems may deem it necessary to start the cycle again by seeking additional stimuli while still staying within the original real-time time constraints.

An agile IS allows for short execution times. Some example attributes that may enable an IS to execute a response in real-time are as follows: Scalable IT components; Modular IT components; Existence of a common underlying framework like middleware, EAI, etc., to integrate existing and legacy IT components; Loosely coupled IT components; Standards for processes, practices, functions, and activities that can be incorporated into IS; Standards for decomposition of functionality into lower level modules or components; IT components and/or modules with a base set of standard functionality; Standards (message formats, protocols, etc.) for information exchange between modules/components; Technical interface (e.g. PCI and other bus standards) standards for IT components; Technical standards (like naming of variables) for building of the modules and/or components; Standards for assessing and certifying the skills of the IS staff (including those of contractors); Service oriented architecture for IS that views all IS components as services; Ability to collaborate with external parties to use services provided by their IS components through advertising of services and specification of the access mechanisms; Existence of security mechanisms to control access to service provided by IS components inside and outside the organization; etc. Additional attributes related to the technology components and personnel would be included.

VALIDATION AND SUPPORT OF THE PROPOSED DEFINITION

The proposed definition of agility and IS agility is very different from the existing definitions and conceptualizations. Though the definition is consistent with the thought process embedded in current and past practitioner IS literature, it has not been conceptualized as it is in this research. As a result, it was considered necessary to obtain initial validation of the definition from the practitioners in the IS area.

Methodology

Given that IS agility is a relatively new area of study and this work is in the initial stages of theory building, a qualitative data collection methodology was employed which can result in better insights to a new phenomena. Interviews with IS executives were conducted to obtain their opinion on the proposed definition. The IS executives targeted were involved with both business and technical aspects of IS in their regular job roles. Multiple interviews were conducted for purposes of literal replication as per Bonoma's guidelines for verification when using qualitative methods (Bonoma, 1985). Each interview was

treated as a case (given that the interviewee was from a different organization) and each interview was expected to be complementary to the other interviews, sufficing the replication to be as literal. The interviewees were selected from an IS executive discussion round-table which had the mission of increasing collaboration between practitioners and academicians on leading edge techniques and research in the IS area. An additional criterion for selection was to interview those executives whose organizations/roles were expected to have a need for IS agility.

For the purposes of validation, the interviewees were first asked to comment upon what they thought IS agility or agility in general was (There was some additional data collected during the interviews.) They were then told about the proposed definition and requested to comment on it. While commenting, they were specifically asked to comment upon the appropriateness of the definition and any proposed changes that they would like to have incorporated in the definition.

Interviewee Demographics

The interviews were conducted in the first and second quarter of 2004. "Table 1: Interviewee Demographics" presents the demographic information of the interviewees. The interviewees represent diversity in organizations in terms of industry and size; diversity in role and responsibilities; and diversity in organizations in terms of their approach to developing and managing IS. For example, while organization #9 tries to be on the forefront of new and developing technologies, organization #8 still uses a large number of legacy systems and is cautious in its use of cutting-edge technologies. The interviewees hold roles that span from strategic, to a mix of strategic and technical, to more specialized technical roles. Insights from this sample, particularly those pointing to the convergence of thoughts on the proposed definition, would provide the needed validation of the definition.

Table 1. Interviewee demographics

#	Interviewee Job Area	Industry	Product / Services	IS Staff Strength	Annual IS Budget	Annual Revenue
1.	Consultant	Consulting, Clients in banking, retailing	Strategic and technical consulting	Clients with IS staff of 125 to 300	Clients with $30 million and above	Fortune 1000 clients
2.	Disaster Recovery	Computer services, Information System services	Hardware manufacturer and IS services	50,000	$3 billion	$73 billion
3.	IT Strategy & Communic-ation	Insurance	Risk management, reinsurance, and insurance brokerage	2,500	$800 million	$8 billion
4.	CIO	Financial services	Retail and commercial banking	30	$18 million	$280 million
5.	Information & Strategic Services	Government	Public Safety	139	$20 million	$1.1 billion (operating budget)
6.	IT Architect	B2B payment intermediary	Controlled spending payment tools (credit cards, gift cards, etc.)	120	$20 million	$1 billion
7.	Software and Application Integration	Healthcare	Hospital operation and management	1500	$500 million	$13 billion
8.	System Analysis and Design	Insurance	Retail and business insurance	5000	$2 billion	$44 billion
9.	Product Integration and Support	Financial services	Service Bureau for banks	400	$250+ million	$2.4 billion
10.	Consultant	Financial services	Strategic recommenda-tions, IT solutions and implementation	Clients with IS staff of 50 to 500	Clients with $15 million to $60 million	Small to mid size banks clients ($250 million to $1 billion)

Data Analysis

The interview recordings were transcribed and the transcripts of the interviews were content-analyzed to determine the presence of certain ideas and/or concepts. The transcripts of the interviews were analyzed and coded into the three categories of: interviewee's definition of IS agility, agreement of the interviewee with the proposed definition, and comments on the proposed definition. To ensure the validity of the coding and to avoid researcher bias in coding, coding by at least one more coder other than the researcher is recommended. Due to resource constraints, one interview transcript was randomly picked and coded by a second coder. There was an 80% agreement between the

coding by the primary researcher and the second coder. This is deemed sufficient for purposes of reliability (Miles & Huberman, 1994). Alternate methods for reducing biases were used during the analyses and coding of all of the ten transcripts. Interviews were analyzed and coded in two steps. The first analysis and coding of the interviews was done about 10 days after the interview was transcribed. This ensured that the analysis and coding was based on the text in the transcript in an objective fashion. This may lead to a loss of some richness in the data but preventing researcher bias was considered most important given that the definition proposed here had a lot of researchers' time and resources invested in it. The second analysis and coding of the interview was done about a week after the first analysis. The results of the two analyses and coding were examined for congruence and discrepancies. No systematic discrepancies were found in the analyses and coding of the ten transcripts for the two steps.

Interviewee Definition of IS Agility

The interviewees forwarded a variety of definitions for agility and IS agility. These were broad in coverage while overlapping with related concepts of flexibility and adaptability. Since the question about the definition was posed at the beginning of the interview, most interviewees (except #9) chose to talk more about agility in general, rather than being very specific to IS agility, though IS was still the central theme of their definitions. The common theme was the ability of an IS to respond quickly/rapidly to changes of different kinds (#1, #3, #4, #6, #10). Agility allows response to events that have not been thought about (#6). Agility (and IS agility) involves changing business processes (#1, #10), product (#1), data (#2), information (#5, #7), human resources (#5), IS itself (#1, #7), and/or platforms (#6). These changes should be made to meet business requirements, objectives, or needs (#2, #3, #4, #6, #8, and #10). Agility was also described as being similar to flexibility (#2, #7). IT was seen to have a pivotal role in enabling agility (#2). Reflecting the trend in the industry, one interviewee (#8) stressed the exploitation of the latest and emerging technologies as an essential component of agility. IS agility was associated with the technological attributes of connectivity (#9), redundancy (#9), upgradeability (#9, #10), open and standards-based (#10), scalability (#10), and resiliency (#10). The organizational aspects of IS agility were also stressed. One interviewee (#10) overwhelmingly stressed that IS agility has more to do with the culture of the organization rather than the technology itself. The importance of linking IS changes to strategic or market changes was stressed by most interviewees (#2, #3, #4, #6, #7, #8, #10) which is also the predominant

theme in the practitioner literature that discuss IS agility.

The time for making these changes was described to be quickly (#1, #3, #6, and #10), as quickly as one thinks (#1), fast (#3), rapidly (#6, #10), timely (#7), in a hurry or less than 6 months (#8), and six to nine months (#9). Interviewee #1 alluded to real-time by saying that the translation from thought to action should happen without going through the many intervening layers. It was explicitly mentioned that the time to change depends upon the context and can vary from instantaneous to days, depending upon the context (#4). IT needs to follow the business which in turn follows the market (#3).

The variety of thoughts and conceptualizations of agility (and IS agility) in the interviews clearly points to the need for a definition that is focused and discriminating and incorporates elements of timeliness in relation to a given context. These elements are part of the definition proposed in this paper. The next section presents the opinion of the interviewees on the proposed definition

Comments on the Proposed Definition of Agility and Information Systems Agility

As stated earlier, since the definition is considered to be very different, compared to the existing or prevalent definitions, agreement with the definition and its endorsement in the very first introduction during the interview was considered to be sufficient evidence of its viability in defining the phenomenon of IS agility.

The responses to the definition of agility ranged from a very good definition that should be disseminated (#1) to an academic definition that may be depicting an ideal situation (#10) primarily on account of the use of real-time. The first impression of real-time to most interviewees was that of instant solution. Interviewees said that real-time needed explaining (#1), real-time needs caution since people usually view real-time as instant (#3), real-time may not be practical (#8), it seemed like a perfect definition (#8), and real-time may be ideal and give an impression that there is some magic out there (#10). However consequent to the explanation, all interviewees agreed with the context-dependent nature of real-time and the fact that it should be looked at in relation to the process to which it is being referred. Interviewees were satisfied with the use of real-time and agreed that real-time is probably the best term to use (#1) though it would need to be explained so as not to cause confusion. Alternates to real-time were "time that is synchronized with the expectations of the organization" (#2), or "meet business requirement in the time frame of that requirement" (#10). They are both congruent to the conceptualization of real-time. Overall, it seemed like the use of real-time was appropriate provided some explanation was included along with the definition.

Overall there was sufficient agreement by the interviewees that the definition made the meaning of agility clearer and provided a structure and/or framework for the study of agility and IS agility. The interviews did not point to pressing need for a modification to the definition, though additional explanation of real-time could provide more clarity. The evidence of congruence of thinking between the interviewees and the researchers provides the needed initial validation of the definition. It supports the claim that IS agility (and agility) as defined in this study is an improvement on what currently exists in academic literature and what is understood in the practice.

CONCLUSION AND FURTHER WORK

The current environment for businesses is volatile and turbulent, characterized by the rapid pace of change. Such an environment, coupled with the dependency of modern organizations on IS, implies that IS agility may lead to significant

advantages for an organization should the organization choose to pursue it and invest in initiatives to make IS more agile. The area of IS agility is an exciting area that is of great interest to the IS practitioners. The academic IS community can make valuable contributions in this area by applying the rigors and principles of scientific research to come up with models that lead to specific and meaningful interventions. This study contributes to this aim.

There is little systematic academic or practitioner research till date on IS agility. This study is an attempt to advance research in IS agility from a prescience to a science stage, and to study it as per formal theory-building standards (Melcher & Schwitter, 1967). A good definition of IS agility would be the first step in this direction. This study revisits existing academic and practitioner work on agility and arrives at its definition based on its core characteristics using a set of primitives. This definition is extended to IS and the application of this definition to arrive at specific attributes and characteristics of an agile IS has been demonstrated. The proposed definition was validated through interviews with IS practitioners. It was found to have merit and can form the basis of future studies. The initial work on the attributes of an agile IS briefly presented in this study has been further extended to provide a better coverage and operationalize the construct of IS agility. The operationalization has been used in a qualitative and quantitative empirical study the results of which would be presented in subsequent work.

IS agility is an important issue that will become more and more important as IS become more and more integrated into every aspect of modern business and society, and as IS become more complex and sophisticated. It is hoped that the work presented in this research will provide a basic framework for future studies in this area to establish it as a formal research stream in academic IS literature.

REFERENCES

Abdul-Nour, G., Drolet, J., & Lambert, S. (1999). Mixed Production, Flexibility, and SME. *Computers and Industrial Engineering, 37*(1-2), 429-432.

Allen, B. R., & Boynton, A. C. (1991). Information Architecture: In Search of Efficient Flexibility. *MIS Quarterly,* 435-445.

Allen, B. R., & Boynton, A. C. (1991). Information Infrastructure: In Search of Efficient Flexibility. *MIS Quarterly, 15*(5), 435-445.

Anonymous. (2006). Real-time Computing. *Wikipedia.* Retrieved June 06, 2006, from http://en.wikipedia.org/wiki/Real-time_computing

Backhouse, C. J., & Burns, N. D. (1999). Agile Value Chains for Manufacturing—Implications for Performance Measures. *International Journal of Agile Management Systems, 1*(2), 76-82.

Bal, J., Wilding, R., & Gundry, J. (1999). Virtual Teaming in the Agile Supply Chain. *The International Journal of Logistics Management, 10*(2), 71-82.

Bessant, J., Francis, D., Meredith, S., & Kalinsky, R. (2001). Developing Manufacturing Agility in SMEs. *International Journal of Technology Management, 22*(1, 2, 3), 28-54.

Billings, R. S., Milburn, T. W., & Schaalman, M. L. (1980). A Model for Crisis Perception: A Theatrical and Empirical Analysis. *Administrative Science Quarterly, 25*(2), 300-316.

Bititci, U. S., Turner, T. J., & Ball, P. D. (1999). The Viable Business Structure for Managing Agility. *International Journal of Agile Management Systems, 1*(3), 190-202.

Bodine, W. E. (1998). Making Agile Assembly Profitable. *Manufacturing Engineering, 121*(4), 60-68.

Bonfield, P. (1995). Building International Agility. *Chief Executive, January/February,* 50-53.

Bonoma, T. V. (1985). Case Research in Marketing: Opportunities, Problems, and a Process. *Journal of Marketing Research, 22*(2), 199-208.

Borsboom, D., Mellenbergh, G. J., & Heerden, J. V. (2003). The Theoretical Status of Latent Variables. *Psychological Review, 110*(2), 203-219.

Brancheau, J. C., Janz, B. D., & Wetherbe, J. C. (1996). Key Issues in Information Systems Management: 1995 SIM Delphi Results. *MIS Quarterly, 20*(2), 225-242.

Brown, J. L., & Agnew, M. (1982). Corporate Agility. *Business Horizons, 25*(2), 29-33.

Byrd, T. A., & Turner, D. E. (2000). Measuring the Flexibility of Information Technology Infrastructure. *Journal of Management Information Systems, 17*(1), 167-208.

Canter, J. (2000). An Agility Based OODA Model for the E-Commerce/E-Business Enterprise. Retrieved Dec 28, 2000, from http://www.belisarius.com/canter.htm

Cho, H., Jung, M., & Kim, M. (1996). Enabling Technologies of Agile Manufacturing and its Related Activities in Korea. *Computers and Industrial Engineering, 30*(3), 323-335.

Christian, P. H., Govande, V., Staehle, W., & Jr., E. W. Z. (1999). Advantage Through Agility. *IEEE Solutions, 31*(11), 26-33.

Christian, W., & Frederick, K. (1996). Why Isn't Your Company Agile? *Manufacturing Engineering, 116*(6), 104-105.

Christopher, M. (2000). The Agile Supply Chain: Competing in Volatile Markets. *Industrial Marketing Management, 29*(1), 37-44.

Coronado, A. E., Sarhadi, M., & Millar, C. (2002). Defining a Framework for Information System Requirements for Agile Manufacturing.

International Journal of Production Economics, 75(1-2), 57-68.

Day, M., Forrester, P., & Burnett, J. (2000). Agile Supply: Rethinking Systems Thinking, Systems Practice. *International Journal of Agile Management Systems, 2*(3), 178-186.

Demeulemeester, E., Reyck, B. D., & Herroelen, W. (2000). The Discrete Time/Resource Trade-off Problem in Project Networks: A Branch-and-Bound Approach. *IIE Transactions, 32*(11), 1059-1069.

Devor, R., Graves, R., & Miles, J. J. (1997). Agile Manufacturing Research: Accomplishments and Opportunities. *IIE Transactions, 29*(10), 813-823.

Dove, R. (1994). The meaning of Life & The meaning of Agile. *Production, 106*(11), 14-15.

Dove, R. (1995a). Agile Cells and Agile Production. *Automotive Production*(October), 16-18.

Dove, R. (1995b). Measuring Agility: The Toll of Turmoil. *Production, 107*(1), 12-14.

Dove, R. (1996a). Building Agility Improvement Strategies. *Automotive Production, 108*(7), 16-17.

Dove, R. (1996b). Critical Business Practices for Agility. *Automotive Production*(June), 16-17.

Dove, R. (1999). Agility = Knowledge Management + Response Ability. *Automotive Manufacturing & Production, 111*(3), 16-17.

Duncan, N. B. (1995). Capturing Flexibility of Information Technology Infrastructure: A Study of Resource Characteristics and their Measure. *Journal of Management Information Systems, 12*(2), 37-57.

Foster, J. S., & Welch, L. D. (2000). *The Evolving Battlefield*. December 2000. Retrieved Sept, 15, 2001, from http://physicstoday.org/pt/vol-53/iss-12/p31.html

Friedlos, D. (2006). *Legacy IT systems a 'ticking time bomb'*. Retrieved May 24, 2006, from http://www.vnunet.com/articles/print/2155608

Galal-Edeen, G. H. (2003). System Architecting: The Very Idea. *Logistics Information Management, 16*(2), 101-105.

Gandossy, R. (2003). The Need for Speed. *The Journal for Business Strategy, 24*(1), 29-33.

Goldman, S. L., Nagel, R. N., & Preiss, K. (1995). *Agile Competitors and Virtual Organizations: Strategies for Enriching the Customer* (First ed.). New York: Van Nostrand Reinhold.

Grove, A. S. (1999). *Only the Paranoid Survive*. New York: Doubleday.

Haeckel, S. H., & Nolan, R. L. (1996). *Managing By Wire: Using I/T to Transform a Business From "Make-and-Sell" to "Sense-and-Respond"*. London, UK: Oxford University Press Inc.

Heilala, J., & Voho, P. (2001). Modular Reconfigurable Flexible Final Assembly Systems. *Assembly Automation, 21*(1), 20-28.

Hibbert, L. (1999). Expecting the Unexpected. *Manufacturing, 12*(6), 39-40.

Hoek, R. I. V. (2000). The Thesis of Leagility Revisited. *International Journal of Agile Manufacturing Management Systems, 2*(3), 196-201.

Hopp, W. J., & Oyen, M. P. V. (2004). Agile Workforce Evaluation: A Framework for Cross-training and Coordination. *IIE Transactions, 36*(10), 919-940.

Huang, C.-C. (1999). An Agile Approach to Logical Network Analysis in Decision Support Systems. *Decision Support Systems, 25*(1), 53-70.

Huang, C.-Y., Ceroni, J. A., & Nof, S. Y. (2000). Agility of Networked Enterprises—Parallelism, Error Recovery, and Conflict Resolution. *Computers in Industry, 42*(2,3), 275-287.

Huang, C.-Y., & Nof, S. Y. (1999). Enterprise Agility: A View from the PRISM Lab. *International Journal of Agile Management Systems, 1*(1), 51-59.

James, T. (2005). Stepping Back from Lean. *Manufacturing Engineering, 84*(1), 16-21.

Jiao, L. M., Khoo, L. P., & Chen, C. H. (2004). An Intelligent Concurrent Design Task Planner for Manufacturing Systems. *International Journal of Advanced Manufacturing Technology, 23*(9/10), 672-681.

Kassim, N. M., & Zain, M. (2004). Assessing the Measurement of Organizational Agility. *Journal Of American Academy of Business, 4*(1/2), 174-177.

Kiesler, S., & Sproull, L. (1982). Managerial Response to Changing Environments: Perspectives on Problem Sensing from Social Cognition. *Administrative Science Quarterly, 27*(2), 548-570.

Kinsella, J. (1998, July). Open Automation: A Perspective on Connection. *Manufacturing Engineering, 121,* 94-95.

Langer, G., & Alting, L. (2000). An Architecture for Agile Shop Floor Control Systems. *Journal of Manufacturing Systems, 19*(4), 267-281.

Langford, H. P., & Scheuermann, L. (1998). Cogeneration and Self-generation for Energy Agility. *Industrial Management + Data Systems, 98*(2), 44-47.

Long, C. (2000). Measuring Your Strategic Agility. *Consulting Management, 11*(3), 25-28.

Markus, K. (2006). What is a Good Definition? Retrieved March 12, 2006, from Structural Equation Modeling Discussion Group [SEMNET@ BAMA.UA.EDU]

Mason-Jones, R., & Towill, D. R. (1999). Total Cycle Time Compression and the Agile Supply Chain. *International Journal of Production Economics, 62*(1,2), 61-73.

McGaughey, R. E. (1999). Internet Technology: Contributing to Agility in the Twenty-First Century. *International Journal of Agile Management Systems, 1*(1), 7-13.

Meehan, M. (2005). 2005: The year SOA broke big. Retrieved 01/16/2006, 2006

Meier, R. L., Humphreys, M. A., & Williams, M. R. (1998). The Role of Purchasing in the Agile Enterprises. *International Journal of Purchasing and Materials Management, 34*(4), 39-45.

Melarkode, A., From-Poulsen, M., & Warnakulsuriya, S. (2004). Delivering Agility through IT. *Business Strategy Review, 15*(3), 45-50.

Melcher, A. J., & Schwitter, J. P. (1967). *Designing an Empirical Research Project: Considerations and Guidelines.* Unpublished manuscript, Kent.

Meredith, S., & Francis, D. (2000). Journey Towards Agility: The Agile Wheel Explored. *The TQM Magazine, 12*(3), 137.

Michelis, G. D., Dubois, E., Jarke, M., Matthes, F., Mylopoulos, J., Papazoglou, M., et al. (1998). A Three-Faceted View of Information Systems: The Challenge of Change. *Communications of the ACM, 41*(12), 64-70.

Miles, M. B., & Huberman, M. (1994). *Qualitative Data Analysis: An Expanded Sourcebook* (2nd ed.). Thousand Oaks, CA: Sage Publication.

Morash, E. A. (2001). Supply Chain Strategies, Capabilities, and Performance. *Transportation Journal, 41*(1), 37-54.

Narasimhan, R. (1999). Manufacturing Agility and Supply Chain Management Practices. *Production and Inventory Management Journal, 40*(1), 4-10.

Noaker, P. M. (1994). The Search for Agile Manufacturing. *Manufacturing Engineering, 113*(5), 5-11.

O'Connor, L. (1994). Agile Manufacturing in a Responsive Factory. *Mechanical Engineering, 16*(7), 54-57.

Ota, M. (2001). The Concepts of Production-Marketing Integration Towards Agile Manufacturing. *International Journal of Manufacturing Technology and Management, 3*(3), 225-237.

Oyen, M. P. V. (2001). Performance Opportunity for Workforce Agility in Collaborative and Non-Collaborative Work Systems. *IEEE Transactions, 33*(9), 761-777.

Pankaj, & Hyde, M. (2003, 2003). *Organizations and the Necessity of Computer Based Information Systems.* Paper presented at the 9th Americas Conference on Information Systems, Tampa, FL.

Pfohl, H.-C. (1997). Logistics: State of the Art. *Human Systems Management, 16*(3), 153-158.

Pullin, J. (2001). How Being Agile is the Best Way Up. *Professional Engineering, 14*(11), 32-33.

Quinn, J. B. (1980). Managing Strategic Change. *Sloan Management Review, 21*(4), 3-20.

Reddy, S. B., & Reddy, R. (2002). Competitive Agility and the Challenge of Legacy Information Systems. *Industrial Management + Data Systems, 102*(1/2), 5-16.

Richards, C. W. (1996). Agile Manufacturing: Beyond Lean? *Production an Inventory Management Journal, 37*(2), 60-64.

Rossi, H. (2006). What is a Good Definition? Retrieved March 12, 2006, from Structural Equation Modeling Discussion Group [SEMNET@BAMA.UA.EDU]

Roth, A. V. (1996, March). Achieving Strategic Agility Through Economies of Knowledge. *Strategy & Leadership, 24,* 30-37.

Sahin, F. (2000). Manufacturing Competitiveness: Different Systems to Achieve the Same Results.

Production and Inventory Management Journal, 41(1), 56-65.

Schonsleben, P. (2000). With Agility and Adequate Partnership Strategies Towards Effective Logistics Networks. *Computers in Industry, 42*(1), 33-42.

Shafer, R. (1999). Only the Agile will Survive. *HR Magazine, 44,* 50-51.

Shafer, R. A., Dyer, L., Kilty, J., Amos, J., & Ericksen, J. (2002). Crafting A Human Resource Strategy to Foster Organizational Agility: A Case Study. *Human Resource Management, 40*(3), 197-211.

Sharifi, H., & Zhang, Z. (1999). A Methodology for Achieving Agility in Manufacturing Organizations: An Introduction. *International Journal of Production Economics, 62*(1), 7-22.

Sieger, D. B., Badiru, A. B., & Milatovic, M. (2000). A Metric for Agility Measurement in Product Development. *IIE Transactions, 32*(7), 637-645.

Sullivan, G. (2005). Integrating Business Intelligence and Financial Management. Retrieved October 30, 2005, from http://www.s-ox.com/news/detail.cfm?articleID=1197

Tennant, R. (2001, April). Building Agile Organizations. *Library Journal, 126,* 30.

Unknown. (2002). Comp.realtime: Frequently Asked Questions (FAQs) 3.6. Retrieved 1/1/03, 2002, from http://www.faqs.org/faqs/realtime-computing/faq/

Vasilash, G. S. (2001). Dedicated Automation to Give Way to Agility. *Automotive Manufacturing and Production, 113*(2), 56-59.

Vastag, G., Kasarda, J. D., & Boone, T. (1994). Logistical Support for Manufacturing Agility in Global Markets. *International Journal of Operations and Production Management, 14*(11), 73-83.

Vernadat, F. B. (1999). Research Agenda for Agile Manufacturing. *International Journal of Agile Management Systems, 1*(1), 37-40.

Vokurka, R. J., & Fliedner, G. (1997). Agility: Competitive Weapon of the 1990s and Beyond? *Production and Inventory Management Journal, 38*(3), 19-24.

Vokurka, R. J., & Fliedner, G. (1998). The Journey Towards Agility. *Industrial Management + Data Systems, 98*(4), 165-171.

Vokurka, R. J., Zank, G. M., & III, C. M. L. (2002). Improving Competitiveness Through Supply Chain Management: A Cumulative Improvement Approach. *Competitiveness Review, 12*(1), 14-25.

Voss, B. (1994). A New Spring for Manufacturing. *Journal of Business Strategy, 15*(1), 54-59.

Yoffie, D. B., & Kwak, M. (2001). Mastering Strategic Movement at Palm. *Sloan Management Review, 43*(1), 55-63.

Yusuf, Y. Y., Sarahadi, M., & Gunasekaran, A. (1999). Agile Manufacturing: The Drivers, Concepts, and Attributes. *International Journal of Production Economics, 62*(1, 2), 33-43.

ENDNOTES

[a]   While there is a reference to flexibility, this study considers agility as distinct from flexibility. They are related though, since both refer to change.

[b]   Waterfall development has gained somewhat more traction with the increase in offshore outsourcing where vendor value proposition is lower costs and a relatively faster development time. One of the authors has industry experience in this area. Usually iterations are allowed but they may result in increased costs.

[c]   One of the authors has had extensive experience in selling offsourcing services from Indian companies. The engagement and business model is heavily oriented towards the waterfall methodology.

[d]   The practitioner and academic literature has been constantly reviewed till the date of submission of this manuscript for new significant definitions through multiple search engine alerts and listservs.

[e]   Information when presented as part of the definitions is taken to imply IS, since IS constitute the primary information processing mechanisms in modern organizations. Though here the IS support the organizational agility.

[f]   This may be attributed to using the Goldman et al. framework when defining agility. Goldman et. al. stress virtual organizations as a primary mechanism for achieving agility.

[g]   It is not necessary that the end result of an agile action be always be what was intended since failures are integral part of any response.

[h]   This problem is similar to distinguishing common cause variation from special cause variation in process control.

APPENDIX 1: EXISTING DEFINITIONS OF AGILITY

1. The search was first conducted using online research databases- ProQuest, ABI/INFORM, IEEE, ACM, and EBSCO. Additional articles were included in the review by referring to the bibliography in the articles collected in the initial search.
2. Articles that provide a definition independently of the referral to previous work have been cited. Published work that is based on principles already cited, or refer to existing definitions that have not been cited especially in the case of recent literature, are not included in this list.
3. Though the list may not be not all-inclusive, it does capture most mainstream academic literature on agility.

Year	Authors	Definition of Agility
1982	Brown and Agnew	• Corporate agility or the ability to react quickly to changing circumstances.
1994	Dove	• Agility is defined as proficiency at change and this proficiency can be measured using the four metrics of cost, time, scope, and robustness.
1994	Noaker	• Agility is a measure of manufacturer's ability to react to fast and sudden, unpredictable change in customer demand for its products and services, and make a profit. • Agile manufacturing is a top-down enterprise-wide effort that supports time-to-market attributes of competitiveness. • An agile enterprise could swiftly reconfigure operations, processes and business relationships swiftly thriving in an environment of continuous and unpredictable change. Agility repostures the fundamental approach to minimize the inhibition to change in any direction.
1994	O'Connor	• Agility allows rapid response to continuously changing customer requirements. • Agile manufacturing provides the ability to thrive and prosper in a competitive environment of continuous and unanticipated change and to respond to rapidly changing markets.
1994	Vastag, Kasadra, and Boon	• Time-based competition and flexibility converge in agile manufacturing.
1994	Voss	• As per the CEO of Texas instruments: Agile manufacturing is essentially a new form of competition. It is based upon using science and engineering to leverage a person's decision making capabilities and it presents a major shift in how we use science and engineering to leverage a worker's skills and dexterity.

continued on following page

Year	Authors	Definition of Agility
1995	Dove	• Agility is the adaptability to thrive (combination of viability and leadership) in a continuously changing and unpredictable business environment. • Agility is change proficiency and 8 types of change proficiencies can be identified: creation, capability change, improvement, migration, capacity change, reconfiguration, performance change, and recovery.
1996	Cho, Jung, and Kim	• Agility is defined as the capability of surviving and prospering in a competitive environment of continuous and unpredictable change by reacting quickly and effectively to changing markets driven by customer designed products and services.
1996	Christian and Fredrick	• Agility approaches competitiveness through coordination, cooperation, and optimization of resources.
1996	Dove	• Change proficiency is the underlying competency of an agile enterprise.
1996	Richards	• Air Force experts characterize agility as the ability to change maneuver state. Maneuverability is referred to as the maximum turn rate. Agility is described as how fast an aircraft can go from one direction to another. • Agility is the ability of the friendly forces to react faster than the enemy. • Agility forum defines agility as the ability to thrive in a competitive environment of continuous and unanticipated change. To respond quickly to rapid changing markets driven by customers valuing of products and services. • Agile manufacturers may be defined as a lean producer that has extended the concept to improve its ability to function as an open system (observe), change its world view accordingly (orient), and make timely and effective decisions (decide), and act on those decisions (act).
1996	Roth	• Strategic agility is the capability to produce the right products at the right time at the right place.
1997	Devor, Graves, and Miles	• Agile manufacturing represents the ability of a producer of goods and services to thrive in the face of continuous change. Agility means that a company is capable of operating profitably in a competitive environment of continuous and unpredictable change. • NSF/ARPA solicitation identified the focus of agile manufacturing as that of improving flexibility and concurrence of all facets of production process and integrating different units of production across a firm or among firms through integrated software and communications systems. • Successful agile enterprises are those that make use of state of change as a means to be profitable.

continued on following page

Year	Authors	Definition of Agility
1997	Pfohl	• Agility as a competence is described as achievement and retention of competitiveness and customer focus through: • Relevancy: The ability to maintain focus on changing needs of the customer. • Accommodation: The ability to respond to unique customer requests. • Flexibility: The ability to adapt to unexpected circumstances.
1997	Vokurka and Fliedner	• Agility refers to the ability to produce and market successfully a broad range of low cost high quality products with short lead times in varying lot sizes which provide enhanced value to individual customers through customization. • Agility is the capability of a company to operate profitably in a competitive environment of continually and unpredictably changing customer opportunities. To be agile a firm needs to be able to deal with unpredictable changes in market or customer demands. Agility enables a firm to respond to any changes in market demand whether it is a change in product characteristic, customer order, or internal company condition. • Agility merges the four distinct competencies of cost, quality, dependability, and flexibility as identified by Hays and Wheelright. As per the sand cone model, agility needs continuous investment in quality, dependability, and flexibility. • Agility is a competitive weapon beyond flexibility. Agility is a capability beyond flexibility. Agility follows flexibility. • Agility is dynamic, context specific, aggressively change embracing, and growth oriented.
1998	Bodine	• Agility means that a manufacturer should be able to produce and distribute products and respond to fluctuations in local demands without increasing the cost of production.
1998	Kinsella	• Agility is the ability to reconfigure lines faster.
1998	Langford and Scheuermann	• Demand for agile manufacturing is to produce high quality market-sensitive products at the lowest possible cost in an environment that has constant dynamic changes.
1998	Meier, Humphreys, and Williams	• Four dimensions of agile competitive strategies: a) Being a total solution provider. b) Having a collaborative production systems. c) Being knowledge-driven. d) Maintaining an adaptive organization.

continued on following page

Year	Authors	Definition of Agility
1999	Abdul-Nour, Drolet, and Lambert	• System agility is defined as the capacity of a company to efficiently benefit from the flexibility of its production lines. • The basic components of an agile system are: a) Total Quality Control. b) Cellular layout. c) Total productive maintenance. d) Reduction of setup times. e) Waste elimination. f) Continuous improvement of process. g) Kaizen, kan-ban, small lot production, etc.
1999	Bal, Wilding, and Gundry	• Agility is the response to coping with uncertainty and it is the basis for achieving competitive advantage in changing market conditions.
1999	Bititci, Turner, and Ball	• Agility is the business' ability to quickly adapt and change in response to rapidly changing environmental conditions.
1999	Blackhouse and Burns	• Agility is the ability of the enterprise to adapt to unpredicted changes in the external environment. One may distinguish between internal and external agility.
1999	Christian, Govande, Staehle, Zimmers	• Agility principles: a) Enabling customer enrichment. b) Cooperation in virtual relationships. c) Adaptive organization and culture. d) Valuing people, skills, and information. • Agility is not a destination but a continuum of ongoing change that must occur to meet the changing demands of customers and consumers.
1999	Dove	• Agility may be succinctly defined as the ability to apply and manage knowledge effectively. • Agility is loosely defined as the ability of an organization to thrive in a continuously changing unpredictable business environment.
1999	Hibbert	• Agility is the ability to thrive in an environment of continual and unanticipated change that is driven by the customer-specified products and services. • Agility principles: a) All agile companies must have the ability to thrive in change, unpredictability, and uncertainty. b) The ability to provide the customer with total solutions. c) Leveraging of people through knowledge and information. d) Ability to cooperate with other companies to raise competitiveness.

continued on following page

Year	Authors	Definition of Agility
1999	Huang	• An agile corporation should be able to respond to market changes.
1999	Huang and Nof	• Agility is a measure that shows how well a system can adjust itself and seek help from other systems. • Agility can be examined along the lines of: business and organizational agility or logistical and operational agility. a) Business and organizational agility is manifested in various virtual alliances formed for various market and customer needs. b) Operational and logistical agility is defined as an extension of flexibility to include collaboration (which is seeking help from other systems) and is focused on error detection and recovery. If the focus is on a single enterprise then agility is same as flexibility.
1999	Mason-Jones and Towill	• Agility means using market knowledge and virtual corporation to exploit profitable opportunities in a volatile market.
1999	McGaughey	• Agility is the ability of an enterprise to respond quickly and successfully to change.
1999	Narasimhan	• Manufacturing agility is described as the ability to produce a broad range of low-cost, high-quality products with short lead times in varying lot sizes built to individual customer specifications. • Agility is characterized as the concurrent realization of cost, quality, dependability, and flexibility competencies of the firm.
1999	Shafer	• Agility is the ability to be infinitely adaptable without having to change. Agile enterprise is ready for anything and is able to simultaneously innovate instantly, organize on-the-fly, and respond instantly to unexpected demands.
1999	Sharifi and Zhang	• Agility, in concept, is comprised of the two factors of "responding to change" and "exploiting change." Agility is the ability to cope with unexpected changes to survive unprecedented threats of business environment and to take advantage of changes as opportunities. Responding to changes and taking advantage of them through strategic utilization of managerial and manufacturing methods and tools are the pivotal concepts. • Agility capabilities: responsiveness, competency, flexibility, and speed.
1999	Vernadat	• Enterprises must be more flexible, responsive, and efficient to continuously evolve and adapt to their markets, be innovative and capture new markets. This is called agility. • Agility can be defined as the ability to closely align enterprise systems to changing business needs in order to achieve competitive performance.

continued on following page

Year	Authors	Definition of Agility
1999	Yusuf, Sarahadi, and Gunasekaran	• Main points in the definition of agility: a) High quality and highly customized products. b) Products and services with high information and value-adding content. c) Mobilization of core competencies. d) Responsiveness to social and environmental issues. e) Synthesis of diverse technologies. f) Response to change and uncertainty. g) Inter- and intra-enterprise integration. • Agility is the ability of a business to grow in a competitive market of continuous and unanticipated change; and to respond quickly to rapidly changing markets driven by customer-based valuing of products and services. • In operational terms, agility can be defined as a synthesis of a number of enterprises that each have some core skills or competencies which they bring to the joint venturing operation, thus enabling cooperative enterprises to respond to quickly changing customer requirements. • Agility is the ability to accelerate the activities on the critical path. • An agile manufacturing system is a manufacturing system with extra-ordinary capabilities to meet the rapidly changing needs of the marketplace. It is a system that shifts quickly among product models or between product lines ideally in real-time to meet customer demand. An agile organization can quickly satisfy customer orders. It can introduce new products frequently and in a timely manner and even get in and out of strategic alliances rapidly. • Agility as defined in this paper is the successful exploration of competitive bases (speed, flexibility, innovation, proactivity, quality, and profitability) through integration of reconfigurable resources and best practices in a knowledge-rich environment to provide customer-driven products and services in a fast changing market environment. • Agility can be divided into elemental agility (resources), micro-agility (enterprise), and macro-agility (inter-enterprise). • There are four key concepts for agile competition: Competition based on core competence management, virtual enterprise information, capability for reconfiguration, and knowledge-driven enterprise.
2000	Christopher	• Possession of high level of maneuverability is termed as agility. • An agile supply chain: a) Is market sensitive. b) Uses IT to share information between suppliers and buyers. c) Has process integration between supply chain partners. d) Is a confederation of partners in a network. • The concept of postponement is a vital element in agile strategy.

continued on following page

Year	Authors	Definition of Agility
2000	Day, Forrester, and Burnett	• Agility is defined as the ability of an organization to thrive in a constantly changing, unpredictable environment (Iacocca Institute). • The agile form of an enterprise is a network of firms working as an operational system where each member of the collective negotiates a task and manages internal process in a way that is beneficial for other collaborators.
2000	Foster and Welch	• Strategic and operational agility is the ability to assemble the needed force rapidly, where they are needed, in the context of armed forces.
2000	Hoek	• The basic dimensions of agility concept are to be tuned along the dimensions of market responsiveness, virtual and information, process and network integration.
2000	Huang, Ceroni, and Nof	• Agility enables enterprises to intelligently change themselves and the way they interact. They can collaborate with each other to best adapt to various customers' demand changes in taste, design, time, and quantity while keeping the costs at a reasonable level. • Agility can be divided into the following: a) Business and organizational agility: Parallel relationships between tasks and resources among distributed organizations. b) Operational and logistical agility: Capability of each enterprise and/or subsidiary to handle its own errors and resolve conflicts while interacting and collaborating with other enterprises. It may be defined along the dimensions of range, response, and collaboration. • Agility can be defined as a measure that indicates how well a system can adjust itself while also seeking help from other systems (enterprise in the network). When an enterprise is not networked, agility and flexibility are the same; but, when the enterprises are networked, even with components with low flexibility, the whole network may be agile. Flexibility is mainly determined by range (alternatives of possible system changes) and response (reaction time needed to respond to changes).

continued on following page

Year	Authors	Definition of Agility
2000	Langer and Alting	• Agile performance can be disaggregated into the following (in the context of manufacturing execution systems): a) Operational agility: Allowing for operational change. b) Structural agility: Allowing for structural changes and reconfiguration. • Agility refers to the ability of a system to accommodate change as an inherent characteristic. Agile performance is measured by how the system deals with change. To be agile means to operate optimally in an environment that is constantly changing. Agile systems are not made to deal with a set of contingencies but change their structure as need arises. Agile manufacturing deals with things that cannot be controlled as opposed to flexibility, which deals with things that can be controlled. An agile system not only has the ability to sustain change but use the opportunities inherent in a dynamic environment. • Agility is a means of thriving in an environment of continuous change by managing complex inter- and intra-firm relationships through innovations in technology, information, communication, organization design, and new marketing strategies.
2000	Long	• Strategic Agility: Restructuring and modifying the conduct of practices. Agility is balancing stability with flexibility. Strategic Agility is comprised of the following: a) Clarity of vision. b) Knowledge of clients. c) Understanding core capabilities. d) Selecting strategic targets. e) Shared responsibility. f) Understanding the competition. g) Taking action.

continued on following page

Year	Authors	Definition of Agility
2000	Meredith and Francis	• Agility has roots in time-based competition, fast-cycle innovation, and intraprenuering. Agility means proactivity, adaptability, flexibility, speed, learning, and skills to provide strategically driven and effectively implemented waves of change. • Agility is a dynamic capability of organization's capacity to gain competitive advantage by intelligently, rapidly, and proactively seizing opportunities and reacting to changes. There are two aspects of agility: strategic (short cycle strategic decision making) and operational agility. • Agility can be comprehensively defined using an agility wheel with four quadrants: a) Quadrant 1 of agile strategy is comprised of wide-deep scanning (to understand pivotal change drivers), strategic commitment (by the top leadership for agile policies), full deployment (all departments should adopt agile policies), and agile scoreboard (performance management & measurement systems factors in agility). b) Quadrant 2 of agile processes is comprised of flexible assets and systems (facilities, systems, and software), fast new product acquisition, rapid problem solving, rich information systems (for shared and effective decision-making). c) Quadrant 3 of agile linkages is comprised of agility benchmarking, deep customer insight (for precipitation of opportunity), aligned suppliers (for a responsive supply chain), and performing partnerships (to enlarge capabilities through partnerships). d) Quadrant 4 of agile people is comprised of adaptable structure (organizational form), multi-skilled flexible people, rapid-agile decision making, and continuous learning. • Characteristics of agile manufacturing are: a) Produces to order. b) Meets customers' specific needs. c) Achieves a speed and flexibility in its functioning matched to the speed and flexibility of the technology it manages. d) Mobilizes and manages all forms of knowledge intelligently. e) Adopts new ways of working when these facilitate agility. f) Creates virtual projects and ad-hoc organizations to add capabilities when needed.
2000	Sahin	• Agility is the capability of operating profitably in an uncertain, unstable, and continuously changing environment. • Agility is the time derivative of maneuverability. • Agility is the ability to respond to unplanned changes by economically producing a variety of products with quick changeover, in any quantity. • Agility is optimization of customer relations. Agility aims to optimize the relationship with the customers by offering a variety of products that satisfy customer specifications on a time-competitive basis.

continued on following page

Year	Authors	Definition of Agility
2000	Schonsleben	• Agile firms are those who understand how to remain competitive by means of proactive amassing of knowledge and competencies.
2000	Sieger, Badiru, and Malatovic	• Agility: Manufacturer's ability to respond quickly and cost effectively to sudden unexpected changes in customer demands. Agility should also be able to guide the concurrent engineering effort. Responsiveness of the companies and the alliances should be measured in terms of factors that capture the status of the product being developed relative to their development time. • Agility can be measured as some function of the time and effort between conceptualization of the product and the delivery of the product.
2001	Bessant, Francis, Meredith, and Kalinsky	• Agility is the organizational capability (dynamic capability) that reflects the ability to learn and adapt. Agility is the dynamic capability that translates to the organization's capacity to gain competitive advantage by intelligently, rapidly, and proactively seizing opportunities and reacting to threats. • Agility is the ability of a firm to respond quickly and flexibly to its environment and to meet the emerging challenges with innovative responses. • Agility relies on being able to respond to two puzzles, both of which are already changing: a) Configuring knowledge, labor, energy, and other resources into artifacts. b) Carry out the activity in a constantly changing environment. Real agility is to keep solving the manufacturing puzzle as it changes. This signifies a dynamic capability.
2001	Heilala and Voho	• Agile manufacturing is achieved through integration of three primary resources into a coordinated, interdependent system. These are: a) Innovative management structure and organization. b) A skill base of knowledgeable and empowered people. c) Intelligent technologies.
2001	Morash	• Agility is a customer closeness strategy in a supply chain supported by demand side capabilities (customer service and quality). Agility is also supported by operational excellence in the supply chain. • Agility quickly and flexibly adjusts supply chain capabilities and their combinations to changing customer needs. • Empirically, agility is distinguished by frequent interactions, collaborations, and communications with the customers.

continued on following page

Year	Authors	Definition of Agility
2001	Ota	• The meaning of agility in the manufacturing process is to execute all the four stages of product planning, product design, production, and distribution, promptly and in a flexible manner.
2001	Oyen	• Agile work systems: Workers are not tied to individual tasks but are cross trained and empowered to move between tasks to follow the workload.
2001	Pullin	• The original concept of agility envisages multi-task machines. These machines are supported by agile employees: those who can react fast, flexibly, and in a high value-adding way.
2001	Tennant	• Agile organizations are marked by committed staff, skilled managers, and commonly held beliefs in the organization's mission.
2001	Vasilash	• Agile means volume and capacity flexibility. The difference between agile, flexible, convertible, and dedicated (in the order specified) is how long it takes to convert from one type of product being produced to another. In an automotive engine manufacturing scenario the time frames can be specified as Agility—3 to 6 months, flexible—6 to 12 months, convertible—12 months, dedicated—12 to 18 months.
2001	Yofee and Kwak	• Agility is a capability that comes into play when there is movement like in Judo. It is more pronounced when the bodies in question are in movement. It is an offensive and/or defensive move to take advantage of the changing situation.
2002	Coronado, Sarhadi, and Millar	• Agility is the capability to grow and prosper in an environment of continuous and unpredictable changes driven by customer designed products and services. • It is the ability to respond to changing customer demand, adapt to changing business climate, flexibility to design processes towards customers and suppliers while enabling decentralized operations.
2002	Shafer, Dyer, Kilty, Amos, and Ericksen	• Agility is defined as being nimble and change-hardy with unparalleled flexibility and adaptability. • Agility can be seen as the three strategic capabilities of the following: a) Initiate: Find and quickly exploit opportunities. b) Adapt: Anticipate and deal with threats and opportunities. c) Deliver: Capacity to operate effectively and efficiently on a day-to-day basis, ability to minimize the effects of distractions associated with constant turmoil and change. • Initiate where possible, adapt when necessary, and deliver always.

continued on following page

Year	Authors	Definition of Agility
2002	Vokurka, Zank, and Lund	• Agility is defined as the ability to market successfully low-cost, high-quality products with short lead times in varying volumes that provide enhanced value to customers through customization. Agility merges the four strategic capabilities of quality, dependability, flexibility, and cost as identified by Hayes and Wheelright. • Agility is a capability to respond to a change in a dimension beyond flexibility. Agility is responding to unanticipated market changes where there is not necessarily a pre-defined procedure.
2004	Hopp and Van Oyen	• Competing on multiple dimensions of cost, quality, delivery time, and product variety requires efficient operations that are tailored to the specific needs of a firm's customers. We refer to the ability to achieve this heightened level of efficiency and flexibility while meeting objectives for quality and customer service as production agility. • Production agility has three aspects: The first facet is inter-firm relations, which include for example, supply chain management, purchasing contracts, and strategic partnerships. The second facet of agility is the firm's resources and infrastructure. Examples of these include information technology, flexible manufacturing systems, improved processes, desirable locations, and effective layouts. The third facet, upon which this paper focuses, is the workforce itself.
2004	Jiao, Khoo, and Chen	• Basically, an agile manufacturing system attempts to integrate product design with the various product realization processes so as to reduce the time to market and be responsive to customer needs.
2004	Kassim and Zain	• Generally, agility is the ability of a firm to face and adapt proficiently in a continuously changing and unpredictable business environment. • Agility is not about how a firm responds to changes, but it is about having the capabilities and processes to respond to its environment that will always change in unexpected ways.
2004	Melarkode, From-Poulsen, and Warnakulsuriya	• Agility is the capacity to anticipate changing market dynamics, adapt to those dynamics, and accelerate enterprise change faster than the rate of change in the market, to create economic value.

continued on following page

Year	Authors	Definition of Agility
2005	James	• Agility throughout your entire organization is meeting the needs of customers you don't even know you have, for products you don't even know anything about, and being able to support that with systems and communications to suppliers that you don't even know exist—that is what agile is about. • Agile manufacturing enterprises are expected to be capable of rapidly responding to changes in customer demand. They should be able to take advantage of the windows of opportunities that, from time to time, appear in the market place. They should also develop new ways of interacting with customers and suppliers. • Agility is an ability to respond to change, uncertainty and unpredictability in the business environment, whatever its source -customers, competitors, new technologies, suppliers or government regulation.

Chapter III
Global Understanding Environment:
Applying Semantic and Agent Technologies to Industrial Automation

Vagan Terziyan
University of Jyväskylä, Finland

Artem Katasonov
University of Jyväskylä, Finland

ABSTRACT

Industry pushes a new type of Internet characterized as the Internet of Things, which represents a fusion of the physical and digital worlds. The technology of the Internet of Things opens new horizons for industrial automation, that is, automated monitoring, control, maintenance planning, and so forth, of industrial resources and processes. Internet of Things definitely needs explicit semantics, even more than the traditional Web—for automatic discovery and interoperability among heterogeneous devices and also to facilitate the behavioral coordination of the components of complex physical-digital systems. In this chapter, the authors describe their work towards the Global Understanding Environment (GUN), a general middleware framework aimed at providing means for building complex industrial systems consisting of components of different nature, based on the semantic and the agent technologies. The authors present the general idea and some emergent issues of GUN and describe the current state of the GUN realization in the UBIWARE platform. As a specific concrete case, they use the domain of distributed power network maintenance. In collaboration with the ABB Company, we have developed a simple prototype and vision of potential add-value this domain could receive from introducing semantic and agent technologies, and GUN framework in particular.

INTRODUCTION

Recent advances in networking, sensor and RFID technologies allow connecting various physical world objects to the IT infrastructure, which could, ultimately, enable realization of the Internet of Things and the ubiquitous computing visions. This also opens new horizons for industrial automation, i.e. automated monitoring, control, maintenance planning, etc., of industrial resources and processes. A much larger, than in present, number of resources (machines, infrastructure elements, materials, products) can get connected to the IT systems, thus be automatically monitored and potentially controlled. Such development will also necessarily create demand for a much wider integration with various external resources, such as data storages, information services, and algorithms, which can be found in other units of the same organization, in other organizations, or on the Internet.

Such interconnectivity of computing and physical systems could, however, become the "nightmare of ubiquitous computing" (Kephart and Chess, 2003) in which human operators will be unable to *manage* the complexity of interactions, neither even architects will be able to *anticipate* this complexity and thus *design* the systems effectively. It is widely acknowledged that as the networks, systems and services of modern IT and communication infrastructures become increasingly complex, traditional solutions to manage and control them seem to have reached their limits. The IBM vision of autonomic computing (e.g. Kephart and Chess, 2003) proclaims the need for computing systems capable of running themselves with minimal human management which would be mainly limited to definition of some higher-level policies rather than direct administration. The computing systems will therefore be *self-managed*, which, according to the IBM vision, includes self-configuration, self-optimization, self-protection, and self-healing. According to this vision, the self-manageability of a complex

system requires its components to be to a certain degree autonomous themselves. Therefore, we envision that agent technologies will play an important part in building such complex systems. Agent-based approach to software engineering is also considered to be facilitating the *design* of complex systems (see Section 2).

Another problem is inherent *heterogeneity* in ubiquitous computing systems, with respect to the nature of components, standards, data formats, protocols, etc, which creates significant obstacles for interoperability among the components of such systems. The semantic technologies are viewed today as a key technology to resolve the problems of interoperability and integration within heterogeneous world of ubiquitously interconnected objects and systems. The Internet of Things should become in fact the *Semantic Web of Things* (Brock and Schuster, 2006). Our work subscribes to this view. Moreover, we believe that the semantic technologies can facilitate not only the discovery of heterogeneous components and data integration, but also the behavioral coordination of those components (see Section 2).

In this paper, we describe our work on the *Global Understanding Environment (GUN)* (the concept introduced in Terziyan, 2003, 2005). This work is conducted in the line of projects of the Industrial Ontologies Group at the University of Jyväskylä including SmartResource (2004-2007, see http://www.cs.jyu.fi/ai/OntoGroup/SmartResource_details.htm) and ongoing UBIWARE (Smart Semantic Middleware for Ubiquitous Computing, 2007-2010, see http://www.cs.jyu.fi/ai/OntoGroup/UBIWARE_details.htm). GUN is a general middleware framework aiming at providing means for building complex industrial systems consisting of components of *different* nature, based on the semantic and agent technologies. A very general view on GUN is presented in Figure 1; a description of GUN will be given in Section 3.

When applying the semantic approach in the domain of industrial automation, it should be obvi-

Figure 1. Global understanding environment

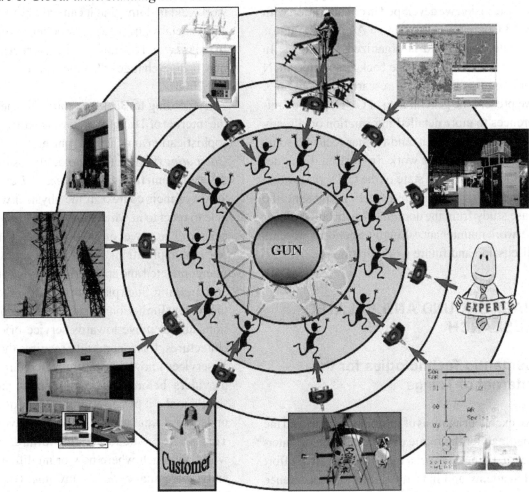

ous that the semantic technology has to be able to describe resources not only as passive functional or non-functional entities, but also to describe their behavior (proactivity, communication, and coordination). In this sense, the word "global" in GUN has a double meaning. First, it implies that industrial resources are able to communicate and cooperate globally, i.e. across the whole organization and beyond. Second, it implies a "global understanding". This means that a resource A can understand all of (1) the properties and the state of a resource B, (2) the potential and actual behaviors of B, and (3) the business processes in which A and B, and maybe other resources, are jointly involved. From the Semantic Web point of view, GUN could probably be referred to as *Proactive, Self-Managed Semantic Web of Things.* We believe that such Proactive Self-Managed Semantic Web of Things can be the future "killer application" for the Semantic Web.

As a specific concrete case for this paper, we use the domain of distributed power network maintenance. We describe our existing prototype and the vision we developed in collaboration with ABB Company (Distribution Automation unit).

The further text is organized as follows. In Section 2, we discuss the background for GUN and comment on related research. In Section 3, we present the general idea of GUN, provide references to more detailed information on already elaborated parts of it, and further focus on some recent issues in our work. In Section 4, we describe the achieved state of the GUN realization in the *UBIWARE Platform*. Section 5 presents the case study from the domain of distributed power network maintenance. Finally, Section 6 presents discussion and future work directions.

BACKGROUND AND RELATED RESEARCH

Semantic Technologies for the Internet of Things

An excellent analysis of the today's status and the roadmap for the future development of the Internet of Things has been made as collective effort of academy and industry during the conference organized by DG Information Society and Media, Networks and Communication Technologies Directorate in Brussels (Buckley, 2006). It was pointed out that the Internet of Things characterizes the way that information and communication technologies will develop over the next decade or so. The Internet of Things represents a fusion of the physical and digital worlds. It creates a map of the real world within the digital world. The computer's view of the physical world may, depending on the characteristics of sensor network, possess a high temporal and spatial resolution. The Internet of Things may react autonomously to the real world. A computer's view of the world allows it to interact with the physical world and influence it. The Internet of Things is not merely a tool to extend the human capability. It becomes part of the environment in which humans live and work, and in doing that it can create an economically, socially and personally better environment. In industry and commerce, the Internet of Things may bring a change of business processes (Buckley, 2006).

According to Buckley (2006), the devices on the Internet of Things will have several degrees of sophistication and the final one makes *Proactive Computing* (INTEL terminology) possible. These devices (sometimes called *Smart Devices*) are aware of their context in the physical world and able to react to it, which may cause the context to change. The power of the Internet of Things and relevant applications arises because devices are interconnected and appropriate service platforms are emerging. Such platforms must evolve beyond the current limitations of static service configurations and to move towards service-oriented architectures. Interoperability requires that clients of services know the features offered by service providers beforehand and semantic modeling should make it possible for service requestors to understand what service providers have to offer. This is a key issue for moving towards an open-world approach where new or modified devices and services may appear at any time. This also has implications on requirements for middleware, as these are needed to interface between the devices that may be seen as services, and applications. This is a key issue to progress towards device networks capable of dynamically adapting to context changes as may be imposed by application scenarios (e.g. moving from monitoring mode to alarm mode and then to alert mode may imply different services and application behaviors). Devices in the Internet of Things might need to be able to communicate with other devices anywhere in the world. This implies a need for a naming and addressing scheme, and means of search and discovery. The fact that devices may be related to an identity (through naming and addressing) raises in turn a number of privacy and security challenges. A consistent set of middleware offering application programming interfaces, communications and other services to applications will simplify the creation of services and applications. Service approaches need to move from a static programmable approach towards a configurable and dynamic composition capability.

In Lassila and Adler (2003), the ubiquitous computing is presented as an emerging paradigm qualitatively different from existing personal computing scenarios by involving dozens and hundreds of devices (sensors, external input and output devices, remotely controlled appliances, etc). A vision was presented for a class of devices, so called *Semantic Gadgets*, which will be able to combine functions of several portable devices users have today. Semantic Gadgets will be able to automatically configure themselves in new environments and to combine information and functionality from local and remote sources. Semantic Gadgets should be capable of semantic discovery and device coalition formation: the goal should be to accomplish discovery and configuration of new devices without a human in the loop. Authors pointed out that critical to the success of this is the existence or emergence of certain infrastructures, such as the World Wide Web as a ubiquitous source of information and services and the Semantic Web as a more machine- and automation-friendly form of the Web.

Later, Lassila (2005a, 2005b) discussed possible application of semantic technologies to mobile and ubiquitous computing arguing that ubiquitous computing represents the ultimate "interoperability nightmare". This application is motivated by the need for better automation of user's tasks by improving the interoperability between systems, applications, and information. Ultimately, one of the most important components of the realization of the Semantic Web is "serendipitous interoperability", the ability of software systems to discover and utilize services they have not seen before, and that were not considered when and where the systems were designed. To realize this, qualitatively stronger

means of representing service semantics are required, enabling fully automated discovery and invocation, and complete removal of unnecessary interaction with human users. Avoiding a priori commitments about how devices are to interact with one another will improve interoperability and will thus make dynamic, unchoreographed ubiquitous computing scenarios more realistic. The semantic technologies are qualitatively stronger approach to interoperability than contemporary standards-based approaches.

To be truly pervasive, the devices in a ubiquitous computing environment have to be able to form a coalition without human intervention. In Qasem et al. (2004), it is noticed that ordinary AI planning for coalition formation will be difficult because a planning agent cannot make a closed-world assumption in such environments. Agent never knows when e.g. it has gathered all relevant information or when additional searches may be redundant. Local closed-world reasoning has been incorporated in Qasem et al. (2004) to compose Semantic Web services and to control the search process. The approach has two main components. The first is Plan Generator, which generates a plan that represents a service composition. The second component, the Semantic Web mediator, provides an interface to the information sources, which are devices in the ubiquitous computing environments.

The advances around the Semantic Web and Semantic Web services allow machines to help people to get fully automated anytime and anywhere assistance. However, most of the available applications and services depend on synchronous communication links between consumers and providers. In Krummenacher and Strang (2005), a combination of space-based computing and Semantic Web named as *semantic spaces* is introduced to provide a communication paradigm for ubiquitous services. The semantic spaces approach introduces a new communication platform that provides persistent and asynchronous dissemination of machine-understandable information, especially suitable for distributed services. Semantic spaces provide emerging Semantic Web services and Semantic Gadgets with asynchronous and anonymous communication means. Distributing the space among various devices allows anytime, anywhere access to a virtual information space even in highly dynamic and weakly connected systems. To handle all the semantic data emerging in such systems, data stores will have to deal with millions of triples. In consequence reasoning and processing the data becomes highly time and resource consuming. The solution is to distribute the storage and computation among the involved devices. Every interaction partner provides parts of the space infrastructure and data.

One question is whether Semantic Web is ready to provide services, which fit the requirements of the future Internet of Things? The original idea of Semantic Web (Berners-Lee *et al.*, 2001) is to make Web content suitable not only for human browsing but also for automated processing, integration, and reuse across heterogeneous applications. The effort of the Semantic Web community to apply its semantic techniques in open, distributed and heterogeneous Web environments have paid off: the Semantic Web is evolving towards a real Semantic Web (*Sabou et al., 2006*). Not only the number of developed ontologies is dramatically increasing, but also the way that ontologies are published and used has changed. We see a shift away from first generation Semantic Web applications, towards a new generation of applications, designed to exploit the large amounts of heterogeneous semantic markup, which are increasingly becoming available. In Motta and *Sabou (2006),* a number of criteria are given, which Semantic Web applications have to satisfy on their move away from conventional semantic systems towards a new generation of Semantic Web applications:

- *Semantic data generation vs. reuse*—the ability to operate with the semantic data that already exist, i.e. to exploit available semantic markup.

- *Single-ontology vs. multi-ontology systems* —the ability to operate with huge amounts of heterogeneous data, which could be defined in terms of many different ontologies and may need to be combined to answer specific queries.
- *Openness with respect to semantic resources*—the ability to make use of additional, heterogeneous semantic data, at the request of their user.
- *Scale as important as data quality*—the ability to explore, integrate, reason and exploit large amounts of heterogeneous semantic data, generated from a variety of distributed Web sources.
- *Openness with respect to Web (non-semantic) resources*—the ability to take into account the high degree of change of the conventional Web and provide data acquisition facilities for the extraction of data from arbitrary Web sources.
- *Compliance with the Web 2.0 paradigm*—the ability to enable *Collective Intelligence* based on massively distributed information publishing and annotation initiatives by providing mechanisms for users to add and annotate data, allowing distributed semantic annotations and deeper integration of ontologies.
- *Open to services*—the ability of applications to integrate Web-service technology in applications architecture.

In a nutshell, next generation Semantic Web systems will necessarily have to deal with the increased heterogeneity of semantic sources (Motta and *Sabou, 2006),* which partly corresponds to the trends related to the Internet of Things roadmap for the future development (Buckley, 2006).

As discussed above, ubiquitous computing systems need explicit semantics for automatic discovery and interoperability among heterogeneous devices. Moreover, it seems that that the traditional Web as such is not enough to motivate the need for the explicit semantics, and this may be a major reason why no killer application for the Semantic technologies has been found yet. In other words, it is not only that the ubiquitous computing needs semantics, but also the Semantic Web may need the emergence of really ubiquitous computing to finally find its killer application. Recently, the US Directorate for Computer and Information Science and Engineering (CISE) and National Science Foundation (NSF) has announced an initiative called Global Environment for Networking Innovations (GENI, http://www. nsf.gov/cise/cns/geni/) to explore new networking capabilities and move towards the *Future Internet*. Some of GENI challenges are: support for pervasive computing, bridging physical and cyberspace with the impact to access the information about physical world in real time, and enabling exciting new services and applications (Freeman, 2006). If the Future Internet will allow more natural integration of sensor networks with the rest of the Internet, as GENI envisions, the amount and heterogeneity of resources in the Web will grow dramatically and without their ontological classification and (semi- or fully-automated) semantic annotation processes the automatic discovery will be impossible.

Semantic Technologies for Inter-Agent Coordination

When it comes to developing complex, distributed software-based systems, the *agent-based approach* was advocated to be a well suited one (Jennings, 2001). From the implementation point of view, agents are a next step in the evolution of software engineering approaches and programming languages, the step following the trend towards increasing degrees of localization and encapsulation in the basic building blocks of the programming models (Jennings, 2000). After the *structures*, e.g., in C (localizing data), and *objects*, e.g., in C++ and Java (localizing, in addition, code, i.e. an entity's behavior), agents follow by

localizing their *purpose*, the thread of control and action selection. An agent is commonly defined as an encapsulated computer system situated in some environment and capable of flexible, autonomous action in that environment in order to meet its design objectives (Wooldridge, 1997).

However, the actual benefit of the agent-oriented approach arises from the fact that the notion of an agent is also appropriate as a basis for the analysis of the problem to be solved by the system developed. Many processes in the world can be conceptualized using an agent metaphor; the result of such a conceptualization is either a single agent (or cognitive) description or a multi-agent (or social) description (Bosse and Treur, 2006). Jennings (2001) argued that agent-oriented decompositions (according to the purpose of elements) are an effective way of partitioning the problem space of a complex system, that the key abstractions of the agent-oriented mindset are a natural means of modeling complex systems, and that the agent-oriented philosophy for modeling and managing organizational relationships is appropriate for dealing with the dependencies and interactions that exist in complex systems.

The problem of crossing the boundary from the domain (problem) world to the machine (solution) world is widely recognized as a major issue in software and systems engineering. Therefore, when it comes to designing software, the most powerful abstractions are those that minimize the semantic distance between the units of analysis that are intuitively used to conceptualize the problem and the constructs present in the solution paradigm (Jennings, 2000). A possibility to have the same concept, i.e. agent, as the central one in both the problem analysis and the solution design and implementation can make it much easier to design a good solution and to handle complexity. In contrast, e.g. the object-oriented approach has its conceptual basis determined by the underlying machine architecture, i.e. it is founded on implementation-level ontological primitives such as object, method, invocation, etc. Given that the early stages of software development are necessarily based on intentional concepts such as stakeholders, goals, plans, etc, there is an unavoidable gap that needs to be bridged. Bresciani et al. (2004) even claimed that the agent-oriented programming paradigm is *the only* programming paradigm that can gracefully and seamlessly integrate the intentional models of early development phases with implementation and run-time phases. In a sense, agent-oriented approach postpones the transition from the domain concepts to the machine concepts until the stage of the design and implementation of individual agents (given that those are still to be implemented in an object-oriented programming language).

Although the flexibility of agent interactions has many advantages when it comes to *engineering* complex systems, the downside is that it leads to certain *unpredictability in the run time system*; as agents are autonomous, the patterns and the effects of their interactions are uncertain (Jennings, 2000). This raises a need for effective coordination, cooperation, and negotiation mechanism. (Those are in principle distinct, but the word "coordination" is often used as a general one encompassing all three; so for the sake of brevity we will use it like that too.) Coordination aims at avoiding negative interactions, e.g. two agents simultaneously accessing the same non-shareable resource, as well as exploiting positive interactions, e.g. one agent performs an action and shares its results so that another agent would not need to repeat the same action. Jennings (2000) discussed that it is common in specific systems and applications to circumvent coordination difficulties by using interaction protocols whose properties can be formally analyzed, by adopting rigid and preset organizational structures, and/or by limiting the nature and the scope of the agent interplay. However, Jennings asserted that these restrictions also limit the power of the agent-based approach; thus, *in order to realize its full potential some longer term solutions are required*. Emergence of such a longer term solution that would

allow flexible yet predictable operation of agent systems seems to be a prerequisite for wide-scale adoption of the agent-oriented approach.

The available literature sketches two major directions of search for such a longer term solution:

- D1: *Social level* characterization of agent-based systems. E.g. Jennings (2000) stressed the need for a better understanding of the impact of sociality and organizational context on an individual's behavior and of the symbiotic link between the behavior of the individual agents and that of the overall system.

- D2: *Ontological* approaches to coordination. E.g. Tamma et al. (2005) asserted a need for common vocabulary for coordination, with a precise semantics, to enable agents to communicate their intentions with respect to future activities and resource utilization and get them to reason about coordination at run time. Also Jennings et al. (1998) put as an issue to resolve the question about how to enable individual agents to represent and reason about the actions, plans, and knowledge of other agents to coordinate with them.

Recently, some progress has been made with respect to D1, resulting, e.g., in elaboration of the concept of a *role* that an agent can play in an organization. However, with respect to D2 very little has been done. Bosse and Treur (2006) discussed that the ontological understanding among agents requires sharing the following different types of ontologies: an ontology for internal mental properties of the agent A, MentOnt(A), for properties of the agent's (physical) body, BodyOnt(A), for properties of the (sensory or communication) input, InOnt(A), for properties of the (action or communication) output, OutOnt(A), of the agent, and for properties of the external world, ExtOnt(A). Using this distinction, we could describe the present situation as following. The work on explicitly described ontologies was almost exclusively concerned with ExtOnt(A), i.e. the *domain ontologies*. MentOnt(A) comes for free when adopting a certain agent's internal architecture, such as Beliefs-Desires-Intentions (BDI) (Rao and Georgeff, 1991). Also, the communication parts of InOnt(A) and OutOnt(A) come for free when adopting a certain communication languages, such as FIPA's ACL and SL. However, BodyOnt, i.e. the vocabulary for describing preceptors and actuators that the agent has available, the sensory part of InOnt, i.e. the agent's perception vocabulary, and the action part of OutOnt, e.g. the agent's acting vocabulary, are not usually treated. However, sharing these ontologies is a necessary precondition for agents' awareness of and understanding each other's actions, i.e. for D2. Already referred to article by Tamma et al. (2005) is one of the first endeavors into this direction, which however only introduced and analyzed some of the relevant concepts, such as resource, activity, etc.

In our work, we attempt to provide a solution advancing into both D1 and D2 and somewhat integrating both. The current state, namely the architecture of the UBIWARE Platform, will be described later. Some basic thinking, leading to it, is presented here.

On the landscape of research in agent-based systems, we can identify two somewhat independent streams of research, each with its own limitations. The first stream is the research in multi-agent systems (MAS); the second stream is the research in agents' internal architectures and approaches to implementation.

Researchers in MAS have contributed with, among others, various methodologies for designing MAS, such as Gaia (Wooldridge et al., 2000), TROPOS (Bresciani et al., 2004), and OMNI (Vázquez-Salceda et al., 2005). For example, OMNI (which seems to be the most advanced with respect to D1) elaborates on the organizational context of a MAS, defines the relationship between organizational roles and agents enacting those roles, discusses how organizational norms, values and rules are supposed to govern the organization's behavior and thus to put restrictions on individual agents' behaviors. However, OMNI touches only on a very abstract level the question about how the individual agents will be implemented or even function; the agents are treated as rather atoms. One reason is that it is (reasonably) assumed that the agent organization's designer may have no direct control over the design of individual agents. The organization designer develops the rules to be followed and enforcing policies and entities, such as "police" agents, while development of other agents is done by external people or companies. One of few concrete implementation requirements mentioned in OMNI is that a rule interpreter must be created that any agent entering the organization will incorporate, somehow. The OMNI framework also includes explicitly the ontological dimension, which is restricted, however, to a domain ontology only, and thus does not provide much new with respect to D2.

The other stream of research, on individual agents, has contributed e.g. with well-known BDI architecture, and introduced *agent-oriented programming* (Shoham, 1993) along with several *agent programming languages (APL)* such as AGENT-0 (Shoham, 1993), AgentSpeak(L) (Rao, 1996), 3APL (Dastani et al., 2003) and ALPHA/AFAPL (Collier et al., 2005). All of those are declarative languages, follow the BDI model, and are based on the first order logic of n-ary predicates. For example, an agent program in ALPHA consists of declarations of the beliefs and goals of that agent and declaration of a set of rules, including belief rules (generating new beliefs based on existing ones), reactive rules (invoking some actions immediately) and commitment rules (adopting a commitment to invoke an action). Sensors (perceiving environment and generating new beliefs) and actuators (implementing the actions to be invoked) are then pieces of external code, in Java. As discussed above, the agent-oriented approach postpones the transition from the domain concepts to the machine concepts until the stage of the design and implementation of individual agents. The advantage of using an APL is that the transition is postponed even further, until the implementation of particular sensors and actuators.

This advantage is, however, the only one that is usually considered. In some approaches, it is assumed that the agents can communicate their plans encoded in an APL. But, otherwise, the role of APL code does not go much beyond the development stage. APL code is assumed to be written by the developer of an agent and either compiled into an executable program or interpreted in runtime but remaining an agent's intrinsic and static property. APL code is not assumed to ever come from outside of the agent in run-time, neither shared with other agents in any way.

Such export and sharing of APL code would, however, probably make sense in the light of findings from the field of MAS, and also in the light of D2. Methodologies like OMNI describe an organizational role with a set of rules, and an APL is a rule-based language. So, using an APL for specifying a role sounds as a natural way to proceed. The difference is that APL code corresponding to a role should naturally be a property of and controlled by the organization, and accessed by the agents' enacting the role potentially even in the run-time. Run-time access would also enable the organization to update the role code if needed. The second natural idea is that the agents may access a role's APL code not only in order to enact that role, but also in order to coordinate with the agents playing that role. As one option, an agent can send to another agent a part of its APL code to communicate its intentions with respect to future activities (so there is no need for a separate content language). As another option, if a role's code is made public inside the organization, the agents may access it in order to understand how to interact with, or what to expect from, an agent playing that role.

However, when thinking about using the existing APLs in such a manner, there are at least two issues:

- The code in an APL is, roughly speaking, a text. However in complex systems, a description of a role may need to include a huge number of rules and also a great number of beliefs representing the knowledge needed for playing the role. Also, in a case of access of the code by agents that are not going to enact this role, it is likely that they may wish to receive only a relevant part of it, not the whole thing. Therefore, a more efficient, e.g. a database-centric, solution is probably required.

- When APL code is provided by an organization to an agent, or shared between agents, mutual understanding of the meaning of the code is obviously required. While using first-order logic as the basis for an APL assures understanding of the semantics of the rules, the meaning of predicates used in those rules still needs to be consistently understood by all the parties involved. On the other hand, we are unaware of tools allowing unambiguous description of the precise semantics of n-ary predicates: sendsMessage(a, b, c)—who is sending what to who.

To summarize the discussion above, in a nutshell our approach is: Let's treat agent programs as data; data that can be stored into a database, queried for, merged, shared between agents, and so on. As with any data in a distributed computer system, there are problems of other-party understanding the meaning of the data and of machine processibility. Therefore, the utilization of the Semantic Web technology is natural. Semantic Web technology makes the meaning of data as explicit and as unambiguous as possible through the Resource Description Framework (RDF) data model that uses binary predicates only, Universal Resource Identifiers (URI), and ontologies.

Ontologies can be explicitly modeled, e.g. using Web Ontology Language (OWL), providing the explicit description of the semantics of predicates and enabling semantic inference. Several RDF databases exist including Sesame, Joseki, and Oracle Spatial RDF.

Therefore, our proposition is to create and use an agent programming language which will be RDF-based. In fact, the Semantic Web community already contributed with several rule-based semantic reasoners, which are in many aspects similar to APLs with the exception that they do not involve acquiring new data, i.e. sensing, or invoking any actions, neither external nor even mental, such as removing data. One example is Tim Berners-Lee's own CWM data processor (http://www.w3.org/2000/10/swap/doc/cwm), another one is Euler inference engine (http://www.agfa.com/w3c/euler/). CWM is a forward-chaining reasoner while Euler is backward-chaining reasoner; however, they are interoperable because both are based on Notation3 (http://www.w3.org/DesignIssues/Notation3.html). Notation3 (or N3) was proposed by Berners-Lee himself as an alternative to the dominant notation for RDF, which is RDF/XML. N3 is a language which is more compact and probably better readable than RDF/XML, and is also extended to allow greater expressiveness. One feature of N3, which goes beyond the plain RDF, is the concept of formula that allow RDF graphs to be quoted within RDF graphs, e.g. {:room1 :hasTemperature 25} :measuredBy :sensor1. An important convention is that a statement inside a formula is not considered as asserted, i.e., as a general truth. (In a sense, it is a truth inside a context defined by the statement about the formula and the outer formulas.) This is in contrast to the plain RDF where every statement is asserted as a truth.

The Semantic Agent Programming Language (S-APL) is in a sense a hybrid of CWM-like semantic reasoners and ALPHA-like agent programming languages. S-APL uses the data model and the notation of N3. Most of CWM constructs are either directly applicable or have equivalents in S-APL. From the CWM point of view, S-APL extends it with common APL features such as BDI architecture, i.e. ability to describe goals and commitments—data items presence of which lead to some executable behavior, and ability to link to sensors and actuators implemented in a procedural language, namely Java. S-APL also includes several solution-set modifiers and counters which have little meaning in the context of pure reasoners like CWM, but can be found e.g. in the standard RDF query language SPARQL. From APLs point of view, S-APL is a language that provides all the features (and more) of exisitng APLs, while being RDF based and thus providing advantages of semantic data model and reasoning.

S-APL is the core language of the UBIWARE Platform. Although this paper provides a description of the UBIWARE Platform, describing S-APL is beyond the scope of the paper. For a detailed description of S-APL, see Katasonov (2008). Note that in Katasonov and Terziyan (2007), we described the old version of S-APL. Although being based on same basic ideas, that version used different notation and was rather primitive as the current one.

THE GLOBAL UNDERSTANDING ENVIRONMENT (GUN)

GUN Basics

Global Understanding Environment (GUN) (Terziyan, 2003; Terziyan, 2005; Kaykova et al., 2005a) is a concept denoting next generation of Web-based platforms which will make heterogeneous industrial resources (documents, services, devices, business processes, systems, organizations, human experts, etc.) web-accessible, proactive and cooperative in the sense that they will be able to automatically plan own behavior, monitor and correct own state, communicate and negotiate among themselves depending on their roles in a business process, utilize remote experts, Web-services, software agents and various Web applications. Three fundamentals of such platform are *Interoperability, Automation* and *Integration*. Interoperability in GUN requires utilization of Semantic Web standards, RDF-based data, metadata and ontologies and semantic adapters for the resources. Automation in GUN requires proactivity of resources based on applying the agent technologies. Integration in GUN requires ontology-based business process modeling and integration and multi-agent technologies for coordination of business processes over resources.

The main players in GUN are the following resources: service consumers (or components of those), service providers (or components of those), and decision-makers (or components of those). All these resources can be artificial (tangible or intangible) or natural (human or other). It is assumed that the service consumers will be able: (a) to proactively monitor own state over time and changing context; (b) to discover appropriate decision makers and order from them remote diagnostics of their condition, so that the decision makers can decide what maintenance (treatment) services are applied to that condition; (c) to discover appropriate service providers and order from them the required maintenance.

Main layers of the GUN architecture are shown in Figure 1 (in Section 1). Industrial resources (e.g. devices, experts, software components, etc.) can be linked to the Semantic Web-based environment via adapters (or interfaces), which include, if necessary, sensors with digital output, data structuring (e.g. XML) and semantic adapter components (XML to Semantic Web formats). Agents are assumed to be assigned to each resource and to be able to monitor semantically enriched data coming from the adapter about states of the resource, decide if more deep diagnostics of the state is needed, discover other agents in the environment, which represent decision makers and exchange information (agent-to-agent com-

munication with semantically enriched content language) to get diagnoses and decide if maintenance is needed. It is assumed that decision making Web-services will be implemented based on various machine learning algorithms and will be able to learn based on samples of data taken from various service consumers and labeled by experts. Utilization of the agent technologies within GUN framework allows mobility of service components between various platforms, decentralized service discovery, FIPA communication protocols utilization, and MAS-like integration/composition of services.

The SmartResource project, which was mentioned above, in its research and development efforts analyzed Global Understanding Environment decomposing it into three main parts:

The first is the *General Adaptation Framework (GAF)* for semantic interoperability. GAF has to provide means for semantic description of industrial resources, including dynamic and context-sensitive information. The central part in GAF is played by the Resource State/Condition Description Framework (RscDF). An implementation of GAF for a specific domain is assumed to include also an appropriate RscDF-based domain ontology, an appropriate RscDF Engine and the family of *semantic adapters to resources* to provide an opportunity to transform data from a variety of possible resource data representation standards and formats to RscDF-based and back. For more details about RscDF and GAF see (Kaykova *et al.*, 2005b) and (Kaykova *et al.*, 2005a).

The second is the *General Proactivity Framework (GPF)* for automation and proactivity. GPF has to provide means for semantic description of the behaviors of individual resources. GPF defines as its part the Resource Goal/Behavior Description Framework (RgbDF). An implementation of GPF is supposed to include also appropriate RgbDF-based domain ontology, an appropriate RgbDF engine and a family of *semantic adapters to behaviors* to provide an opportunity to transform data from a variety of possible behavior representation standards and formats to RgbDF-based and back. See more on RgbDF in (Kaykova *et al.*, 2005c). The Semantic Agent Programming Language (S-APL), which is the core language of our platform, can be seen as a simplified realization of RgbDF.

The third is the *General Networking Framework (GNF)* for coordination and integration. GNF has to provide means for description of a group behavior within a business process. It specifies the Resource Process/Integration Description Framework (RpiDF), and an implementation of GNF is supposed to include also an appropriate RpiDF-based domain ontology, an appropriate RpiDF engine and a family of *semantic adapters to business process*es to provide opportunity to transform data from a variety of business process representation standards and formats to RpiDF-based and back. The work on GNF is still ongoing

in the UBIWARE project. Some of important GNF-related issues will be discussed in the next subsection. See more about contextual extension of RDF in (Khriyenko and Terziyan, 2006).The main ideas behind these three frameworks and the conceptual difference between RscDF, RgbDF and RpiDF are shown in Figure 2.

As it was mentioned above, the GUN environment is supposed to have decision making resources, which utilize some machine learning algorithms. By getting data from some external industrial resources (devices, machines, etc.), such algorithms are to be able to build models for diagnostics and performance prediction of these devices. Natural heterogeneity and distribution of these algorithms and models result to another important challenge of GUN environment, which is to provide an opportunity for use of automated algorithms (learning and decision making), and for

Figure 2. The three frameworks in the global understanding environment

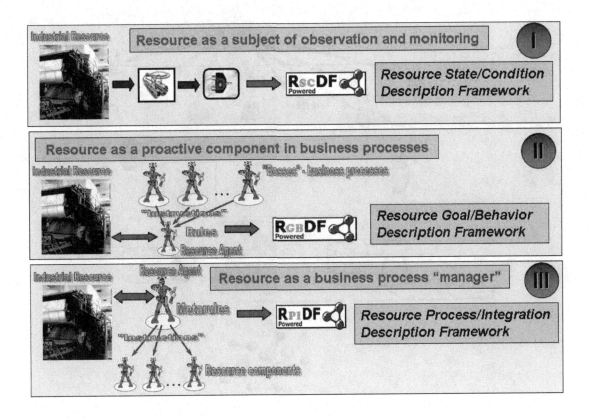

models discovery, sharing, reuse, interoperability, invocation, integration and composition.

GUN Issues

Industrial World (as a natural part of the World of Things) consists of a variety of entities: simple and complex products, machines, tools, devices and their components, Web-services, human workers and customers, processes, software and information systems, standards, markets, domain ontologies, and others. Thus, the Industrial World contains all type of entities: physical, biological, and digital. On the other hand, the World of GUN also consists of a variety of entities: agents for managing Industrial World (IW) or GUN resources, resource histories semantically enriched with metadata, GUN ontologies, adapters for

connecting with IW resources, tools, platforms, standards, executable software components, engines and rules employed by agents, multi-agent commitments and conventions, internal and global standards. GUN is meant for intelligent control over the Industrial World.

To each entity (resource) of the Industrial World, the Global Understanding Environment assigns a Resource Agent, which is assumed to "take care" of the resource and to implement GUN-level proactivity of the resource behavior. Thus, each of the IW resources can be GUN-supported if there is an opportunity to physically and semantically connect the resource to GUN. Heterogeneous IW resources, due to being represented by agents, become in a sense homogeneous in the GUN environment and naturally interoperable with other IW resources. Each GUN agent

Figure 3. The 3-layered GUN architecture for managing industrial resource

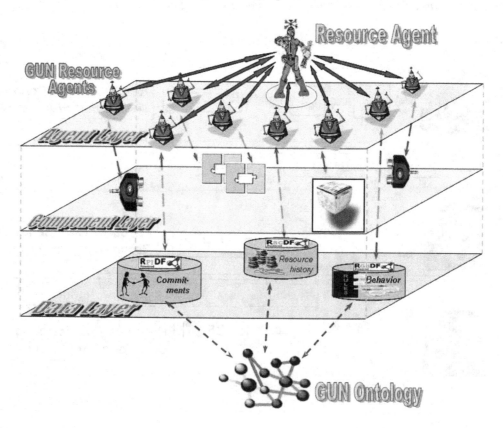

responsible for an industrial resource, *Resource Agent*, communicates with other agents, either with other resource agents or with *GUN resource agents*, and may even have no direct contact with any other software or other entities. Each GUN agent responsible for a GUN resource, *GUN Resource Agent*, necessarily communicates not only with other agents but also with the corresponding GUN resource directly.

In Figure 3, the 3-layered GUN architecture for a particular industrial resource management is shown (do not confuse with the architecture of a resource agent itself, which is 3-layered as well—see Section 4). The Agent Layer contains a resource agent who is responsible for a resource and also several GUN agents responsible for various software components needed for resource sensing, adaptation, condition monitoring, decision-making, maintenance, etc. Each GUN resource agent is connected to an appropriate software component on the Component Layer (e.g. resource sensor adapter, resource actuator adapter, alarm manager, etc.) and is able to invoke it whenever needed. Alternatively, it can be connected to an appropriate semantic storage on the Data Layer (automatically annotated resource history, resource proactive behavior, or resource commitments with other resources). Data Layer components are linked to the GUN ontology (either distributed or centralized), which contains necessary reusable patterns for resource history, resource behavior and resource coordination. Each resource agent keeps record of the resource states and own mental states in a semantically-rich RscDF-based format with link to the industrial domain ontology. Each resource agent keeps a set of needed rules and behavior patterns according to its role in a business process in a semantically-rich RgbDF-based format with link to GUN ontology. Each agent can keep needed adapters, histories, behavior sets, software components, commitments and reusable coordination patterns (in RpiDF-based format) and other GUN resources on own platform. Shared ontology guarantees interoper-

ability and understanding among resource agents. Industrial world will be represented in the GUN environment with a distributed history database, which can be queried by agents and is the subject of agent communication. All the components of the Component Layer and the Data Layer can be exchanged between the resource agents, flexibly composed and reconfigured on-the-fly as result of context-driven agent coordination on the Agent Layer.

The history for a resource contains (see Figure 4) temporal tracks of semantically annotated: resource states as result of sensing and measurements; symptoms as detected by an embedded alarm system; diagnoses made by various experts or Web-services; maintenance (treatment) plans and activities made by experts or Web-services to fix recognized problems. Such a smart history may be not only subject to querying, sharing, integration, etc, but also can provide useful patterns (discovered by data-mining tools), which can be used for predictive diagnostics, maintenance, etc.

The General Networking Framework considers an opportunity of ontological modeling of business processes as integration of the behavioral models of various business actors (agents representing smart resources in the Web) in such a way that this integration will constitute the behavioral model of an agent responsible for the *alliance* of the components. This means that such a corporate agent will monitor the behaviors of the proactive components against the constraints defined in the integration scenario. Such model is naturally recursive and this means that the corporate agent can be a component in a more complex business process and will be itself monitored by an agent from a more higher level of the hierarchy. The hierarchy of agents can be considered as possible mapping from the part-of ontological hierarchy of the domain resources (see Figure 5). Note that we do not assume centralized decision making, but only centralized supervision of compliance.

Figure 4. Resource history and the process of its management

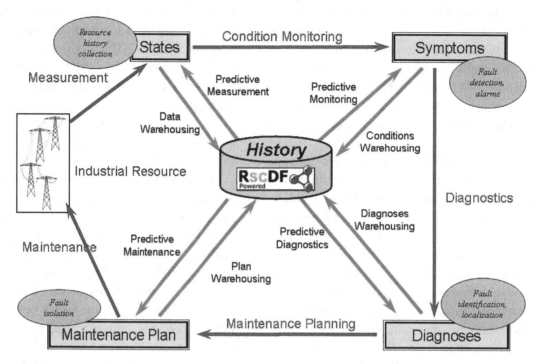

Figure 5. Part-of hierarchy of resources results in corresponding hierarchy of agents

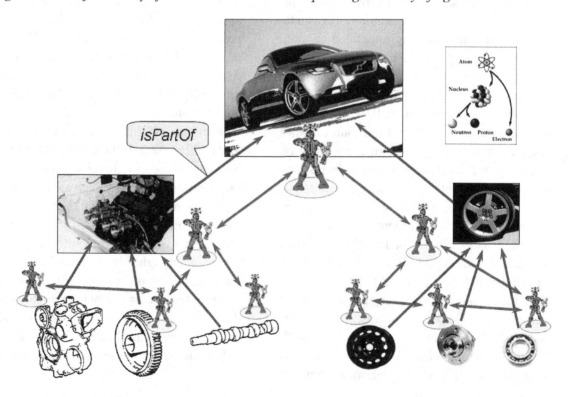

Figure 6. Multiple roles of a resource in the Industrial World and appropriate agent-clones in GUN

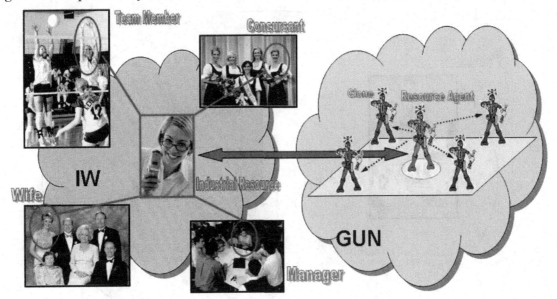

Another important concern is: What is a process in the GUN environment? Consider the following two axioms of GUN:

Axiom 1: Each resource in a dynamic Industrial World is a process and each process in this world is a resource.

Axiom 2: Hierarchy of subordination among resource agents in GUN corresponds to the *part-of* hierarchy of the Industrial World resources.

As all GUN resources, a process has own properties that describe process's state, history, sub processes and belongingness to upper-process (super-process). Thus, following the principles of GUN resource, each process should be assigned an agent that serves this process, similarly to any other resource. GUN's Top Agent is the one, which resource to be taken care of is the Industrial World as whole. Such agent will be on the top of the hierarchy of resource agents.

Each industrial resource can theoretically be involved into several processes, appropriate commitments and activities, which can be either supplementary or contradictory. This means that the resource is part of several more complex resources and its role within each is probably different. Modeling such resources with GUN can be done with the resource agent that can make clones of itself and distribute all necessary roles among them (see Figure 6).

Each industrial resource, which joins some commitment, will behave according to the restrictions that the rules of that commitment imply. The more commitments individual resource takes, the more restriction will be put on its behavior (see Figure 7).

An important feature of the General Networking Framework is the smart way of managing commitments (processes and contracts) of proactive resources to enable cooperation of them and to reach the group's goals along with the individual ones.

Summarizing we can say that GUN vision assumes proactivity of all the heterogeneous resources (humans, devices, services) in the World of Things and intends to provide reusable

Figure 7. Individual vs. team resource freedom

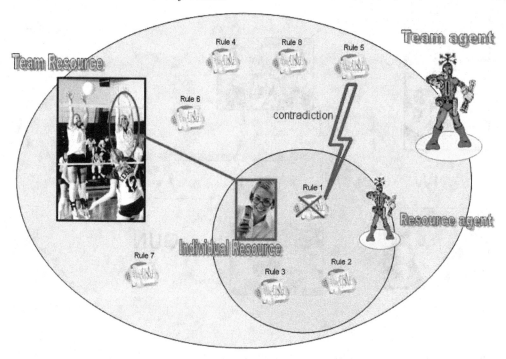

behaviors and reusable coordination patterns to all the resources, making them components in a self-organized process of automatic creation of complex dynamic reconfigurable systems for different industrial purposes. GUN vision allows considering everything as a smart agent-driven resource, which are not only physical objects, but also processes, mathematical models, ontologies and even messages in communication. The last one be used to allow if needed dynamic smart routing, where a smart message itself (not the nodes) decides where to go further within a network, is able to collect own history and communicate with others.

In the following section, we provide more details on the implementation issues focusing on integration of MAS platforms with semantic representation of reusable behavioral patterns for the resource agents.

THE CURRENT STATE OF THE REALIZATION

This section describes the currently achieved state of the GUN realization in the UBIWARE platform. The central to the platform is the architecture of a SmartResource agent depicted in Figure 8.

The basic 3-layer agent structure is similar to, for example, the Agent Factory's ALPHA/AFAPL (see Section 2). There is the behavior engine implemented in Java, a declarative middle layer, and a set of sensors and actuators which are again Java components. The latter we refer to as *Reusable Atomic Behaviors (RABs)*. We do not restrict RABs to be only sensors or actuators, i.e. components sensing or affecting the agent's environment. A RAB can also be a reasoner (data processor) if some of the logic needed is impossible or is not efficient to realize with the S-APL means, or if one wants to enable an agent to do some other kind of reasoning beyond the rule-based one.

The middle layer is the S-APL beliefs storage. As explained in Section 2, the main factor that differentiates S-APL from traditional APLs like AgentSpeak or ALPHA is that S-APL is RDF-based. An additional immediate advantage is that in S-APL the difference between the data and the program code (rules and plans) is only logical but not any principal. They use the same storage, not two separate. This also means that: a rule upon its execution can add or remove another rule, the existence or absence of a rule can be used as a premise of another rule, and so on. None of these is normally possible in traditional APLs treating rules as special data structures principally different from normal beliefs which is n-ary predicates. S-APL is a very symmetric in this respect—anything that can be done to or with a simple statement can also be done to any structure of any complexity.

Technically, our implementation is built on the top of the Java Agent Development Framework (JADE, Bellifemine et al. 2007), which is a Java implementation of IEEE FIPA specifications. The S-APL behavior engine is an extension (subclass) of JADE's Agent class, while the base class for all RABs is an extension of JADE's SimpleBehavior class.

As Figure 8 stresses, an S-APL agent can obtain the needed data and rules not only from local or network documents, but also through querying S-APL repositories. Such a repository, for example, can be maintained by some organization and include prescriptions (lists of duties) corresponding to the organizational roles that the agents are supposed to play. Such externalization of behavior models has several advantages:

- Increased flexibility for control and coordination. Namely, the organization can remotely affect the behavior of the agents through modifying the behavior models. Another advantage is that the models can always be kept up-to-date.

Figure 8. The agent architecture

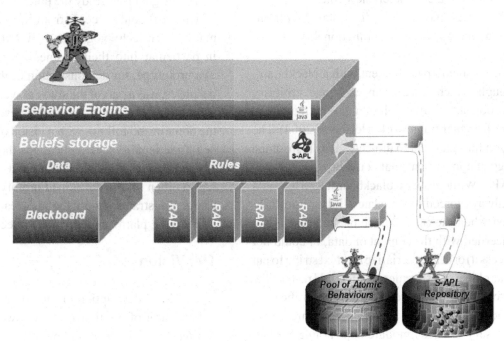

- An agent may 'learn' how to play a new role in run-time; it does not need to be pre-programmed to do it.
- Inter-agent behavior awareness. How is discussed in the in Section 2, the agents not enacting a particular role can still make some use of the information encoded in its behavior model. One reason is to understand how to interact with, or what to expect from, an agent playing that role.

In our implementation, such querying is performed as inter-agent action with FIPA ACL messaging, but does not involve any query or content languages beyond S-APL itself.

As can be seen from Figure 8, agents also can to load RABs remotely. This is done as an exception mechanism triggered when a rule prescribes engaging a RAB while the agent does not have it available. Thus, organizations are able to provide not only the rules to follow but also the tools needed for that. The obvious additional advantages are:

- An agent may 'learn' new behaviors and so enact in a completely new role.
- Agents may have a "light start" with on-demand extension of functionality.

We also equip each agent with a blackboard, through which RABs can exchange arbitrary Java objects. Similar solution can be found e.g. in the Cougaar framework (Helsinger, 2004). The reason for that is not to unnecessarily restrict the range of applications that could be realized with S-APL. Without such a blackboard, RABs would be always forced to translate all data into RDF (even when the S-APL code of the agent is not concerned with the content of data, or could not process it) or at least serialize it as text string to put the as object of a statement. This could restrict the performance and, more importantly, significantly reduce the wish to use S-APL. Blackboard is also necessary to accommodate objects like Socket,

HttpServletResponse or similar to enable an agent to process and respond to HTTP requests, which may be needed in many applications. With the blackboard extension, the developers of a specific application can use S-APL in different ways:

- Semantic Reasoning. S-APL rules operating on S-APL data.
- Semantic Data. RABs (i.e. Java components) operating on S-APL semantic data.
- Workflow management. RABs operating on Java blackboard objects, with S-APL used only as workflow management tool, specifying what RABs are engaged and when.
- Any combination of the three options above.

A CASE: DISTRIBUTED POWER NETWORK MAINTENANCE

This section describes a case study in the domain of distributed power network maintenance we have been performing, starting from early 2006, in collaboration with ABB (Distribution Automation). The goal is to study the potential add-value which ABB could receive from introducing Semantic Web technologies and GUN framework in particular into their business. Development of a prototype, for demonstration of the concept purposes, was a part of the study as well. The first subsection provides a very brief description of the domain and follows with a vision of potential new functionality and applications that could be created based on GUN. The second subsection reports then on the developed prototype, which also demonstrates some of the basic features of the UBIWARE platform described in Section 4.

The Vision

A very brief description of the domain follows. A basic unit of monitoring in a power network is a *feeder*, which is a section of the power line including all the poles, conductors, insulators, etc. The start and the end point of a feeder are *substations*, whose task is to transform the electric power e.g. from high-voltage to medium-voltage or from medium-voltage to low-voltage. In addition to the transformer, any substation naturally includes the devices monitoring and protecting both the incoming and the outgoing feeders. Such *protection relays* automatically monitor the state of the feeder in terms of voltages and currents, are able to disconnect the feeder if a significant *disturbance* is registered, and to automatically re-close the circuit after a specified time (and to break it again if the disturbance persists).

Persistent disturbance is usually a sign of a *fault* in the network, which could be e.g. earth fault (conductor falling of the ground), short-circuit (could be caused e.g. by a tree falling on a line with bare conductors), or open circuit (broken line). Restoration of the network, after a fault occurs, includes *fault detection*, *fault localization* (estimating the geographic location of the fault), and of course fault removal. In meanwhile, network reconfiguration may also be performed, with a goal of e.g. minimizing the number of customers who will suffer outage of power until the fault is removed.

As mentioned, the fault detection is performed by protection relays. The rest is performed in the *operation centers* with participation of human *operators*. In case of a fault, protection relay sends an alarm to the operation center and also sends a dataset with recorded disturbance: several-second history of all the monitored parameters with a high frequency of sampling (0.5 ms or so). A certain operation center controls a sub-network of the integral power network. The operators use systems, which belong to the MicroSCADA Pro product family, like DMS 600 or MicroSCADA Pro Distribution Management System and SYS 600, which is MicroSCADA Pro Control System. These systems provide an integrated graphical view over the sub-network, provide data acquisition from the substations and remote control over the relays, switches, etc. The

systems like DMS also include implementations of various algorithms: for fault localization, for calculation of optimal reconfiguration of the network and other.

ABB is a vendor of hardware and software for power networks. The medium-voltage sub-networks are owned, controlled and maintained then by some local companies, e.g. Jyväskylän Energia for the city of Jyväskylä, and Vattenfall for all the rural areas around. It is noticeable that the operation centers of different companies have no connection to each other, so information exchange among them is nearly impossible. In the case of a fault affecting two different sub-networks, such information exchange, though, may be very important, for all of fault localization, network reconfiguration, and network restoration. Introducing an inter-organizational GUN system could solve this issue (Figure 9). The information flow will go through the agents representing the sub-networks in the GUN environment. Utilization of Semantic Web technologies will allow such interoperability even if the sub-networks use software systems from different vendors (ABB is not the only one), and thus maybe different data formats and protocols.

The second scenario in our vision is related to *a new business model* that ABB could implement. At present, all ABB expertise gets embedded into hardware or software systems and sold to the customers as it is. A new business model would be to start own Web-service providing implementation of certain algorithms, so the ABB customers will utilize those algorithms online when needed (Figure 10). ABB will be always able to update algorithms, add new, and so on. The GUN environment will ensure interoperability and coordination between such Web-service and customers' software systems, and also a relative ease of implementation of such a solution—because it will not require changes in existing software systems, only extension with GUN. Noticeable that, if semantically defined, such Web-service can potentially be utilized across the globe even

Figure 9. Scenario: sub-networks' interoperability

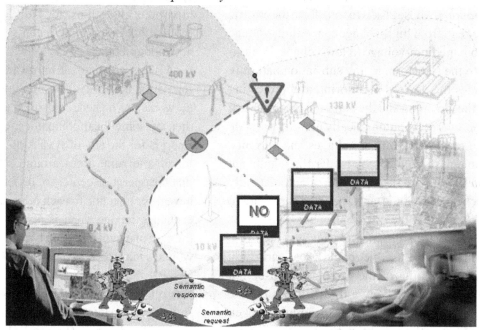

Figure 10. Scenario: a new business model

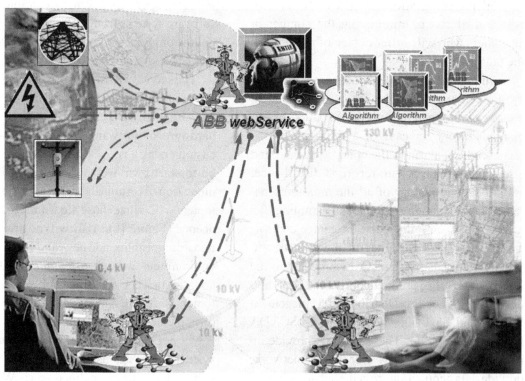

by the customers who never purchased any of ABB hardware or software.

The third scenario in our vision is related to the possibility of integrating data, which is currently utilized in the power network management (network structure and configuration, feeder relay readings), with contextual information from the external sources (Figure 11). Such integration can be used for:

- *Risk analysis.* Information about whether conditions, ongoing forest works, or forest fires can be used for evaluating existing threats for the power network. This may be used to trigger an alert state for the maintenance team, or even to do a precautionary reconfiguration of the network to minimize possible damage.
- *Facilitation of fault localization.* The output of fault localization algorithms is not always certain. The information about threats for the power network that existed at the time when the fault occurred (which thus may have caused the fault) may greatly facilitate the localization. In some situations, contextual information alone may even be sufficient for localization.
- *Operator interface enhancement.* Contextual information may be used also to extend the operators' view of the power network. For example, satellite imagery can be used for geographic view (instead of locally stored bitmaps as it is in the DMS); also, dynamically-changing information can be accessed and represented on the interface.

The last scenario is our vision is about the possibility of transferring the knowledge of human experts to automated systems, by means of various data mining tools (Figure 12). In the

Figure 11. Scenario: integration with external information services

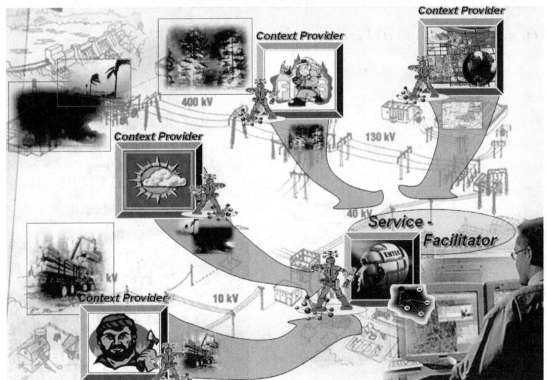

power network management case, one scenario that seems to be highly appropriate for such knowledge transfer is the following. In present, it is always a decision of a human expert which of the existing fault localization algorithms will perform the best in the context of the existing configuration of the power network and the nature of the fault. Such decisions made by an expert, along with the input data, could be forwarded to a learning Web-service. After a sufficient learning sample, this Web-service could start to be used in some situations instead of the human expert, e.g. in situations when a faster decision is needed or when the expert is unavailable.

The Prototype

We also developed a prototype, mainly for the purpose of the concept demonstration, both for ABB and their customers. The prototype includes the following smart resources, represented by the corresponding agents:

- Operator. A human operator monitoring and controlling the power network. In addition to the traditional interfaces—DMS/MicroSCADA—the operator is provided with an additional interface by the operator' agent (see below).
- Feeders. Each feeder (section of the power network) is represented by an agent. Those agents are responsible for answering operator's requests for the state of the feeder, and also for sending alerts when a disturbance is registered. Technically, feeder agents are accessing feeders' data from the MicroSCADA system.
- Network Structure Storage. The DMS system is utilizing a database for storing the data on the power network including the network graph structure, detailed data on substations, feeders, etc. The network storage agent is responsible for interaction with that database for answering operator's requests for the network graph (for visualization) and e.g. for detailed data on a substation.

Figure 12. Scenario: expert's knowledge transfer

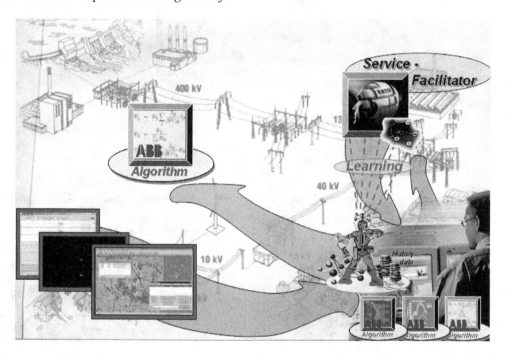

- Fault Localization Services. We assume the scenario presented in Figure 10 will be eventually realized. The fault localization can be then performed by an external entity, e.g. a Web-service, which will also be represented in GUN environment by a corresponding agent (the service itself is a stub in the prototype).

- Weather Service. A service providing constantly updated weather conditions and forecast for a geographic location. We utilized one provided by the Finnish Meteorological Institute.

- Forest Fire Alert Service. A service that is supposed to issue alerts when there is a forest fire (a stub in the prototype). The agent representing this service is responsible for automatic forwarding such alerts to the operator's agent.

- Geographic Service. Provides the geographic map data in Geography Markup Language (GML), if operator's agent requests.

- Repository of Roles and Pool of Atomic Behaviors. See Section 4.

In the prototype, both the repository of roles and the pool of atomic behaviors are managed by the same agent with the role "OntologyAgent". Also, there is only one single repository of the roles, which is also, in fact, a simplification. Consider the scenario of the fault localization by an external service. The agent representing such a service has to necessarily play at least two different roles. One is "our localization service seller" for the company developed the service, say, ABB. The other is "localization service agent" for the company running a power network, say, Jyväskylän Energia. It is because the agent needs to represent the interest of ABB, sell the service for them; but it is also obliged to deliver the service according to the rules, protocol, etc. specified by Jyväskylän Energia. Obviously, it is reasonable that each of cooperating organizations

Figure 13. An agent's start-up

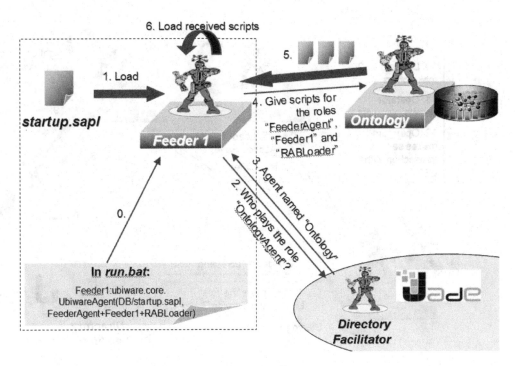

will maintain its own repository of the roles it defines. However, for a prototype, implementing this was not so important.

Figure 13 shows the process of starting up an agent. The same process is followed for every new agent on the UBIWARE platform. From the startup batch file of the platform, an agent receives only the names of the roles that it has to play (the same holds also for cases when an agent in created in run time). For the example in Figure 13, the agent called "Feeder1" gets to know that it has play the general role "FeederAgent"—common for all the feeder agents, and a particular role "Feeder1"—needed for that other agents will associate this agent with the feeder ID1, and including a set of beliefs and rules specific for getting connected to and managing that particular feeder. Additionally, it is supposed to have a capability "RABLoader"—needed for remote loading of RABs. First, the agent "Feeder1" loads the startup.sapl script, which is again common for all the agents. According to that script, the

agent contacts the Directory Facilitator to find the agent who plays the "OntologyAgent" role. The Directory Facilitator maintains a mapping between agents and roles they play. After the OntologyAgent named "Ontology" is discovered, it is contacted and asked to deliver the three scripts needed. After the delivery, "Feeder1" loads the scripts and starts to work according to them. It also registers itself with the Directory Facilitator, so that other agents will be aware that it now plays those roles.

Figure 14 depicts a more complex scenario of auction for selection of a service provider, in this case a fault localization service. Using the Directory Facilitator, the operator's agent discovers that there are two competing agents on the platform that provide the fault localization service. The operator's agent checks its script for a rule resolving such a situation and discovers that, in case of several localization services, an auction has to be performed (for other roles, random select is done). The agent first sends to

Figure 14. Auction for selection of the service provider

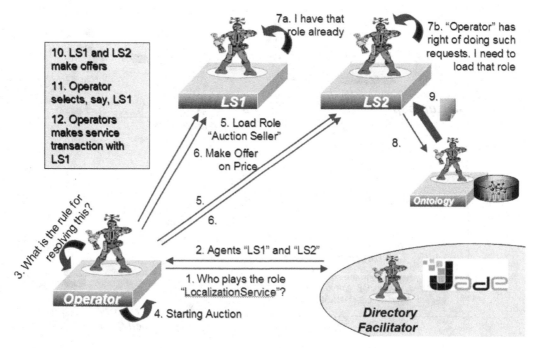

Figure 15. Interface of an operator provided by his/her agent (2 versions)

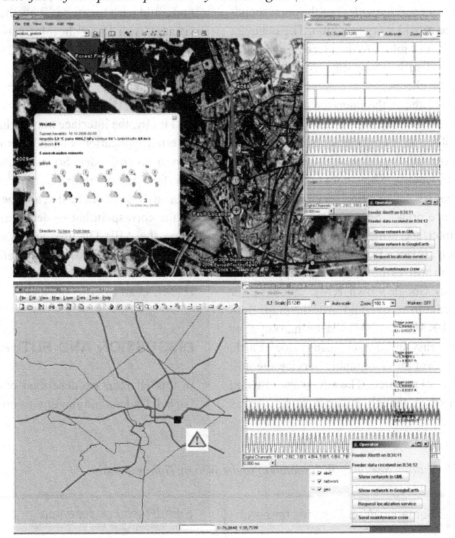

both localization agents a special request "Load Role OneStepAuctionSeller", and then a request to make an offer on, say, price of the service. The agent "LS1" has loaded the role "OneStepAuction-Seller" from the beginning, but the agent "LS2" did not. So, "LS2" contacts the OntologyAgent and requests the needed script now. A simple check of rights is performed just before that: with the Directory Facilitator "LS2" checks whether the requesting agent "Operator" is working in the role that empowers it to make this particular request,

"OperatorAgent" in this case. The agent "LS1" makes its offer immediately, while "LS2" does that after it gets the script and, likely, the corresponding RAB. Then, the operator's agent selects one of the providers and commits the service transaction with it. This scenario demonstrates that roles can be loaded also dynamically.

Obviously, "LS1" and "LS2" needed to enact the "LocalizationService" role earlier. The behavior model corresponding to it will enable the agent to actually deliver the service in the step

12. Also, "LS1" and "LS2" needed to enact some roles like "our service seller" of the corresponding service provider organization. The behavior models of those roles are the places from which they, e.g., get such information as what price to ask from the clients.

Figure 15 shows the interface of an operator generated by the operator's agent. The interface consists of the following elements. First, there is a small command window with buttons "Show network in GML", "Show network in GoogleEarth", "Request localization service" and "Send maintenance crew". Second, there is the main graphic interface, which comes in two options. One option utilizes a freeware GML viewer. The other option utilizes the GoogleEarth application, which uses Google's own KML language for defining data to be overlaid over the map. Both GML and KML are XML-based markups, so transition is easy. In the case of using GoogleEarth, participation of the Geographic Service agent is, obviously, not required. The advantage of using GML map data, though, is that it can be used as

input for some analysis if needed. For example, one could wish to estimate how the forest fire can progress with time—the information about where lay the boundaries of forests and open spaces or lakes is then important, and may be encoded in GML. In contrast, a satellite image will provide little help in that case.

Finally, the interface may include some other external applications that the operator's agent can pop-up when needed. So, using the main graphic interface, the operator can request the real-time data on the state of a feeder, and the data delivered by the corresponding feeder agent is visualized using the ABB Disturbance Draw application. The operator can also request detailed description of a substation, which will be represented with HTML in an Internet browser window.

DISCUSSION AND FUTURE WORK

In this chapter, we described our work on the Global Understanding Environment, a general

Figure 16. Shifting Semantic Web roadmap to the Web of Things domain

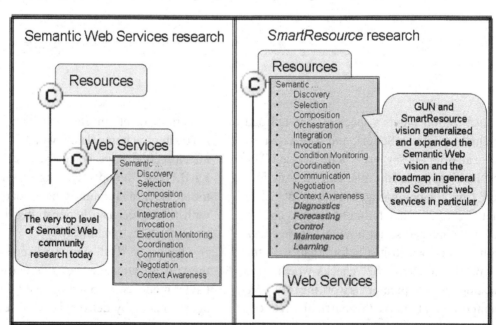

Figure 17. Three dimensions of developing RDF towards the Web-of Things domain

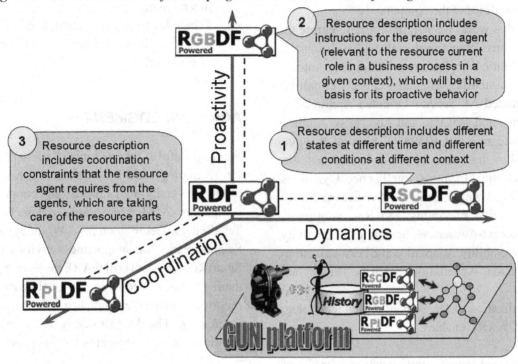

middleware framework aiming at providing means for building complex industrial systems consisting of components of different nature, based on the Semantic Web and agent technologies. From the Semantic Web point of view, GUN could probably be referred to as Proactive Self-Managed Semantic Web of Things. We believe that such Proactive Self-Managed Semantic Web of Things can be the future killer application for the Semantic Web.

The shift from the Web of documents and software to the Internet of Things should affect the Semantic Web research roadmap. So far, the concepts of (semantic) discovery, selection, composition, orchestration, integration, invocation, execution monitoring, coordination, communication, negotiation, context awareness, etc. were mainly applied to the Web-services domain. In future, however, all these concepts should be modified to be applicable also to a resource from the Internet of Things. Also, some new things should

be taken into account, such as e.g. (semantic) diagnostics, forecasting, control, maintenance, learning, etc. (see Figure 16).

Our research on GUN in the SmartResource project (2004-2006) has pointed out the need of updating RDF as the basic Semantic Web framework—in three dimensions: regarding context-sensitivity and dynamics, proactivity, and coordination (see Figure 17).

Our plans include further development the UBIWARE platform towards of a general domain-independent tool allowing creation of self-managed complex industrial systems consisting of mobile, distributed, heterogeneous, shared and reusable components. Those components can be smart machines and devices, sensors, actuators, RFIDs, web-services, software, information systems, communication networks, humans, models, processes, organizations, etc. Such middleware will enable various components to automatically discover each other and to configure a system with complex functionality based on the atomic functionalities of the components.

In this work, we will naturally integrate the Ubiquitous Computing domain with such domains as Semantic Web, Proactive Computing, Autonomous Computing, Human-Centric Computing, Distributed AI, Service-Oriented Architecture, Security and Privacy, and Enterprise Application Integration. UBIWARE aims at bringing the following values to the industrial automation domain: Openness, Intelligence, Dynamics, Self-Organization, Seamless Services and Interconnectivity, Flexibility and Re-configurability, Context-Awareness, Semantics, Proactivity, Interoperability, Adaptation and Personalization, Integration, Automation, Security, Privacy and Trust.

Utilization of the Semantic Web technology in UBIWARE enables:

- Reusable configuration patterns for ubiquitous resource adapters;
- Reusable semantic history blogs for all ubiquitous components;
- Reusable semantic behavior patterns for agents and processes descriptions;
- Reusable coordination, integration, composition and configuration patterns;
- Reusable decision-making patterns;
- Reusable interface patterns;
- Reusable security and privacy policies;

In this chapter, we had focused, among other things, on proactive agent-driven functionality of industrial resources supported by the UBIWARE platform. The existing architecture allows an agent to decide which role it should take in changing context, download and apply reusable semantic description of behavior appropriate to the role. Many interesting issues remain with respect to this for further study, for example:

- Possible conflicts between the roles simultaneously played by the same agent, i.e. what

in this case should be the self-coordination mechanism;
- Principles and concrete benefit of using the code describing a behavior model of one agent by other agents.

ACKNOWLEDGMENT

We are grateful to Tekes (Finnish National Agency for Technology and Innovation), Agora Center of the University of Jyväskylä, and cooperating companies (ABB, Metso Automation, Fingrid, TeliaSonera, TietoEnator, Inno-W, and Jyväskylä Science Park) for supporting activities of the SmartResource and UBIWARE projects. Special thanks to ABB for collaboration on the case study reported in this paper, and permission to publish the results. Thanks to Oleksiy Khriyenko for creating some of the figures for this paper.

REFERENCES

Bellifemine, F. L., Caire, G., & Greenwood, D. (2007). *Developing Multi-Agent Systems with JADE*. Wiley

Berners-Lee, T., Hendler, J., & Lassila, O. (2001). The Semantic Web. *Scientific American, 284*(5), 34-43.

Bosse, T., & Treur, J. (2006). Formal interpretation of a multi-agent society as a single agent. *Journal of Artificial Societies and Social Simulation, 9*(2).

Bresciani, P., Perini, A., Giorgini, P., Giunchiglia, F., & Mylopoulos, J. (2004). Tropos: An agent-oriented software development methodology. *Autonomous Agents and Multi-Agent Systems, 8*(3), 203-236.

Brock, D. L., & Schuster, E. W. (2006). *On the Semantic Web of things*. Semantic Days 2006. Norway, April 26, 2006.

Buckley, J. (2006). *From RFID to the Internet of Things: Pervasive Networked Systems*, Final Report on the Conference organized by DG Information Society and Media, Networks and Communication Technologies Directorate, CCAB, Brussels (available in: http://www.rfid-consultation.eu/docs/ficheiros/WS_1_Final_report_27_Mar.pdf).

Collier, R., Ross, R., & O'Hare, G. M. P. (2005). Realising reusable agent behaviours with AL-PHA. In *Proc. 3rd Conference on Multi-Agent System Technologies (MATES-05), LNCS 3550*, 210–215.

Dastani, M., van Riemsdijk, B., Dignum, F., & Meyer, J.-J.Ch. (2003). A programming language for cognitive agents: Goal directed 3APL. *Proc. First International Workshop on Programming Multi-Agent Systems, LNCS 3067*, 111-130.

Freeman, P. A. (2006). *Statement before the Committee on Science of the U.S. House of Representatives*, Hearing on Innovation and Information Technology: The Government, University and Industry Roles in Information Technology Research and Commercialization, Austin, Texas (available in: http://www.house.gov/science/hearings/full06/May%205/ Freeman.pdf).

Helsinger, A., Thome, M., & Wright, T. (2004). Cougaar: A scalable, distributed multi-agent architecture. In *Proc. IEEE International Conference on Systems, Man and Cybernetics, 2*, 1910–1917.

Jennings, N. R., Sycara K. P., & Wooldridge, M. (1998). A roadmap of agent research and development. *Autonomous Agents and Multi-Agent Systems 1*(1), 7-38.

Jennings, N. R. (2000). On agent-based software engineering. *Artificial Intelligence 117*(2), 277-296.

Jennings, N. R. (2001). An agent-based approach for building complex software systems. *Communications of the ACM 44*(4), 35-41.

Katasonov, A. (2008). *UBIWARE Platform and Semantic Agent Programming Language* (S-APL): Developer's guide, Online: http://users.jyu.fi/~akataso/SAPLguide.pdf.

Katasonov, A., & Terziyan, V. (2007). SmartResource Platform and Semantic Agent Programming Language (S-APL). In *Proc. 5th Conf. Multi-Agent Technologies (MATES'07), LNAI, 4687*, 25-36.

Kaykova O., Khriyenko O., Kovtun D., Naumenko A., Terziyan V., & Zharko A. (2005a). General Adaption Framework: Enabling Interoperability for Industrial Web Resources. *International Journal on Semantic Web and Information Systems, 1*(3), 31-63. Idea Group.

Kaykova O., Khriyenko O., Naumenko A., Terziyan V., & Zharko A. (2005b). RSCDF: A Dynamic and Context Sensitive Metadata Description Framework for Industrial Resources. *Eastern-European Journal of Enterprise Technologies, 3*(2), 55-78.

Kaykova O., Khriyenko O., Terziyan V., & Zharko A. (2005c). RGBDF: Resource Goal and Behaviour Description Framework. In *Proc. 1st International Conference on Industrial Applications of Semantic Web, Springer, IFIP, 188*, 83-99.

Khriyenko O., & Terziyan V. (2006). A Framework for Context-Sensitive Metadata Description. *International Journal of Metadata, Semantics and Ontologies, 1*(2), 154-164.

Kephart J. O., & Chess D. M. (2003). The vision of autonomic computing. *IEEE Computer 36*(1), 41-50.

Krummenacher, R., & Strang, T. (2005). Ubiquitous Semantic Spaces, In *Conference Supplement to the 7th Intl. Conf on Ubiquitous Computing (UbiComp 2005)*, Tokyo.

Lassila, O. (2005a). Applying Semantic Web in Mobile and Ubiquitous Computing: Will Policy-Awareness Help? In *Proc. Semantic Web Policy*

Workshop, 4th International Semantic Web Conference, Galway, Ireland. (pp. 6-11).

Lassila, O. (2005b). Using the Semantic Web in Mobile and Ubiquitous Computing. In *Proc. 1st IFIP Conference on Industrial Applications of Semantic Web,* Springer IFIP. (pp. 19-25).

Lassila, O., & Adler, M. (2003). Semantic Gadgets: Ubiquitous Computing Meets the Semantic Web, In: D. Fensel et al. (eds.), *Spinning the Semantic Web,* MIT Press. (pp. 363-376).

Motta, E., & Sabou, M. (2006). Next Generation Semantic Web Applications. In *Proc. 1st Asian Semantic Web Conference (ASWC),* Beijing, China.

Qasem, A., Heflin J., & Mucoz-Avila H. (2004). Efficient Source Discovery and Service Composition for Ubiquitous Computing Environments. In: *Workshop on Semantic Web Technology for Mobile and Ubiquitous Applications,* ISWC 2004.

Rao, A. S., & Georgeff, M. P. (1991). Modeling rational agents within a BDI architecture. P*roc. 2nd International Conference on Principles of Knowledge Representation and Reasoning* (KR'91), (pp. 473-484).

Rao, A. S. (1996). AgentSpeak(L): BDI agents speak out in a logical computable language. *Proc. 7th European Workshop on Modelling Autonomous Agents in a Multi-Agent World, LNCS 1038,* 42-55.

Shoham, Y. (1993). Agent-oriented programming. Artificial Intelligence, 60(1), 51–92.

Sabou, M., Lopez, V., & Motta, E. (2006). Ontology Selection on the Real Semantic Web: How to Cover the Queens Birthday Dinner? In *Proceedings of EKAW,* Podebrady, Czech Republic.

Tamma, V. A. M., Aart, C., Moyaux, T., Paurobally, S., Lithgow-Smith, B., & Wooldridge, M. (2005). An ontological framework for dynamic coordination. *Proc. 4th International Semantic Web Conference'05, LNCS, 3729,* 638-652.

Terziyan V. (2003). Semantic Web Services for Smart Devices in a "Global Understanding Environment", In: *On the Move to Meaningful Internet Systems 2003: OTM 2003 Workshops, LNCS, 2889,* Springer-Verlag, (pp.279-291).

Terziyan V. (2005). Semantic Web Services for Smart Devices Based on Mobile Agents. *International Journal of Intelligent Information Technologies, 1(*2), 43-55, Idea Group.

Vázquez-Salceda, J., Dignum, V., & Dignum, F. (2005). Organizing multiagent systems. *Autonomous Agents and Multi-Agent Systems 11*(3), 307-360.

Wooldridge, M. (1997). Agent-based software engineering. *IEE Proceedings of Software Engineering, 144*(1), 26-37.

Wooldridge, M., Jennings, N. R., & Kinny, D. (2000). The Gaia Methodology for Agent- Oriented Analysis and Design. *Autonomous Agents and Multi-Agent Systems, 3*(3), 285-312.

FURTHER READING

Schuster, E.W., Allen, S.J. and Brock, D.L. *Global RFID,* Springer, October 2006

Knowledge Media Institute publications on the concept of "Real Semantic Web", available in: http://kmi.open.ac.uk/publications/publications.cfm?id=110.

Aware.IT publications on the synergies of pervasive computing and the Semantic Web, available in: http://www.awareit.com/blog/index.php?/pages/publications.html

Publications of the TAPAS Project (Telematics Architecture for Play-Based Adaptable System), available in http://tapas.item.ntnu.no/wiki/index.php/Publications

USEFUL URLS

Public web-site of the SmartResource project: http://www.cs.jyu.fi/ai/OntoGroup/SmartResource_details.htm

Public web-site of the UBIWARE project: http://www.cs.jyu.fi/ai/OntoGroup/UBIWARE_details.htm

IBM Research—Autonomic Computing: http://researchweb.watson.ibm.com/autonomic/

Semantic Web on The World Wide Web Consortium (W3C): http://www.w3.org/2001/sw/

IEEE Foundation for Intelligent Physical Agents (FIPA): http://www.fipa.org/

Chapter IV
Targeting E-Commerce to Chinese Audiences and Markets:
Managing Cultural and Regional Challenges

Jeffrey Hsu
Fairleigh Dickinson University, USA

ABSTRACT

The market for e-commerce to Chinese audiences is one which has tremendous potential, given the fact that the number of potential users and customers is projected to exceed that of English-speaking Western users. However, managing the host of cultural issues that come up is an important need which must be met. This chapter examines the cultural issues which are relevant to sites targeted at China and Chinese-speaking audiences, including user and consumer behavior patterns, categorizing China using Hofstede's cultural dimensions, examining traditional and historical attitudes, and addressing business issues including trust, payment, and infrastructure challenges. In the chapter design principles based on these are proposed, as well as an examination of the differences between the cultures of China, Taiwan, Hong Kong, and Singapore.

INTRODUCTION

The influence of China is certainly one which has had an impact upon the world in terms of history, culture, and the global economy. This includes not only the influence of mainland China proper, with a population of over one billion, but also in other countries which speak Chinese, and from countless communities of "overseas Chinese" which exist throughout the world.

Many experts predict that China will have the second largest population of web surfers, after the US (McCarthy, 2000), and currently, the Internet population in China is doubling every six months (CNNIC, 2001). The population of Internet users in China is rivaling the United States and western countries in terms of growth. While it may be assumed by some that English-language sites, together with European languages and Japanese, make up the majority of what is on the web, however, the fact is that Chinese language and content sites comprise as many, or more sites than those in English and Japanese. This enormous, yet perhaps less recognized emerging market for the Web is the Chinese-language population, well over a billion of them in mainland China alone, spread out throughout China, Taiwan, Hong Kong, and Singapore, and with many more "Overseas Chinese" throughout the world. According to Global Reach, the population of Internet users who speak and read Chinese and Japanese will have exceeded English language users in 2005 (Global Reach, 2004). As such, the ability to effectively market to this audience is important in our global market economy.

In fact, the Chinese market may evolve into one of the largest in the world, even though currently it is in the earlier of development. Back in 2000, there were close to 9 million computers connected to the Internet in China (CNNIC, 2000), and the number of users exceeded 22 million (CNNIC, 2001). Based on a more recent report, there were at least 80 million Internet users in China reported in 2003, up from 68 million in 2002 (UNCTAD 2002) with the number increasing since then. The latest update puts the estimate at 210 million (Jesdanun 2008).

All of this growth occurred since 1996, and China is now considered one of the top five nations in terms of Internet use, and some experts predict, that China is making strides towards having the second largest population of web surfers in the world. Clearly, there is a vast potential market which has yet to be expanded and tapped to its fullest potential.

Certainly, when dealing with users who speak and use a foreign language, and also have grown up with an entirely different culture, background, and expectations, there are a host of considerations which come into play. The issues relating to the translation between English and other Western languages to Chinese, together with the mechanics and issues involved with the effective display and management of Chinese fonts online, are issues which can be solved with the employment of a translator, and in consultation with technical guides on properly displaying Chinese characters on the web.

However, there are a number of other issues, relating to the cultural aspects of Chinese culture and society which can impact the design and content of web sites which are directed towards Chinese audiences. Some of these issues include the basic differences between Chinese and American/Western cultures, family and collective orientations, religion and faith, color, symbolism, ordering and risk/uncertainty. Attitudes and perceptions about the Internet, shopping, and buying also come into play, as well as some traditions and methods of doing business which have been ingrained into Chinese culture.

Although they are sometimes perceived as being similar or identical, attention is given to the differences between the cultures of China, Hong Kong, Taiwan, and Singapore. Related theories and frameworks, and their relevance to Chinese e-commerce, are also discussed. This chapter will focus on these issues and provide practical guidelines and advice for those who want to reach out to Chinese audiences, whether for marketing, e-commerce, or other needs.

CULTURE AND E-COMMERCE

While there are a number of issues and impacts which relate to the use of the Internet in China and in Chinese-speaking nations, culture is the area on which this chapter focuses. The influence of culture can be an important factor in determining the success of a web site or e-commerce business, since instead of working within the cultural confines of a single nation, such as that of the United States, cultural boundaries are crossed. Consequently, there are frequently a number of issues and considerations which come into play, which if understood and implemented, can help to enhance effectiveness, reach, and acceptance of the site and business.

Broadly stated, the definition of culture includes not only the material features of the human environment, but the conceptual features—the ingrained beliefs, science, myths, religions, laws, and other tenants, held by a group of people. Culture can also, in the case of business, relate to the perceptions and attitudes which a group of people or a country have about money, credit, and mutual trust between customers and merchants, towards institutions such as banks, or the government as a whole, and in terms of shopping behavior. As such, the importance of culture cannot be over-emphasized, since it was found that problems can occur if crucial elements are omitted, which can happen when people from one culture unconsciously apply their own rules to another culture. Cultural differences can also determine which potential users are more likely to go online, and who are most likely to shop once on the Internet (Stafford et al, 2004; Lohse et al., 2000).

One perspective which has been employed is to examine the applicability of theoretical dimensions, such as that derived from Hofstede's book (1997), in which culture is likened to mental programs, or "software of the mind," using the analogy of computer programming. More detail on Hofstede's work and its relationship with Chinese e-commerce and web design is discussed later in this chapter.

As mentioned earlier, the need to factor in the effect of culture is important, since in many cases the goal of a web site is to market something—a product, service, or idea. According to Mooij (1998), culture is a fundamentally important aspect of marketing, and the success or failure may depend on effectively employing cultural elements. Moreover, it is important for marketers of one cultural system to understand and adopt the cultural strategy of the system/nation it is attempting to market to (Penazola, 1998). There are a number of cultural aspects which need to be addressed, whether they be attitudes, behavior, or values. Marketing strategies and tactics, which may work quite effectively in one culture, could result in dismal failure in another.

Before embarking on any kind of international e-commerce venture, it is important to properly targeting the local culture, use meaningful symbols and meanings, manage social relations, and understand the cultural nuances, identities and ethnic preferences (Penazola, 1989; Bouchet, 1995). In addition, aspects as family orientation, importance of Confucianism, and group orientation make up a unique approach to life and viewing the world, which results in important differences that China has from Western cultures (Scarborough, 1998; Lai, 2001).

Certainly, these cultural aspects as they relate to China and Chinese audiences, are complex and encompasses many variables; however the study of these would be useful towards improving and maximizing any efforts made in terms of China-focused web sites and e-business.

HOFSTEDE'S DIMENSIONS OF CULTURE

One of the earliest and most well-known major studies into culture and individual countries was Geert Hofstede's Dimensions of Culture. The work was conducted at IBM in 53 countries between the years 1978-1983. This pioneering work was used to identify a number of theoretical variables which were designed to measure cultural factors. The theory which was developed from this data, were used to form five cultural dimensions, power-distance, collectivism versus individualism, femininity versus masculinity, uncertainty avoidance, and long versus short term orientation. These represent cultural differences which are manifested in values, symbols, and what a culture would value more, or less.

Power-distance (PD) refers to the amount of inequity, or imbalance between those with power and those without, within a culture. High levels of power distance are more closely associated with authoritarian governments, central power, hierarchical structure, and wide differences between the power, status, and affluence of individuals. A culture with fewer of these differences, and less imbalance, would be designated as have a lower power-distance. China was categorized as being high power-distance (Hofstede, 1997).

Individualism versus Collectivism looks at whether the culture is focused more towards the individual or towards a collective group (society as a whole). The success, motivation, and general orientation of the society can be focused either more towards the individual, personal interests, and personal improvement (individualism). On the other hand, a collective culture emphasizes the needs of society or group over the individual, and therefore tends to encourage dominance and established laws and regulations; consequently de-emphasizing privacy and individual freedoms. China is considered to be a culture with a greater emphasis on collectivism. As a result, the needs of the group of community are given greater attention than the needs of the individual (Hofstede, 1997).

Femininity versus masculinity examines the gender roles and their influence in the country's culture. As is expected, masculinity is associated with aggressiveness, competition, and career enhancement, while femininity trends to emphasize family, modesty, and quality of life. China is generally regarded as a masculine culture (Hofstede, 1997).

Uncertainty avoidance (UA) examines, in a culture, how much stress or anxiety is generated by unknown or uncertain events. A high uncertainty avoidance culture would display greater anxiety towards uncertainty, and therefore would emphasize higher levels of emotion, more emphasis on rules, and day to day affairs rather than strategies about the future. The opposite of this would be a low UA culture, where people are less anxious, emotional, and there is more informality and emphasis on strategic planning. It is interesting to note that high UA cultures tend to view new or unusual events as threatening, and one which is to be avoided as it is "dangerous." On the other hand, there is a more curious and laid-back approach to these same "new things" in low UA cultures. China is regarded as a country which is high on the scale in terms of uncertainty avoidance (Hofstede, 1997).

Long versus short term orientation (LTO) was a later addition to Hofstede's dimensions, and has a connection with the study of Asian countries and their emphasis on Confucian principles. China, therefore has a distinctly long-term orientation in its culture (Hofstede, 1997).

The application of these characteristics can be used in practical terms, in designing more effective web sites for Chinese audiences. High power distance cultures would prefer and expect web pages which are highly structured, emphasize nationalism and authority, and give attention to leaders and rather than to the common person.

Other emphases include a tolerance for security restrictions, and secure areas for "higher status" users.

Since China is a collective society, the emphasis is likely to be on group goals and achievement, social agendas, and official statements and symbols. Masculinity is conveyed using traditional distinctions between age and peer groups, emphasis on competition and achieving success, and emphases on work-related (rather than family) concerns (Hofstede,1997).

High uncertainty avoidance would be reflected in pages and sites which emphasize simplicity, fewer choices, less data, "easy" navigation, and means to help users avoid errors. China, being a nation which has a long-term orientation, would be more receptive to sites and pages that emphasize practical value and information, having goals which may take longer to fulfill, and sites which might take longer to use and navigate, rather than one which would necessarily provide immediate results.

It was found that there are differences between China, Taiwan, and Hong Kong in terms of rating using Hofsdtede's dimensions. Some studies tend to suggest that China and Hong Kong tend to exhibit higher levels of long-term orientation and masculinity compared with Taiwan, and that Taiwan also tends to show signs of having higher levels of uncertainty avoidance and individualism than Hong Kong or China (Chen, Wu, and Chung, 2008).

CULTURE AND CHINESE WEB DESIGN

Many of the previous analyses of culture tended to focus on issues of language and customs issues (Lo and Gong, 2005; Dr. Ecommerce, 2001). However, the realm of culture as it relates to China is more complex and can involve a number of interrelated factors and variables.

Some of the studies discussed the concept of web communication standardization, which emphasized standardized ways of representing information and operations, even across international and cultural boundaries. Contrasted to this is the belief that cultural factor differences, which can be represented in the content, appearance, and the level of interactivity on a web site, can be critical to their effectiveness (Lo and Gong, 2005). This latter focus, which is discussed in another study under the term cultural congruity, claims that it will improve the web user's experience to bring in cultural elements which are relevant to the audience being targeted (Luna et al., 2002). As a starting point, it would be useful to examine what are some of the distinctive aspects of Chinese culture, especially those which could relate in some way to the marketing and effectiveness of web sites. Chinese culture is unique, and has a long history reflected by two commonly used terms: *Zhong Guo*, the Chinese word for the country itself, means "the center of the world," expressing belief that China is unique and an important force in the world, and, *Guo Qing* reflecting the fact that China is a special, important country which has its own forms of distinctiveness and uniqueness.

In the case of Chinese versus Western culture, some of these differences are described by Xing (1995). In general, Chinese culture is characterized as being intuitive, aesthetic, introverted, self-restrained, dependent, procrastinating, implicit, patient, group-oriented, and emphasizing continuity. This is in contrast to Western cultures, which are thought of as being more rational, scientific, extroverted, aggressive, independent, active, explicit, impatient, individualistic and change-oriented.

Appadurai's (1991) Five Dimensions of Cultural Flow, and King's Towns and Landscapes (1991), are other relevant theories of globalization. Appadurai attempted to capture the ways in which cultures relate to and influence each other.

These are the Five Dimensions of Global Cultural Flow (1991) dimension: Ethno-scapes (Flows of people—users and the Internet), Finanscapes (Currency and stock exchanges—Internet and e-commerce), Ideo-scapes (The distribution and proliferation of state and counter-state messages over the Internet), Mediascapes (Images of media and information), and Techno-scapes (Technological products and equipment for the Internet).

King (1991) claims that the Internet allows "the global diffusion of information, images, professional cultures and sub-cultures, supported by international capital flows." Both of these models support the concept that culture exists on, and is an important component of, the Internet, and should be taken into account whenever a web site is intended to be globalized.

The influences of Chinese philosophy, including Confucianism (mentioned below), Taoism, and Buddhism even in our modern-day society still carry weight. These help to bring about a sense of practicality, together with philosophical views of life, into Chinese culture.

Some of the traditional values which are important to be aware of when interacting with Chinese culture include respect for the elderly and social status, "face", the use of color, and various traditions which are associated with various aspects of life. A high level of respect for elders and the elderly, more respect given to those with high social status, together with education being highly valued, are all traditional characteristics of Chinese culture. In addition, the desire to avoid embarrassment ("save face") is also a tradition which has endured over the ages (Lee, 1986).

Unlike the United States and other Western cultures, Chinese culture is influenced by Confucianism, in which societal harmony, and respect for family and elders, are considered important. As discussed by Xing (1995) and Hofstede (1997), many Chinese attach a sense of importance to being a part of a group, rather than emphasizing their own individuality. In addition, the emphasis is on the moderate, "middle" path to things, instead of being to one or the other extreme.

There are a number of other characteristics of Chinese culture which are of importance when examining e-commerce in China. These include conservative thinking, respect for conformity and authority, brand loyalty, and a general resistance to new products and ideas. Compared to Western societies, the Chinese are generally more conservative, tend to avoid uncertainty, and prefer continuity and more moderate views of the world (Scarborough, 1998; Jing, 1993).

Also, the attitude towards marketing and advertising differs in that authority and the opinions of peers and neighbors matter. Social aspects such as conformity to norms and worries about the opinions of others are more a factor than in the West (Jing, 1993; Yau, 1988). Brand loyalty seems to be rather strong in Chinese cultures (Yang, 1989). In connection with this, tradition seems to be considered more important than innovation, and some new products and services may be met with some resistance and skepticism, especially if it is viewed as being "socially unacceptable" at that early stage (Yang, 1989). It would also be possible to generalize these tendencies to the fact that the Chinese are more concrete and traditional in their thinking, as opposed to the West, where there may be a stronger influence of abstract thinking and imagination (Li, 1998).

Other factors include the importance of emphasizing the geographical areas of Chinese Internet users, the role of language, and transitional aspects of Chinese culture. According to a study conducted by Lai (2001), many Chinese Internet users are more interested in and concerned with the news and information which relates to their immediate geographical area. For instance, if someone resides in Shanghai, he or she would have greater interest in Internet delivered content if it is focused on central China and Shanghai rather than Harbin or Jiangxi, for example. Local services, or those which focus on a certain region, and deliver information such as local news, weather, or chat would therefore have the most appeal. For instance, in the Sina.com site, the highest hit rates were reported on the Beijing and Shanghai local news and information, and also "city union" chat services (Sina Survey in Major Cities of China, 2001).

Language also appears to be a key factor. While many of the sites which currently existing on the Internet are in English and Western-culture oriented, many experts predict that the Internet will become increasing globalized, and that the influence of China will contribute to this major shift (Gupta, 2001). Language is an important part of China's cultural tradition, and therefore the effective use of Mandarin Chinese in Chinese web sites appears to be of critical importance (Woodfield, 1995)

This is particular true in mainland China (People's Republic of China), where Mandarin is considered the official and main language, unlike Hong Kong or Singapore, where there is a much stronger bilingual emphasis, and many people are well versed in both Chinese, English, and other languages. While it is true that many Chinese, especially those who are younger and college educated, have studied and can communicate effectively in English, it appears that overall, the preference and emphasis of communications is in Chinese.

This could be attributed not only to the ease of communicating in the native language, but also due to a sense of tradition and pride in being Chinese. Moreover, there are expressions, phrases, nuances and shades of meaning in Chinese which cannot always be expressed in the same way in English.

Inherent in this is the difference between linguistic translation and cultural translation. Simply converting English text to Chinese characters, for example, is a far simpler task than accounting for many of the differences noted in

the respective cultures, whether the difference between the U.S. and China, or the difference between China and Taiwan, for example (Bin, Chen, and Sun, 2003).

CHINESE WEB USAGE

It should be noted that most of the users of the Internet in China are from the major cities, such as Beijing, Shanghai, and Guangzhou. Even though the majority of the population resides in rural areas, the main concentration of Internet users can be found in the cities and urban areas. As a result, a strong focus on urban issues, concerns, and interests should therefore be taken into account when designing for a Chinese audience e-commerce site.

As might be expected, more males than females (roughly twice as many) are online, and most of they are young. The majority of Internet users are less than 25 years of age, have a college education (or are students), and/or have a professional employment in government or industry.

As for usage, the main uses for the Internet in China are to communicate via e-mail messaging, and the like; obtain information about various subjects and do research online; and for entertainment (such as playing on-line games, etc.) Most of the usage in China is centered on these communication, information gathering/research and entertainment purposes.

The concept of purchasing items online, while commonplace in many countries, is still not a recognized means of shopping in China, however that may be slowly beginning to change. The few items which are more frequently purchased over the Internet such as books and audio CDs which are generally low priced goods which can be purchased online and delivered to via postal mail to one's home (Wong, Yen, and Fang 2004).

TRUST AND OTHER CHALLENGES

Since e-commerce is in fact a new form of doing business, the cultural aspects of Chinese society as they relate to business and trust is important to examine.

While the market in China for the Internet is indeed huge, and many Chinese are eagerly getting online every day, only a small percentage, (roughly 20%) have done any shopping online. Part of this is the limited use of credit cards in China, which contributes to making e-commerce transactions more difficult than in the United States and Europe. Since it is difficult to conduct electronic transactions when goods must be paid for in cash, the main form of payment has been either to use some form of COD (collect on delivery), to place orders online and to pay and take delivery of them offline, usually at a local store (Bin, Chen, and Sun, 2003). A larger issue is the notion of trust. One potential problem when attempting to further e-commerce is the lack of trust within Chinese society. The notion of ordering a product, sight-unseen, using some form of credit (e.g. credit card), and then expecting delivery in the future, is something which is contrary to the expectations and attitudes of Chinese consumers. The Internet, together with merchants who exist primary online, are simply not highly trusted by potential online shoppers (Bin, Chen, and Sun, 2003).

On a broader scale, Chinese business is accustomed to maintaining personal relationships known as good *guanxi* ("relationship" in Chinese). The definition of *guanxi* could be expressed as the existence of personal connections in order to secure favor in business relations (Brunner, Chan and Zhou, 1989). While important in interpersonal relationships, *guanxi* is especially critical in business, where having guanxi can considerably improve how well a firm can do. Clearly, this is one aspect of a business relationship which is not the most easily accomplished using the Internet.

In addition, in Chinese business there is often a need or expectation for face to face contact in order to build up a sense of trust. This relates back to the earlier discussion of Hofstede's notion of individualism-collectivism, where Chinese culture, based on the underpinnings of Confucianism, is generally collective. Confucianism also is in favor of the evaluating a partner's past and present behavior, which is a prerequisite for trust. Therefore, when dealing with uncertainty, which is the case of business, the need still exists for some kind of face to face contact. This is further supported by the connection between collectivism and high power-distance, which is contrary to the expectation that e-commerce is a low power-distance activity. Clearly, one of the problems that e-commerce is facing in China may be due to a lack of trust both in the online retailers and in the concept of buying something without face-to-face contact and without *guanxi*.

Other differences and challenges in terms of Chinese e-commerce concern transaction trust, the lack of ability to bargain, and reduced socialization effect of e-commerce (Efendioglu and Yip, 2004).

The tradition of Chinese business of cash transactions, receiving goods when purchased, and of knowing your merchant or customer personally (guanxi) is something which is hindering the growth of e-commerce (Davies and Howard, 1995). Simply put, the basic foundations of trust are not present in electronic transactions conducted over the Internet. Also missing is a critical desire to bargain, and to get the best price possible through haggling and on-the-spot negotiations. Finally, there is little or no socialization, personal relationship, discussion, or other interaction prior to, during, and after an online transaction (Efendioglu and Yip, 2004).

Concerns about privacy and security are also more acute among Chinese. A strong reluctance to provide personal information, a lack of trust in the security of credit cards, and also a lack of trust in the banking system and the government in general, also contribute to the slow development of e-commerce in China. Debt, in general, such as that which can happen due to the use (or over-use) of credit cards, is also considered a negative state, and one to be avoided (Efendioglu and Yip, 2004).

PAYMENTS AND INFRASTRUCTURE

In a nation long accustomed to cash transactions, credit cards have remained largely the domain of foreign tourists, hotels, and some restaurants. The widespread availability of credit cards is not yet a phenomenon which exists, so not only is electronic payment not yet a reality, it will not become so until there is a well-developed technological infrastructure for processing large volumes of credit card transactions. The credit card penetration rate in China is around 1%, a very low figure by any standard (Ortolani, 2005). One reason for this may be the perception that credit cards are insecure, and the fact that running up a debt using a credit card is a negative financial state (Fannin 2003; Tan and Wu 2002).

Since credit cards are not widely in use, ordering online is made more difficult in that most of the transactions need, consequently, to be completed using some form of payment on delivery method, such as cash on delivery (COD). One option which is growing in use is the payment for goods at the post office, where the pickup of goods can also be done. This is an especially good option for those persons who do not have home mail delivery, and is growing in popularity (Wong, Yen, and Fang 2004).

Only with the development of a high-volume and widely available technology-based payment infrastructures, together with widespread availability and use of credit cards, can e-commerce in China can grow in terms of larger volume and greater acceptance.

In connection with this, shipping goods to households in China is far more difficult in China compared with the U.S. and other Western nations. There are few large-scale shipping companies comparable to UPS or Federal Express in China, and the Post Office (regular and express mail) remains one of the main viable shipping methods available to Chinese merchants. Moreover, the shipping and logistics system in China is less efficient, and what would take a few days in the U.S. could take a week or several weeks. (Su and Adams 2005; Jiang and Prater 2002; Goh and Ling 2002).

DESIGN ASPECTS OF CHINESE WEBSITES

There are a number of different variables and factors which go into the design of Chinese web and e-commerce sites, and a number of different approaches can be used to examine this. One approach is to examine the characteristics of Chinese websites, both by themselves, and in contrast and comparison to English-language American websites. This, together with recommendations based on theories and cultural characteristics, could provide insight into what Chinese users expect and prefer. Lo and Gong (2005) examine the role of cultural impact on web site format and layout. The results of this study, which in particular examined four variables: interactivity, color usage, page layout, and site content, as they relate to both Chinese and U.S. websites. As such, there was the goal of contrast and comparison between these two dominant web site audiences.

Color usage concerns the choices and usage of colors for web pages, backgrounds, and for various logos and images. How heavily colors in general are used, and the types of colors used are some of the options and choices to be examined. In general, Chinese websites frequently showed a preference for red and black, while American websites tended to use a wider range of colors. In particular, foreground colors tended to included red more often than other colors (Lo and Gong, 2005).

Page layout examines the use of webpage components, including buttons, icons, windows, rollovers, and means of navigation. It was found that Chinese websites tended to include significantly more animations, banners, and other webpage components than American sites. It could be concluded that Chinese sites tend to be denser in terms of page elements, can be more cluttered, and seemed to use less white space than American sites. Overall, Chinese sites tended to be considerably more active in terms of web page elements. Navigation tended to be primarily top-down, perhaps reflecting the tendency for Chinese characters traditionally to be written from the top of the page to the bottom (as opposed to left to right). Navigation is also primarily guided by text links rather than using GUI buttons and icons in Chinese sites (Lo and Gong, 2005).

Site content refers to both the overall strategy and purpose of the site, as well as the specific type or category of the website. A strategy could be for sales, or information dissemination, or entertainment, while the category could be a storefront, portal, or service-oriented site. Interactivity concerns any features which allow the user to interact with the system, such as feedback, search, FAQs, and online ordering. Generally, Chinese sites tended to be information-oriented, and but varied in terms of interactivity.

Singh, Hao and Hu (2003) take Hofstede's dimensions and suggest various web features and elements which would be suitable given China's cultural characteristics. The more extensive use of animation, using bright and bold colors, and displaying cultural and national symbols (flag, Great Wall of China, landmarks, etc.) help to support the concept that there are cultural markers which can help to define a country's website look and feel (Barber and Badre, 1998).

In addition, China's focus on collectivism, uncertainty avoidance, high power distance, and masculinity also tend to support and favor the inclusion of certain web site elements. Collectivism or group emphasis would support the use of chat rooms, newsletters, community event and relation information, family themed information, and symbols of national identity (Singh, Hao, and Hu, 2003).

Uncertainty avoidance could be supported by including many different kinds of customer service and support features, to help manage the uncertainty of users on the site. In addition, the emphasis on traditional beliefs and ideas, together with a focus on familiar names and local brands/merchants would help to increase usage and acceptance. Introducing users to new products, ideas and concepts through trials and downloads would also help to relieve the effects of uncertainty, in a culture where people are wary of and may even feel threatened by anything new (Singh, Hao, and Hu, 2003). High power distance could suggest the receptivity of photos and symbols of leadership, hierarchical structures, symbols of status and of high standing in the community. Masculinity could be reflected by any symbols or images relating to traditional male/female gender roles, together with the use of games and quizzes which present a kind of challenge (Singh, Hao, and Hu, 2003).

REGIONAL ISSUES FOR CHINESE WEB/E-COMMERCE SITES

In the previous sections, discussions were focused on the effective use of cultural aspects to improve web sites for e-commerce and other purposes in China. In this section, some of the differences between the major Chinese-speaking regions are discussed.

China. Users in Mainland China generally are young, college-educated, and reside in the major cities. They generally prefer to surf and use the Internet in Mandarin Chinese, and currently there are emphases on more traditional and risk-adverse products and services (books, audio CDs, computer-related products). However, the markets are changing and the situation may be different in a few years. Since most mainland Chinese understand and use their language using simplified Chinese characters, it is important that any web sites being developed for use in mainland China, use simplified Chinese characters. Traditional Chinese may not be understandable by many mainland Chinese, with the exception of some older individuals.

The effects of government control, restrictions, and censorship are also factors to consider, so it is advisable to consider what is allowed before posting anything up on a web site.

Hong Kong. Because of its cosmopolitan nature and British influence (a former British colony), the use of English is more widespread in Hong Kong as compared with China, and more Western influences have taken hold. Therefore, the use of both Chinese and English on the site, or having two language versions for the same site, might be appropriate. In addition, Hong Kong being in the South of China, and having as its native dialect Cantonese, has its own written version of Cantonese which is combined with Mandarin. The interpretation of this language requires both a knowledge of spoken Cantonese and written Mandarin (Chang, 2000). The fact that Hong Kong is a part of China makes it important to understand the cultures of both.

Taiwan. Taiwan, more formally, the Republic of China, is the government which prior to 1949 ruled mainland China. While currently considered by China to be one of its provinces, but a separate nation from its own perspective, Taiwan uses Traditional Chinese characters, and users there would likely not only have difficulty understanding simplified characters, but would also have a negative reaction to reading simplified Chinese. The use of traditional, rather than simplified Chinese characters is required. In addition, the sensitive political situation which exists between China and Taiwan is another factor to keep in mind.

Singapore. Singapore is more like Hong Kong in that its orientation is more inherently global. A former British colony, it has been on the forefront of the Internet revolution, and currently has not only a well-developed Internet infrastructure, but a nation with the largest numbers of Internet surfers in Asia. It is also one of the most information-driven economies in the world. Web surfers, like those in other Chinese-speaking countries in Asia, are generally, young (29 or younger), are more than likely male, and have at least a secondary school education. The types of applications most favored and used in Singapore include many of the same which Americans favor—e-mail, chat, news, games, and obtaining information for various needs. Much like the US, books and computer products appear to be the top purchases online, however surfers in Singapore tend to purchase more food and grocery products online than Americans.

Singapore, because of its unique mix of multiculturalism, influence of technology, and Westernization, has somewhat different orientation than China, for example. There is a much stronger influence of modernization, Westernization of the youth, a predominantly masculine culture, and a stronger influence of individualism.

Another interesting phenomenon which is unique to Singapore is the concept of "kiasuism" (Milakov, 1995), which is described as being "going for one's own interest, at the expense of the common good." This could be captured more concisely as being "success-driven," or as being "extremely competitive." The fast-moving nature of Singapore and the desire to succeed is one of the traits which has become ingrained into Singapore culture, and perhaps can be captured in terms of success and advancement oriented products and services via the web.

Also, there are subtle language issues to be considered for Singapore as well. People in Singapore, because of the multitude of cultures and nationalities, have developed their own kind of slang called "Singlish." This combines English with words and expressions from languages including Malay, Mandarin Chinese, and from various Chinese dialects. The result is a mixed language which is generally unique to Singapore. While not an official language by any means, it has been reported by some various businesspersons from outside Singapore that an understanding of "Singlish" was important to their success of their projects and business endeavors (Milakov, 1995).

CONCLUSION

In this chapter, a number of issues and considerations with relation to Chinese cultural and web site/e-commerce design were discussed, and clearly, these should be noted when creating a website or e-commerce site for Chinese audiences.

To start, the Chinese value the use of their own language. Whether it be simplified or traditional Mandarin Chinese, the use of the language implies a respect for and understanding of Chinese culture. Because of technology developments, it is not difficult technically to display Chinese, although it may require the services of an effective translator in order to be certain that the language being presented is correct and culturally sound. For instance, a firm providing a site entirely in English, to a Chinese audience, because of a perceived expectation that most Chinese learn English in school, may produce a negative result. The proper use of specific fonts and character types, together with an understanding of cultural and societal differences between mainland China, Taiwan, Hong Kong, and overseas Chinese in other parts of the world, is important as well.

An understanding of Hofstede's Dimensions of Culture also yield insights into the cultural differences between China and other nations, especially the United States and others which have exhibited large growth in terms of e-commerce and online business. The concepts of power distance, masculinity, uncertainty avoidance, and collectivism were discussed in relation to China, and various web design recommendations are suggested.

Other models and concepts of Chinese culture, including a background in Confucianism, and unique traits of the Chinese, are also relevant in understanding the culture, and the reactions to e-commerce, the Internet, and online buying.

Other cultural aspects include a lack of trust between buyers and sellers, the absence of guanxi, reduced interpersonal communications when doing business, and concerns about privacy, personal information, running up a debt, and using credit cards.

The lack of an electronic payment infrastructure, in a society where cash reigns and credit cards are not widespread, makes online transactions difficult. In addition, inadequate shipping and delivery methods are also a challenge.

Design techniques and suggestions, based on various studies, research, and theoretical approaches are presented. Finally, some critical differences between China, Taiwan, Hong Kong, and Singapore are presented.

In conclusion, while marketing to or interacting with China and Chinese audiences over the Internet is a complex task, involving many different cultural factors and considerations, the potential for this market is huge, and one which can yield great benefits and opportunities in the years to come.

REFERENCES

Appadurai, A. (1991). In A. D. King, (ed.), *Culture Globalisation and the World-System*. Macmillan Press Ltd, SUNY-Binghampton.

Barber, W., & Badre, A. (1998). Culturability: The Merging of Culture and Usability. Retrieved from http://www.research.att.com/conf/hfweb/.

Bin, Q., Chen, S., & Sun, S. (2003). Cultural Differences in E-Commerce. *Journal of Global Information Technology Management, 11*(2), 48-55.

Bouchet, S. (1995). Marketing and the Redefinition of Ethnicity. In J. Costa, & G. Balmossy, (eds.), *Marketing in a Multicultural World.* London: Sage Publications.

Brunner, J. A., Chan, C. S., & Zhou, N. (1989). The role of guanxi in negotiation in the Pacific Basin. *Journal of Global Marketing, 3*(2), 58-72.

Chang, S. F. (2000). *A Study of Cultural Influences on Singapore-Chinese Use of E-Commerce.* Major Thesis, RMIT.

Chen, Y., Wu, J., & Chung, Y. (2008). Cultural impact on Trust. *Journal of Global Information Technology Management, 11*(1), 28-48.

CNNIC (2001, 2000). Semi-Annual China Internet Report, 2000.

Davies, H., & Howard, L. (1995). The Benefits of Guanxi. *Industrial Marketing Management, 24*, 207-213.

Dr. Ecommerce (2001). What are the key cross cultural differences that will affect E-Commerce Web site development. Retrieved from http://www.jpb.com/drecommerce/answers/00340.html.

Efendioglu, A., Yip, V. (2004). Chinese Culture and E-Commerce. *Interacting with Computers, 16*, 45-62.

Fannin, R. (2003). The eBay of China, *Chief Executive*, Aug/Sep. 2003, 31-32.

Global Reach (2004). Global Statistics on World Online Populations by Languages. Retrieved from http://global-reach.biz/globstats/evol.htm.

Goh, M., & Ling, C. (2002). Logistics Development in China. *International Journal of Physical Distribution and Logistics Management, 33*(10), 886-917.

Gupta, A.F. (2001). Internet and the English Language, from http://www.fas.nus.edu.sg/staff/conf/poco.paper6.html.

Hofstede, G. (1997). *Cultures and Organizations: Software of the Mind.* McGraw-Hill.

King, A. D. (1991). (ed.) *Culture Globalisation and the World-System.* Macmillan Press Ltd, SUNY-Binghampton.

Jesdanun, A. (2008). China Catching Up to US in Number of Web Surfers. *Associated Press/ECT News Network*, 1/21/08.

Jiang, B., & Prater, E. (2002). Distribution and logistics development in China. *International Journal of Physical Distribution and Logistics Management, 32*, 9, 783-798.

Jing, L. B. (1993, July 10). The influence of Chinese culture on marketing management, Economics Studies, *36*.

Lai, J. (2001). *Marketing Web Sites in China.* Minor Thesis, RMIT.

Lee, S. M. (1986). *Spectrum of Chinese Culture.* Pelanduk Publications (M), Selangor Darul Ehsau.

Li, C. H. (1998). *China: The Consumer Revolution.* New York: Wiley.

Lohse, G., Bellman, S., & Johnson, E. (2000). Consumer Buying Berhavior on the Internet. *Journal of Interactive Marketing, 14*(1), 15-29.

Lo, W. N., & Gong, P. (2005). Cultural Impact of E-Commerce Web sites. *Issues in Information Systems, VI*(2), 182-188.

Luna, D., Peracchio, L., & de Juan, M. (2002). Cross-Cultural and Cognitive Aspects of Web Site Navigation. *Journal of the Academy of Management Science, 30*(4), 397-410.

McCarthy, T. (2000). China's Internet Gold Rush, *TIME Magazine*, Feb 28 2000, 20-23.

Milakov, S. (1995). *Asian Games.* Coolum Beach: Gull Publishing, 19.

Mooij, M. (1998). *Global Marketing and Advertising.* California: Sage Publications.

Nathan, A. (1998). *China's Transition.* New York: Columbia U. Press.

Ortolani, A. (2005). Chinese begin Paying by Cellphone. *Wall Street Journal,* Feb 2, p. 1.

Penazola, (1998). L. N. Immigrant Consumer Acculturation. In Srull, (ed.), *Advances in Consumer Research.* Provo, UT: Assn. For Consumer Research.

Scarborough, J. (1998, November). Comparing Chinese and Western Culture Roots. *Business Horizons.*

Sina Survey in Major Cities in China, (2001).

Singh, N., Zhao, H., & Hu, X. (2003). Cultural Adaptation on the Web. *Journal of Global Information Technology Management, 11,* 3, 63-80.

Stafford, T., Turan, A., & Raisinghani, M. (2004). International and Cross-Cultural Influences on Online Shopping Behavior. *Journal of Global Information Technology Management, 7*(2), 70-87.

Su, Q., & Adams, C. (2005). Will B2C E-commerce developed in one culture be suitable for another culture. *Proceedings of ICEC'05,* X'ian China, August15-17, 236-243.

Tan, Z. and Wu, O. (2002). Globalization and e-commerce: factors affecting e-commerce diffusion in China, *Communications of the AIS, 10,* 4-32.

UNCTAD (2002). *Report on China.*

Wong, X., Yen, D., & Fang, X. (2004). E-Commerce Development in China and its Implication for Business. *Asian Pacific Journal of Marketing and Logistics, 16,* 3, 68-83.

Woodfield, A. (1995). The Conservation of Endangered Languages. CTLL Seminar of University of Bristol.

Yang, C. F. (1989). A Conception of Chinese Consumer Behavior, in Hong Kong Marketing Management at the Cross-Roads, Hong Kong: Commercial Press. (pp. 317-342).

Yau, O. H. (1988). Chinese culture values: Their dimensions and marketing implications. *Journal of Marketing, 22,* 44-57.

Xing, F. (1995). The Chinese Cultural System, in *SAM Advanced Management Journal, 60*(1), 14-20.

Chapter V
Enterprise Resource Planning System:
Issues and Implementation

Edward T. Chen
University of Massachusetts Lowell, USA

ABSTRACT

Enterprise Resource Planning (ERP) is the method of trying to unify all processes within an organization into one software system or database. Enterprise Resource Planning Projects should not be entered into lightly. Not only are ERP projects a new software program to learn, but they are a new way of thinking. This chapter provides a brief history of ERP; follows by the advantages and disadvantages of ERP for organizations considering the adoption of ERP. The next section introduces various strategies of ERP implementation with a list of ERP software vendors. ERP is a long-term IT investment. The total cost of ownership is analyzed and discussed with several cases of ERP implementation.

INTRODUCTION

Enterprise Resource Planning (ERP) is the method of trying to unify all processes within an organization into one software system or database. Whether the process is part of manufacturing, financial,

human resources, or customer service, ERPs attempt to capture all of the processes within two or more departments with a common software program and/or database (Davenport, 1998). Before the advent of ERP it was very common for organizations to have several different software programs each designed to support the needs of individual departments. These programs may have been purchased programs or programs designed by the IT staff of the organization. The IT staff would not only have to support the individual programs but also have to design programs and interfaces so that each of the individual programs could communicate with each other if possible.

Since there are multiple programs, it is not uncommon for the customer information to be keyed into multiple different programs. For example, Sales department takes an order and keys the customer information into its system, the Finance department receives a copy of the order and keys the customer information into its system, the Shipping department receives the product and sales paper work and keys the customer's shipping information into its system, etc. The purpose of the ERP System is to have one centralized location where all of the customer's information is stored and accessible to all departments (Linthicum, 1999; Jacobs and Whybark, 2000).

HISTORY OF ERP

ERPs came about as a way to reduce costs within organizations in the early 1990s. Called organization "re-engineering" or "business process redesign", ERPs helped to streamline processes (Davenport, 1993; Davenport, 1998; Hammer and Champy, 1993; Hammer, 1997). The IT staff would no longer need several application specialists on staff to support the multiple software programs running. Organizations would no longer need as many administrative personnel in each department since there would be one common database shared by multiple departments.

When ERP Systems were first developed, IT professionals were anticipating a "one-size fits all" software development that could capture the functions of all departments across the board (White, 2002). The first versions of ERP in the early 1990s tied together logistics and production.

By 1995, software vendors were hearing requests from organizations to have a marketing and sales solution added to the ERP platform. For those customers that already owned ERPs, vendors offered add-on application solutions. For new customers, vendors created total solutions that tied Logistics, Production, Marketing and Sales all into one program. Vendors focused their newer versions on the recommendations of their users. Once organizations implemented ERP software, the vendors were able to take advantage of the "relationship" by imposing mandatory upgrades every twelve to eighteen months. Organizations had no other choice but to comply since it is not economically viable to discontinue use of an existing ERP or switch to a new vendor.

By the time 1999-2000 rolled around, ERP vendors saw a slow down in sales of ERP solutions. This was due, in a large part, to the Y2K scare. Those organizations that were interested in ERP solutions either hurried up to implement prior to 2000 or waited to ensure that the ERP vendors had successfully solved the Y2K problem within their programs. Several organizations also took the money that would have been used for ERP implementation and used it to ensure that their existing systems would survive the stroke of midnight January 1, 2000 and thus their respective ERP projects were delayed a year.

In the early to mid 2000s there has been a decline in sales of ERP solutions as a result of a "saturation" of the market. Due to the cost and complexity of ERP systems, historically only large organizations have been able to afford a total ERP package. The larger organizations also have the personnel resources to devote to the ERP project. In order to combat the declining sales, vendors are now designing ERP solutions catered to small to medium sized organizations with scaled down versions of the total ERP package that is designed for the large organizations. These scaled down versions of the ERP solutions would require less IT support and thus fewer personnel (Koh and Simpson, 2007).

ADVANTAGES OF ERP

As with any new technology you will see a level of advantages and disadvantages. To understand why an organization would undertake the large all encompassing task of implementing an ERP system, you need to review the advantages of an ERP system and then decide if these advantages would be in the best interests of your organizations.

From an IT approach, an ERP system makes perfect sense. If an organization purchases an ERP system to replace outdated departmental systems throughout the organization, the IT staff no longer has to support several different software programs. The ERP system also creates a central repository for all organizational information, no need for IT to maintain mainframe or multiple servers from the various applications. The IT staff is also alleviated of the task of having to create multiple interfaces for the various programs within the organization.

From an end-user or power user approach, an ERP system can streamline processes throughout the organization by creating a one time entry process. Prior to the advent of ERP, most organizations operated in departmental silos where information was only shared within the individual departments and upwards to management. Departments often had to re-key information that was already inputted by another department to get the customer information into their departmental computer system. With ERP, all departments now have access to all the information that is needed within one centralized database. An example would be the process of taking a sales order from receipt to invoice. Most organizations have an order or customer service department that would key all the necessary information into the ERP system. Once the order is keyed into the system, the finance department and the production floor now have visibility of the order. Production will start building the product by allocation of all of the necessary materials from inventory. The finance department will then review the customer's financials to ensure that the customer will pay the balance due. Once Finance and Production are done with their parts, the product is given to the shipping department to ship to the customer and the order is closed out. At any time throughout the process, anyone within the organization can view the status of the order. Prior to an ERP system, each department would not have this level of visibility into the status of the order within the other departments (Koch, 2006).

From a management perspective, ERP programs can capture a snapshot of the current status of the entire organization. Management no longer has to wait for different divisions to report on the status of their departments. Management now has the ability to see this information in real time. The ability to see the company information in real time allows for organizations to be more agile and respond quicker to changes within the organization or within the industry. This benefit can also be felt at the corporate level. ERP systems allow for information to be shared by different departments or different facilities globally. The CEO of an organization has the sales information of not only the corporate office, but every other office internationally, at his or her fingertips. ERP Systems also reduce operating costs by consolidating IT and Administrative tasks. Organizations are no longer required to carry as large an IT staff since there are fewer software applications to support and maintain. Administrative staff no longer needs to have multiple personnel devoted strictly to data entry since all customer information will only need to be keyed in once (Willcocks and Stykes, 2000).

DISADVANTAGES OF ERP

Along with the advantages of adding an ERP system to your organization comes some disadvantages. ERP systems can be very time consuming and can cost organizations millions of dollars. Organizations may have to spend a considerable amount of money on hardware needed to support the new ERP platform or needed to consolidate the existing hardware. Many organizations also hire ERP consultants, another added expense to an already expensive project, to aid with the implementation project within the organization. A key factor in ERP implementation is not whether or not the software works but how the organization uses the software. ERP programs by themselves are application programs. Only when they are used properly do they actually have a defined value. Contrary to popular belief, ERP programs are not designed to solve organizational problems (Gunson and de Blasis, 2007).

On top of the significant costs to the organization, ERP implementations are very time consuming to the personnel. ERP System implementations generally require some form of Business Process Re-engineering (BPR) to redesign the current processes. The organization needs to decide which of the current processes can effectively fit within the new ERP System and which processes will not effectively fit within the new system and thus need to be re-designed. BPRs allow for a rapid overhaul of an entire process from start to finish (O'Leary, 2000). BPRs are started by a manager who states a case for making the major re-engineering. The manager presents the issues that are faced in the current system and explains what steps are needed in order to solve the problem. Once the case is made, the current process is analyzed to ensure that there are no missing issues or concerns. The manager then develops a new process along with key metrics used to determine whether or not the new process is successful. The manager then develops a transition plan and implementation of the BPR begins. Most BPRs are generally met with resistance from the personnel. Personnel tend to resist any modifications to existing processes that may create more work for them or may benefit a different department over their own (Pearlson and Saunders, 2006).

Another disadvantage of ERP implementation is the toll the project takes on the personnel. Teaching a few people a new process is hard enough as it is let alone training an entire organization to

think a different way. Since ERPs stretch across various departments, most organizations see a marked drop in productivity across the board (Edwards and Humphries, 2005). Departments that were once fluid are now experiencing delays in the tasks that used to take minimal amounts of time. This generally results in frustration with the new program throughout the organization (Stoddard and Jarvenpaa, 1995). Another issue that can arise is conflicts between departments over ownership of certain processes. Should this be a Finance process? Should this process be a Sales process? Etc. Not to mention the fact that now everyone has visibility throughout the organization. No one can hide. If you have not done your job yet, not only does everyone within your department know, but the entire organization knows. "Big Brother" is watching!

At the management level there are a few disadvantages to ERP implementation. The Return on Investment (ROI) of an ERP project is very difficult to measure. Most ERP advantages are intangibles that do not necessarily result in monetary savings or increased sales (Epicor, 2003). It is difficult for senior management, most of who rely on facts and figures to determine success of an ERP project. It may also take several years for an ERP system to be running smoothly and thus take years for any ROI to be realized. Another disadvantage of ERP is the potential loss of any competitive advantage, especially if the implementation is a vanilla implementation. Your nearest competitor may be operating with the same ERP software as yours and may even be utilizing it better (Donovan, 2007).

ERP IMPLEMENTATION STRATEGIES

Once an organization has chosen an ERP vendor, they now need to step back and determine the best course of action for implementing the program. Senior management needs to take into account several factors when determining the appropriate implementation strategy. "Do we need this new program implemented immediately?"; "Is this an ERP program that will be shared with other facilities?"; "Do we have enough personnel on hand to handle the implementation plus keep up with their other job functions?"; "What, if any, modifications do we need to make to get ready for the ERP implementation?" Most articles speak of a chocolate (customized ERP software platform) and a vanilla (non-customized software platform) forms of implementation (Markus and Tanis, 2000; Grenci and Hull, 2004). Parr and Shanks (2000) actually feel that there are three different ERP implementation categories as follows:

- Comprehensive—The most aggressive approach, Comprehensive implementation is very popular among global organizations. True to its name, the Comprehensive implementation involves installing the full functionality of the ERP program. Due to the complexity of implementing one software program at multiple facilities globally, the level of ERP customizations and the level of BPRs for implementation are high. Most Comprehensive implementations take 5+ years to implement and are extremely expensive.

- Middle of the Road—This implementation category shares characteristics of both the Comprehensive and Vanilla implementations. Similar to Comprehensive implementation, Middle of the Road implementation can be used in organizations that have multiple facilities. Similar to Vanilla implementation, Middle of the Road implementation uses a scaled down version of the ERP program. BPRs and customizations are still used but not nearly to the extent that they are used in the Comprehensive approach. Middle of the Road implementations can take 3-5 years and cost up to $3 million.

- Vanilla—The least aggressive of the implementation, Vanilla implementation is used

when an ERP system is only being implemented at one facility and there are not a large number of users. Little to no customization or BPRs is used. Vanilla implementation is for organizations that want to use the bare bones format of the ERP program. Due to the simplicity of the implementation it only takes 6-12 months to install and cost about $1-2 million.

In order for an ERP implementation to be successful, Michael Hawksworth (2007), President and CEO of MSS Technologies, stated there are six steps that need to be achieved: Define Success, Set Priorities, Avoid Modifications, Prepare for Change, Gain Executive Support, and Budget Dollars and People. Defining success metrics and gaining executive support seem to go hand-in-hand. Too often people just assume that if the software is up and running then the implementation was successful. In order to ensure that the ERP system's implementation is successful, senior management needs to take an active role in the implementation by setting goals and measurement metrics to ensure that the organization is heading towards the goals set by management. With active senior management throughout implementation, not only will management be able to ensure that the ERP program will capture all the information management wants to capture, but the level of personnel resistance to the project will lessen.

Setting priorities, avoiding modifications, and preparing for change all play off of each other. When undergoing a large project such as ERP implementation, you need to determine what issues need to be addressed prior to the implementation, what issues can be addressed right after implementation, and what issues need to be put on the back burner until the implementation is solidified. Once you have set you priorities, you need to review the issues on your priority list from top to bottom and determine whether or not it is possible to avoid modifications (Huang, et al., 2004). Modifications to the ERP system actually end up costing the organization more money than re-engineering the current processes. Once you have set the priorities and determined whether or not modifications to the ERP are needed, you can now prepare your organization for change. End users feel the effects of an ERP implementation the most. In order to get the end users ready for the new ERP program, the ERP project team needs to make sure the users are fully trained. The project team, along with senior management needs to also ensure that the end users understand how this new ERP system will be beneficial to the organization. Open communication with the end users as to the benefits of the new system may lessen the resistance to change.

Last but not least is the need to budget dollars and people. Due to the complexity of organization-wide implementation, it is necessary to pull your major players in each department into the project. Major players are employees within each department who not only have strong knowledge of the company, industry and current processes, but are also well respected throughout the organization. These major players may be able to influence acceptance of the implementation. Once you have a project team, management then needs to determine how much day-to-day work needs to be taken away from the project team members and re-assigned to other employees. Other employees within the department will have to pick up some extra work or perhaps management needs to hire more resources (Hofstede, 2001; Davison, 2002).

SOFTWARE VENDORS

As the technology improves and the market grows, more and more vendors are getting into the ERP marketplace. The ERP market is estimated to be a staggering $36 billion in 2008 and vendors are fighting to get a larger piece of the pie. Some customers, when evaluating potential vendors, will go straight to the top option to partner with

the leader in the ERP industry. The belief is that if the vendor is the market leader, then they must have the best technology and the greatest amount of experience with ERP systems. Some customers, on the other hand, will take the time to research each and every vendor and go with the vendor they find to be the best fit for their organization and their organization's goals. The following is an examination of some of the main vendors within the ERP market place (Motiwalla and Thompson, 2008).

SAP

Founded in 1972, SAP is the market leader for ERP solutions. Priding itself on being the industry leader because SAP can provide software solutions for practically every industry, SAP has over 12 million users worldwide. Based out of Waldorf, Germany, SAP employs over 30,000 people in 50 countries (www.sap.com).

Oracle/Peoplesoft

Commonly considered the second most popular solution within the ERP market place, Oracle has been around for about as long as SAP. Oracle software is the chosen software of 98 out of 100 Fortune 100 companies. Headquartered in Redwood, California, Oracle is the first software provider to develop a 100% Internet based ERP system. Oracle currently employs over 40,000 people in more than 100 countries (www.oracle.com).

Microsoft Dynamics

Coming a little late to the game, software powerhouse Microsoft has developed its own ERP solution called Microsoft Dynamics. Microsoft Dynamics' appeal amongst customer is the fact that Microsoft Dynamics works like the standard Microsoft suite programs that most computer users globally are familiar with. Since Microsoft Dynamics is similar in function to the standard

Microsoft Office Suite, Microsoft Dynamics is stated to be one of the easier ERP programs to implement and configure and train personnel on (www.microsoft.com/dynamics).

Infor

Founded in 2002, Infor employs over 8,000 people in 100 different companies. Infor is actually deemed to be the third largest ERP solution provider. According to Jim Shepherd (2006), Infor is "The $2B Enterprise Application Company You've Never Heard of." Headquartered in Alpharetta, Georgia, Infor has risen to its level of success by conducting smart acquisitions and assimilating software businesses. Infor's most recent acquisitions were SSA Global, Systems Union, and Extensity. Infor's key strength is its focus on ERP solutions for specific industries, size segments, and geographies (www.infor.com).

Lawson

Founded in 1975, Lawson has over 4,000 customers in 40 countries. Headquartered in Saint Paul, Minnesota, Lawson offers ERP solutions that are tailored to specific industries. In 2001, Lawson became a public company and has been acquiring several smaller ERP solution companies such as Intentia, Armature, Closedloop, and Numbercraft in order to gain a larger market share. Lawson's strengths are its focus on flexible architecture, analytics and web-addressable applications (www. lawson.com).

QAD

Headquartered in Santa Barbara, California, QAD employs close to 2,000 people worldwide. QAD, which was founded in 1979, focuses on creating ERP solutions for a narrow range of industries (Automotive, Consumer Products, Electronics, Food & Beverage, Industrial Products, and Life Sciences). By focusing on a narrow

range of industries, QAD can develop a close working relationship with their customers and develop software solutions based on customer input recommendations. QAD strives to make its programs simple to learn and easy to implement (www.qad.com).

TOTAL COST OF ERP OWNERSHIP

One of the most difficult things about ERP implementations is the struggle to get a firm understanding of the Total Cost of Ownership (TCO). Pearlson and Saunders (2006) define TCO as "a technique that attempts to comprehend all costs associated with owning and operating an IT infrastructure." TCO looks past the basic cost of the software program and the associated licenses, to the other costs that arise as part of the implementation. TCO looks at hardware costs—desktops, printers, servers, network connections, etc. as well as "soft" costs such as technical support, employee training, hardware repairs and upgrades, etc.

As more and more organizations are embracing ERP solutions, TCO has become a major factor in the ERP decision making process and the ERP strategy development process. In July of 2006, Aberdeen Group, an organization that is devoted to researching business processes, conducted a research project on TCO of ERP Systems. Surveying over 1100 companies of all sizes, Aberdeen limited their research to only 689 of these companies due to the fact that almost 500 of the companies surveyed reported using 2 or more ERP Systems. Aberdeen then focused their report on 5 ERP vendors due to the fact that all 5 vendors had at least 100 customers participating in the study. The 5 vendors Aberdeen focused on were: SAP, Oracle, Lawson, Infor, and QAD.

For the purpose of this study, Aberdeen used 3 metrics to determine total cost of ERP implementation: amount spent on software, amount spent on external services, and internal costs. Aberdeen calculated the average cost of the software and external services divided by the number of average users. As expected, there was a coorelation between the amount of money spent on the implementation and the average price per user. The smaller the ERP implementation, the more money it cost per user. This is due to the fact that volume discounts are common in ERP vendor pricing. The only caveat to this was the discovery that organizations that had revenues of over $1 billion actually spent more per user than those in the $500 million to $1 billion range. Aberdeen attributed this to two key factors: (1) Implementations in organizations of this size can be more complex than the typical implementation, and (2) Companies that have revenues in excess of $1 billion have more money to spend and can purchase more licenses.

Aberdeen goes on to analyze each organization by Average number of Users per Vendor, Vendor Costs Relative to Closest Average number of Users per Vendor, Vendor Costs Relative to Closest Average number of Users, Cost per Utilization by Company Size, Cost per Utilization by Vendor and Cost of Performance by Vendor. SAP led the pack when it came to highest number of modules used, but Lawson led when it came to Software Costs per User. Infor had the best Total Cost of Software and Services per User, but QAD led the Cost per Percentage Point of Performance Improvement Gains (Jutras, 2006).

CASES OF ERP IMPLEMENTATION

Implementation of ERP systems is a tricky task for an organization to undertake. Nearly 90% of all ERP implementations are late and over budget and the success rate of ERP implementations is about 33% (Fulla, 2007; Motiwalla and Thompson, 2008). With the cost of ERP implementation typically in the millions, ERP implementation failure can significantly impact an organization's stability and can in extreme cases cause the failure of an organization.

Tata Refractories

An example of a successful implementation was that of Tata Refractories in India. Prior to the implementation, Tata had no ERP system in place and use of computers within the organization was minimal. The refractories industry experienced a downturn in the 1990s and Tata needed to come up with a solution to remain competitive within the industry and even possibly gain a competitive advantage. Tata looked into implementing an ERP system as a way to cut costs throughout the organization as well as a way to keep a closer eye on the overall success of the organization.

Tata's management team researched several solutions and decided to implement Baan IV C4 within the organization. Tata's management team felt that Baan's solution would be a good fit due to the fact that Baan could handle India's taxation and duty structure norms. Since Tata did not have a pre-existing ERP system, Tata decided not to customize Baan too much and actually focused on re-engineering their organization to fit Baan's software program where possible. The overall implementation was a success due in part to the lack of a legacy system. With no legacy system in place, Tata's management team could focus on the implementation and did not have to worry about the transfer of information from the old software program to the new one. Tata re-engineered its processes to fit within Baan. Tata had adopted the best business practices followed the world over by streamlining core activities, cutting costs, and gaining significant competitive advantage. Some of the benefits realized by Tata were the ability to see financial numbers for the previous month by the second day of the current month, real-time visibility of inventory levels, faster processing times, etc. (Express, 2003).

FoxMeyer Drugs

An example of an implementation gone completely wrong is the classic FoxMeyer Drugs SAP implementation. With sales of over $5 billion, FoxMeyer decided to implement SAP R/3 in order to increase efficiency. FoxMeyer's legacy system was reaching the end of its product lifecycle and FoxMeyer was anticipating receiving a large contract from University HealthSystems Consortium (UHC) so FoxMeyer wanted to implement a new system that could handle the increased volume of transactions the UHC contract would bring. After doing its research, FoxMeyer decided to go with SAP R/3 in 1994. FoxMeyer was one of the early adopters of SAP R/3, a new platform that SAP had just launched in 1994. Estimated to save the organization $40 million annually, SAP R/3 was wrought with problems throughout the entire implementation.

According to Scott (1999), there were four key risk factors that combined were the main catalysts for the failure of ERP. The first catalyst was customer mandate, which deals with user and management adoption to the new process. Executive level adoption to the process was high, but end user adoption to the process was very low. Morale problems surfaced throughout the organization as SAP R/3 struggled to keep up with the volume of orders. The second catalyst was the scope of the project. SAP R/3 was a new program that through initial testing phases had shown that it would be able to handle the volume of orders that FoxMeyer would need to sustain its business; but once the software was implemented, R/3 could only handle 10,000 orders per night versus the 420,000 orders per night that FoxMeyer's legacy system could handle. Third catalyst was execution of the implementation. Since R/3 was a new platform for SAP, there were a limited number of skilled and knowledgeable personnel. FoxMeyer relied on its SAP consulting firm, Andersen Consulting, to implement R/3. Andersen, along with SAP, used the FoxMeyer implementation as a "training ground" for their consultants and used FoxMeyer as their guinea pig. The turnover rate for consultants at FoxMeyer was extremely high. The last catalyst for the failure was the

environment. FoxMeyer failed to keep control of the implementation since it allowed Andersen to run the whole implementation with few, if any, direct FoxMeyer employees involved.

With all of the issues above, it is commonly believed that FoxMeyer would step back and realize that they were heading down the wrong road, take the SAP program offline, re-engineer what did not work, and start all over. The original projected costs for the program was approximately $65 million and since then FoxMeyer threw another $10—$20 million onto the project for re-engineering, while it would have been painful, should not have bankrupted the organization. By the time FoxMeyer realized they were in trouble, no one wanted to do anything to fix the situation. The CEO and the CIO both felt strong personal ties to the project and refused to believe that there were any problems that couldn't be easily fixed. The CEO and CIO were trying to force a square peg into a round hole and ignored all signs pointing to the fact that it would not work. Over commitment to a project is almost as bad as under commitment. Andersen and SAP were also to be blamed for the failure of the implementation. Feeling that a "successful" implementation of SAP R/3 on this large of a scale would be great publicity for both companies, Andersen and SAP put their own interests ahead of their customer's. In the end, FoxMeyer ended up filing for bankruptcy in 1996 and ended up filing lawsuits against SAP and Andersen for their part in the downfall of a billion dollar company.

FLIR Systems

FLIR Systems, an infrared imaging company based out of Portland, OR decided in 2004 to implement one ERP system throughout the organization. With four major manufacturing facilities, FLIR's corporate team wanted visibility at all four facilities. The Portland facility was using Baan, and the Boston, MA facility and the Danderyd, Sweden facility were both using

Avante by Epicor. The Santa Barbara, CA facility, a private company that was recently purchased, did not have an ERP system in place. The Santa Barbara facility kept track of orders, customers, and inventories via Microsoft Excel spreadsheets. When senior management wanted information on the performance of a particular facility, it was often difficult to obtain one report that accurately captured all of the activities of each facility. The corporate team was used to reports via Baan, the Boston and Sweden facilities had to rely on reports generated through Crystal, a third party software that extracted the necessary information from the Avante data storage system. Crystal's reporting system had a 24 hour lag so any information keyed into the Avante system today would not be visible to Crystal until tomorrow. The California facility only captured the most rudimentary data about orders, customers, etc. When management requested information from the California facility it often took days upon days to get the requested information.

The Executive team decided that the organization had grown to a point where one universal ERP System was necessary. One of the key metrics required of the new system would be the ability to obtain reports in "real-time". Corporate would no longer have to wait 24—48 hours or even 72+ hours to obtain information requested. Subject Matter Experts from each department and each facility were selected and after meeting for two weeks to list the requirements of each facility, the Subject Matter Experts (SMEs) along with the executive team analyzed the potential solutions and went with SAP.

The implementation phase was conducted in a phased approach at the corporate level, but a "Big Bang" approach at each facility (Grenci and Hull, 2004). Corporate decided that the Portland facility would implement SAP first, followed by Santa Barbara, Sweden and then Boston last. By implementing the first instance of SAP at the corporate office, FLIR corporate could work out any major software issues prior to implement-

ing at the other facilities. Corporate also had more control over the first crucial stages of the implementation. Corporate could ensure that the program was capturing all of the information that the executive team would need to operate effectively. There was little to no resistance from the personnel since the executive team was based out of the Portland facility and took an active role in the implementation (Hayes, Okonkwo, and Utecht, 2004).

The next facility to implement was the Santa Barbara facility. The Santa Barbara facility was given extra time to implement due to the lack of previous ERP experience. Since the Portland facility was able to resolve most of the initial software issues prior to the Santa Barbara implementation, the main issue that needed to be addressed was the software communication between each facility. The IT staffs from Portland and Santa Barbara had to make sure that any processes keyed into the SAP system at the Santa Barbara facility could be viewed by the personnel in the Portland. The Santa Barbara and Portland staffs worked around the clock to resolve any communications issues and finally got the communications system operating smoothly. The implementation was met with a little resistance at the personnel level but that was expected and anticipated due to the Santa Barbara facility's lack of ERP experience.

Next up was the Sweden facility. Since the Sweden and the Boston facility were operating out of the same legacy system, Avante, FLIR decided to keep Avante installed at their facilities for 6 months after "Go Live" but only in a "Display" mode so that users would have easy access to historical information. Sweden's implementation has been fraught with difficulties. Due to the culture in Sweden, the Swedish facility shuts down for 4 weeks in July. The implementation plan was to have SAP "Go Live" upon the workers return from their summer shut down. This created huge issues across the entire facility. Workers were provided a good amount of training prior to the summer shutdown and conversion, but as the saying goes:

"Use it, or lose it." After 4 weeks of shutdown, most workers forgot a significant amount of the processes of the new system and needed to be re-trained. On top of this was the fact that although their facility was shut down for 4 weeks, the rest of the world was not. The Swedish facility came back into operations with a large back log of orders that had accumulated while they were on shut down and no one knew how to operate within the new system. Customers worldwide were getting extremely frustrated with the delays, personnel were frustrated with the processes of SAP, and the corporate was frustrated with the Swedish facility's poor shipment numbers. In order to help Sweden out, FLIR Corporate agreed to temporarily take a few SAP processes offline and re-activate certain modules of Avante so that Sweden could catch up. FLIR Corporate only agreed to this under the caveat that the Sweden facility brought the offline modules back online as of the beginning of 2008.

The last facility to "Go Live" was the Boston facility. The overall implementation on the technical level was seamless. Since SAP was implemented in three other facilities prior to the Boston facility, all technical issues were known ahead of time and easy to resolve. After the issues at the Sweden facility, senior management took a vested interest in ensuring that everyone was on board at the Boston facility and that there would be little to no resistance to the implementation. Boston was scheduled to "Go Live" October 8th, 2007and they met their schedule. First thing Monday morning, October 8th, 2007, SAP was live in Boston. This is when the issues started to arise. The main issue that arose during the implementation was the quality of the training provided to the personnel. The heads of each department were to nominate one person from each department to be the Subject Matter Expert for their department and develop the appropriate training materials for the other people in their group. Some departments did a great job and the transition was seamless. Some departments fell

flat on their face (Lengnick-Hall, Lengnick-Hall, and Abdinnour-Helm, 2004).

One example of this was the Order Services Department, which handles the sales order processing for new camera purchases. The Manager of this department was hired early last year primarily due to the fact that this person had SAP experience. Management thought that the SAP experience would be a great skill that could be leveraged by the entire department. The Order Services Manager was made the SME for her department and was in charge training all of the people within the department on the ins and outs of SAP and how to effectively process orders within SAP. While the SME had knowledge of how to use SAP, she had very limited amount of knowledge of FLIR's day-to-day operations. The training courses designed by the SME contained only rudimentary knowledge of SAP and no real correlation to how SAP would operate outside the facility (Soh, Kien, and Tay-Yap, 2000; Davison, 2002). So far removed from FLIR's actual operations, the SME conducted one 3-hour training on a process that had nothing to do with the department she was training. Once "Go Live" came around, the Order Services Department came to a screeching halt because the level of training was inadequate to cover the processes that were needed. Orders that should have taken an average of 1-2 weeks to process were now taking 4-6 weeks to process (Edwards and Humphries, 2005).

CONCLUSION

Enterprise Resource Planning Projects should not be entered into lightly. Not only are ERP projects a new software program to learn, but they are a new way of thinking. Facilities that are used to thinking only about what is going on at their own plants now have to start thinking on a global level. While the day-to-day user of the new ERP may just view a new ERP as just another software program to learn, management needs to view ERP as a very useful tool that can help the organization to remain competitive in this ever changing world.

In the case of FLIR Systems, we would have to say that overall the implementation was successful. It employed a system development life cycle approach to implement the ERP system across four divisions. Due to the distinct corporate culture in Sweden division, FLIR has to re-train its employees to guarantee a successful usage of the ERP system. There is always a newer technology out there for ERP application. Hence, we need to continuously equip end-users with proper mindsets and skills to maximize the usability of the ERP system.

REFERENCES

Davenport, T. H. (1993). *Process Innovation: Reengineering Work Through Information Technology.* Boston: Harvard Business School Press.

Davenport, T. H. (1998). Putting the Enterprise into the Enterprise Systems. *Harvard Business Review,* 121-135.

Davison, R. (2002, July). Cultural Complications of ERP. *Communications of the ACM, 45*(7), 109-110.

Donovan, R. M. (n/d). *Why the controversy over ROI from ERP?* Accessed December 5, 2007. http://www.rmdonovan.com/pdf/perform.pdf

Edwards, H., & Humphries, L. (2005, Oct.-Dec.). Change Management of People & Technology in an ERP Implementation. *Journal of Cases on Information Technology, 7*(4), 144-160.

Epicor Software Corporation (2003). The ROI of ERP: Proven Implementation Methodology Is the Determining Factor. Accessed December 5, 2007. http://www.crm2day.com/library/EpZZpEFkpAPBNvjUTC.php

Express Computer, (2003). *Tata Refractories: Another ERP Success Story.* Indian Express Group. Mumbai, India. Accessed December 5, 2007. http://www.expresscomputeronline.com

Fulla, S. (2007). Change Management: Ensuring Success in Your ERP Implementation. *Government Finance Review, 23*(2), 34-40.

Grenci, R., & Hull, B. (2004, Fall). New Dog, Old Tricks: ERP and the Systems Development Life Cycle. *Journal of Information Systems Education, 15*(3), 277-286.

Gunson, J., & de Blasis, J. P. (2007). *The Place and Key Success Factors of Enterprise Resource Planning (ERP) in the New Paradigms of Business Management.* University of Geneva. Accessed December 5, 2007. http://www.crm2day.com/library/EpFlAAAkElDCUAUBZU.php

Hammer, M., & Champy, J. (1993). *Reengineering the Cooperation.* New York: Harper Collins.

Hammer, M. (1997). *Beyond Reengineering: How the Process-Centered Organization Is Changing Our Work and Our Lives.* New York: Harper Collins.

Hawksworth, M. (2007). *Six Steps to ERP Implementation Success.* Accessed December 5, 2007. http://hosteddocs.ittoolbox.com/WP-2007-08-6StepstoERPImplementationSuccess.pdf

Hayes, R., Okonkwo, P., & Utecht, K. (2004). Enterprise Resource Planning and the Competitive Advantage: The Ease of Integrating Information between Corporate Headquarters in the United States and Factories in Mexico. *Competitiveness Review, 14*(1/2), 13-17.

Hofstede, G. (2001). *Culture's Consequences: Comparing Values, Behaviors, Institutions, and Organizations Across Nations.* 2nd ed., London: Sage

Huang, S., Chang, I., Li, S., & Lin, M. (2004). Assessing Risk in ERP Projects: Identify and

Prioritize the Factors. *Industrial Management and Data Systems, 104*(8/9), 681-688.

Jacobs, F. R., & Whybark, D. C. (2000). *Why ERP?* Boston: McGraw-Hill.

Jutras, C. (October 2, 2006). *The Total Cost of ERP Ownership.* Aberdeen Group.

Koch, C. (2006). *ABC: An Introduction to ERP.* CIO. Available at http://ww.cio.com/article/print/40323

Koh, S. C. L., & Simpson, M. (2007). Could enterprise resource planning create a competitive advantage for small businesses? *Benchmarking, 14*(1), 59-76.

Lengnick-Hall, C. A.; Lengnick-Hall, M. and Abdinnour-Helm, S. (2004). The Role of Social and Intellectual Capital in Achieving Competitive Advantage Through Enterprise Resource Planning (ERP) Systems. *Journal of Engineering and Technology Management, 21*(4), 307-330.

Linthicum, D. S. (1999). *Enterprise Application Integration.* Boston: Addison-Wesley.

Markus, M. L., & Tanis, C. (2000). The Enterprise System Experience—From Adoption to Success. In R. W. Zmud (ed.), *Framing the Domains of IT Management: Projecting the Future through the Past.* Cincinnati, OH: Pinnaflex Education Resources, Inc. (pp. 173-203).

Motiwalla, L., & Thompson, J. (2008). Enterprise Systems Management: ERP Implementation in Organizations. New York: Prentice Hall Publications.

O'Leary, D. E. (2000). Enterprise Resource Planning Systems. London: Cambridge University Press.

Parr, A., & Shanks, G. (2000). A Taxonomy of ERP Implementation Approaches. *Proceedings of the 33rd Hawaii International Conference on System Sciences*, Monash University.

Pearlson, K., & Saunders, C. (2006). *Managing & Using Information Systems: A Strategic Approach*, 3rd Edition. Hoboken, New Jersey: Wiley & Sons, Inc.

Scott, J. E. (1999, August). The FoxMeyer Drugs' Bankruptcy: Was it a Failure of ERP?" *Proceedings of the Association for Information Systems Fifth Americas Conference on Information Systems*, Milwaukee, WI, 223-225. Available at http://homepage.cs.uri.edu/courses/fall2007/csc305/Schedule/FoxMeyer1.pdf

Shepherd, J. (December 14, 2006). *Infor: The $2B Enterprise Application Company You've Never Heard Of.* AMR Research.

Soh, C., Kien, S. S., & Tay-Yap, J. (2000). Cultural Fits and Misfits: Is ERP a Universal Solution? *Communications of the ACM, 43*(4), 47-51.

Stoddard, D., & Jarvenpaa, S. (1995, July). Reengineering Design Is Radical, Reengineering Change Is Not. *Harvard Business School, case* 196-037.

White, J. W. (2002). *Making ERP Work the Way Your Business Works.* Addison, TX: Fuego.

Chapter VI
A Secure Characteristics of Wireless Ad–Hoc Networks

Sandip Vijay
I.I.T. Roorkee, India

S. C. Sharma
I.I.T. Roorkee, India

ABSTRACT

This chapter reviews the secure characteristics of mobile devices that can use wireless networks (ad-hoc) almost any where and any time, by using one or more wireless network technologies. Currently, most computers communicate with each other by using wired networks. This approach is well suited for stationary computers, but it is not appropriate for mobile devices. These technologies enable the use of infrastructured networks (3GPP) and ad-hoc networks. Furthermore, the authors describe the gateway specification, requirement for implementation for ad-hoc networks. The minimum, essential, and additional functional requirements for effective functionality of gateway are presented in tabular form. At the end, the future functional requirement and the features of multiple ad-hoc networks are also described.

INTRODUCTION TO WIRELESS AD-HOC NETWORKS

An ad-hoc network is a self-configuring network of wireless links connecting mobile nodes. These nodes may be routers and/or hosts. The mobile nodes communicate directly with each other and without the aid of access points, and therefore have no fixed infrastructure. They form an arbitrary **topology,** where the routers are free to move randomly and arrange themselves as required. First, the devices can freely move in the network, second, the devices can leave and join the network at any time. This type of network can change constantly. Finally, the network disappears when the last devices leave the network (Arkko, J. et al., 2004). The decentralized nature of wireless ad hoc networks makes them suitable for a variety of applications where central nodes cannot be relied on, and may improve the scalability of wireless ad hoc networks compared to wireless managed networks, though theoretical and practical limits to the overall capacity of such networks have been identified. Minimal configuration and quick deployment make ad hoc networks suitable for emergencies like natural disasters or military conflicts. The presence of a dynamic and adaptive routing protocol will enable ad hoc networks to be formed quickly (Buddhikot, M. et al., 2003).

Isolated wireless ad-hoc networks are not suitable for today's applications that require accessing services in the Internet. To overcome this limitation, one or more devices in the wireless ad-hoc network can provide a gateway to an external network. This external network can be the Internet or a local area network (LAN), which may or may not be an infrastructured network. Wireless networks are more vulnerable to misuse than wired networks. In a wireless network, all devices share the same radio band. If two or more devices transmit simultaneously, the communication fails. In addition, a malicious device may be present in the network. It can analyze the communication in the network and do several attacks by sending invalid data. It can masquerade as another device, or it may do various Man-in-the-Middle (**MitM**) or Denial-of-Service (**DoS**) attacks. In particular, it can even block all communication by constantly interfere the transmission. Several security mechanisms partially protect communication in WLAN. **WLAN** may provide security on the lower layers that corresponds the physical and link layers of the Open Systems Interconnection (OSI) reference model. These mechanisms protect communication authenticity, integrity and confidentiality by using cryptographic methods. Moreover, these mechanisms depend on the WLAN technology. On the other hand, security can be provided independently on upper layers. However, none of these mechanisms protect against DoS attacks because it is impossible to prevent a malicious device from interfering the

transmission in a wireless ad-hoc network. It is also possible that not all devices can communicate directly in the wireless ad-hoc network. Such a scenario is shown in Fig. 1. in which device B can communicate with devices A and C directly, but devices A and C cannot communicate directly. This has an impact on the network-layer and application-layer protocols. In the network-layer, not all devices can communicate directly with each other by using IP addresses. Moreover, some applications do not work unless the communication is link-local. For example, Dynamic Configuration of **IPv4** Link-Local addresses requires link-local communication to successfully configure and maintain IPv4 addresses.

Routing enables communication between devices that cannot communicate directly. In the ad-hoc network, this is done by using an ad-hoc routing protocol. There are two types of routing protocols for ad-hoc networks: Proactive and Reactive. In proactive routing, routes are actively maintained, and they are available when needed. In reactive routing, routes are discovered on demand. An ad-hoc network can be isolated, or it can have a gateway that provides a connection to another network. Consequently, the devices must be able to communicate when the gateway is available and when it unavailable.

THE AD-HOC NETWORK ENVIRONMENT

This section introduces the gateway and its environment, and it describes the used ad-hoc network environment first from the lowest layer upwards and then from the logical point of view. The users use wireless devices to communicate with other users in proximity. The devices use Wireless Local Area Network (WLAN) to form a wireless ad-hoc network. The devices can be desktops, laptops, and mobile phones. The communication takes place within a group of two or more people. The communication group may be

Figure 1. Communication link between different networks using gateway

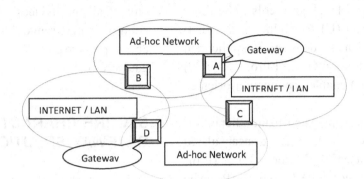

formed for one communication session only or for many communication sessions. The communication group may remain unchanged during the communication, or it may change constantly. The communication can be personal, professional, or between unknown people. Friends and relatives can use the devices for personal communication. Company employees can use them to organize a project meeting. The users can also use them to communicate temporarily with unknown people.

The users may also need to use services that are not available in the wireless ad-hoc network. They may need to browse web pages, send and receive email, and communicate with other users that are not present in the wireless ad-hoc network. These services are available in infrastructured networks, such as in the Internet or in intranets. A user usually communicates with the infrastructured network through an access network, e.g. through a cellular network. However, this option is available only to the customers of the operator that provides the access network.

WLAN Technology: WLAN is based on the **IEEE 802.11** standard (IEEE Std 802.11i, 2004) that defines a family of WLAN standards. More specifically, it is based on the 802.11b standard (ISO/IEC 7498-1:1994 ed., 1994) that enables the

data transfer rate of 11 Mbps making the performance comparable to that of a wired LAN. In addition, the ad-hoc network is implemented by using the Independent Basic Service Set (IBSS) type of network. This allows devices within range communicate only directly. However, devices must use the same physical channel to communicate, and they must use choose to use the same ad-hoc network because the standard allows coexistence of many networks in the same physical channel. Although WLAN implements the functionality of the physical layer and the link layer, to enable the use of network-layer addresses in the current link, the network-layer addresses must be mapped into Ethernet addresses by using An Ethernet Address Resolution Protocol (ARP) (Kaufman, C. et al., 2004) or Neighbor Discovery (ND) (Kent, S. et al., 1998).

Network Layer: In the network layer, the communication is based on IP. More specifically, either IPv4 (Cheshire, S. et al., 2004) or IPv6 (Conta, A. et al., 1998) is used. It is also possible to use a dual stack in which both IPv4 and IPv6 are used. Also Internet Control Message Protocol (ICMP) (Deering, S.,1998) is used along with IPv4 for various purposes, e.g. testing the reach ability of a host. Similarly, ICMPv6 (Conta, A. et al., 1998) is used along with IPv6.

Transport Layer and Session Layer: The Internet Protocol provide unreliable packet delivery of upper level protocols. The User Datagram Protocol (UDP) (Calhoun, P., 2004) enables connectionless delivery of application data. The Transmission Control Protocol (TCP) (Aboba, B., 2004) enables connection-oriented communication.

IP can also be encapsulated inside other protocols. When IPsec is used, IP can be encapsulated by using Authentication Header (AH) or IP Internet Key Exchange (IKE). Moreover, IP can be encapsulated by using IP Encapsulation within IP and Generic Routing Encapsulation (GRE).

Presentation Layer and Application Layer: Using the network requires several services that are provided in the application layer. These services are service discovery service, address configuration, and domain name service (DNS). The service discovery service allows gateway clients to discover the gateway. The address configuration service allows clients to negotiate unique IP addresses. DNS is used to resolve host names and IP addresses in the external network. The next sections describe first services and then logical network structures.

Devices: This work considers devices that are laptops with a WLAN interface, and the operating system used is Linux. In addition, using mobile devices based on the *Symbian* operating system is an optional solution that is considered here.

A gateway can also provide access to an infrastructured network. A gateway can be either wired or wireless. A wired gateway is usually based on Ethernet but other technologies can also be used. A wireless gateway can offer network access, for example, by using 3G or WLAN.

Network Structure: In the wireless ad-hoc network, the communication is restricted to the *linklocal* communication, but the gateway is used enable communication between the wireless ad-hoc network and the infrastructured network. The communication works properly only if all the devices are within each other's communication range. The gateway may also be able to provide globally routable addresses to the gateway clients.

SECURE CHARACTERISTICS OF GATEWAY SOLUTIONS

In this section, we describe the potential gateway solutions, compare them, and select the most suitable solution for the environment described above.

3GPP System and WLAN Interworking: The 3GPP System and WLAN Interworking specification allows 3G devices to use WLAN as a radio access technology. The specification describes Authentication, Authorization, and Accounting (AAA) through the 3GPP system, the use of an infrastructured network through a WLAN, and Packet Switched (PS) services through a Public Land Mobile Network (PLMN).

Figure 2 presents the trust model entities in the 3GPP System and WLAN interworking: user, WLAN access provider, and cellular operator. The user uses the 3G functionality of the cellular operator through the WLAN access provider. The WLAN access provider offers WLAN connectivity to the user and an access network to the cellular operator. The WLAN access provider can also be a part of the cellular operator. The cellular operator provides 3G services to the user through the WLAN access provider. The user-operator trust relation (U-O) is based on a legal agreement between the user and the cellular operator. The operator-WLAN trust relation (O-W) is based on roaming agreements or other agreements, or it is internal to the cellular operator if the WLAN access provider is part of the cellular operator. Finally, the user-WLAN trust relation (U-W) is derived from U-O and O-W. Next, we describe the 3GPP system and WLAN interworking architecture in more detail and explain how it is modified to provide a gateway implementation for the environment described above.

Architecture: Figure 3 presents the simplified architecture. A user can access an infrastructured network directly through WLAN or through a Packet Data Gateway (PDG). This requires that the user is successfully authenticated and authorized for access by using the 3GPP AAA server. The 3GPP system and WLAN interworking provides two reference models: the non-roaming and the roaming reference model. In the non-roaming model, a user uses WLAN connected to the 3GPP home network. In contrast, in the roaming model, a user uses WLAN connected to the 3GPP visited network. Here, a user can access the PDG either in the 3GPP home network or in the 3GPP visited network.

Authentication, Authorization, and Accounting: Using 3GPP system and WLAN interworking requires that the cellular operator trusts the WLAN access provider. The cellular operator must allow the WLAN access provider to use its AAA server to authenticate and authorize the users. This also allows the WLAN access provider to generate accounting information that can be used for billing and other purposes. A WLAN access point (AP) uses the AAA information

Figure 2. The trust model in 3GPP system and WLAN interworking

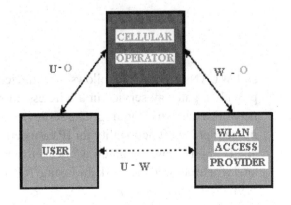

in the AAA server of the 3GPP home network by using an AAA protocol. Both RADIUS and DIAMETER can be used to transport the AAA information over IP.

Authentication is based on the Extensible Authentication Protocol (EAP) that supports multiple authentication methods. Authentication is done by using a Universal Subscriber Identity Module (USIM) or by using a Subscriber Identity Module (SIM). Using EAP between a 3G device and an AAA server is shown in Figure 4. The authentication information is transported between a device and an AAA server. Between a device and AP, EAP is transported over a WLAN protocol. In a 802.11 WLAN, the EAP Over LANs (EAPOL) is used.

Further, between AP and an AAA server, EAP transported over an AAA protocol. In addition, there can be proxies between AP and the AAA server. The AAA proxy is responsible for obtaining the AAA information from the appropriate AAA proxy or server. Proxies can participate in authorization by further restricting access, and they can store accounting information.

Communication Integrity and Confidentiality: In 802.11 WLAN, link-layer communication integrity and confidentiality are based on the IEEE 802.11i specification. This specification enhances WLAN security by introducing the use of Advanced Encryption Standard (AES). However, according to the Wi-Fi Alliance's white chapter, old IEEE 802.11 hardware may not be able to support it.

In the network layer, communication integrity and confidentiality between WLAN and PDG can be provided by using IPsec. Using IPsec the mechanism to set up a secure tunnel between WLAN and PDG is not yet finalized. However, it does propose a solution. First, a security association is made by using the Internet Key Exchange (IKEv2) Protocol, and PDG is authenticated by using public key cryptography with certificates. Second, a device can be authenticated by using EAP with USIM or SIM. Alternatively, IKEv2

Figure 3. Simplified 3GPP system and WLAN interworking architecture

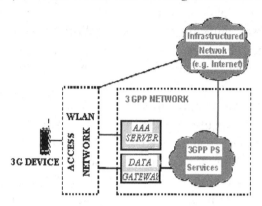

Figure 4. EAP between a 3G device and an AAA server

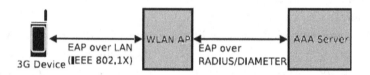

Figure 5. 3GPP System and WLAN Interworking as a gateway

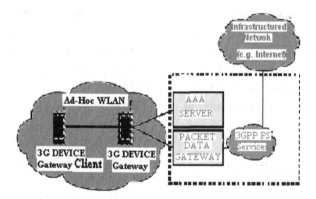

or the older version, IKE is used, and both the device and PDG mutually authenticate each other with certificates.

Using 3GPP System and WLAN Interworking as a Gateway: The modified 3GPP system and WLAN interworking allows a 3G device to provide a gateway service in a wireless ad-hoc network as shown in Figure 5. The 3G device uses its standard 3G functionality for IP connectivity and DNS. It allows the gateway clients to access an infrastructured network by using Network Address Translation (NAT).

It also provides a caching DNS service and advertises the gateway service by using ICMP Router Discovery Messages or Neighbor Discovery. Finally, IPsec provides communication integrity and confidentiality between the gateway and the gateway client.

Authentication, Authorization, and Accounting: As the gateway acts as a client to the cellular operator, the gateway and the cellular operator mutually authenticate and authorize each other by using the standard 3G functionality. The cellular operator also checks that the gateway is authorized to use the AAA server. This allows the gateway and the gateway client to mutually authenticate and authorize each other by using EAP with USIM or SIM as the gateway and the gateway client establish an IPsec tunnel by using IKEv2. The gateway can also further restrict its use by denying access. In addition, the cellular operator stores the total accounting information of the gateway by using standard 3G functionality. This information represents the total amount of network traffic through the gateway, that is, the traffic caused by the gateway clients the traffic caused by the gateway itself. In addition, the gateway can be allowed to generate accounting information on behalf of the gateway clients. The amount of traffic caused by the gateway is obtained when the amount of client traffic is subtracted from the total amount. However, this requires that the cellular operator trusts that the gateway generates the accounting information correctly.

Alternatively, the gateway does not generate accounting information, and only the total amount of network traffic through the gateway is available.

Local 3G Radio Link: A 3G device can use its own 3G radio link to access an infrastructure network, and it can use a WLAN interface to access the wireless ad-hoc network. Consequently, the device is a multi-homed host that has a valid IP address in both networks. The device must have routes to both networks, but it does not need to provide routing between the networks. Authentication, authorization, and accounting are based on existing 3G functionality. Each device that needs to access the infrastructured network must mutually authenticate with the cellular operator by using USIM or SIM.

Generic Gateway: A multi-homed device can act as a gateway that enables communication between the wireless ad-hoc network and the infrastructured network as presented in Figure 6. As the gateway provides access to an infrastructured network by using NAT, it does not need to configure IP addresses for the gateway clients. IPsec provides Communication integrity and confidentiality between the gateway and the gateway client. The gateway can advertise its availability by using ICMP Router Discovery Messages or Neighbor Discovery. In short, the gateway is just a router. This approach is so generic that it is applicable with any network technology that enables IP based communication.

Authentication, Authorization, and Accounting: The gateway and the gateway client mutually authenticate and authorize each other as they establish an IPsec tunnel by using IKE with certificates. The AAA information may reside in the gateway or in a remote AAA server. Optionally, the gateway generates accounting information.

Application-Level Gateway: In a wireless ad-hoc network, the gateway can also provide access to an infrastructured network on the application level. The gateway can be a generic proxy for all applications, or it can provide an application-specific proxy for each application.

The gateway can provide a generic SOCKS proxy that can provide IP connectivity for all applications that support the SOCKS protocol. The SOCKS proxy is shown in Figure 7. To access an infrastructured network, a gateway client uses the SOCKS protocol to communicate with a SOCKS proxy which in turn communicates in an infrastructured network on behalf of the

Figure 6. Generic Gateway for wireless ad-hoc and infrastructured network

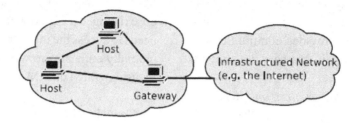

Figure 7. The generic SOCKS proxy (Application level gateway)

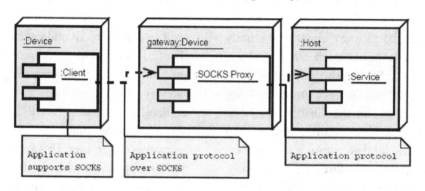

Figure 8. Application-specific proxies for ad-hoc networks

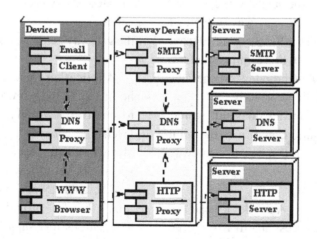

client. Alternatively, a gateway can provide an application-specific proxy for each application as shown in Figure 8. This requires that the client can use the protocol through a single proxy only. Here, a gateway client uses an application-specific protocol to communicate with a proxy which in turn communicates in an infrastructured network on behalf of the client. However, using application-specific proxies is possible only with known applications and compatible software versions.

Optionally, an application-specific proxy is transparent. A transparent proxy is shown in Figure 9. Using a transparent proxy does not require any modification to a gateway client. Here, a gateway client assumes that it can access an infrastructured network by using the IP address of an infrastructured network as a destination address. The gateway intercepts the application-specific communication sent by a gateway client, and it acts as a client on behalf of the gateway client in an infrastructured network. It relays the application-specific communication from an infrastructured network to a gateway client as if it came from the infrastructured network.

Authentication, Authorization, and Accounting: Although some applications provide proxy authentication, IPsec can provide authentication and authorization for all applications, and it can also provide communication integrity and confidentiality between the gateway and the gateway client. Optionally, the gateway can also use a remote AAA server. The application-specific proxies do not store traditional accounting information, but they can do application-specific logging that provides application-level information.

OTHER SOLUTIONS

Striegel, Ramanujan, and Bonney describe a protocol-independent gateway for wireless ad-hoc networks. This gateway can support various ad-hoc routing protocols in the wireless ad-hoc network. The gateway routes traffic between the wireless ad-hoc network and the Internet. It enables Internet access by using either NAT or Mobile IP. However, this solution does not provide any security. Nilsson et al. discuss how IPv6 and Ad-hoc On-Demand Distance Vector Routing (AODV) can be used for Internet access. In this solution, the gateway allocates a globally routable prefix for the ad-hoc network. However, this disables coexistence of multiple gateways because there can be only one global prefix.

This specification describes a gateway for wireless ad-hoc networks. The business model of the gateway is shown in Figure 10. The gateway is available only to authenticate and authorized users, and the users can choose which devices are authenticated and authorized to provide the gateway. The integrity and confidentiality of the gateway communication can be protected in the wireless ad-hoc network. It works with most frequently used applications. It does not require any changes to the external network. Several important choices were made for the gateway implementation. NAT provides a generic solution for accessing external services from the private network, and it works with most frequently used applications. The gateway implementation can provide security for all applications with IPsec. However, using IPsec significantly decreases the performance, and demanding applications may not deliver adequate performance with IPsec. The gateway implementation also provides a DNS service that can resolve host names and addresses in the ad-hoc network and in the infrastructured network without any changes to existing applications. In the gateway business model, there are four roles (Described in figure 11): the user, the gateway Figure 10: The business model of the gateway for ad-hoc and infrastructured networks.

The operator provides IP based access to the infrastructured network. The operator may charge a monthly fee or according to the transferred data. In addition, if the gateway provider is visiting a foreign network, the foreign network may charge the roaming costs. The use cases illustrate the

Figure 9. Transparent proxy for wireless ad-hoc communication

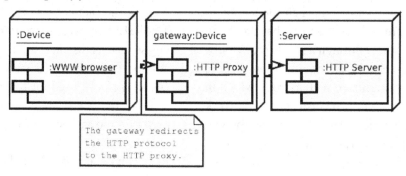

Figure 10. The business model of the gateway for ad-hoc and infrastructured networks

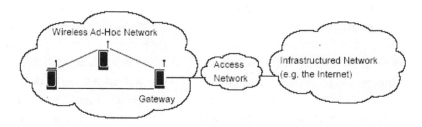

Figure 11. The roles of gateway business model for ad-hoc networks

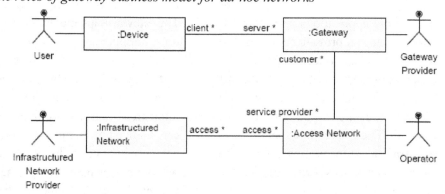

basic functionality of the gateway. The use cases are shown in Figure 12. The actors are the users, gateway providers and the operator. The user uses the gateway to access the infrastructured network. The gateway provider provides the gateway to the users. The operator provides access to the infrastructured network.

User a function includes discovers, connect and disconnect. The user discovers the available gateways. The user connects to the gateway. This enables the DNS service and IP based access to the infrastructured network. The user disconnects from the gateway. The user does this explicitly, or this may occur implicitly when the gateway is unavailable.

Figure 12. Use cases for gateway specification in infrastructured and ad-hoc networks

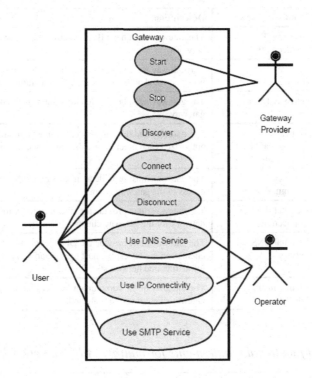

REQUIREMENTS FOR GATEWAY SPECIFICATION

There are two types of requirements: functional requirements and nonfunctional requirements. The minimum functional requirements are given in Table 1. There are also additional requirements that extend the usability of the gateway. They do not belong to the minimum requirements; nevertheless, they are mandatory. The additional functional requirements are given in Table 2. The gateway must also conform to the non-functional requirements given in Table 3. Finally, optional functional requirements are not implemented, but they describe features that may be implemented in the future. These requirements are given in Table 4.

THE GATEWAY ARCHITECTURE

The architecture of the gateway is shown in Figure13. The access network enables communication with the infrastructured network, and it provides services such as DNS and SMTP.

Wireless Ad-Hoc Network: In the wireless ad-hoc network, WLAN is based on the IEEE 802.11b standard which enables data transfer rate of 11 Mbps. WLAN is operated in IBSS mode which enables ad-hoc communication without using network infrastructure.

Access Network: The gateway can communicate with the infrastructured network through the access network. Optionally, it provides the SMTP service.

Security: The architecture from the security point of view is shown in Figure14. To enable opti-

Table 1. Functional requirement for multiple Ad-Hoc networks

ID	Name	Description
A1	Gateway IP Connectivity	The gateway must have IP connectivity to the infrastructured network.
A2	Gateway DNS Service	The gateway must be able to use the DNS service that can resolve host name and addresses in the infrastructured network.
A3	Gateway Discovery	The gateway must be able to allow gateway clients to discover the gateway.
A4	Mutual Authentication and Authorization	The gateway and the gateway client must mutually authenticate and authorized each other before the gateway client use the gateway.
A5	Gateway Configuration	The gateway must provide all necessary configurations for network access to the gateway client.
A6	External IP Connectivity	The gateway must provide the IP connectivity to the infrastructured network for the gateway clients.
A7	External DNS Services	The gateway must provide the DNS services that the gateway clients can use to resolve host names and addresses in the infrastructured networks.
A8	Communication Integrity	The integrity of the communication between the gateway and the gateway client must be protected.

Table 2. Additional functional requirements for multiple Ad-Hoc networks

ID	Name	Description
B1	SMTP Services	The gateway must provide a SMTP service in the wireless ad-hoc Network.
B2	Multiple Gateways	More than one gateway must be able to coexist in the same wireless ad-hoc networks.

Table 3. Non-functional requirements for multiple Ad-Hoc networks

ID	Name	Description
N1	Link-Layer independence	The gateway must be independent of the link-layer technology.

mal settings for different network configurations, the gateway supports the following security levels defined in the SESSI project (Defined in table 5.): (a) None: No security is provided. (b) Authentication: Authentication, authorization, and integrity are provided. (c) Confidentiality: Authentication, authorization, integrity, and Confidentiality are provided. However, the firewall is not a part of the gateway implementation.

THE INTERNAL ARCHITECTURE OF GATEWAY

The Internal Architecture describes the architectural components of the gateway. The gateway and the gateway client are similar enough to share the same implementation. This implementation can be started as a gateway or a gateway client. The internal architecture of the gateway implementation is shown in figure15. The network interfaces

Table 4. Optional functional requirements for multiple Ad-Hoc networks

ID	Name	Description
X1	Ad-Hoc Routing	The gateway must use an ad-hoc routing protocol and provide access to the infrastructured network through zero or more intermediate nodes.
X2	Routable IP Address	The gateway must provide a routable IP address to the gateway clients. The address must also be routable from the infrastructured network.
X3	Authoritative DNS service	The gateway must provide the DNS service to the infrastructured network that resolves host names and addresses in the wireless ad-hoc network.
X4	Inter-Ad-Hoc Gateway	The gateway must enable IP based access between two or more wireless ad-hoc networks.
X5	Inter Ad-Hoc DNS service	In the wireless ad-hoc network, the gateway must provide the DNS service that resolve host names and addresses in those ad-hoc networks that the gateway provides IP based access too.
X6	IPv4 and IPv6	The gateway must support both IPv4 and IPv6.

Figure 13. Gateway architecture

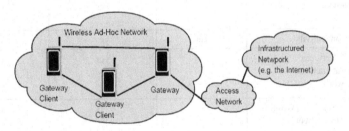

used by the gateway are shown in Figure 7. The DNS proxy uses the loopback interface to provide DNS locally in the current device.

Virtual Interface using IPsec in tunnel mode between the gateway and the gateway client creates virtual interfaces that enable communication through the IPsec tunnel. This requires that the tunneled data is communicated by using concrete interfaces such as WLAN interfaces. The WLAN interface enables communication in the wireless ad-hoc network. Therefore, WLAN must support the ad-hoc mode. WLAN is used for link local communication only. It can start gateway component as a gateway or as a gateway client.

As a gateway, it provides start the gateway and stop the gateway functions.

The external interface allows the gateway to communicate with the infrastructured network. The gateway manager controls the other gateway components. It is a program that provides a command line interface.

On the other hand, as a gateway client, it provides connect to the gateway and disconnect from the gateway functions. The service discovery service enables gateway discovery in the wireless ad-hoc network. The gateway manager uses the service discovery service for two purposes:

Figure 14. Security solution for infrastructured and ad-hoc networks.

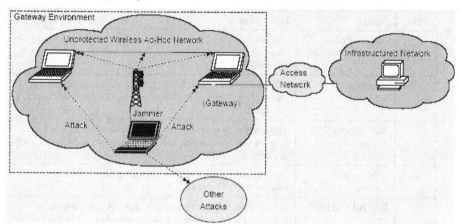

Table 5. Security levels supported by the gateway for multiple Ad-Hoc networks

Services	Authorization	Authentication	Confidentiality
Gateway Discovery	yes	yes	yes
IP Connectivity	yes	yes	yes
DNS Services (Infrastructured Network)	yes	yes	yes
DNS Services (Wireless Ad-Hoc network)	yes	no	no

- When the gateway component acts as a gateway, the gateway manager uses the service discovery service to advertise the gateway to the gateway clients. When the gateway component stops acting as a gateway, it stops advertising the gateway.
- When the gateway component acts as a gateway client, the gateway manager uses the service discovery service to discover available gateways.

The gateway advertises itself by using an SLP URL. The gateway client uses the same URL to discover gateways. The URL is defined as follows: service:gateway.sessi::://IP_ADDRESS.

Here, the suffix .sessi defines the naming authority. _Security:_The service discovery service must be able to provide mutual authentication, mutual authorization, communication integrity, and communication confidentiality within the service discovery protocol.

DNS Proxy : The DNS proxy provides a DNS service that can resolve host names and addresses in an infrastructured network and in a wireless ad-hoc network within the link-local scope. The deployment of the DNS proxies is shown in Figure 8. The DNS proxy distinguishes queries between the wireless ad-hoc network and the infrastructured network by applying the following rule:

Figure 15. The internal architecture of the gateway

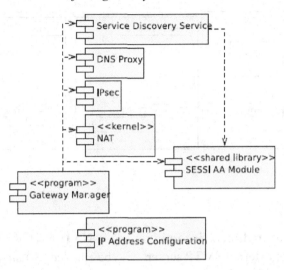

Figure 16. Network Interfaces for infrastructured networks communicating with ad-hoc

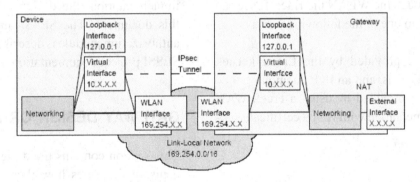

1. The query is resolved locally in the wireless ad-hoc network with mDNS. if either of the following conditions is met:
   - The IP address is a link-local address within the range of 169.254.0.0/16.
   - The host name ends with the suffix .local.
2. Otherwise, the query is resolved externally with DNS. *Security* : IPsec protects the DNS protocol between the gateway and the gateway client. In addition, when the device boots, the DNS proxy is started along with other networking components. The design of the DNS proxy is given in Figure 17. An application resolves host names and addresses by using the resolver library which is an integral part of BIND. The DNS proxy can be provided by one of the following implementations: (a) *named*, which is an integral part of BIND (b) *pdnsd*, which is a lightweight DNS server (c) *djbdns*, which is another DNS server

Moreover, the DNS proxy is modified to use mDNS to resolve local host names and addresses in the wireless ad-hoc network. The mDNS implementation is based on Rendezvous.

Figure 17. The deployment of the DNS proxies

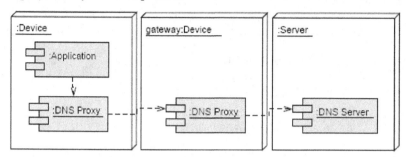

SMTP: The gateway redirects incoming SMTP connections to the external SMTP server by using destination NAT (DNAT).

IPsec: When the gateway acts as a client or a server, it uses IPsec that enables secure communication through the WLAN interface. IPsec can be provided in one of the following ways:

• IPsec is provided by the Linux kernel, KAME tools, and an IKE daemon.

• IPsec is provided by using a FreeS/WAN implementation with X.509 certificate support

NAT: NAT is provided by the kernel. It can be enabled by using iptables.

SESSI: Authentication and Authorization Module because the SESSI authentication and authorization module is based on an existing implementation, the design is not included in this document. The SESSI authentication and authorization module is described in detail in the SESSI project documentation.

GATEWAY DESIGN CRITERION

This section contains the design of the components. It describes how these components are

Figure 18. Design layout of the DNS proxy

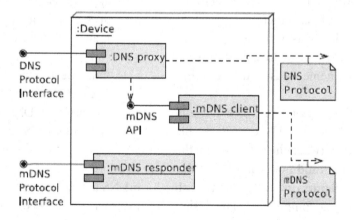

Figure 19. The deployment of the SMTP server

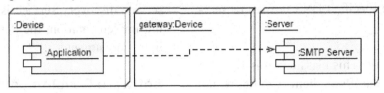

Figure 20. Gateway manager implementation

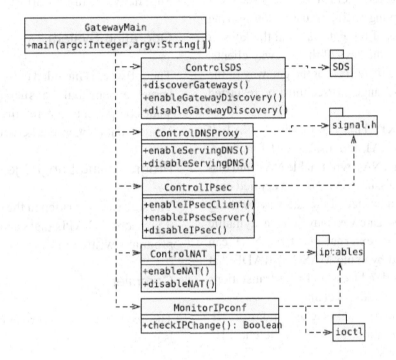

implemented. It also describes which tools and libraries are used.

Gateway Manager: The gateway manager controls the gateway components. The design of the gateway manager is given in Figure 11. Next, the classes of the gateway manager are introduced.

ControlSDS: ControlSDS controls the service discovery service. It provides the following functions:

- discover Gateways: Discover available gateways in the wireless ad-hoc network.

- enable Gateway Discovery: Enable gateway discovery. This allows gateway client to discover the gateway.

- disable Gateway Discovery: Disable gateway discovery. This prevents gateway clients from discovering the gateway.

Control DNS Proxy: This class controls the DNS proxy. It provides the following functions:

- enable Serving DNS: Enable the DNS proxy to use the specified DNS proxies or servers.

Control IPsec: This class controls IPsec. It provides (a) **enableIPsecClient:** Configure and enable IPsec for the gateway client. (b) **enableIPsecServer:** Configure and enable IPsec for the gateway. (c) **disableIPsec:** Disable IPsec for the gateway or the gateway client. Before IPsec is enabled, the following settings must be configuring d for IP address of the gateway and the keys of the gateway and the keys of the gateway clients. Moreover, if the IP address of the gateway or the gateway client changes, IPsec must be restarted or reconfigure d.

Control NAT: This class controls NAT. It provides enableNAT and disableNAT functions. Where the enableNAT will Enable NAT and disableNAT will Disable NAT. NAT is applied only to the external interface of the gateway by using iptables. As the gateway may have a dynamic IP address for its external interface, NAT can be implemented by using MASQUERADE that drops all network address and port translations if the external IP address changes.

MonitorIPconf : This class monitors IP address configuration. It provides the checkIPChange functions

Check if the IP address has changed. Checking the IP change can be implemented in two alternative ways:

1. The function uses iptables to monitor the messages related to obtaining and claiming an IP address. This allows the gateway manager to take action immediately, but this solution is dependent on the IP address configuration protocol.
2. The function periodically checks the IP address by using the ioctl function available on UNIX platforms. This results in a delay, but this solution is independent of the IP address configuration protocol.

Service Discovery Service: Because the service discovery service is based on an existing implementation, the design is not included in this document.

Software Development

Design Principles

Simplicity, Minimum Effort, Independence.

Operating System

The software is intended to be run on Linux. The kernel version should be as new as possible because some components may require functionality that is unavailable in earlier kernel versions.

Programming Language

The software is written in the C++ language, but it provides a C APIs that can also be used from programs written in C.

Compiler

The gcc C/C++ compiler version 1.1.1 or higher is used.

CONCLUSION AND FUTURE WORK

The gateway manager provides a centralized approach for managing changes in the ad-hoc network because it can reconfigure or restart services based on existing implementations. However, building and designing new services from scratch for ad-hoc networks can enable more seamless operation as the services can independently manage changes in the ad-hoc network. Alternatively, static IP addresses can be provided to existing implementations in the network layer. If IP addresses are available, the IP based service discovery service can be used to discover both infrastructural services and application-specific services. Consequently, only one service discovery service is needed. The implemented DNS proxy enables resolving host names and addresses in the wireless ad-hoc network and in the external network without any changes to existing applications. Because the addresses may change in the wireless ad-hoc network, the DNS proxy must use small TTL values or disable caching for local host names and addresses. Alternatively, the DNS proxy must monitor the network and keep the cache up to date. Although IPsec can protect the DNS protocol, it cannot protect the mDNS protocol that uses multicasting. The gateway can also be extended to use private addresses in the wireless ad hoc networks and to use tunnels between the networks. Here, the gateways are used to build a large private network in which NAT is not needed. Also, infrastructured networks with private or global IP addresses can join the private network. Nevertheless, other infrastructured networks are accessed through NAT. Although the gateway implementation only provides half of this functionality, it is one step towards global IP connectivity.

The gateway implementation provides a secure generic solution for accessing the infrastructured network from the ad-hoc network, and it provides multiple security levels for different network environments. It works with most frequently used applications.

Next, the most appropriate gateway solution is chosen from the previously presented gateway solutions according to a brief comparison. A 3G device can use its local 3G radio link to provide the gateway service to it. When configured correctly, it can directly access both the ad-hoc network and the infrastructured network. However, this option is available to 3G devices only. Moreover, to use the gateway based on 3GPP System and WLAN Interworking, the device must be a 3G device. From the technical point of view, this solution is obsolete because the device does not need to

use this solution because it can use its local 3G radio link to provide the gateway service to itself. However, this solution can be meaningful from the business perspective. For example, if the devices are used in a foreign country, one of the devices might have a local USIM or SIM that enables Internet access at a moderate charge. Still, this solution is not very useful under normal circumstances. Although the application-level gateway is independent of the network technology, it depends on the applications. The gateway must support all applications that are used. In addition, when a new application is added, a new proxy must be added. Consequently, as the application-level gateway supports a fixed set of applications only, it lacks generality, and it is not practical for evolving applications. In contrast, the generic gateway is independent of the device type, the network technology, and the applications. Therefore, it is the preferred gateway solution.

REFERENCES

Aboba, B., Blunk, L., Vollbrecht, J., Carlson, J., & Levkowetz, H. (2004). Extensible Authentication Protocol (EAP). *IETF RFC 3748.*

Aboba, B., & Dixon, W. (2004). *IPsec-Network Address Translation (NAT) Compatibility Requirements.* Tech. rep., IETF.

Arkko, J., & Haverinen, H. (2004). *Extensible Authentication Protocol Method for 3rd Generation Authentication and Key Agreement (EAPAKA).* Internet draft, IETF.

Arkko, J., Kempf, J., Sommerfeld, B., Zill, B., & Nikander, P. (2004). *Secure Neighbor Discovery (SEND).* Internet draft, IETF.

Bernstein, D. (2004) *DJBDNS: Domain Name System tools. BIND9.NET. DNS, BIND, DHCP, LDAP* and Directory Services.

Buddhikot, M., Hari, A., Singh, K., & Miller, S. (2003). MobileNAT: A New Technique for Mobility across Heterogeneous Address Spaces. *In Proceedings of the 1st ACM international workshop on Wireless mobile applications and services on WLAN hotspots.* ACM Press. (pp. 75- 84).

Calhoun, P., Loughney, J., Guttman, E., Zorn, G., & Arkko, J. (2003). *Diameter Base Protocol.* RFC RFC3588, IETF.

Cheshire, S., Aboba, B., & Guttman, E. (2004). *Dynamic Configuration of IPv4 Link-Local Addresses.* Internet draft, IETF.

Cheshire, S., & Krochmal, M. (2004). *Multicast DNS.* Internet draft, Apple Computer, Inc. http:// files.multicastdns.org/draft-cheshire-dnsext-multicastdns.txt.

Conta, A., & Deering, S. (1998). *Internet Control Message Protocol (ICMPv6) for the Internet Protocol version 6 (ipv6) specifications.* RFC 2463, IETF.

Crispin, M. (1996, December). Internet Message Access Protocol—Version 4rev1. RFC 2060, IETF.

Deering, S. (1991, September). *ICMP Router Discovery Messages.* RFC 1256, IETF.

Deering, S., & Hinden, R. (1998, December). *Internet Protocol, Version 6 (IPv6) Specification.* RFC 2460, IETF.

Eastlake, D. (1999, March). Domain Name System Security Extensions. RFC 2535, IETF.

Farinacci, D., Li, T., Hanks, S., Meyer, D., & Traina, P. (2000, March). *Generic Routing Encapsulation (GRE).* RFC 2784, IETF.

Glenn, R., & Kent, S. (1998, November). *The NULL Encryption Algorithm and Its Use With IPsec.* RFC 2410, IETF.

Guttman, E., Perkins, C., Veizades, J., & Day, M. (1999, June). *Service Location Protocol, Version 2.* RFC 2608.

Harkins, D., & Carrel, D. (1998, November). *The Internet Key Exchange (IKE).* RFC 2409, IETF.

Haverinen, H., & Salowey, J. (2004, October). *Extensible Authentication Protocol Method for GSM Subscriber Identity Modules (EAPSIM).* Internet draft, IETF.

Hertzog, R. (2004, November). *Overview of zcip source package.* Referred: 26 Nov 2004.

Huttunen, A., Swander, B., Volpe, V., DiBurro, L., & Stenberg, M. (2004, May). *UDP Encapsulation of IPsec ESP Packets.* Internet draft, IETF.

IEEE. IEEE Std 802.11 1999, Part 11: Wireless LAN Medium Access Control (MAC) and Physical Layer (PHY) Specifications, IEEE Std 802.11 1999 ed. IEEE, 1999.

IEEE. IEEE Std 802.11b-1999, Part 11: Wireless LAN Medium Access Control (MAC) and Physical Layer (PHY) Specifications: Higher-Speed Physical Layer extension in the 2.4 GHz Band, IEEE Std 802.11b-1999 ed. IEEE, 1999.

IEEE. IEEE Std 802.1X-2001, Port-Based Network Access Control, IEEE Std 802.1X-2001 ed. IEEE, 2001.

IEEE. IEEE Std 802.3-2002, Part 3: Carrier sense multiple access with collision detection (CSMA/ CD) access method and physical layer specifications, IEEE Std 802.3-2002 ed. IEEE, 2002.

IEEE. IEEE Std 802.11i-2004, Part 11: Wireless Medium Access Control (MAC) and Physical Layer (PHY) specifications—Amendment 6: Medium Access Control (MAC) Security Enhancements, IEEE Std 802.11i-2004 ed. IEEE, 2004.

ISO. Information technology- Open Systems Interconnection—Basic Reference Model: The Basic Model, ISO/IEC 7498-1:1994 ed., 1994.

Kaufman, C. (2004, September). *Internet Key Exchange (IKEv2) Protocol.* Internet draft, IETF.

Kent, S., & Atkinson, R. (1998, November). *IP Authentication Header*. RFC 2402, IETF

Kent, S., & Atkinson, R. (1998, November). *IP Encapsulating Security Payload (ESP)*. RFC 2406, IETF.

Kivinen, T., Huttunen, A., Swander, B., & Volpe, V. (2004, February). *Negotiation of NAT-Traversal in the IKE*. Internet draft, IETF.

Klensin, J. (2001, April). *Simple Mail Transfer Protocol*. RFC 2821, IETF.

Leech, M., Ganis, M., Lee, Y., Kuris, R., Koblas, D., & Jones, L. *SOCKS Protocol Version 5*. RFC 1928, IETF.

USEFUL URL: WEBSITES

http://www.3gpp.org/ftp/Specs/archive/33fiseries/33.234/33234-621.zip .

http://www.3gpp.org/ftp/Specs/archive/23fiseries/23.234/23234-620.zip .

http://www.ietf.org/rfc/rfc3748.txt

http://www.ietf.org/rfc/rfc3715.txt

http://www.apple.com/macosx/features/rendez-vous/

http://www.ietf.org/internet-drafts/draft-arkko-pppext-eap-aka-13.txt .

http://www.ietf.org/internetdrafts/draft-ietf-send-ndopt-06.txt .

http://cr.yp.to/djbdns.html

http://www.ietf.org/rfc/rfc3588.txt .

http://www.bind9.net/

http://www.ietf.org/internet-drafts/draft-ietfzero-conf-ipv4-linklocal-17.txt .

http://www.ietf.org/rfc/rfc2463.txt.

http://www.ietf.org/rfc/rfc2060.txt .

http://www.ietf.org/rfc/rfc1256.txt .

http://www.ietf.org/rfc/rfc2460.txt .

http://www.ietf.org/rfc/rfc2535.txt .

http://www.ietf.org/rfc/rfc2784.txt

http://www.ietf.org/rfc/rfc2410.txt .

http://ietf.org/rfc/rfc2608.txt .

http://www.ietf.org/rfc/rfc2409.txt .

http://www.ietf.org/internet-drafts/draft-haver-inen-pppexteap-sim-14.txt .

http://packages.qa.debian.org/z/zcip.html

http://www.ietf.org/internet-drafts/draft-ietf-ipsec-udp-encaps-09.txt .

http://www.ietf.org/internet-drafts/draft-ietf-ipsec-ikev2-17.txt .

http://www.ietf.org/rfc/rfc2402.txt .

http://www.ietf.org/rfc/rfc2406.txt .

http://www.ietf.org/internet-drafts/draftietf-ipsec-nat-t-ike-08.txt .

http://www.ietf.org/rfc/rfc2821.txt .

Chapter VII
A Survey on Approaches to Adaptation on the Web

Jorge Marx Gómez
Oldenburg University, Germany

Thanh Tran
Karlsruhe University, Germany

ABSTRACT

Approaches to adaptation have been proposed by many different research communities, Hypermedia System and Intelligent Tutoring in particular. The task of adaptation breaks down to a mediation of resource provision and resource demand. In doing so, it is necessary to obtain some representation of them, either directly or through intermediate models that can be further processed to arrive at this information. Correspondingly, major differences in adaptation approaches manifest themselves in the employed sources, the way they are represented and the techniques used to derive the user demand from them. Therefore, we like to structure this survey according to these model-related aspects.

INTRODUCTION

Approaches to adaptation have been proposed by many different research communities, Hypermedia System and Intelligent Tutoring in particular. The task of adaptation breaks down to a mediation of resource provision and resource demand. In doing so, it is necessary to obtain some representation of them, either directly or through intermediate models that can be further processed to arrive at this information. Correspondingly, major differences in adaptation approaches manifest themselves in the employed sources, the way they are represented and the techniques used to derive the user demand from them. Therefore, we like to structure this survey according to these model-related aspects.

In particular, it starts with an initial overview of the approaches, which are distinguished in terms of the number of sources that are employed to model the different aspects of adaptation. Other major differences shall become more apparent in subsequent sections devoted to one specific model-related aspect. There is one section that puts the underlying techniques into generic categories. These techniques for model processing are determined by the chosen formalisms for model representation, which are discussed subsequently in a separate section. Thereafter, specific attributes that have been used to capture the different sources are presented. Here, the focus necessarily rests on the user and the domain model because generic information and techniques for the representation of other sources are simply not available from the surveyed approaches. The survey ends with a final discussion on the relative strengths and weaknesses of these approaches—from which consequences and requirements for the proposed ontology can be derived.

OVERVIEW OF ADAPTATION APPROACHES

Single-Model Adaptation

Adaptive functionalities of many general information systems, commercial recommendation systems in web stores (EBay, 2005) (Amazon, 2005), are implemented through filtering-based approaches (Schafer, Konstan, Riedi, 1999). As discussed below, they exploit information extracted from usage as well as from the content of the resources in order to suggest further items potentially interesting to the user. In this regard, filtering denotes the mining of (meta-)

relationships between users and contents useful for recommendations.

Collaborative Filtering

This filtering approach bases on the extraction of similarities among users through the analysis of profiles reflecting users' past behavior. It supports the recommendations of items that have been used (selected, read, acquired, liked etc.) by similar users. In other words, users recognized as being similar are assumed to have the same preferences, i.e. are interested in the same items. Accordingly, the individual profile is populated with the entire preferences of a user class—see details on this approach and applications in (Good et al., 1999) (Herlocker et al., 1999) (Konstan et al., 1997).

Content-Based Filtering

This approach bases on the extraction of relationships between the user and the resources. Rather than making recommendations on the basis of other users' preferences, it proposes items that match the user profile. As suggested by the name, the focus lies on information about the content of the resources. In fact, the approach can be reduced to the mining of similarities among items because most of the time, the profile contains only items previously visited by the user. So, items are recommended that are similar to the ones used in the past (Pemberton, Rodden, Procter, 2000).

In Syskill & Webert for instance, a system for identifying interesting resources, the user rates a number of documents from a content domain on a binary "hot" and "cold" scale. Resources similar to those with hot ratings are computed using words probabilities, a measure that has been derived from this learning set of documents (Pazzani, Muramatsu, Billsus, 1996). Surveys conducted in (Schafer, Konstan, Riedi, 1999) (Montaner, Lopez, Dela, 2003) provide details on many other examples of this type of approaches.

Multi-Dimensional Approaches

Instead of drawing recommendations from one single information source, approaches taken in specific areas, particularly in Instructional Systems, utilize information of different dimensions: the user, the application, their environments and the interaction between them. More information means that potentially, the quality and quantity of discovered patterns can be enhanced and with them go the accuracy and granularity (fine-tuning to the individual user) of recommendations. The subsequent presentation focuses on the dimension that is distinct to each particular approach.

Combining Domain and User Model

This is a combination of the user dimension with another aspect of the application: the resources it provides. Applying either one of these approaches separately results in shortcomings (see the discussion at the end of this chapter) that, to a great extent, can be addressed by a hybrid approach. Conceptually, such a combination would have to extract relationships both among users and between users and content. Recommendations are made on the basis of preferences of other users and of the correspondence between the items and the user profile (Pemberton, Rodden, Procter, 2000) (Cunningham et al., 2001).

Probabilistic Latent Semantic Models (PLSA) is such a concept that integrates information about the domain with user data. It is based on latent factors, which are probabilistically associated with entries of a session-page matrix as well as entries of a keyword-page matrix. In this fashion, these factors capture the underlying rationale of the navigational path not only in terms of the usage patterns of pages put also in terms of the semantic relationships among their contents. The degree of such relationships can be revealed by the examination of the associated conditional probabilities. These values, e.g. probability of observing the user segment U_i, the attribute A_j or the page P_m

given the latent factor z_k, are incorporated into a joint probability model. Applying the Expectation-Maximization algorithm on this model yields probability estimates that allow for the characterization of user segments, the identification of the segment best matching the current session and ultimately, for making recommendations as follows: each user segment is an *n*-dimensional page-vector. Identifying the segment most suitable to the user reduces the number of relevant pages to *n*. In the next step, the best pages out of these *n*-pages are selected and recommended to the user (Jin, Zhou, Mobasher, 2004).

Extending the Domain Model with Presentation and Narrative Information

Apart from these models, (Houben, 2000) (Frasincar, Houben, Vdovjak, 2001) (Ossenbruggen et al., 2001) (Cannataro, Pugliese, 2001) (Little, Geurts, Hunter, 2002) (Henze, Dolog, Nejdl, 2004) introduce the use of a presentation model that should enable the on-the-fly assembly of content units. Optimally, it should incorporate enough information for the system to determine what chunks of information are to be selected and in what structure they are to be inserted for an adaptive use.

(Cannataro, Pugliese, 2001) for instance, proposes a layered model termed XAHM. The domain model organized as a digraph consisting of Elementary Abstract Concepts (EAC), which in turn, is decomposed into one or more Presentation Description (PD). A PD is a generic template for a page that includes information about the atomic content units, their layouts, formats and access rights. This description enables the composition of an individual page comprising of actual fragments, called Presentation Unit (PU).

In detail, this digraph contains sets of nodes, arcs and weights denoting EACs, their relationships and the strength of each relationship. The probabilistic interpretation of the arcs' weights permits a classification of users according to their browsing behavior—similar to the PLSA approach. This is because internally, the user is reflected in the system as a particular path of the graph, viz. the user is represented in terms of the visited resources. Having assigned user to a profile in this fashion, the system generates an individual presentation according to the information in the associated PD.

In supporting this type of ad-hoc presentation generation, (Conlan et al., 2002) suggests the use of another model: the narrative model. Such models define the structure for assembling content units that can be applied interchangeably depending on the content, the goal of the user or the purpose of the application.

We consider both the presentation and the narrative model as an augmentation of the domain model concept. As implied in XAHM, the presentation model is equal to a model about resources of the domain, except for the difference that it captures not only information about the content using Elementary Abstract Concepts but also the structure and presentation-related issues through the concepts of Presentation Descriptions and Presentation Units. Also, the narrative model in this regard, is just an explicit description of the content structure.

The Task Model

Besides information related to the content and the user, (Brusilovsky, Cooper, 2001) introduces a task model and related information such as goal, role and methods. This paper gives a summary of a system, which has the aim to select and present technical papers that are relevant to the users' task context. The task model is hierarchically structured into task, subtask and steps related to the process of maintenance. Likewise, the domain model captures a hierarchy of components that are subjects of the content. Elements of the task model are connected with elements of the domain model via the "involve" relationship, that is, a task involves some components. Content units are asso-

ciated (indexed) with concepts both of the domain and the task model. The system selects content units according to the user's current context and the information contained in the user model, which measures the individual user's experience w.r.t. the tasks and the components.

Other Models Used in Adaptation

In (Henze, Dolog, Nejdl, 2004), interactions between user and application are stored in an observation model. In the same manner, Aerts and De Bra assert that the knowledge about adaptation should be manifest itself in the form of rules. The rationales of adaptive actions are expressed in form of conditions and consequences within a so-called teaching model.

This is not really new, because user feedbacks and adaptation logic are essential and have always been implicitly incorporated into the systems. The explicit specification of them however, brings advantages that will be discussed at the end of this chapter.

Finally, the Cuypers engine, presented as part of the Hera framework in (Houben et al., 2003), adopts a system profile that models the network resources and the presentation capabilities of the platform in terms of bandwidth, recognized formats etc. This way, adaptation takes relevant conditions prevalent in the systems' and users' environment into account.

TECHNIQUES FOR MODEL PROCESSING

State-of-the-Art Techniques

Statistical Matching Techniques

At some stage of the adaptation process, approaches surveyed above involve the computation of some similarity measures. For instance in collaborative filtering, it is needed to match items to the user profile, in content-based filtering, it is used to find a match among items and in PLSA, the assignment of the current session to a predefined user segment also requires such a measure. In Bibster for instance (Broekstra et al., 2004), adaptation involves the primary task of measuring similarities among concepts and users. Several similarity functions operate on three layers: at the lowest layer, data values of the resource's features are examined. At the Graph Layer, relations between resources are taken into account. Finally, at the Ontology Layer, also ontological information such as the class hierarchy is incorporated into the comparisons.

Depending on the representation formalisms and content of the model (see subsequent sections) different formulas might be applied for the computation of a distance measure between two values. Among many others, the following have been tested for adaptation:

- Cosine Similarity, discussed in (Salton, McGill, 1983) (Salton, Buckley, 1988) and used in (Chen et al., 2000)
- Mean Squared Differences (Shardanand, Maes, 1995)
- Pearson r correlation coefficient (Shardanand, Maes, 1995)
- Spearman Rank correlation coefficient (Herlocker et al., 1999) (Herlocker, Konstan, Riedl, 2000).

Machine-Learning-Based Classification Techniques

Classification is a broader task that conceptually, includes some form of matching. As implied by this definition of Statistical Classification (Wiki, 2005), any classification result can theoretically be reproduced by applying a set of appropriate matching operations. So, instead of applying successively the one of the above formulas, items can be directly categorized using dedicated classification algorithms that involve some of the above low-level formulas.

In (Krulwich, Burkey, 1995), this is done by means of a decision tree that basically, constitutes a set of if-then rules. Applying these rules successively through the entire tree on a resource eventually leads to the final decision: interesting or not interesting.

(Henze, 2000) demonstrates the use of such a Bayesian network to calculate the users' knowledge. The nodes are variables representing the system's belief about user properties, which are expressed in terms of Knowledge Items (KI). The arcs denote their probabilistic influence relationships. The computation of a value for a particular node factors in Conditional Probability Distributions of all parent nodes that have been derived from empirical testing data and estimations of domain experts. So, the final values `known` and `unknown` of the variable `knowledge of „inheritance"` is determined by the combination of values of its parents, which are `expertise in object-orientation` and `difficulty of "inheritance"`. Henze also adopts a specialized clustering algorithm for this classification as the high number of variables in this adaptation problem renders the application of Bayes' Theorem in its pure form unmanageable.

(Jennings, Higuchi, 1993) demonstrate the use of a neural network to classify users. Other classification algorithms potentially useful for adaptation includes K-nearest neighbor, Boosting, Support vector machines, Hidden Markov models and linear classifiers such as Fisher's linear discriminant, Logistic regression, Naive Bayes classifier and Perceptron (Wiki, 2005).

Furthermore, due to the imprecise, incomplete and heterogeneous data collected from usage, [Soft Computing Approaches] reviews and suggests some soft computing techniques that conceptually, are more appropriate in dealing with the uncertainty and fuzziness of "ill-defined" problems—user modeling in particular. For instance, Fuzzy Logic provides a mechanism to mimic human decision-making that can be used to infer user goals and plans. Fuzzy Clustering allow user to be part of more than one stereotype at the same time. For a detailed discussion of these and other soft computing techniques, please refer to the mentioned paper.

Semantic-Based Retrieval and Reasoning

While most of the techniques implemented in current state-of-the-art systems are of the former category, the following examines recent theoretical approaches yet to be implemented in commercial systems. They adopt SW-technologies to perform adaptation on the basis of knowledge models, which are marked-up in such a way that allows the system to retrieve existing and derive new information. For now, this reasoning is restricted to RDF-entailments, viz. inference about type and subclass relationships. This could advance when KR formalisms other than RDF is used instead. This style of processing is illustrated in details by a closer look at these representative approaches:

The Hera Specification Framework

The approach underlying Hera (Frasincar, Houben, Vdovjak, 2002) involves the use of ontology for modeling. The domain, which is about artifacts of a museum, is represented in terms of RDF-concepts that together, form a conceptual model (CM). Specifically, there are statements about `Artifact`: it has `subclass` such as `Sculpture`, `Furniture`, and `Costume`, is `exemplified` by a `Technique` and is `created` by a `Creator`. A `Painting`, another `subclass` of `Artifact`, depicts a `Theme`, is `painted` by a `Painter` and has an `Image` as `Picture`. These ontology concepts are used as meta-information for resources presented to the user during a virtual tour. That is, an item, represented internally as an instance of the ontology, is populated with concrete values: e.g. `The Stone Bridge is a Painting` that has `x02.jpeg` as `Picture`, is painted by `Painter _ ID01` and is exemplified by `Technique _ ID09`.

While this CM describes the what, there is another model building on top of it that describes how user can navigate over the resources—called the Application Model (AM). It built on three concepts: `Slice`, `Link` and `Anchor`. Each Slice represents a presentation unit that is associated with a particular concept, e.g. Slice. Painting.main and Slice.Technique.main. The Link Link.exemplified.by that connects them both corresponds to the relationship specified in the CM. Thus, the AM can be considered as a simple mapping that transforms concepts and semantic relationships of the underlying CM into units and possible navigation paths.

The generation of the presentation is performed by asking against the AM RQL queries that can exploit the RDF-semantic. Doing so retrieves the data as well as the implied navigation structure, viz. the specific Slice, Link and the Link's destination, which is another slice that materialized itself as a link or sub-slice of the presentation unit.

Adaptation in the system takes into account the User Profile (UP), comprising of pre-configured user settings and the User Session, which is dynamically updated to capture the slices already visited by the user. Conditions attached to attributes of the slice allow the adaptation engine to determine which slice' components are really to be made visible to the particular user.

The Personal Reader

(Henze, Nejdl, 2002) proposes adaptation rules that operate on three different, relatively simple logic-based models: domain, user and observation. The domain comprises of `Documents` that contain `Concepts`, viz. D hasConcept C. Relationships among `Concepts` is expressed with `depends`, meaning one `Concept` is required to understand one another. A concept is assumed to be learned whenever the corresponding document has been visited by the user. This relation is captured by a rule that let the system derives new user knowledge, i.e. if `visited` than `learned`. Then, documents are marked up and recommended on the basis of the following adaptation rules:

- It is `recommended` for learning if all prerequisite concepts of this document are `learned`.
- It `might be understandable` if at least some of the prerequisites have already been learned by the user.
- It `will become understandable` if the user has learned at least one of the document's concepts.

This approach is further developed in (Henze, Nejdl, 2002). The domain model comprising of `Concept` and `Document` is further augmented with the concepts `DocumentType`, `DocumentRole` and `ConceptRole` to represent specific types such as `Course Material`, `Exercise` and `Exam` and to reflect the particular role of a concept in the document, e.g. `Introduction` and `FullDescription`. The user model is made more sophisticated by a detailed specification of the learner's `Performance` and its relations to other concepts of the domain such as `Document` and `Concept`. Furthermore, another two simple ontologies are introduced to capture concepts and relationship concerning with the observations and the presentation. Base on concepts in these models, more sophisticated rules for adaptation have been designed, e.g.

- a `Concept` is `learned` if the `User` has a `Performance`, which is related to the `Concept` in question,

- a `Document` is the best example if it covers each `Concept` of the current `Document` and contains additional `Concepts` not already `learned` by the `User`.

In Personal Reader (Dolog et al., 2003) (Dolog et al., 2004), an implementation of the above concept, adaptation takes the form of searching for resources within a closed corpus and adaptive generation of recommendations. In particular, when the user reads a `Document`, the system recommends other resources containing related `Concepts`. For this purpose, adaptation rules also take advantage of RDF entailments such as `is a` and `is subclass of`. The system identifies concepts by a rule stating that given a `Concept`, one another is related to it if it is the super-concept, sub-concept or its sibling w.r.t. a given maximum distance. This obviously requires an ontology about concepts and their relations. For now, this is a simple taxonomy of concepts related with each other through the property `subConceptOf`.

Another interesting concept discussed in Personal Reader is open-corpus adaptation: instead of operating on a limited and fixed number of known resources, the system reaches out to the internet to search for further resources potentially interesting to the user. For this, the system is supposed to construct appropriate queries, adapt them to the user profile and if necessary, relax them during the querying process when the number of results is below a threshold.

Model Representation Formalisms

Models can be presented by a natural language or some abstract syntax using literals and (or) non-literals. This syntax determines whether the model is also meaningful to machine, e.g. models expressed in natural language vs. logic-based models. Most of the following formalisms are extracted from (Montaner, Lopez, Dela, 2003), which surveys information stored in user profiles employed in state-of-the-art recommendation systems. We extend them with up-to-date examples and semantic formalisms. Except for semantic models, information conveyed by the following formalisms become only useful when human interpretations of the content are translated to concrete algorithms.

- Vector space model: With this model, resources are represented with a vector of features, usually words or concepts. They can be associated with a value, e.g. Boolean or a real number. While Boolean value mostly denotes the existence of a feature, real numbers represent the frequency, relevance or probability of the feature. In Wemate (Chen, Sycara, 1998) for instance, documents are represented as vectors, with each dimension stands for a word and values indicating the relative term frequency. Document similarities can then be determined by the distance of the respective vectors in the vector space.
- Matrix model: Matrix is mostly employed in adaptive systems to represent user-item ratings. Each cell (u, i) of the matrix stands for a rating representing the evaluation of the item i by the user u or if empty—there is no such evaluation.
- Weighted n-grams: N-grams represent a consecutive sequence of symbols—words in particular. Counting their occurrences in a learning set enables the computation of probabilities of word combination, i.e. the probability that one word occurs after one another (or after some others when n greater than 2). For detailed discussion and how such formalism is used for text categorization, see (Cavnar, Trenkle, 1994). In PSUN (Sorensen, McElligot, 1995), fixed-length consecutive series of n words are extracted from texts and organized as nodes in a network with weighted edges. The co-occurrence of word combinations captured in this network is used to derive a context representation of the words.

The following models are referred to in (Montaner, Lopez, Dela, 2003) as Classifier-based models. This category encompasses all models that have a structure imposed by the respective classifiers. In other words, a particular structure is required for the classification algorithm to yield meaningful results.

- Artificial neural networks: An artificial neural network is an interconnected group of artificial neurons. It composed of input, processing elements (containing mathematical or computational model for information processing) and output nodes (Hepner et al., 1990). Boone uses such a network to represent and process feature vectors of messages to filter irrelevant e-mails.
- Bayesian network: A Bayesian network is a directed acyclic graph in which nodes represent propositional variables and arcs represent dependencies. The leaf nodes represent observable propositions. Subsequent node's value is a function of the values of the preceding nodes it depends upon (Jensen, 1996). Example of Bayesian network being used for user modeling is given in [State-of-the-art techniques to adaptation] and discussed at length in (Henze, Nejdl, 1999) (Henze, Nejdl, 2002).
- Decision tree: A decision tree is another way to represent and classify data. It resembles the tree structure consisting of a set of nodes and a set of directed edges that connect the nodes. The internal nodes stand for questions, the edges answers to those questions, and the leaf nodes represent the final answer—also called decision. A decision tree is employed in ContactFinder (Krulwich, Burkey, 1995), InfoFinder (Krul-

wich, Burkey, 1996) and Lifestyle Finder (Krulwich, 1997) to find and recommend contact, documents and lifestyles.

• Weighted associative networks: An associative network consists of a set of nodes representing some terms (resources). The organization of these resources in a set of weighted and connected nodes allow for the derivation of associated recommendations based on the current node. The dissertation (Belew, 1986) offers a very detailed elaboration on machine learning with associative network for adaptive information retrieval.

• Weighted semantic networks: As opposed to the former, this network has instead of only one single link type, different generic link types. Wordnet for instance, an online lexical database developed at the Princeton University (Miller, 1995), is organized using multiple semantic relations such as synonymy, hyponymy and antonym. In SiteIF (Stefani, Strappavara, 1998), every node stands for a concept, arcs between nodes denote co-occurrence relations among them and the weights represent a specific level of interests of the user w.r.t. that concept. Ifweb (Asnicar, Tasso, 1997) is another system using this type of formalism, albeit for a different purpose: to represent user profiles.

This classification is rather complete, but misses recent development in semantic-based modeling. Approaches discussed in [Semantic-based Retrieval and Reasoning], e.g. (Frasincar, Houben, Vdovjak, 2002) (Henze, Dolog, Nejdl, 2004) (Dolog et al., 2003), employ ontology as the representation formalism. As a whole, concepts and relations of the ontology form a network, especially OWL and RDFS ontology. However, as opposed to the previous formalism where thinking and modeling is really driven towards the network structure, ontology modeling is rather

frame-based. The network structure is a result of the underlying frame paradigm rather than the paradigm itself. Besides frame, which his geared towards representing object, rules seem to become the foremost formalism to model process oriented knowledge (SWRL):

• Frame: frames is an abstraction concept that is geared towards object, allowing knowledge engineers to think about the domain in terms of objects, object classes and relations among them—see (Fikes, Kehler, 1985) for a detailed discussion of the role of Frame in reasoning and KL-ONE (Brachman, Schmolze, 1985), one of the first KR-language capitalizing on Frame.

• Rules: Basically, rules composed of two parts: conditions and consequences. Such a structure seems to be more appropriate to capture (causal) dependencies of objects. For instance, a rule may resemble a process, an associative patterns or a universally valid inference pattern.

MODEL CONTENT

The User Model

In general, the user model is an abstraction of the user in terms of her (his) properties. These characteristics are associated with a value of specific types, e.g. Probabilistic, Boolean, Discrete and Nominal (Jameson, 1998). Also, (Brusilovsky, 1996) introduce the notion of aptitudes, denoting that a value might be transient, situational-dependent or permanent.

In the simplest form commonly found in filtering-based approach, the only characteristic of the user model is *ratings*, e.g. of news articles in (Konstan et al., 1997). Other approaches (Paiva, Self, 1995) (Houben, 2000) (Torre, 2001) (Frasincar, Houben, Vdovjak, 2001) (Conlan et al., 2002) (Dolog et al., 2004) (Henze, Dolog, Nejdl,

2004) make use of many more characteristics best described by the following attempts in user profile standardization: IEEE Personal and Private Information (PAPI) (IEEE, 2002), IMS Learner Information Package (LIP) (IMS, 2002) and the General User Model Ontology (GUMO) (Heckmann et al., 2005).

PAPI and LIP partially overlap in the following aspects:

- Security Information: covers information about authentication, credentials and access rights.
- Personal Information: PAPI specifies a "Personal" category that covers contact information such as names, contacts and addresses. The corresponding category in LIP, named "Identification", represents demographic and biographic data about the user.
- Preferences: In PAPI, "Preference" indicates the types of devices and objects, which the learner is able to operate on. "Accessibility" that refers to more general learning preferences, is a similar but broader category in LIP. It includes preferences, language capabilities, disabilities and eligibilities.
- Abilities: Conceptually, this can be interpreted as a general characteristic that measures what the user has done, knows, is able to do and the likes. This corresponds to the categories "Portfolio" and "Performance" in PAPI. The former is for accessing previous experiences. The latter is for storing information about their performance. Categories in LIP analogue to them are "Activity", "Competence", "QCL" and "Transcript". The first contains any learning related activity in any state of completion. The second serves as a slot for skills, experience and the knowledge acquired. "QCL" and the last deliver specific measures and proofs of the user's abilities in form of qualifications,

certifications, licenses and transcripts from recognized authorities.

- Relation: The category called "Relations" in PAPI registers associations of the user to other people. The corresponding LIP-concept termed "Relationship" captures relationships between any data elements instead.

In addition, LIP introduces some more characteristics that might be applicable for adaptation, such as:

- Goal: A category that represents learning, career and other objectives of the user.
- Interest: Any information describing hobbies and recreational activities.
- Affiliation: represents information records about membership in professional organizations.

In compassion, GUMO is an ontology-based approach that covers much of the characteristic above and other aspects. Most interestingly, GUMO follows the UserML approach where user models are composed of statements of the form *subject{UserModelDimension}object* (Heckmann, Krueger, 2004). In this regard, GUMO specifies the Basic User Dimensions. Examples of subclasses of this dimension denoting characteristics not already discussed above are Role, Emotional State, Physiological State, Characteristics and Facial Expression.

The Domain Model

In the surveyed approaches, e.g. (Cannataro, Pugliese, 2001) (Weber, Brusilovsky, 2001), model that concerns the underlying resources is referred to as the domain model. This is probably because in reaching a representation of the underlying resources, concepts extracted from them are used for modeling. As the resources might belong to a specific domain, these concepts form together a domain vocabulary.

As implied by [Adaptive Functionalities], there are three different aspects to the presentation of resources: content, structure and layout. While the last is relatively independent, i.e. can be applied to any content and structure, the first two are inherently related: the structure is determined by the relationships among and within content units. For instance, the structure of a page is frequently given by the sequential arrangements of its components. Alike, the complex structure of a book (a web domain) manifest itself in the hierarchical (graph-liked) arrangements of the contained pages. The arrangement is not arbitrary but instead, represents a particular narrative structure intended by the author that normally, based on the semantic of the content. This implies that a page form a content unit that is put together so as to form a particular narrative. In an adaptive system, this narrator might be the system—when adaptive navigation is supported. In this respect, content unit can be distinguished in terms of granularity, e.g. with the lowest beginning at word level that might go up to the level of sentence, paragraph, page, section, chapter and so on. Word-level assembly is probably what we human do when expressing our thoughts. W.r.t. current technologies, the lowest appropriate level for adaptive content assembly to be performed by machine might be higher than that.

In XAHM (Cannataro, Pugliese, 2001), two levels of granularity are distinguished: pages and basic multimedia fragments. The relationships among them are inherent in an upper layer, modeled as weighted directed graphs of extracted concepts. Similarly, resources are represented as nodes of a conceptual network in ELM-ART (Weber, Brusilovsky, 2001). Each unit in the conceptual network has a slot containing the text for the page and the information relating this page to others units in the form of prerequisite concepts, related concepts, and outcomes.

In summary, these approaches model the structure of content units in terms of relations among concepts organized as graphs. The content itself is represented through the concepts. This representation could be enhanced with presentation related information, e.g. by means of Presentation Description such as in (Cannataro, Pugliese, 2001).

Further attributes proposed for the description of content are for the most part, covered by the Dublin Core Schema (DC) (Weibel et al., 1998) and the Learning Objects Metadata Standard (LOM) (LOM, 2001).

DC is designed to promote the widespread adoption of interoperable metadata standards that enable more intelligent information discovery for digital resources. It is a specification of set of 15 attributes—including Title, Identifier, Language and Comment—to be used as a standard vocabulary for describing resources. The Simple DC supporting the use of the elements as attribute-value-pairs is distinguished from the Qualified DC, which employs additional qualifiers to further refine the description of a resource.

As an extension of DC, LOM considers the specific needs encountered in describing learning resources. It is a more complex schema that defines a structure divided into nine categories that in turn contain sub-elements as follows:

- General: title, language, keyword, coverage, etc.
- Life cycle: author, publisher, version, etc.
- Meta-metadata: metadata scheme, language, identifier, etc.
- Technical: format, size, requirements, etc.
- Educational: learning time, difficulty level, interactivity level, etc.
- Rights: price, copyright, etc.
- Relation: relationships with other resources, such as has part, requires, has version etc.
- Classification: taxonomy, purpose, etc.
- Annotation: date, etc.

This means that concepts used for modeling the content correspond to "keyword" or "subject" in LOM. In this regard, (Dolog et al., 2005) identifies a need of a controlled vocabulary, particularly such one that is internationally accepted. If such a standard exist, applications will be able to share an agreement not only about the attribute to be used but also their possible values. As a consequence, resources become interoperable. The paper introduces the use of ACM (ACM, 2005) for the exchange of resources across applications in an open-domain setting. Basically, ACM represents a taxonomy of terms in the field of computer science that has already existed for several decades. The following figure shows a small fraction of this taxonomy:

Using RDF, concepts from this hierarchy are specifies as a instances of `Lom cls:Taxonomy`. Together, the form the vocabulary for annotating learning resources via `dc:subject`.

DISCUSSION ON THE APPROACHES TO ADAPTATION

Drawbacks of Filtering-Based Approaches

In terms of the penetration to practical and commercial scenarios, filtering-based approaches appear to be state-of-the-art. Nevertheless, they are not very effective and provide only restricted fine-tuning to the individual user. (Terveen, Hill, 2001) summarizes the following shortcomings w.r.t. filtering-based approaches:

In content-based–filtering, recommendations are made based on objective measures about the similarity of products. However, preferences are mostly influenced by subjective attributes of the item in reality, e.g. a spicy taste. Another problem is overspecialization as the system always recommends more of what the user has already indicated a liking for.

Collaborative filtering assumes user of the same group to have similar interest. Certainly, this assumption contradicts any efforts of fine-granular adaptation as distinctive preferences cannot be taken into account. Also, it requires a sufficient large amount of existing data to operate with due to the new-item and sparsity problem: the former materializes the facts that there is no way to recommend any new item appropriately until more information can be obtained from user's behavior. The latter is prevalent when the number of users is small relative to the content volume in the system. This has the consequence that only few products are examined by users, i.e. the coverage of ratings become to sparse thinning the set of recommendable items. Moreover, recommendation let users reading only the documents of interest, which even intensify thus sparsity.

Advantages of Multi-Model Approaches

Nevertheless, (Terveen, Hill, 2001) also shows that both approaches are rather complementary:

Figure 1. An extract of the ACM taxonomy

- C. Computer Systems Organization
- D. Software
  - D.0 GENERAL
  - D.1 PROGRAMMING TECHNIQUES
    * D.1.0 General
    * D.1.1 Applicative (Functional) Programming
    * D.1.2 Automatic Programming
    * D.1.3 Concurrent Programming
    * D.1.4 Sequential Programming
    * D.1.5 Object-oriented Programming
    * D.1.6 Logic Programming
    * D.1.7 Visual Programming
    * D.1.m Miscellaneous
  - D.2 SOFTWARE ENGINEERING
  - D.3 PROGRAMMING LANGUAGES
  - D.4 OPERATING SYSTEMS
  - D.m MISCELLANEOUS
- E. Data

Source: ACM taxonomy (ACM, 2005)

subjective ratings of user groups could counterbalance the lack of subjective data about the resources. New resources can be recommended on the basis of their content. In return, content-based filtering could eliminate the sparsity problem because recommendation would not depend merely on ratings of other users.

Still, incorporating even more information and sources could theoretically, generate recommendations that can be tuned more effectively to the user. This is the core idea of multi-dimensional approaches. Filtering approaches and their combination rely on information about the user and the domain. In best case, a resource is deemed relevant to the user because it denotes some real object or represents some information or knowledge that has been searched for or visited by the user. Previous section shows that when enhanced with the task context, further hints can be recognized by the system as to what is relevant and required for the user's objective, e.g. to accomplish the task. Likewise, information related to the environment let the system adapt the presentation to technological requirements such as bandwidth, display size etc. Also, it has been shown that when designed to capture the necessary details, the domain model could encapsulate information sufficient to generate the adaptive presentation on-the-fly.

Drivers for Semantic in Adaptive Hypermedia Systems

(Herlocker, Konstan, Riedl, 2000) asserts that nowadays adaptive systems are black boxes, computerized oracles which give advice but cannot be questioned. Most of the algorithms employed are to complex and compute latent factors, heuristics that only approximately, or probabilistically, capture the relations between entities and the rationales underlying users' behavior. Consequently, it is difficult to explain the reasons behind a particular recommendation. Discussed semantic-based approaches have shown that recommendations could be generated on the basis of rules instead.

Underlying inferences then can be analyzed, provided with a proof and make publicly available for the user to inspect. This could improve their trust towards the system.

Furthermore, obtaining model information is difficult in general. We noticed that in most approaches promoting sophisticated user models can be found in the field of Instructional Systems, where possibly, the overall duration and the type of interaction permits the extraction of much of the relevant information. For example, the notion of a task concept appears to be reasonable. But the task concept employed in (Brusilovsky, Cooper, 2001) built on a hierarchy of activities that is characteristic to the application. This however, does not really apply to the typical hypermedia application that serves for a multitude of general purposes. The number of possible tasks might exceed the number manageable and the users are not for the long-term exposing only few usable information.

To this end, the observed trend towards the explicit specification of model information, e.g. interaction model in (Henze, Dolog, Nejdl, 2004), facilitates the exchange and therefore, the collection of such information. However, this requires involved parties to talk the same language. Conventionally, standard, commonly agreed upon schemas come into play. Using semantic models instead, entailed information can be used by inference engines to perform automatic merging of (non-standardized) schema.

This is particularly important for hypermedia application on the web. As discussed previously, the key driver of adaptation is the need for a personalized view on the mass content of the internet so as to face the problem of "loss in information space". Obviously, the point of entry for the user, e.g. a portal, a personal web assistant etc., is then expected to be able to syndicate and adapt content from various sources. While the former is through standardized content exchange, the system needs to understand the content for accomplishing the latter.

For now, this "understanding" is achieved through keyword matching on the basis of similarity measures. That means a resource might be interesting because it contains concepts that match with the ones relevant to the user. A semantic approach in contrast, makes recommendation due to similarities in terms of the concept semantic. For this purpose, the ontology provides vocabularies, which are defined through axioms that constrain its interpretation. With OWL for instance, the system would infer that two concepts are alike due to similarities of their definitions—instead of a mere matching in denotation. Instances of these concepts are then similar if there have similar properties and similar values for these properties. This semantic processing capability could enable the system to reconcile concepts contained in resources with concepts representing the user's need. From them, it can infer further information and incorporate them all into rules representing very generic adaptation logic.

There are already concepts laid out for reaching such a vision of knowledge-based hypermedia systems that automatically exchange and generically exploit semantic information for adaptation. The simple conceptual architecture proposed in (Bra, Aroyo, Chepegin, 2005) for instance, implicates supports for the information acquisition by virtue of specialized semantic services. While these concepts and the existing SW-technologies are not yet mature to accomplish that vision of information processing in its entirety, we think that it is worth experimenting. This is why we elaborate on an ontology proposal for the domain of adaptive hypermedia application.

REFERENCES

ACM (2005). *The ACM Computing Classification System*. 1998 Version. Available at http://www.acm.org/class/1998/, 07.01.2005.

Amazon (2005). *Amazon start page*. http://www.amazon.com/gp/homepage.html/103-4263439-7624613, 06.01.2005.

(Asnicar, F., & Tasso, C. (1997). ifWeb: A Prototype of User-Model-Based Intelligent Agent for Document Filtering and Navigation in the World Wide Web. In *Proceedings of the Workshop Adaptive Systems and User Modelling on the World Wide Web*. User Modelling Conference 97.

Belew, R. K. (1986). *Adaptive Information Retrieval: Machine Learning in Associative Networks*. Ph.D. dissertation, Computer Science Dept., University of Michigan. Ann Arbor. Michigan.

Brachman, F. J., & Schmolze, J. G. (1985). An overview of the KL-ONE knowledge representation system. *Cognitive Sci., 9.2*. S. 171-216.

Broekstra, J., Ehrig, M., Haase, P., van Harmelen, F., Menken, M., Mika, P., Schnizler, B., & Siebes, R. (2004). Bibster—A semantics-based bibliographic peer-to-peer system. In *Proceedings of the WWW'04 Workshop on Semantics in Peer-to-Peer and Grid Computing*.

Brusilovsky, P. (1996). Methods and Techniques of Adaptive Hypermedia. In *Proceedings of User Modelling and User-Adapted Interaction, 6*, S. 87–129. Kluwer academic publishers.

Brusilovsky, P., & Cooper, D. W. (2001). Domain, task, and user models for an adaptive hypermedia performance support system. In *Proceedings of the 7th international conference on intelligent user interfaces*. San Francisco, California, USA. S. 23-30.

Cannataro, M., & Pugliese, A. (2001, August). A flexible architecture for adaptive hypermedia systems. In proceedings of the IJCAI's Workshop on Intelligent Techniques for Web Personalization.

Cavnar, W., & Trenkle, J. (1994). N-Gram-Based Text Categorization. In *Proceedings of the 3rd Annual Symposium on Document Analysis and*

Information Retrieval (SDAIR 94), S. 161-175, Las Vegas, NV, USA, April 11-13.

(Chen, L., & Sycara, K. (1998). Webmate: A Personal Agent for Browsing and Searching. In *Proceedings of AGENTS '98*, S. 132–139. ACM.

Chen, Z., Meng, X., Zhu, B., & Fowler, R. (2000). WebSail: From On-Line Learning to Web Search. In *Proceedings of the 2000 International Conference on Web Information Systems Engineering.*

Conlan, O., Wade, V., Bruen, C., Gargan, M. (2002). *Multi-model, Metadata Driven Approach to Adaptive Hypermedia Services for Personalized eLearning.* Malaga, Spain, Mai 2002, S. 100–111.

Cunningham, P., Bergmann, R., Schmitt, S., Traphoner, R., Breen, S. & Smyth, B. (2001). *WebSell: Intelligent Sales Assistants for the World Wide Web.* In E-2001.

De Bra, P., Aroyo, L., Chepegin, V., (2005). The Next Big Thing: Adaptive Web-Based Systems. In *Journal of Digital Information, 5*, 247.

Dolog, P., Henze, N., Nejdl, W., & Sintek, M. (2003). Towards the adaptive semantic web. In Proceedings *of the 1st Workshop on Principles and Practice of Semantic Web Reasoning.*

Dolog, P., Henze, N., Nejdl, W., & Sintek, M. (2004). *The personal reader: Personalizing and enriching learning resources using semantic web technologies.* Technical report, University of Hannover. Hannover, Germany.

Dolog, P., Gavriloaie, R., Nejdl, W. & Brase, J. (2005). *Integrating Adaptive Hypermedia Techniques and Open RDF based Environments.* Available at www.kbs.uni-hannover.de/Arbeiten/Publikationen/2002/www2003-10.pdf.

Ebay (2005). *EBay start page.* http://www.ebay.com. 06.01.2005.

Fikes, R., & Kehler, J. (1985, September). The role of frame-based representation in reasoning.

Comm. of the Assoc. for Computing Machinery, 28(9).

Frasincar, F., Houben, G., & Vdovjak, R. (2001). An RMM-Based Methodology for Hypermedia Presentation Design. In *Proceedings of the Fifth East-European Conference on Advances in Databases and Information Systems (ADBIS '01).* Springer.

Frasincar, F., Houben, G. J., & Vdovjak, R. (2002). Specification framework for engineering adaptive web applications. In *The Eleventh International World Wide Web Conference, WWW.*

Good, N., Schafer, J. B., Konstan, J. A., Borchers, A., Sarwar, B., Herlocker, J., & Riedl, J. (1999). Combining collaborative filtering with personal agents for better recommendations. In *Proceedings of the AAAI '99 Conference on Artificial Intelligence*, Orlando, FL, 1999, S. 439-446.

Heckmann, D., & Krueger, A. (2004). *A User Modeling Markup Language (UserML) for Ubiquitous Computing, 2004.* Available at www.dfki.de/~krueger/PDF/UM2003.pdf.

Heckmann, D., Schwartz, T., Brandherm, B., & Schmitz, M. (2005). *Wilamowitz-Moellendorff, M., GUMO—the General User Model Ontology.* Available at w5.cs.uni-sb.de/~schmitz/publications/UM05_Gumo.pdf.

Henze, N., & Nejdl, W. (1999). *Adaptivity in the KBS Hyperbook System. Workshop on Adaptivity and User Modeling on the WWW, International Conference on User Modeling UM'99.*

Henze, N. (2000). *Adaptive Hyperbooks: Adaptation for Project-Based Learning Resources.* PhD thesis, University of Hannover.

Henze, N., & Nejdl, W. (2002). Knowledge modeling for open adaptive hypermedia. In *Proccedings of the 2nd International Conference on Adaptive Hypermedia and Adaptive Web-Based Systems (AH 2002),* Malaga, Spain.

Henze, N., Dolog, P., & Nejdl, W. (2004). Reasoning and Ontologies for Personalized E-Learning in the Semantic Web. *Educational Technology & Society, 7*(4), S. 82-97.

Hepner, G. F., Logan, T., Ritter, N., & Bryant, N. (1990). Artificial neural network classification using a minimal training set: comparison to conventional supervised classification. *Photogrammetric Engineering and Remote Sensing, 56*(4), S. 469-473.

Herlocker, J. L., Konstan, J. A., Borchers, A., & Riedl, J. (1999). An algorithmic framework for performing collaborative filtering. In *Proceedings of SIGIR '99 Conference on Research and Development in Information Retrieval*, ACM Press, New York, NY, 1999, S. 230-237.

Herlocker, J., Konstan, J. & Riedl, J. (2000). Explaining Collaborative Filtering Recommendations. In *Proceedings of ACM 2000 Conference on Computer Supported Cooperative Work*.

Houben, G. (2000). HERA: Automatically Generating Hypermedia Front-Ends for Ad Hoc Data from Heterogeneous and Legacy Information Systems. In *Proceedings of the Third International Workshop on Engineering Federated Information Systems*. Aka and IOS Press.

Houben, G., Barna, P., Frasincar, F., & Vdovjak, R. (2003). *Hera: Development of Semantic Web Information*. Available at SiteCeer http://citeseer.ist.psu.edu/cachedpage/675475/1, 06.01.06.

IEEE P1484.2/D7, 2000-11-28. (2002). *Draft standard for learning technology. Public and private information (papi) for learners (papi learner)*. Available at: http://ltsc.ieee.org/wg2/. Accessed on October 25, 2002.

IMS (2002). IMS learner information package specification. Available at: http://www.imsproject.org/profiles/index.cfm. Accessed on October 25, 2002.

Jameson A. (1998). *User Modeling: An Integrative Overview*. Tutorial ABIS98: Workshop on Adaptivitiy and User Modeling in Interactive Software Systems, FORWISS Report.

Jennings, A. & Higuchi, H. (1993). A User Model Neural Network for a Personal News Service. *User Modeling and User-Adapted Interaction 3*, S. 1–25, 1993.

Jensen, F. V. (1996). *An Introduction to Bayesian Networks*. New York: Springer.

Jin, X., Zhou, Y., Mobasher, M. (2004). *A Unified Approach to Personalization Based on Probabilistic Latent Semantic Models of Web Usage and Content*. Available at Citeseer http://citeseer.ist.psu.edu/715309.html.

Konstan, J. A., Miller, B. N., Maltz, D., Herlocker, J. L., Gordon, L., & Riedl, J. (1997, March). GroupLens: Applying collaborative filtering to Usenet news. In *Communication of the ACM, 40*(3), S. 77-87.

Krulwich, B., & Burkey, C. (1995). ContactFinder: Extracting Indications of Expertise and Answering Questions with Referrals. *Working Notes of the 1995 Fall Symposium on Intelligent Knowledge Navigation and Retrieval*, S. 85–91, Technical Report FS-95-03, The AAAI Press.

Krulwich, B., & Burkey, C. (1996). Learning User Information Interests through Extraction of Semantically Significant Phrases. In *Proceedings of the AAAI Spring Symposium on Machine Learning in Information Access*. Stanford, CA.

Krulwich, B. (1997). LifeStyle Finder: Intelligent User Profiling Using Large-Scale Demographic Data. *AI Magazine 18*(2), 37–45.

Little, J., Geurts, & J. Hunter (2002, September). Dynamic Generation of Intelligent Multimedia Presentations through Semantic Inferencing. In *6th European Conference on Research and Advanced Technology for Digital Libraries*, S. 158-189. Springer.

LOM (2001, April). *LOM, Draft Standard for Learning Object Metadata*. IEEE P1484.12/D6.1. 18.

Miller, G. A. (1995). WordNet: A Lexical Database. *Communication of the ACM, 38*(11): S. 39-41.

Montaner, M., Lopez, B., & Dela, J. L. (2003). A taxonomy of recommender agents on the internet. *Artificial Intelligence Review 19*(2003), 285-330.

Ossenbruggen, J. van, Geurts, J., Cornelissen, F., Rutledge, L., & Hardman., L. (2001, May). Towards Second and Third Generation Web-Based Multimedia. *In Proceedings of the Tenth International World Wide Web Conference (WWW10)*. Hong Kong: ACM Press, S. 479-488.

Paiva, A., & Self, J. (1995). TAGUS: A User and Learner Modeling Workbench. *International Journal of User Modeling and User-adapted Interaction, 5*(3), 197-224. Kluwer Academic Publishers.

Pazzani, M., Muramatsu, J., & Billsus, D. (1996). Syskill & Webert: Identifying Interesting Web Sites. In *Proceedings of the Thirteenth National Conference on Artificial Intelligence*, S. 54–61.

Pemberton, D., Rodden, T., & Procter, R. (2000). GroupMark: A WWW recommender system combining collaborative and information filtering. In *Proceedings of the 6th ERCIM Workshop*, Florence, Italy, Oct.25-26.

Salton, G., & McGill, M. (1983). Introduction to Modern Information Retrieval. New York, NY: McGraw-Hill Publishing Company.

Salton, G., & Buckley, C. (1998). Term-Weighting Approaches in Automatic Text Retrieval. *Information Processing and Management, 24*(5), 513–523.

SAP (2005). *SAP Komponenten und Werkzeuge von SAP NetWeaver: SAP NetWeaver Portal*, 05.01.2005 http://www.sap.com/germany/solutions/netweaver/components/netweaverportal/index.epx/.

Schafer, J. B., Konstan, J., & Riedi, J. (1999). Recommender Systems in E-Commerce. In *Proceedings of the ACM Conference on Electronic Commerce*. New York, NY: ACM Press, 158-166.

Shardanand, U., & Maes, P. (1995). Social Information Filtering: Algorithms for Automating 'Word of Mouth'. *In Proceedings of CHI'95*, S. 210–217.

Sorensen, H., & McElligot, M. (1995). PSUN: A Profiling System for Usenet News. In *CKIM'95 Workshop on Intelligent Information Agents*.

Stefani, A., & Strappavara, C. (1998). Personalizing Access to Web Wites: The SiteIF Project. In *Proceedings of HYPERTEXT'98*.

Terveen, L. G. & Hill, W. (2001). Beyond Recommender Systems: Helping people help each other. In Carroll, J. (ed.), *HCI in the New Millennium*. Addison Wesley.

Torre I. (2001). Goals, tasks and Application domains as the guidelines for defining a framework for User modelling. In *User Modelling 2001, LNCS*, Springer Verlag, (pp. 260-262).

Weber, G., & Brusilovsky, P. (2001). ELM-ART: An adaptive versatile system for Web-based instruction. In *Proceedings of the International Journal of Artificial Intelligence in Education, 12*(4). Special Issue on Adaptive and Intelligent Web-based Educational Systems, S. 351-384, available at http://www.sis.pitt.edu/~peterb/papers/JAIEDFinal.pdf, 2001.

Weibel, S., Kunze, J., Lagoze, C., & Wolf, M. (1998). *Dublin Core Metadata for Resource Discovery*. Number 2413 in IETF. The Internet Society, September.

Wiki (2005). *Statistical classification*. http://en.wikipedia.org/wiki/Statistical_classification. 05.01.2005.

Chapter VIII
A Personalized Portal on the Basis of Semantic Models and Rules

Jorge Marx Gómez
Oldenburg University, Germany

Tran Duc
Karlsruhe University, Germany

ABSTRACT

A portal is a Web-based single point of access that delivers information and applications to a user on its own and by the integration of external services. With most portals, various users in the role of customer, supplier, employee, and so forth, can configure the available content and the functionalities in their own way and access them over multitude of devices—mobile phone, PDA, and PC to name a few (Priebe; Pernul, 2003). Whereas this type of portal can be seen as an adaptable system, adaptive portals shall adapt themselves to the individual user.

INTRODUCTION

In general, portal implementations resemble a multi-tier architecture. Figure 1 shows such an architecture that has been adopted from (Sun Microsystems, 2005a) and slightly modified to represent the extension with semantic data sources. Apparently, the respective tiers are the client, the data sources, and the server that can be further decomposed into a web and a domain layer.

THE WEB LAYER

Various types of client that sit on different devices with different supports in terms of content markup languages requests content by virtue of a communication protocol. The most common protocol on the internet is the HTTP, which, combined with SSL, cater for a secured exchange of data between the server and the client machine. These HTTP request are then processed by the web container situated at server side. Using other protocols, such as SOAP, RMI and IIOP, specific clients could directly invoke the services managed by the application container (Sun Microsystems, 2005b)—which are illustrated as domain components in figure 1.

Meanwhile, the Model-View-Controller (MVC) has become the foremost pattern for structuring the web tier. This design pattern involves a division of a functional module into three components with different responsibility. The view obtains data from the model and presents it to the user. The model encapsulates data and functionality of the domain logic, e.g. of one or several domain components. The controller is the central component in that it maps request data into operations of the model and notifies the view of respective changes. Among other merits, this division implies an isolation of the presentation logic from the domain logic. That means, changes in the UI can be implemented without modification of the underlying processing logic—which is valuable since drivers and rates of changes of the web tier, viz. the user interface, and the domain are different. Please refer to (Krasner; Pope, 1988) for a more detailed discussion on MVC.

Common implementations of the MVC-architecture are based on servlets, JSPs and portlets.

Figure 1. A generic portal architecture, Source: Sun Microsystems, 2005a

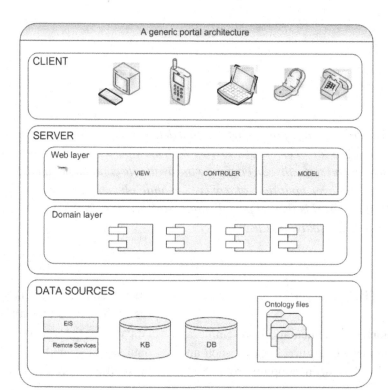

Mostly, there is a servlet, which receipts all incoming requests and delegates them to the responsible portlet. Typically, the latter is responsible for one specific module, e.g. rendered as a window within the portal. For this module, there is a corresponding JSP that encapsulates the static content and generates the dynamic content—marked-up in the language appropriate for presentation at the client device, e.g. VXML for voice and HTML for visual content. Both portlet and JSP require a servlet engine such as Apache Tomcat. This is because technically, the former is simply an adaptation of the servlet concept and the latter, is internally translated to and run as a servlet. While this engine is an essential container required for the execution of the servlet logic, the following section discussed two additional optional platforms—the application and the portal container (Sun Microsystems, 2005c).

THE DOMAIN LAYER

In fact, the web-tier controller could implement the entire logic for model processing. However, in complex enterprise portal solution, the actual processing is rather delegated to domain components, which run on an application server. In a J2EE platform, these components are referred to as business objects that encapsulate the business logic. They are implemented as beans, e.g. entity beans, session beans and message-driven beans, which are supported by platform services such as naming, security, persistence and transaction. That is, while the components realize the specific functionalities, tasks common to all component such as the persistent storage of data, are provided by the EJB container (Sun Microsystems, 2005d).

In addition to such a container that offer services common to the deployed applications, a portal container can be plugged in on top to extends the platform with services common to portal components. Within the Websphere

portal architecture for instance, the entire portal presentation is realized by one single component called the portal servlet. This servlet delivers the combined static and dynamic content coming from various portlets to the final user. The pre-processing is performed by virtue of assembly services that are provided by the container in the form of aggregator modules. Another example of such platform functionalities is the security service designed for specific portal requirements in terms of content access, e.g. propagation of access rights for single sign-on (IBM Corporation, 2006). Since adaptive behaviors shall be common to all portal content and functionalities, they shall be realized as platform services as well.

THE DATA LAYER

Portal components retrieve and store information at a lower layer—the data sources. As shown in the figure, data sources could encompasses anything: persistent stores such as files and databases, legacy systems, Enterprise Information Systems (EIS) and other applications and remote services. Communication with these sources are handled using protocols, e.g. SOAP for web services, or APIs such as JDBC for databases.

However, such standardized protocols and uniformed APIs are not always available. Sources often need to be addressed in a specific way—as imposed by the proprietary API. This is where connectors come into play. The J2EE concept of Data Access Object (DAO) for instance, involves the abstraction and encapsulation of all access to data sources. A DAO implement the specific access mechanism required to work with a particular data sources and expose their functionalities through a more simpler and generic API. Thus, the DAO completely hides the data source implementation details from its clients, e.g. from the business components that connect to the source through the DAO API. This loose coupling has many advantages including transparency of data access, an easier migration to other sources and reduction of code complexity in business components because data access complexities is managed uniformly in DAOs (Sun Microsystems, 2005e).

In particular, accessing data in this fashion implies that the architecture of a semantic portal bear no difference to a normal portal. The concept of DAO can be extended to create a centralized data access layer that includes the use of semantic data sources. Such a source could be a single ontology file containing schema information. It could be a knowledge base (KB), which, as implied in, breaks down to two main components: The one that actually responsible for the storage of data, i.e. relational databases in most cases. The other component make inferences over the knowledge to inferred facts not explicitly asserted. Access and manipulation of these facts are performed directly by means of (semantic aware) query languages such as RQL, SeRQL and RDQL or via method invocation on KB-specific APIs, e.g. as given in Sesam and Ontobroker (Broekstra; Kampman; van Harmelen, 2002). In any cases, specific DAO implementations, or connectors in general, can be employed to abstract away the specific mechanism required for dealing with a particular semantic data source.

A PERSONALIZED KNOWLEDGE PORTAL PROTOTYPE

The main objective of the portal is to provide access to knowledge content in a personalized way so as to illustrate the adaptive functionalities realizable with the proposed ontology. The portal is built on Liferay, an open source portal architecture that already includes various common services as well as modules encapsulating specific content and functionalities. Whereas only a few are visible in figure 2, many of these functional modules have been adopted, e.g. Document Management, Wiki, Journal, Calendar and Project, to form a suite of tools for the personalized knowl-

edge management. The prototype extends this suite with adaptive functionalities, which in this experiment, are realized as functional modules. As shown in the screenshot below, the extension encompasses

- a module for the generation of recommendations,
- a module for the presentation of the content,
- a search module for content retrieval
- And a navigation component that illustrates the environment of the currently active content unit.

With these modules, the user shall be enabled to navigate though the immediate content space, search for a specific content, follow links to recommended contents and interact with the content shown in a separate window.

Most of the interactions probably take place in the Adapted Content window, in which the selected content retrieved from a relational database is shown. Figure 2 contains an example for a complex content unit, which was shown as a link in the Adapted Recommendations and was activated by the user before. Apparently, only the titles of subcomponents are made visible in the case of the complex content. These links can then be activated by the user to stretch the actual content of each part—as shown for `Introduction`. This style of adaptive content corresponds to the additional content method implemented with the stretch-text technique.

The interactions with each of these modules are processed by the system and passed to the data sources. Results of the processing are returned in form of recommendations as shown in the Adapted Recommendations module. This module gives a listing of titles of content units deemed by the system as relevant w.r.t. the current context. In this case, a content-based adaptation has been performed by virtue of a specific rule. The screenshot shows recommendations encompass-

Figure 2. A personalized portal prototype

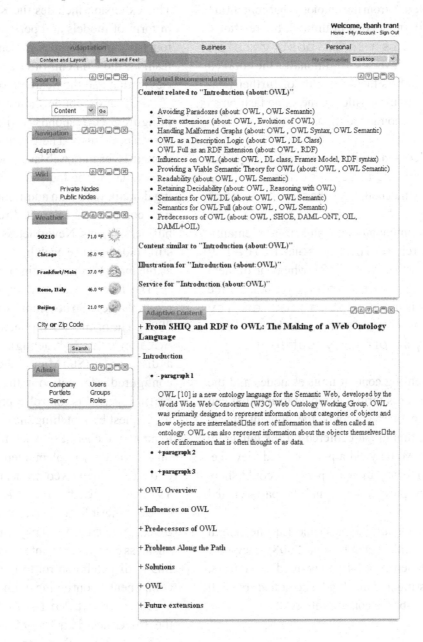

ing content about relations, in which the entity OWL described in the currently active content, viz. Introduction, is involved. This style of adaptive structure resembles the method of global guidance. Instead of related content, the KB contains enough information to make recommendations for similar and illustrative content. This can be further extended to make service recommendations based on the activity the user is currently involved in, as proposed.

Content entities and relations of the KB span a hyperspace. The navigation module shall illustrate the position of the current content unit within this space. We know from the ontology that content are related with other content through the relations, `has part`, `is pre`, `is post version of` and their inverses. Additionally, the entailed semantic enables the derivation of further relationships, e.g. using rules in the same fashion as for making recommendations:

- Two content units `c1` and `c2` are similar, viz. `is similar content (c1, c2)`, when both `has` the same `entity` as `subject`
- Two content units `c1` and `c2` are semantically related, viz. `is semantically related (c1, c2)`, when one of them is a `content about entity`, the other is a `content about entity relation` and both have the same `entity` as `primary subject`.

Representing content units as nodes and the relations as arcs form a complex graph that can serve as an overview over the content space. Rendering this graph centered on the currently active unit would yield a personalized view, i.e. an adaptive orientation support that could show the relevant parts to go to and the parts visited before.

Finally, we are adopting the Lucene search engine (Lucene Search Engine, 2008) to support keyword-based retrieval of hypermedia resources. An interesting and much advanced feature shall be semantic-based content retrieval.

THE PROTOTYPE'S ARCHITECTURE

As mentioned, Liferay provides the basic portal skeleton in the forms of common services and functional modules. The following figure illustrates the general architecture as given by this platform. It focuses on the relevant part that reflects adaptive functionalities added to Liferay. This extension includes the KB, various DOAs in form of models and persistence services and four functional modules implemented in the MVC fashion: the Content, the Recommendation, the Navigation and the Search module.

With one exception, the architecture illustrated in figure 3 corresponds to the generic one discussed previously. There is a data access layer, a domain layer and a web layer. However, rather than encapsulating the logic and data of the underlying domain within an additional web-tier model, web components interact directly with domain business objects. Nevertheless, the MVC-pattern still holds because each business object act than as the model—the domain tier model.

The Liferay web tier implementation bears resemblance to Struts-framework (Apache Struts, 2006). The primary component of this layer is the `action servlet`, acting as the front controller as discussed in (Sun Microsystems, 2005c). Using configured information in the form of `action mappings`, this controller processes all incoming request by matching the corresponding URI to an action class. So, when the user activates a link in the view implemented by `Recommendation.jsp`, this controller maps the request to a `ViewContentPorletAction`. All action classes inherit from `org.apache.struts.action.Action`. They encapsulate calls to business components, interpret the outcome, and finally dispatch control to the appropriate view component. Continuing with the example, the `ViewContentPorletAction` would call the `HypermediaService`, the `InteractionService` thereafter and finally, the `ViewRecommendationPorletAction`. The first service provides method to retrieve the requested hypermedia, e.g. `findHypermediaByTitle()`. Relevant information related to interaction—as specified in the ontology—such as the requesting user, the requested and the current content etc. are passed to the second service via `updateInteraction()`. Eventually, this

Figure 3. The personalized knowledge portal architecture

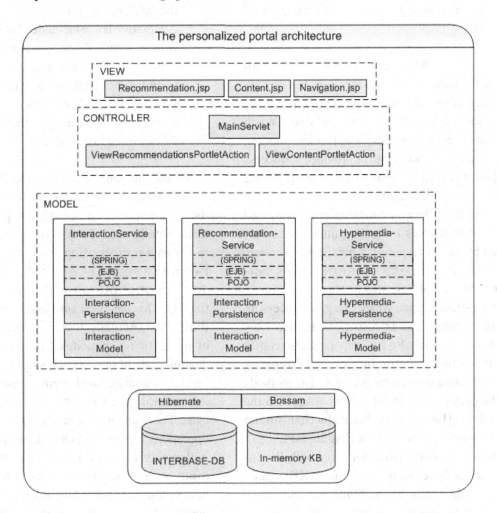

leads to changes in the KB, which are incorporated into adaptation by the final call on `ViewRecommendationPortletAction` to update the list of recommendations. In summary, methods of both `ViewContentPorletAction` and `ViewRecommendationPortletAction` are invoked, causing the rendering of the corresponding views, viz. `Content.jsp` and `Recommendation.jsp`. The views are updated using information that has been returned by the domain components, and received and put by the controllers into the request context.

All the logic implemented in the web-tier controller breaks down to a passing of information collected from interactions between user and application by virtue of methods calls on domain components. The actual processing is performed at domain level. Here are the objects that capture the data, the services that make the data persistent and the services encapsulating the logic of data processing. For instance, when the `InteractionService` receives information related to the current interaction, it computes

- the actual events, e.g. whether it has been an `activate`, an `execute` or other atomic types of `application interaction`
- the `timeout` of the last event

- And other properties not apparent from the interaction, e.g. `is post process of`.

Currently, POJO implementations are provided for these functional services. For our experimental use, this is a way to circumvent the need for a heavyweight EJB container. When container services are important, corresponding EJB implementations shall be provided and access to them can then be configured using the Spring framework (Spring 2007).

Results of the computations are propagated to the data sources by calling methods as provided by the corresponding persistence service, `InteractionPersistence` in this case. Due to the call of `ViewRecommendation-PortletAction`, which delegate processing to `RecommendationService`, also `RecommendationPersistence` also comes to play in this scenario. In general, all types of access to data sources are performed as methods of the persistence services. They wrap both the underlying Hibernate persistence mechanism and the knowledge access of the Bossam API.

Information is distributed over both the Interbase database and the in-memory KB created and managed by Bossam. Since the ontology is imported by Bossam, all entities and properties specified there are available in the KB. Additionally, some of these entities are also managed in the data base (DB) such as the User—with some different properties. This information are combined and reflected in the respective models of the domain layer, e.g. `InteractionModel` and `HypermediaModel`. They are used by the persistence service to retrieve and manipulate information of both data sources.

The reasons for this design are as follows:

- Only adaptation related information should be held in the KB. Otherwise, the size would increase unnecessarily, bearing a negative but avoidable impact on the performance of the inference engine.

- Adaptation is a value-added but not essential feature. When the processing time exceeds a threshold, business objects should be able to return enough information to realize core functionalities. Therefore, some information needs to be maintained in the KB—redundantly when necessary.

Using the same example, the `InteractionPersistence` would write data from the `InteractionModel` as computed and instantiated by the `InteractionService` to the data sources using `InteractionHibernatePersistence` for the DB and `InteractionBossamPersistence` to the KB. This has been simplified for the sake of illustration. Actually, there are several subtypes of interaction—as modeled in the ontology. In dealing with these subtypes, specific persistence services associated with them are used instead of the general `InteractionPersistence` class. These underlying services map data access operations to a set of SQL queries and Bossam API methods such as `ask()` and `tell()`. As a result, a set of new facts representing the recent interactions are updated to the memory and made persistent for further usage in the DB.

Subsequently, `RecommedationPersistence` retrieves new recommendations from the KB, which are finally returned to controller of the web tier and displayed in the view. To be exact, it does so by telling the underlying Bossam service to run a forward chaining inference session over the adaptation rules and facts, including the ones just loaded, and to materialize entailed facts, viz. make them available in the main-memory KB. Conditions of the rules that have become true in the mean time cause the engine to infer new recommendations, as shown in the Adapted Recommendations module in figure 2.

Note that much of the processing that would have been done in the domain layer is shifted to the engine managing the knowledge source. OWL entailments and rules encapsulate the logic that otherwise, need to be hard-coded in programs. For instance, `InteractionService` computes some subtypes by an analysis of the information received from the web tier. As demonstrated for several concepts in the ontology, some of these classification tasks have been achieved by the specification of sufficient properties for the DL engine to infer the types. Likewise, the rules reproduce much of the adaptation logic, which otherwise has to be implemented in domain services using if-the-else constructs. Nonetheless, it should be clear from the discussion in that a semantic approach has other merits. The semantic models provide a vocabulary for the services to communicate with each other. Annotated resources can be understood, exchanged and reused by semantic services that thrive and cooperate in the realm of unbounded interoperability to find and adapt the most appropriate information to the user.

LIMITATIONS AND POSSIBLE EXTENSION

The functionalities described above are only for illustrative purpose. They give an impression of what type of adaptation is possible when retrieving the knowledge available from the KB. However, it cannot be considered as a product ripe for practical use due to the following reasons:

- Adaptive functionalities are implemented as functional modules. More reasonably, adaptation shall be realized as a service run in the portal container that takes all available functionalities and content resources into account. Adaptive behavior should be considered as an aspect, which can be associated to any objects of the portal architecture.

- The performance in the generation of recommendations is not suitable for real-life applications. Despite working on meta-data of only few documents and one user, the system requires several minutes of processing to update the recommendations. This is mostly due to the processing of rules and facts entailed in the KB.

- The quality of recommendations is dependent on this processing. The reasoner currently employed is rather tailored towards rules processing. A few OWL classifications are not processed correctly with Bossam. This can be solved when using pure DL reasoner such as Racer and Fact instead. For the future, a more appropriate reasoner that can cope both with DLP rules and OWL entailments is required. Such an engine must also support persistency and reasoning on a large A-Box (Baader; Calvanese; McGuinness; Nardi; Patel-Schneider, 2003).

- Instead of the in-memory KB, asserted and inferred facts shall be made persistent. A relational database can be employed for this purpose when switching to platform such as Instance Store and Sesame.

- The navigation module is to be realized as a dynamic graph that illustrates relevant relationships and concepts of the entire ontology and given the context of the user, adapt this overview accordingly. For instance, the nodes corresponding to the derived recommendations can be highlighted and realized as links for the user to browse to the underlying resources. In general, adaptive information shall be incorporated to reduce the number of arcs and nodes to obtain a concise representation of the relevant content space.

- There are only a few documents stored in the database. They have been annotated by hand using meta-data for `content` as specified in the ontology. In future, a tool-based annotation shall be taken into account. This is valuable when the respective tool is bundled in a suite that also support the management of the underlying vocabulary, viz. to modify, merge and test the ontology. Most important, this suite shall enable newly created knowledge to be checked for consistency against the KB, since from inconsistency, any facts (including non-senses) are derivable.

- Adaptation anticipates the need only with respect to the current context. The user may want to change it and initiate a new context by a search for a completely unrelated entity, e.g. due to change in task and objective. When possible, the keyword-based search mechanism shall be extended to factor in the content semantic.

An extension towards the automatic crawling of content and content-metadata shall be considered to match up with the information need of the user. Entities that have been identified from previous searches can be use to make this retrieval more goal-directed. Besides sophisticated adaptation, this shall become the major advantage of such a semantic approach. A semantic portal is indeed a progress, when semantic interoperability anticipated for the semantic web can be exploited for the automatic and flexible inclusion of external content to provide the user a single point of access to any relevant information.

CONCLUSION AND OUTLOOK

We have surveyed many approaches to adaptation and argued that to achieve fine-tuned adaptation in an open environment of the web, a semantic approach is more appropriate. The elicitation of adaptive knowledge and rationales in form of explicit semantic models facilitates their reuse. The employed ontology vocabulary ensures an unambiguous interpretation of the model semantic. This is the basis for a semantic interoperability, which facilitate the exchange of model (meta-) information among cooperative services. Most importantly, content data and metadata can then

be understood and automatically included into the adaptive system.

On the basis of initial proposals built on the knowledge representation (KR) and reasoning framework underlying the semantic web vision, we have developed a full-fledge OWL ontology for the adaptive hypermedia application domain that captures every aspects valuable for adaptation. This knowledge is incorporated into SWRL inference rules that embody the logic for the generation of adaptive recommendations. The dependencies between entities that make up the context could be exploited to perform content-based and task-based adaptation. The developed prototype gives an impression of the effectiveness and transparency of this semantic-based adaptation. All these proposals cannot be considered as to be complete. Nonetheless, they have been designed to maximize extensibility. When possible, we have incorporated existing standards, design principles, recommended languages and limitations in expressivity and widely accepted technologies. This way, these proposals can be leveraged to more comprehensive solutions and for the adoption of specific requirements.

With this experiment, we have shown that the application of semantic web technologies has great potential for such personalized information processing and delivery. At the same time, we recognized many requirements that are to be resolved to arrive a full semantic web vision where intelligent services and agents exchange, exploit and reason about meaningful information. We like to discuss the two most essential issues that shall be addressed in future:

- Provision and interoperability of meta-data: The most important limitation of the current prototype is the lack in adaptive content. In order to be useful, the adaptive system must be able to include external content. However, there is not much annotated content available yet. The development shows that this will probably change in the near future: techniques for programmatic, semi and fully automated annotation have been extensively researched and promising tools have been developed such as W4F (Sahuguet; Azavant, 2001), X Wrap (Liu; Pu; Han, 2000) and Lixto (Baumgartner; Flesca; Gottlob, 2001). The progress is signalized by the continuing rise of available (RDF) annotated metadata in several sources, e.g. the peer-to-peer network Edutella (Neid; Wolf; Qu; Decker; Sintek; Naeve; Nilsson; Palmer; Risch, 2002). Nevertheless, even if meta-data can be stripped out from the content by means of knowledge-mining, further works are necessary. The meta-data needs to be mapped to concepts of the respective domain ontology—if there such one at all, viz. subjects of the content mapped to individuals of the corresponding domain. In this respect, using ontology-driven annotation framework such as Cream (Handschuh; Staab; Maedche, 2001) right at the start could be the solution to this problem because such mappings would become an integral task part of the annotation process itself.

- Technologies for reasoning and meta-data storage: In particular, the main issues are reasoning and persistency of large DL A-Boxes, integration of DL and rules and performance of reasoning. Many technologies such as Sesame and KAON offer storage for semantic meta-data. The corresponding query language and API can only exploit RDFS entailments. Recent proposals such as OWLIM accommodate OWL entailments but no persistency appropriate for real application scenarios (Broekstra, 2005). InstanceStore seems to be a more appropriate solution for the storage and reasoning requirements of our prototype. However, is still unknown as how to extend reasoning to such a large A-Box. Furthermore, the prototype also requires an engine that sup-

ports the processing of rules. A reasoner that can process both the semantic of description logic (DL) expressions and rules is very valuable. The AIFB is working on an inference engine (KAON2) that operates on a subset of both, viz. disjunctive Datalog. This however, implies a transformation to this subset, which necessarily result in loss of semantic when the models are two expressive. One could use a DL and logic programming (LP) reasoner together instead. But then, a sophisticate communication platform is required to optimize and possibly, minimize the knowledge exchange. Due to these limitations, we have employed the more convenient Bossam reasoner. It supports many of the required OWL-entailments and can process the Description Logic Program (DLP) rules in the adaptation model. But even our basic setting, we have already recognized problems in performance. In future, a generic strategy for distributed reasoning may be a solution. The KB can be decomposed into logical parts that are processed separately by a dedicated reasoner (instance). These partitions must then be designed in such a way that minimizes the cooperation so that the resulting communication overhead would not exceed the gain in performance.

REFERENCES

Baader, F., Calvanese, D., McGuinness, D. L., Nardi, D., Patel-Schneider, P. F. (2003). *The description logic handbook: theory, implementation, and applications*. Cambridge University Press.

Baumgartner, R. Flesca, S., & Gottlob, G. (2001, September). Visual Web Information Extraction with Lixto. In *Proceedings of the 27th International Conference on Very Large Data Bases*, S. 119-128.

Broekstra, J., Kampman, A., & van Harmelen, F. (2002). *Sesame: a Generic Architecture for Storing and Querying RDF and RDF Schema*. To appear in the 1st International Semantic Web Conference (ISWC2002), June 9-12, Sardinia, Italy.

Broekstra, J. (2005, July). *Storage, Querying and Inferencing for Semantic Web Languages*. PhD Thesis. Vrije Universiteit Amsterdam. SIKS Dissertation Series 2005-09. ISBN 90-9019-236-0.

Handschuh, S., Staab, S., & Maedche, A. (2001). Cream—creating relational metadata with a component-based, ontology-driven annotation framework. In *Proceedings of 1st International Conference on Knowledge Capture*, (pp. 76-83). ACM Press.

IBM Corporation. *IBM Websphere Portal Server Product Architecture*. www.ibm.com/pvc/tech/whitepapers, 18.01.06.

KAON—*Karlsruhe Ontology and Semantic Web framework*, http://kaon2.semanticweb.org/, 20.02.2007.

Krasner, G. E., & Pope, S. T. (1988). A cookbook for using the model-view-controller user interface paradigm in Smalltalk-80. *Journal of Object-Oriented Programming, 1*(3), S. 26-49.

Ling, L., Calton, P., & Wei, H. XWRAP (2000). *An XML Enabled Wrapper Construction System for Web Information Sources. In International Conference on Data Engineering ICDE*, S. 611- 621.

Lucene Search Engine. http://lucene.apache.org/java/docs/, 16.01.2008

Neidl, W., Wolf, B., Qu, Ch., Decker, S., Sintek, M., Naeve, A., Nilsson, M., Palmer, M., & Risch, T (2002, May). Edutella—A P2P Networking Infrastructure Based on RDF. *Proceedings of the Semantic Web Workshop, 11th Intl. WWW Conference*.

Priebe, T., & Pernul, G. (2003). Towards Integrative Enterprise Knowledge Portals. In *Proc. of the Twelfth International Conference on Information and Knowledge Management (CIKM 2003)*. New Orleans, USA.

Sahuguet, & Azavant, F. (2001). Building intelligent Web applications using lightweight wrappers. *Data and Knowledge Engineering, 3*(36), 283-316.

Spring Framework. http://www.springframework.org/about/, 02.02.2007

Apache Struts. http://struts.apache.org/, 20.01.06.

Sun Microsystems (2005a). *Guidelines Designing Enterprise Applications with the J2EE Platform*, Second Edition. Particularly: J2EE Platform Overview. http://java.sun.com/blueprints/guidelines/designing_enterprise_applications_2e/introduction/introduction3.html#1042891, 18.01.06.

Sun Microsystems (2005b). *Guidelines Designing Enterprise Applications with the J2EE Platform*, Second Edition. Particularly: J2EE Platform Overview. http://java.sun.com/blueprints/guidelines/designing_enterprise_applications_2e/client-tier/client-tier.html#1089105, 18.01.06.

Sun Microsystems (2005c). *Guidelines Designing Enterprise Applications with the J2EE Platform*, Second Edition. Particularly: The web tier. http://java.sun.com/blueprints/guidelines/designing_enterprise_applications_2e/web-tier/web-tier.html#1094260, 18.01.06.

Sun Microsystems (2005e). *Core J2EE Pattern Catalog*. Core J2EE Patterns—Data Access Object. http://java.sun.com/blueprints/corej2eepatterns/Patterns/DataAccessObject.html, 19.01.06.

Sun Microsystems (2005d). *Guidelines Designing Enterprise Applications with the J2EE Platform*, Second Edition. Particularly: J2EE Platform Overview. http://java.sun.com/blueprints/guidelines/designing_enterprise_applications_2e/ejb-tier/ejb-tier.html#1055251, 18.01.06.

Chapter IX
British Consumers' Attitudes and Acceptance of Mobile Advertising

Sylvie Laforet
University of Sheffield, UK

Hannah Limahelu
University of Sheffield, UK

ABSTRACT

This wireless advertising is considered to be an important alternative advertising medium in the future, due to its numerous advantages over traditional media. However, little research has been conducted on consumer acceptance of this medium in particular, in the United Kingdom. This study explores consumers' attitudes towards and acceptance of mobile advertising, using focus group interviews. Results indicate that British consumers generally do not accept mobile advertising. Although mobile adverts are seen as interesting, eye catching, and motivating consumers to browse. Consumers who accept the technology do not see the need to have adverts on their mobiles. Those who dislike this medium are comfortable with using the Internet through their PCs as they do not see the benefits of mobile advertising, due to its small screen and speed limitation. Managerial considerations are also discussed.

INTRODUCTION

Rapid development of technology has brought the possibility of mobile phone to be used as an advertising device. Almost half of the population in every country in the developed world possesses mobile phones (Bigelow, 2002). The number of customers using mobile phones is higher than internet users, which is estimated at 465 million people and 365 million people respectively worldwide (Yunos *et al.,* 2003). This means that mobile ads can cover more consumers than the internet.

The advance of technology has converged so that the internet can be accessed by mobile telephony. This technology has been very successful in Japan. In 1999, it witnessed the launch of a product called 'I-mode' from the largest mobile operator, NTT DoCoMo. I-mode offers a broad range of internet services, including email, transaction services such as ticket reservation, banking and shopping, as well as infotainment and directory services. In January 2004, there were 44.7 million 'I-mode' subscribers (Okazaki, 2004).

From a marketing point of view, this medium brings several advantages. Firstly, advertising messages can be delivered anytime and customers will always get the messages. Secondly, because of its mobility and time sensitivity adverts on location-based can be broadcasted, such as where the nearest restaurant is to their targeted customers. In addition, interactivity and advanced personalisation provides an opportunity to target and customise messages to individual customer with a high level of confidence that they will reach their intended audience. But the most important benefit is its ability to accurately hit the targeted customers. However, a major weakness is the limited screen size when compared to PCs it has limited space available to display a message and hence, the advert (Yunos *et al.*, 2003, Hardaker and Graham 2001). Transmission speed is another issue which reduces advertising impact. Users might cancel, delete, or ignore a wireless access

page that loads ads too slowly (Yunos *et al.,* 2003). Several technologies such as 2.5G and 3G have addressed this issue (Browless, 2001). Nevertheless, following the success of wireless advertising in Japan, global wireless advertising revenue is predicted to grow from $750 million in 2001 to $16.4 billion by 2005. Europe, the Asia-Pacific and North America are expected to be the core markets, with wireless advertising revenue of $5.98 billion, $4.71 billion and $4.56 billion respectively in 2005 (Barnes, 2002). However, without the consumer acceptance of the medium, its success may not be predetermined. To-date, little research has been conducted on consumers' attitudes and acceptance of wireless advertising especially, in the UK. This study explores consumers' attitudes in relation to mobile advertising.

A review of literature is presented on attitudes towards advertising, web advertising followed by a description of the methodology, results, discussion and recommendation.

ATTITUDES TOWARDS ADVERTISING AND WEB ADVERTISING

Early research on attitudes towards advertising indicates that consumer beliefs play an important role in their attitudes towards advertising (e.g. Bauer and Greyser, 1968; Pollay and Mittal, 1993; Ducoffe, 1995). MacKenzie and Lutz (1989) have developed a five construct model of beliefs for attitude. However, Tramifow and Fisbein (1994, 1995) argue, that consumers' attitudes towards advertising are not only influenced by their beliefs but also, their emotion/feeling or affective which, will influence their behaviour.

Lund *et al.* (2002) using Pollay and Mittal's (1993) belief's construct as a component to explain attitude but also found education, age and income to have an influence on behaviour. Their findings indicate the belief factors—product information, hedonic pleasure, and social role and image—relate positively to subjects' attitudes towards web advertising. While web users' beliefs about materialism, non-sense and value corruption relate negatively to their attitudes towards web advertising. Another factor affecting the effectiveness of web advertising is, the higher the respondents' income and education the more negative their reported behaviour towards web advertising.

Haghirian *et al.*, (2005)'s unpublished work focuses on Austrian consumers' attitudes toward SMS advertising via mobile devices. Their study employs Ducoffe (1996)'s belief factors to analyse attitude. The results show that advertising value and advertising message content have the largest impact on attitude towards advertising via mobile devices.

Okazaki (2004) studies consumers' perception of wireless advertising in Japan and examines the formation of Japanese mobile users' attitudes to pull-type wireless advertising and their willingness to 'click' such ads. He suggests consumers' willingness to access depends on their attitude towards the ads, content credibility and external search. Attitude towards ads is conceptualised as a consequence of two psychological motives in wireless internet adoption: perceived infotainment and perceived irritation. The external search depends on gender, age and monthly allowance. The sample was divided into three groups, i.e. e-newsletter subscribers, email users and voice users, according to their demographic data. The findings expose that e-newsletter subscribers show the most positive perceptions on all the constructs.

The principal characteristics of e-newsletter subscribers indicate that unmarried young females living with their parents and high disposable income may be playing an important role in wireless internet adoption in Japan.

In the West, the research mainly focuses on the nature and implications, challenge and opportunities of wireless advertising (Barnes, 2002; Yunos *et al*, 2003). Up until now, there have been no published researches on attitude towards wireless advertising in the UK. Although the wireless technology already exists in the UK, the number of users has not yet as widespread in Europe. From the marketer point of view, it is only a matter of time before wireless advertising becomes an effective tool in their arsenal. It is important therefore, to investigate from the consumer perspective, belief, attitude, intention behaviour and acceptance of this medium, which will ultimately determine the success or failure of this medium.

ATTITUDES TOWARDS WIRELESS ADVERTISING

Pollay and Mittal (1993) formulated seven beliefs that drive attitudes. These seven factors represent three personal uses of advertising: 1. product information refers to quality, accuracy, timeliness and usefulness for the consumer. 2. Hedonic/pleasure refers, to entertaining features. 3. Social role and image. Wireless advertising, like other forms of media advertising, promotes social and lifestyle messages through associated status, portrayal of ideal users, social reaction to purchase and brand image. The issue here would be the type of wireless advertising that will give the marketers the information about consumers' lifestyle in addition, to four social effects of advertising: good for the economy, materialism (e.g. browsing the wireless advertising can induce impulse purchase), falsity/non-sense (refers to credibility of this medium) and value corruption.

The Ducoffe (1995) model has three perceptual antecedents, namely: entertainment, informativeness and irritation which refers to consumers feeling irritated or distracted, or maybe even overwhelmed when the wireless advertising provides an array of confusing information and they will react negatively (Stewart and Pavlou, 2002). Another possible annoyance would be unwanted messages, commonly known as spam (Dickinger *et al.,* 2004). Spam intrudes into consumers' privacy and stifle consumers' acceptance. These categories are employed by Brackett and Carr (2001) in cyberspace advertising and also, in mobile advertising by Haghirian *et al.,* (2005).

This study uses Pollay and Mittal's (1993) seven–factor and Ducoffe (1995) model, as it is not possible to analyse some factors from Pollay and Mittal, like the value corruption and good for economy, because it is only a predictive tool for the future and therefore, more difficult to collect the data from focus groups.

The affective component of attitude is about the feelings and the factors analysed in relation to consumer acceptance of wireless internet itself as a medium and wireless advertising. The behavioural component is not only a part of consumers' acceptance of wireless internet but also, their acceptance of wireless advertising itself.

The cognitiye, affective and behavioural components of attitude tend to be consistent (Hawkins, 2001). However, the degree of apparent consistency between measures of cognition and affect, and observations of behaviour may be reduced by a favourable attitude. This requires a need or motive before it can be translated into action (Hawkins, 2001). Howcroft *et al.,* (2002) mention that one of the important factors in encouraging the use of online Banking is to charge lower fees. Lower fee is also an important aspect in this case.

To predict possible future behaviour, some research has examined past behaviour. Recent research (e.g., Orbell *et al,* 1997) has reintroduced the construct of past behavior as a determinant of future behavior. For example, Albarracin and Wyer (2000) found that past behaviour directly influences future behaviour, but it is independent of outcome-specific cognition. Karjaluoto *et al.* (2002) show that prior experience with computers and technologies, as well as attitude towards computers, influence both attitude towards online banking and actual behaviour. Lee and Lee (1995) examine current consumers' behaviour towards television to predict the possibility of future in-

teractive television. Therefore, in this study our assumption is that the current behaviour towards the internet on PC will affect the behaviour towards mobile internet. The future attitude towards wireless, with reference to mobile advertising will be reflected from the current attitude towards mobile advertising.

METHODOLOGY

This study uses a qualitative approach to explore consumers' attitude towards mobile advertising. Qualitative research is best used in the context of new product development (Gordon and Langmaid, 1988). As the data gathered through this method help understand the strengths and weaknesses of a new product in order to guide product improvement.

Focus groups were used as a means of data collection, since the data collected from a focus group interview is often richer and fuller than the data available gathered from an individual interview (Lederman, 1990). Furthermore, focus group interviews are compatible with the key assumptions of the qualitative paradigm (Morgan, 1988). Also, in this study, the intent of focus groups is not to elicit principles or interests that will be extended to a wider populations, instead, the purpose is to conduct an interactive discussion that will elicit a greater, more in-depth understanding of perceptions, beliefs, attitudes and experiences of mobile advertising. Participants of the focus groups were young adults, below 30 years old. Since it has been found that, young people are heavy users of mobile services (Dickinger *et al.,* 2004). They use new technology and are quick to adopting new innovations (Okazaki, 2004).

Focus groups usually consist of six to ten members (Morgan, 1998). In this study, each group had 8 people, with the projection that some of them might not turn up. There were three groups in total this number is considered acceptable (Bryman and Bell, 2003).

The venue for the focus group was University of Sheffield, where the authors were based on the 12th, 17th and 18th of August 2005 at 2 pm. The invitation targeting younger people was previously posted at random to households registered on Sheffield town's electoral list.

Before the focus groups started, all participants were provided with a brief description of the research at the beginning of the discussion along with some points of what we were going to discuss in the focus group. The word "wireless internet" had been defined as access to the internet through mobile phones, so participants could clearly understand the topic and scope of discussion. They were asked to try the mobile internet so they can have a hand-on experience. Two mobile web page advertising were shown to them. Mobile phones, Nokia 6600 and Sony Ericsson p800 were used in the sessions. The discussion was recorded by audio and videotaped.

The moderator was guided by a number of research questions and some probing points. The discussion uncovered unexpected yet, relevant issues and concerns. The set of questions were asked in many different ways.

Transcripts and indexing of the recording of the conversations was made and to allow analysis to be carried out at a later date. However, the process was quite complex and there was no such thing as a perfect transcript of a tape recording as also, confirmed by the literature (e.g. Silverman, 1993).

A major challenge was data analysis applied to this method of research, as there are problems surrounding issues of 'interpretation'. Bristol and Fern (1996) explain that researchers have to adopt a variety of methods in order to make sense of the data generated. The aim of focus groups is to allow for the convergence of lives and experiences. Grounded theory was used as a strategy for the research. One of the outcomes of grounded theory is that, it represents real world phenomena which, is not based on previous researches (Bryman and

Bell, 2003). As it can also be seen that mobile advertising is a new research topic and to date, there is very little research in this area.

RESULTS AND DISCUSSION

Consumer Attitude to Mobile Internet

Before examining consumers' attitude and acceptance of mobile advertising, their attitude and acceptance of mobile internet must be established. If consumers do not want to use the medium, then that medium will not be effective for advertising. Focus group participants' reaction towards the medium itself can be divided into two groups: those who accept and those who reject this medium. Those who accept this medium mention some advantages of having mobile internet. Their answers are grouped according to the following topics.

Ubiquity of Devices

'.....like its really handy ...... to use ...' (Man, age 22).

'If you are out somewhere ....and cannot use the internet on the PC, then it's quite good if you just need to know something.........information or news or something like that...' (Woman, age 19).

This confirms the literature that by using this device people can connect to the internet anytime and every where (Browless, 2001).

Convenience is another factor for the consumer.

'... most people are looking for convenience, so I think that in a few years time, we can do everything on our mobile, just like you do on your computer' (Woman, age 28).

'If you've got something there in front of you, that you can check your email on why would you then, wait 10 minutes till you got home to do it' (Man, age 29).

'You would just do it there and look it up, very convenient.' (Woman, age 20).

Location Information

Having a mobile phone will give consumers location information.

'.....If I can switch that phone like you say and, press the button to tell me where I am and tell me where the nearest cash machine is very easily...' (Woman, age 27).

This result is consistent with previous research on internet medium e.g. Browless (2001), Chaffey (2003) and Yunos *et al*, (2003).

However, the limitation of a mobile phone has made consumers resist this technology as demonstrated, in the following comments from participants.

Smaller Screen

Majority of participants said they get annoyed because of the smaller screen.

'...... a computer has a nice keyboard, mouse and all that, it just seems awkward to see something so small. It would be nicer if it was big....' (Woman, age 25).

'...........I just found it painfully slow to access, to locate anything also the images are quiet small. I just found it's very painful at that time......' (Man, age 19).

This result is consistent with Yunos (2003), Hardaker *et al.*, (2001).

Transmission Speed

They also feel that '....... I prefer to use the computer, because the broadband speed is faster....' (Woman, age 22).

This confirms with Yunos, *et al.* (2003), that transmission speed affects users' acceptance of wireless ads.

Factors Influencing Consumer Adoption of Mobile Internet

Easy to Use

'.... but for me to want to use the mobile internet I need services that are useful and easy to use....' (Man, age 28).

'It has to be a good design, easy to use interface, easy to close things that you don't want to see and if that is true I am more likely to use it...' (Woman, age 27).

Reliability

It is important for customers to know that they can use this product every where.

'.....I think if it's for me it depends on ....The availability of the internet everywhere? Could I use that on the train to London, all the way through? Those kind of things or if it's going to be that reliable' (Man, age 22).

One of the success iMode in Japan was due to trust, perceived value of investment and the leveraging of technological infrastructure such networks and handsets (Barnes, 2002).

Product Experience

With any new product introduction, consumers' past experience will influence adoption.

'.....The thing is that we all feel that internet at home is easy to use, but it's just because we..., I think it's partially because we already invested a lot of time learning how to use the internet and computer, so we are comparing something that we have a lot of experience to something with no experience. Maybe if we play around with that phone for a day maybe tomorrow we will be saying hmm.... It's actually quite good......' (Man, age 29).

According to Barnes (2002), by offering low cost per message of an iMode telephone friends can also easily share their devices for trialling.

Consumer Attitude to Mobile Advertising—Consumer Belief, Feelings (Affect) and Intentional Behaviour to Mobile Advertising

Consumer Belief of Mobile Advertising

Product Information

In general, focus group participants agreed that mobile advertising gives certain information about the product.

'. ... Information about something, probably gives you one side .... to get certain aspect' (Woman, age 20).

'...they have a focus they want to inform me about this' (Man, age 22).

However some information in advertising is not considered relevant.

'...it is not considered as useful information' (Man, age 26).

One of the ways to make the information in advertising valuable for consumers is that the content of mobile advertising be tailored to their interest (Robins, 2003; Haghirian and Inoue, 2007). This issue was raised in the focus groups, some of the focus group participants said, that:

'I think we must be slightly interested in looking for adverts from the start' (Woman, age 19).

'I do, I do ignore most of the ads but, but, there are like particular things that I am interested then I use the internet to find out about and hmmm..... like hardware or something for computer and when I come to specific pages I'm more likely to see the adverts that interest in me' (Man, age 26).

When the medium can give location information as above mentioned, this kind of information will bring greater value for the consumer.

'.....if I can ... ... press the button and tell me where am I and tell me where the nearest cash machine is very easily..... I think that is a good service' (Woman, age 24).

This result confirms Stewart and Pavlou (2002) research which suggests the importance of interactive media, like the internet as an information broker that allows customers to acquire real-time account information that was previously not available. This also confirms the studies by Brackett and Carr (2001) and Ducoffe (1996) that informativeness is positively associated with advertising value, when addressing consumers via mobile devices.

Hedonic/Pleasure

The question put to participants was: by comparing these two websites (ignoring one Yahoo and other Orange) just imagine that both of them is orange, one with ads and the other without ads on the webpage, which one would you prefer?

Majority of the participants said, they preferred Orange ads.

'*....it makes me wants to browse as well....*'(Man, age 25).

This result confirms Raman and Leckby (1998)'s study which suggests interesting ads will bring positive experience and increase browsing.

Participants were also asked which kind of web advertising they prefer to click. Some said they would enjoy seeing something funny and cleverly done.

'*... I pay attention to advertising campaigns that's quite cleverly done, like if it's a funny advert*' (Man, age 22).

This confirms the research from Katterbach (2002) that entertainment is also a crucial factor for wireless marketing. This also confirms the studies by Brackett and Carr (2001) and Ducoffe (1996) that entertainment is positively associated with advertising value when addressing consumers via mobile devices.

Social Role and Image

When participants were asked about whether web advertisement would give them information about lifestyle. Their response was:

'*as long as it's your niche market, if it hits your demographic and it's really punched something, or your way of life that you are interested, I will click on it*' (Woman, age 24).

'*I thought if it was a subject that I had particular interest in like, designer clothes, if I saw a website advertising say cheap designer clothes or something like that…I am going to have a look, to see if there is anything that might be of interest*' (Man, age 23).

But when participants were asked the same question for mobile advertising, although they may

still have the same belief to that of web advertising, their response concerning mobile advertising was different. Some participants did not have a problem with the medium but, the medium did not appeal to them.

Materialism

When participants were asked whether web advertisement can induce impulse buying, their response was positive. A number of participants had the experience of impulse buying, many to do with cheap flights advertised on the web. This demonstrates that when advertisements hit the right target they raise consumer interest. The smaller screen of mobiles however has brought a negative reaction for many participants. The smaller screens reduce the ads appeal.

Falsity/Non-Sense

Participants were asked whether they trust the information advertised on the web.

Many did not trust the information from web adverts.

'*... I think people are quite knowledgeable now about adverts or things like that, that they are now not very credible or trustable...*' (Woman, age 23).

Most of them had bad experiences from web advertising, as illustrated by the following:

'*..... when you see term and condition with that, so you think well, I probably have to spend quiet a lot of money on their website...*' (Woman, age 20).

'*Some advertising will spread virus rather than information....*' (Man, age 22).

They are afraid that product quality is very low and/or buy the wrong thing.

'... Find with the fact that what you see on the computer screen you don't really trust very much about what they looking at, because you don't know what that could be, or that you come up in the wrong place, So advertising like that is not good because you can't trust it' (Man, age 19).

They fear that after seeing the advert they go to the website and could not find the information that they need.

'... Click once, click it, but it still doesn't give us the information we want' (Woman, age 22).

However some participants said they would trust web adverts if it came from a reputable company.

'....Offering from a firm whose reputation I know of, it's not a major firm but book store as we know like Amazon and internet company that has a reputation... I am very dubious to buy from unknown sites that I have never heard.....' (Woman, age 25).

'It depends on what kinds of ads like an MSN or something around that, I wouldn't trust them, but if I was on web pages that I look for and there are web ads, I do look at it, for example in climbing web pages and usually they have ads , that I want like travelling, then I may be trust it' (Man, age 26)

'....I think what is useful is when you search from Google, hmm.... Company who pays a lot of money to become the first result for five first results I think that is very useful because if you were searching for used cars or something and the company who comes on the very first time is going be very useful....' (Woman, age 19).

This is consistent with the literature (e.g. Goldsmith *et al.*, 2000) it seems the company's

credibility and the bearer of the message is important factors to build credibility in consumer perception of the medium.

They usually double check the information they got from web advertising

'... Normally, I would, if I saw ads or something and I thought that looks interesting, I would then try to find out about it. I wouldn't take, what I saw, I couldn't do that without research. If it looks interesting, then I would do some research on the internet and find out what it is....' (Man, age 22).

Some participants trust wireless advertising even less.

'...I think I probably trust less perhaps than web ads, but I would imagine, if probably the ads will be from a similar company, I don't think I would trust them.....' (Man, age 27).

This confirms that credibility is important for advertising value. Building this trust is not easy, it is a complex process that involves technology and business practices but, it is crucial for growth and success of mobile commerce (Siau and Shen, 2003). Since communication with consumers via their mobile devices is a very young phenomenon and has a background of consumers already sceptic to any kinds of advertising through the internet. This will have an impact on their beliefs towards advertising in any internet medium.

Irritation

For many participants, they receive a huge number of adverts on the web which is often of no interest to them or of informational value.

'...Because there are so many adverts on the internet popping up so you just get numb to them...' (Man, age 21).

'... I mainly ignore most of the ads and get annoyed with that....' (Woman, age 25).

Participants prefer not to have advertising on their mobile site because of the small screen and they think that they had enough advertising from other sources. In addition, they said that the advertising can slow the speed of download.

'... but because it's all photo and stuff, I think that it might be getting slower because a lot of hassle....' (Man, age 27).

'The adverts on the smaller screen will make you have to scroll down for the information that actually you looking for on the website' (Woman, age 25).

'...Because when you listen to the adverts page on your phone, then you have a bit of information that you actually ask for ..... but could bump down with information that you are asking, you have to keep scrolling down...then it is annoying.' (Woman, age 22).

Consumer Feelings (Affect) Towards Mobile Advertising

Consumers' feelings towards mobile advertising can be divided into two groups: those who like it and those who do not like it. For the former they prefer mobile adverts to web page adverts because these are more interesting, eye catching and motivate them to browse.

'...I prefer Orange because it's just eye catching and you see something visual...' (Woman, age 19). Another says *'......I think it makes me want to browse....'* (Woman, age 25).

'.... I quite like the character on the screen and stuff...' (Man, age 29).

However, for many participants, there are numerous reasons as to why they reject mobile advertising:

Screen Size

Some participants are not used to the size of the screen, since they always compare with internet in PC's which has wider screen and they think that the ads on a mobile page is not appealing. The smaller screen also makes them feel uncomfortable to see all the menus.

'....You see, If I would accidentally come across something that I was not looking for whilst sitting on the train, and I saw the advertisement, I would probably like to get more information and examine it further I probably will look into pc's, you know what I mean. I just think it's the experience to look at them on the page on the mobile phone. I don't find it appealing at all.' (Woman, age 23).

Also they think that without the advertisement on the webpage of the mobile, the web page itself looks more structure, classic and emptier. It is easy to read the menu on the webpage.

'I am quite keen to look at ads in normal websites on the bigger screen but on the little screen I am not actually interested to click on the ads,' (Man, age 20).

'...Yahoo : It looks emptier and it has more on it, Orange : That has just got a lot of graphic, but not much information on it, which is not easier to find out where you want to go...' (Woman, age 25)

'.........It makes sense really, because .... I found the scrolling a bit uncomfortable, so I prefer not to have ads at all.....' (Woman, age 19).

This confirms the research from Bruner and

Kumar (2000) that website complexity influences consumer attitudes, where complexity has a negative impact and interestingness has a positive impact on attitudes towards websites. In addition to this observation, simpler website backgrounds have a significantly more positive impact on consumer attitudes towards the ad, brand, website and purchase intention (Stevenson *et al.*, 2000).

Speed

Participants think that by having ads on their mobile will slow down the speed to down load therefore, they prefer not to have the ads.

'.... *but because it's all photos and stuff, I think that it might be getting slower, it's a lot of hassle....'* (Man, age 26).

Necessity

Most of the focus groups' participants think that it is unnecessary to have adverts on their mobile page, since they think that they only use mobile internet in emergency situation—for example checking emergency email, therefore they think that they do not have much interaction with the advert and they will ignore it.

Consumer Intentional Behaviour (Behavioural) to Mobile Advertising

Participants have positive and negative intentional behaviour. The positive intentional behaviour is towards the mobile internet itself,

'If I had it on my phone, I definitely would use it .....' (Man, age 21).

The positive intentional behaviour towards mobile ads is that they will click the ads.

'.... *if you look at the ads on the mobile internet, by following the link, you normally can find more about it, so in these cases I would say yes. In a few years time this is just going to be like the internet on the computer....'* (Man, age 29).

On the negative intentional behaviour they resist using internet on the mobile and also, avoid clicking on mobile ads.

Relationship between Consumer Belief, Feelings and Intentional Behaviour to Mobile Advertising

In terms of intentional behaviour, the result can be divided into three categories. First, the audience has positive beliefs and feelings, and their intentional behaviour is also positive. Second, the audience has positive beliefs and behaviour but their intentional behaviour is negative. The third group is people who are sceptical about the medium.

The reasons behind the inconsistency between beliefs, feeling and intention behaviour towards mobile advertising is cost consideration. They fear that if they click the adverts they have to pay whether the advert is valuable to them or not.

In relation to mobile advertising as a medium, there is also inconsistency even though they like the product but, they are less likely to subscribe to this service, due to perceived lack of necessity or personal benefit.

'I wouldn't pay 4 pounds for a month, if it's free then I would use it, but 4 pounds a month I can spend on something else' (Woman, age 22).

Past Behaviour

This research has shown that future consumer behaviour towards mobile advertising will be reflected from the current attitude towards internet advertising. When participants were asked what they think and feel towards mobile advertising and internet advertising, two different answers were obtained.

Some participants felt little difference between the two the only difference is the medium.

'..... I think, if it's done and you can standardize the internet on your phone, than you probably will treat both of them a like.....' (Woman, age 26).

'...... Yes, you just approach it in the same way, you may be able to get a pop up on your mobile or something you know you will treat it the same way that you do on the internet. If you click something you also will click that on the mobile....' (Man, age 20).

'..... Yes, it is the same thing with the smaller format....' '....I kind of imagines me doing what I am doing in my home computers browsing pages.....' (Woman, age 24).

On the other hand there are some consumers who still prefer to see ads through PC's.

'...I still can not imagine sending long email by text; I think it is quicker by using the computer in the library. I think it will take a long time to do that....' (Woman, age 26).

CONCLUSION AND RECOMMENDATIONS

The focus of this study was to explore British consumers' attitude towards mobile advertising and their acceptance of mobile internet, as a new advertising medium. Results showed that British consumers do not accept mobile internet as an advertising medium although mobile adverts are seen as interesting, eye catching and, motivating consumers to browse as well as convenient. The

benefits of such a medium are discarded. Consumers who accept mobile internet do not see the need to have adverts on their mobiles and, those who dislike this are comfortable with using the internet through their PCs. They also do not see the benefits of mobile advertising, due to its small screen and speed limitation.

Consumer beliefs towards mobile advertising are highly impacted from their beliefs towards internet advertising. Most of them feel irritated with internet advertising, but when it comes to the specific web page that they are interested in, they agree that the advertisements give them additional value of information, lifestyle and materialism. However some of them believed that internet advertising is less credible compare to any other media. Consumer beliefs towards internet advertising are similar to their beliefs towards mobile advertising. However, their feeling is mainly affected by the small screen and slow speed. The intentional behaviour is reflected by their beliefs and feelings. However, other consideration raises, due to cost and the credibility of the adverts results in inconsistency between intention behaviour and, the feelings and beliefs of the consumers.

It is recommended that for those consumers who do not see mobile internet as a necessity, creating consumer needs should be companies' priority as well as advertising mobile phones as part of consumers' life style. For those consumers who dislike this technology, changing attitudes could be done by educating and informing them of the advantages of having mobile internet such as, convenient to use when travelling. Lowering service cost may also lead to consumer adoption of the service and consumer trial can be increased, through social networks that can lead to increase in number of users (Barnes, 2002). Other strategies involve providing information that is valuable to consumers and tailored to their needs as well as, using creative eye catching adverts (Haghirian and Inoue, 2007) and building trust towards mobile advertising. As Mobile phone is considered as a personal belonging, companies need to be able to deliver advertisements that match the individual's interest. Also, messages need to be developed carefully otherwise, they will not create interest in themselves or in the product. As bandwidth increases, advertisers will have to be innovative in their campaigns to overcome the limitations of handsets with small screens" (DeZoysa, 2002). Thus they have to employ eye catching adverts, as above mentioned. From the focus group discussion, internet advertising generally has lost its credibility, unless the advertisement comes from a well-known website or from a reputable company. Therefore, it is important to build mobile advertising credibility. However building trust is a complex process that involves technology and business practices but, it is crucial for growth and success of mobile commerce (Siau and Shen, 2003).

This study has two limitations: first, it does not differentiate the difference between two types of advertising: pull and push advertising. The current advertising are available in mobile advertising is pull advertising. The sample of mobile internet used in the focus groups was in 2G. Therefore, this may influence the perception of consumers towards mobile advertising itself. Also, one of the mobile phones that had been used for a sample is Sony Ericson p800 has a touch screen (similar like PDA) and has a wider screen, which might affect consumer perception of mobile internet.

Future research could be coupled with quantitative research as mobile internet adoption grows, to provide a generalisation of consumer perception and acceptance of mobile internet and mobile advertising across the population. As well as research on consumer perception of wireless advertising in comparison with advertising in traditional media and, which type of wireless advertising is most effective for wireless advertising.

REFERENCES

Albarracin, D., & Wyer, R. S., Jr. (2000). The cognitive impact of past behaviour: Influences on beliefs, attitudes, and future behavioural decisions. *Journal of Personality and Social Psychology 79*, 5-22.

Barnes S. J. (2002). Wireless digital advertising: nature and implications. *International Journal of Advertising, 21*(3), 399-419.

Bauer, R., & Greyser, S. (1968). *Advertising in America: The Consumer View*. Graduate School of Business Administration, Division of Research, Harvard University, Boston, MA.

Bigelow, L., (2002). A Brand in Your Hand. *Admap, 426*, 47-50.

Brackett, L. K., & Carr, B. N. (2001). Cyberspace Advertising vs. Other Media: Consumer vs. Mature Student Attitudes. *Journal of Advertising Research, 41*(5), 23-32.

Bristol, T., & Fern, E. F. (1996). Exploring the Atmosphere Created in Focus Group Interviews: Comparing Consumers' Feelings Across Qualitative Techniques. *Journal of the Market Research Society, 38*(2), 185-195.

Browless (2001). Wireless Internet Revolution: Anywhere, Anything, Anytime.—Hull: Butler Group.

Bruner II, G. C., & Kumar, A. (2000). Web Commercials and Advertising Hierarchy of Effects. *Journal of Advertising Research, 40*(1/2), 35-44.

Bryman, A., & Bell E. (2003). Business Research Methods. Oxford University Press, Oxford.

Chaffey, D. (2003). *E-Business and E-Commerce Management*. London: Prentice Hall.

Dickinger, A., Haghirian, P., Murphy, J., & Scharl, A.,(2004). An investigation and conceptual model of SMS marketing. *Proceedings of the 37th Hawaii International Conference on System Sciences,* Hawaii, January.

Ducoffe, R. H. (1996). Advertising Value and Advertising on the Web. *Journal of Advertising Research, 36*(September/October), 21-36.

Ducoffe, R. H. (1995). How Consumers Assess the Value of Advertising. *Journal of Current Issues and Research in Advertising, 17*(1), 1-18.

Goldsmith, R. E., Lafferty, B. A., & Newell, S. J. (2000). The impact of corporate credibility and celebrity credibility on consumer reaction to advertisements and brands. *Journal of Advertising, 29*(3), 43-54.

Gordon, W., & Langmaid, R. (1988). *Qualitative market research: a practitioner's and buyer's guide.* Gower, London.

Hardaker G., & Graham G. (2001). Wired marketing: energizing business for E-Commerce. London: Wiley.

Haghirian, Parissa, & Madlberger, M. (2005). *Consumer attitude toward advertising via mobile devices—an empirical investigation among Austrian users.* http://is.lse.ac.uk/asp/aspecis/20050038.pdf, 5th June 2005.

Haghirian, P., & Inoue, A. (2007). An advanced model of consumer attitudes toward advertising on the mobile internet. *International Journal Mobile Communications, 5*(1), 48-67.

Hawkins, D., Best, R. J., Coney, K. A. (2001). Consumer behavior: Building marketing strategy. 8th ed., Irwin McGraw-Hill, London.

Howcroft, B., Hamilton, R., & Hewer, P. (2002). Consumer attitude and the usage and the adoption of home-based banking in the United Kingdom. *International Journal of Marketing, 20*(3), 111-121.

Karjaluoto, H., Matilda, M., & Pento, T. (2002). Factors underlying attitude formation towards online banking in Finland. *International Journal of Bank Marketing, 20*(6), 261-272.

Lederman, L. C. (1990). Accessing Educational Effectiveness: The Focus Group interview as techniques for data collection. *Communication Education, 39*(2), 117-127.

Lee, B., & Lee, R. S (1995). How and Why People Watch TV: Implications for the Future of Interactive Television. *Journal of Advertising Research* (November/December), 9-18.

Lund, D., Wolin, L. D., Kargaonkar P. (2002). Beliefs, Attitudes and Behaviour Towards Web Advertising. *International Journal of Advertising, 21*(1).

MacKenzie, S. B., & Lutz, R. J. (1989). An empirical examination of the structural antecedents of attitude toward the ad in an advertising pretesting context. *Journal of Marketing Research, 23*(2), 48-65.

Morgan, D. (1988). Focus groups as qualitative Research. London: Sage.

Okazaki, S. (2004). How Do Japanese Consumers Perceive Wireless Ads? A Multivariate Analysis. *International Journal of Advertising, 23*(4), 429-454.

Orbell, S., Hodgkins, S., & Sheeran, P. (1997). Implementation intentions and the theory of planned behaviour. *Personality and Social Psychology Bulletin, 23*, 945-954.

Pollay, R. W., & Mittal, B. (1993). Here's the Beef: Factors, Determinants, and Segments in Consumer Criticism of Advertising. *Journal of Marketing, 57*(July), 99-114.

Raman, N. V., & Leckenby, J. D. (1998). Factors affecting consumers' "Webad" visits. *European Journal of Marketing, 32*(7/8), 737-748.

Robins, F. (2003). The Marketing of 3G. *Marketing Intelligence & Planning, 21*(6), 370-378.

Siau, K., & Z. Shen (2003). Building Customer Trust in Mobile Commerce. *Communications of the ACM, 46*(4), 91-94.

Silverman, D. (1993). Interpreting Qualitative Data: Methods for Analaysing Talk, Text and Interaction. London: Sage.

Stevenson, J. S., Bruner II, G. C., & Kumar, A. (2000). Web Page Background and Viewer Attitudes", *Journal of Advertising Research, 20*(1/2), 29-34.

Stewart, D. W., & Pavlou, P.A. (2002). From Consumer Response to Active Consumer: Measuring the Effectiveness of Interactive Media.

Journal of the Academy Marketing Science, 30(4), 376-396.

Trafimow, D., & Fishbein, M. (1994). The importance of risk in determining the extent to which attitudes affect intentions to wear seat belts. *Journal of Applied Social Psychology, 24*, 1-11.

Trafimow, D., Fishbein, M. (1995). Do people really distinguish between behavioural and normative beliefs? *British Journal of Social Psychology, 34*, 257-266.

Yunos, H. M., Gao, J. Z., Shim S. (2003). Wireless Advertising's Challenges and Opportunities. *IEEE Computer Society, 36*(5), 30-37.

Chapter X
Determinants of ERP Implementations:
An Empirical Study in Spanish Companies

Javier de Andrés
University of Oviedo, Spain

Pedro Lorca
University of Oviedo, Spain

Jose Emilio Labra
University of Oviedo, Spain

ABSTRACT

This chapter aims to determine the factors influencing the decision of implementing an ERP system in a country where technology awareness and the technological development are not as high as those of some others. Firstly, the authors assume that adopters make rational choices but the authors also introduce an alternative innovation model based on the imitation perspective. A questionnaire was sent to the Spanish listed companies and the ERP; adopting firms were compared with a matched control group. The main results indicate that the only factors stemming from the rational-choice perspective, whose influence is relevant, are firm size and the ROI ratio. Also, the authors found that the introduction of the euro and the Y2K issue had an influence in the ERP decision. The influence of the sectoral adscription was supported partially. These findings evidence a certain influence of the imitation effect. The results of this chapter could eventually be extrapolated to the countries whose national culture is similar to that of Spain.

INTRODUCTION

Advances in computer science and telecommunications have crystallized in a set of innovations in management that allow us to improve the communication of information as much inside companies as between the company and the external users. Among them there are the Enterprise Resource Planning (ERP) systems. ERP systems can be defined as customizable, standard application software which includes integrated business solutions to the core processes (e.g. production planning and control, warehouse management, etc.) and the main administrative functions (e.g. accounting, human resource management, etc.) in a company. ERP systems are comprised of a suite of software modules, with each module typically responsible for gathering and processing information for a separate business function. The basic features of these systems are modularity, complementarity and managerial capacity.

The diffusion of ERP systems has grown exponentially over the last few years. Since 1997, the world market for ERP systems has experienced high growth rates (Eckhouse, 1999). According to the European e-Business Report, companies using ERP systems in seven EU countries reached 28 percent in 2005 (European Commission, 2005). This rate is even higher for the companies of the pharmaceutical and automotive sectors. This expansion has also taken place on the Spanish market. By 2002, 70 percent of the biggest Spanish firms had implanted ERP systems (Grupo Penteo, 2003). What reasons underlie this ERP implantation in Spanish listed companies?

The innovation literature is dominated by an efficient choice model which is based on the assumption that users make rational choices guided by goals of technical efficiency (March, 1978; Grandori, 1987). Nevertheless, some researchers have presented forceful arguments for using multiple perspectives in innovation research. These provide better explanations of innovation than does the efficient choice model (Poole and Van de Ven, 1989; Abrahamson, 1991). They present alternative innovation models based on an institutional perspective of organizational theory.

This paper follows the organizational innovativeness (OI) research line and seeks to determine the factors that have influenced the decision of implanting an ERP system at individual level. These factors have not received much attention in prior research and, thus, have been investigated in only few studies (Brown et al. 2000; Ross and Vitale, 2000; Knapp and Shin, 2001). In addition, this research analyzes the diffusion process of the ERP systems in a country that is not highly developed technologically as some others. So, our results can be extrapolated to other similar economies, as the bulk of prior research has focused on ERP diffusion in the USA and other countries where technological awareness is higher than in Spain, especially among top management.

Hofstede (1983) identified four dimensions for the description of culture: power distance index, individualism index, uncertainty avoidance index and masculinity index. Later, a fifth dimension was added to this framework: long-term orientation, but it has not been very used in empirical research works. Two of these dimensions may have an influence on the reasons behind the implementation of an ERP system: power distance and uncertainty avoidance. Power distance is higher in Spain than in other European countries (Germany and UK) and the USA. This is an obstacle to open communication, true involvement-winning contexts and transparency of the "rules of the game". It also inhibits employee perception of positive and exemplary behaviour by management. Uncertainty avoidance is clearly higher in Spain than in other European countries (Germany and UK) and the USA. This indicates that Spanish companies tend to prevent creativity, proaction and innovative attitudes. Strong uncertainty avoidance hampers the emergence of new ideas and even more the implementation of innovations. The implementation of a new way of management might be seen as one of these new organisational innovations, and, therefore, will be more common in low uncertainty avoidance countries. In fact, Boldy et al. (1993) report that risk-taking was not in the top ten most desirable managerial attributes among Spaniards. To sum up, strong uncertainty avoidance at the societal level appears to penetrate organizations and managerial behaviour.

Hofstede (1983) asserts that high power distance and strong uncertainty avoidance produce centralized pyramidal organizational structures, where a powerful person will be sought to resolve uncertainties for the others who are risk-averse, and where there exist rules that the powerful can ignore. Although containing some hyperbole, the Hofstede inference roughly describes the reality of Spain which appears in the comparative literature.

Thus, the present study aims to determine, from a dynamic viewpoint, the factors that have influenced the decision to implement an ERP system in Spanish companies from the perspective of the characteristics of the adopters.

In pursuit of our goal, the next section explains the hypotheses regarding the reasons that influence the implementation of ERP systems. Section 3 describes the procedures for the selection of the sample, and the empirical methods used. The results are detailed in Section 4. Finally, section 5 contains the main conclusions of the paper.

HYPOTHESES DEVELOPMENT

Wolfe (1994) categorizes organizational innovation literature in three research approaches: i) diffusion of innovation (DOI) research (addresses the diffusion of an innovation over time and/or space); ii) organizational innovativeness (OI) research (addresses the determinants of the innovativeness of organizations); and, iii) process theory (PT) research (addresses the process of innovation within organizations). These approaches are not separately focused because while the key

aim of the DOI literature is to understand when and why innovations are adopted or rejected, OI contributes to identify characteristics of adopters, and PT research helps to discern the stages and processes involved in organizational innovation. This paper follows the OI research line, as we try to determine the factors that influence the decision of implementing an ERP system.

Regarding the selection of the possible explanatory variables, the adoption of a single perspective, whatever that might be, limits the scope of the researcher's inquiry and thus limits the extent to which he/she can capture the innovation process, which will be complex, nonlinear, tumultuous, and opportunistic (Poole and Van de Ven, 1989; Wolfe, 1994). In addition, as mentioned above, the special features of Spanish national culture make it unadvisable to include only the factors related with the costs and benefits of ERPs. So, apart from the efficient choice perspective we have considered the imitation perspective. The hypotheses stemming from both of these are developed in the following paragraphs.

Efficient Choice Perspective

In this approach the virtues of the innovation are the motive force behind adoption. Managers will adopt an innovation if they believe that it will, all things considered, enhance their utility. So, they must believe that the innovation may yield some relative advantage to the idea it supersedes.

Modern ERP packages permit wide variation in implementation both in terms of how systems from different vendors are mixed and how transaction processes are implemented. This is important for large global enterprises concerned with many geographically dispersed and unique markets. As an option for such firms, ERP software solutions can be "built" using multiple software systems and databases. These components may still originate from a single vendor, but often multiple software vendors are involved. ERP systems are designed to solve the problem of the fragmentation of information, particularly in large corporate organisations, and integrate all the information flows within a company (McAdam and Galloway, 2005). Problems of coordination and control are exacerbated when organizations are formally divided into large numbers of functional units. A multi-system or multi-structure solution may give a firm the opportunity to purchase "best in class" versions of each operating module (Bendoly and Jacobs, 2004). Therefore, ERP systems are extremely useful in the integration of global companies. As a proxy of the internationalization of a company we chose the amount of its exports[a]. So, we postulate,

H_1: Exporting firms are more likely to implement an ERP system

For the test of this hypothesis, we define the variable EXPORT, which is the quotient between the overseas sales and the total sales of the firm.

Another question to consider is that ERP implementations demand a huge amount of financial resources and only the largest firms possess such sources of funds. Also, large firms have a greater need for innovation technologies than small ones because their control and monitoring costs are higher (Mitra and Chaya, 1996). The meta-analytic review carried out by Damanpour (1992) suggested a positive association between organizational size and innovation. In addition, size has been found to be directly related to complexity (Marsh and Mannari, 1989), and complex organizations are more innovative because they have a greater variety of specialists and more differentiated units (Damanpour, 1992)[b]. In DOI studies, the size of a firm has been used as a proxy for organizational complexity, stack resources, specialization, and scale (Tornatzky et al. 1983). Therefore, the following hypothesis is formulated:

H_2: Bigger firms are more prone to implement an ERP system

Several measures are possible for firm size, such as total revenue or sales, number of employees, or total assets (Damanpour, 1992). In the remainder of this paper we report the results obtained using total assets as the proxy for firm size (in the same way as in Mabert et al., 2003a). So, we define the variable SIZE as the total assets of the firm, expressed in € millions. Tests conducted using the other two measures produced comparable levels of significance.

Furthermore, it must be considered that both an industry's competitive dynamics and how a firm competes in accordance with same, have a great influence on the firm's strategic decisions (Porter, 1987). Competitive pressure is one of the most cited reasons for implementing an ERP system (Deloitte Consulting, 1999; O'Leary, 2000), because the need to develop and sustain a competitive advantage in the marketplace is what drives successful business strategies. In fact, Mabert et al. (2003a) found that all the companies they analyzed had done some form of ROI or economic value added analysis to justify their ERP system. Thus:

H_3: Firms decide to implement an ERP system in response to a poor financial condition

As a proxy for financial health we used the ROI ratio. If H_3 holds, ROI should be significantly lower for the group of ERP adopting firms. Nevertheless, as was stated above, one of the reasons for hypothesizing that big firms are more likely to implement an ERP is their easier access to the financial resources needed for the implementation. As financially healthier companies possess bigger sources of funds, there are also theoretical reasons to presume that H_3 may not hold.

Another factor related to the efficient choice perspective is the efficiency in a firm's operations.

Research has found that technological investments are associated with a decrease in total costs (Alpar and Kim, 1990), and internal coordination costs (Shin, 1999). So, ERP adoption can be a solution for inefficient firms, as well as for financially unhealthy firms. Thus:

H₄: Inefficient firms are more likely to adopt an ERP system

As a proxy for the efficiency in a firm's operations we computed the EFFIC variable, which we define as the quotient between operational costs and net sales. However, in respect of profitability, a high level of efficiency could mean a greater availability of resources, which would therefore favour the adoption of expensive innovations such as ERPs. So, there are also theoretical reasons to presume that H_4 may not hold.

Finally, it is noticeable that ERP has also been found effective in reducing inventory costs (Appleton, 1997; Brakely, 1999). In fact, one of the benefits which is more often mentioned by the companies who decided to adopt this innovation is inventory reduction (Deloitte Consulting, 1999; Grupo Penteo, 2003). So, companies in which the inventory is an important part of their assets should have an extra motivation to implement an ERP system. Hence:

H₅: Firms having large inventories are more likely to implement an ERP system

As a proxy for the importance of the inventory we defined the variable INVENTORY, which is the quotient between the inventory and the total assets.

Imitation Perspective

Abrahamson (1991) recognizes influences on organizations in a group exerted by organizations outside the group. This is due, for example, to the discourse associated with fashions. This discourse promises performance enhancement, or the threat of bankruptcy in the case of non-adoption. It also emphasizes well known uses and features successful users of the concept in question. It stresses the concept's universal applicability and presents it as timely, innovative, and future-oriented, and also as an easily understandable commodity with a catchy title (Benders and Van Veen, 2001).

The imitation perspective assumes conditions of uncertainty among organizations in a group. In times of high uncertainty organizations may seek change and are more likely to imitate other organizations (DiMaggio and Powell, 1983). Adopting actions similar to those taken by other organizations affords management a measure of credibility, especially if the actions provide some publicity (Kimberly, 1981). As O'Neill et al. (1998) point out, firms may adopt inefficient innovations based on their fear that other firms will use them successfully; also, firms may conclude that the cost of adopting an inefficient innovation is less than the cost of not adopting it.

As we have shown, ERP systems should contribute to enhance firm performance through efficiency and effectiveness gains. However, the implementation of ERP systems is not exempt from adverse consequences. Since people are on average risk-averse, the uncertainty will often result in a postponement of the decision until further evidence can be gathered (Rogers, 1962). When a company implements an ERP system, other competitors try to eliminate its advantage as soon as possible (Poston and Grabski, 2001). Repeated successes among organizations adopting a change prompt other organizations to consider the same change, especially in competitive environments (Kimberly and Evanisko, 1981). At the beginning, few companies will implement ERP, but later on more companies will do so. So the adopter distribution will follow over time a bell-shaped curve, the derivative of the S-shaped diffusion curve, and approach normality. Therefore, the following hypothesis is formulated:

H_{6a}: *The number of ERP adopters in each year can be fitted to a normal distribution*

Furthermore, it should be taken into account that for many companies, the implementation of an ERP system was a technological tool to solve the Y2K issue (Deloitte Consulting, 1999; Ross and Vitale, 2000; Davenport et al., 2002). The Y2K problem forced many companies to carry out deep changes in their computer systems. The same can be said of the introduction of the euro, in a transitional period from January 1, 1999 to December 31, 2001. So, these events also demanded a renovation of the company's information systems. For these reasons, we will postulate:

H_{6b}: *Year 2K effect and the introduction of the euro favoured the adoption of ERP systems*

For the contrast of H_{6b}, we considered the year the ERP was implemented. If this hypothesis holds, then the majority of the implementations would have been completed before 2000.

Furthermore, as was stated in the previous section, it can be argued that most firms adopt an ERP system in order to imitate other companies from their same environment. This was evidenced in the research by Granlund and Malmi (2000), who studied the ERP implementations in Finnish companies. Furthermore, O'Leary (2000) concluded that due to this imitation effect, ERP systems support mainly specific industries, for instance, oil, gas, banking, health care and chemical industries. Hence, we propose:

H_{7a}: *The ERP penetration rate depends on the sector of activity we consider*

To contrast this hypothesis, we studied the sectoral assignation of the ERP adopting and non-adopting firms. As in this study we analyzed a small sample, only two sectors were considered (services and manufacturing firms).

Finally, it can be supposed that the ERP fad was only occurred in the most recent years, as, earlier, only few firms were ERP adopters. So, we can hypothesize that early adopting firms took the ERP decision on the basis of their financial and operational features, while firms with a later adoption were more likely to be influenced by the fad. Then, we propose:

H_{7b}: *Firms with a later ERP adoption were more influenced by the fad than early adopters*

We tested this hypothesis by regressing the year of implementation on a series of financial indicators. The details are explained in the following sections.

SAMPLE SELECTION AND EMPIRICAL METHODS

Sample Selection

To carry out the research, a questionnaire was sent to the Spanish companies listed in the Continuous Market with the purpose of finding out which of them have an ERP system, who their supplier is and when they implemented it. Companies with a partial implementation were counted in the group of ERP adopters (in the same way as in Granlund and Malmi, 2002, and Hyvönen, 2003).

A total of 127 questionnaires were sent by mail during February, 2005. 42 usable answers were obtained, a 33.07% rate, which we can consider satisfactory (Hyvönen, 2003; Mabert et al., 2003b; Hawking et al., 2004). The average response time was one day, and in many cases the response was received on the same day the mail was sent. No statistically significant differences were noted between the time of response of adopting and non-adopting firms.

The analyzed sample, made up by the companies that answered the questionnaire, represents

Table 1. Distribution of the sample companies and the continuous market companies

SECTOR	Sample companies (%)	Continuous market companies (%)
1. Oil and energy	9.52	7.09
2. Basic materials, industry and construction	30.95	29.92
3. Consumer goods	21.43	25.20
4. Consumer services	21.43	17.32
5. Financial services and real estate*	9.52	14.17
6. Technology and telecommunications	7.18	6.30

* Only real estate

faithfully the continuous market companies, just as is shown in Table 1.

The companies that responded were compared with those that did not in variables such as total assets and net sales. No statistically significant differences among them at the 5% level[c] were found. So we can consider that this was a cross-section sample.

The results of the questionnaire reveal that by 2003, 66.6% of the companies in the sample possessed ERP systems. This rate is very near to the 70% that in 2003 Grupo Penteo (2003) quantified for the large Spanish firms.

According to Spanish legislation, listed companies are required to submit their annual accounts to the *Comisión Nacional del Mercado de Valores* (CNMV), the Spanish Securities Commission. This information is available on the CNMV web page (www.cnmv.es). We made up a database by extracting the information needed to test the hypotheses. For each variable, we considered the average of the two years prior to the fiscal year the implementation was in operation. In our opinion this procedure eliminates, at least partially, the undesirable distortions in the accounting figures caused by non-permanent changes in the environment of the firm.

Following the recommendation of Barber and Lyon (1996) for each company that implemented

an ERP system, a similar non-ERP firm in terms of sector and size was randomly selected in order to complete a matched pairs design[d]. For the sectoral assignation we used the CNMV sectoral breakdown, effective from January, 2005 (see www.cnmv.es)[e].

Empirical Methods

For the testing of hypotheses H_1 to H_5, first of all some descriptive information on the considered variables was calculated, for each one of the considered groups (ERP firms and non ERP firms). Then, we carried out some univariate tests in order to assess if the observed differences between the two groups are statistically significant for any of the variables used to test the hypotheses. Due to the low power of the small sample, we discarded the use of nonparametrical procedures such as the Wilcoxon signed-rank test. So, we carried out a paired samples t-test.

As a prior examination of the data revealed that the distribution of all the variables is skewed due to extreme values, we reduced the influence of these by restating outliers to the 5th and 95th percentiles. This procedure reduces the conservatism of the parametric t statistic and is recommended by, among others, Balakrishnan *et al.* (1996), Barber and Lyon (1996) and Hunton *et al.* (2003).

Furthermore, in order to achieve a better understanding of the relationship between the analyzed variables and the implementation of an ERP system, some multivariate models were applied. The aim was to detect combinations of values for certain variables that could increase (or decrease) the probability of a firm implementing an ERP system in the subsequent years.

Firstly, we applied an Artificial Intelligence algorithm for the induction of classification trees. From the different models, we chose See5 algorithm. This is the latest version of the different induction systems developed by Quinlan (1979, 1993, 2004, among others)[f]. Quinlan's algorithms are Artificial Intelligence standards. See5, as well as its previous versions (ID3 and c4.5 algorithms), has been widely used in the fields of accounting and finance, especially in research works related to the assessment of credit risk and those that study the choice of accounting methods (see, among others, Liang et al., 1992; McKee, 1995; Gorzalczany and Piasta, 1999).

See5 is a useful tool as it identifies groups of ERP and non-ERP firms that share common financial features. However, we must highlight that the classification tree provided is merely descriptive. The reason lies in the small size of the sample, which makes unfeasible the use of resampling strategies, such as bootstrapping. So, we completed the analysis with the application of an inferential model and we estimated a backwards stepwise logit regression model. The dependent variable of this model is a dummy variable which equals one in the case of a firm implementing an ERP system and zero otherwise. We used the variables previously considered in both the univariate analysis and See5 algorithm as the set of independent variables of the logit model. As for the univariate tests, the influence of outliers was reduced by restating extreme values to the 5th and 95th percentiles, respectively. The estimated model is:

$$B = \alpha + \sum_{i=1}^{n} \beta i * Y_i$$

Where Y_i are the independent variables and α and β_i are the parameters estimated by the model.

Then, the probability of a company implementing an ERP model being $= \frac{1}{1+e^{-B}}$

Regarding the hypotheses that stem from the imitation perspective, for the contrast of H_{6a} (the diffusion of the ERP model can be fitted using a normal distribution) we carried out a Shapiro-Wilk normality test (Shapiro and Wilk, 1965). This procedure is more adequate for a small sample, as is the case of the present research.

For Hypothesis H_{6b} we estimated a confidence interval for the mean of the variable that indicates the year of implementation. Our aim was to evidence that the majority of the implementations occurred in the years prior to 2000 and prior to the introduction of the euro.

For the contrast of Hypothesis H_{7a} (the penetration of ERP depends on the sector we consider), we constructed a crosstabulation, upon which we performed Cramer's Φ test.

For the test of H_{7b} (firms with a later adoption were influenced by the fad but firms with an early adoption took the ERP decision on the basis of their financial / operational features), we regressed the year of implementation on the indicators used for the test of the hypothesis, which stem from the efficient choice perspective (H_1 to H_5). If H_{7b} holds, then the coefficients of the estimated regression function should be statistically significant. Prior to the estimation of the model, and following the same procedure used in both the logistic regression and the univariate tests, we reduced the influence of outliers by restating extreme values to the 5th and 95th percentiles, respectively.

Table 2. Descriptive measures and results of the paired samples t-tests (hypothesis H₁ to H₅)

Variable	NON ERP FIRMS					ERP FIRMS					t (sig.)
	Mean	Std Dev	Q1	Q2	Q3	Mean	Std Dev	Q1	Q2	Q3	
EXPORTS	0.246	0.261	0.000	0.147	0.468	0.301	0.274	0.013	0.330	0.555	0.894 (0.381)
SIZE*	747.6	756.0	239.7	364.1	1020.1	1398.7	1544.6	93.1	782.6	2175.8	2.178 (0.040)
ROI	0.140	0.085	0.070	0.128	0.178	0.187	0.106	0.133	0.157	0.249	1.859 (0.076)
EFFIC	0.939	0.160	0.894	0.940	0.963	0.891	0.108	0.825	0.919	0.959	-1.162 (0.258)
INVEN-TORY	0.138	0.108	0.055	0.109	0.187	0.137	0.115	0.032	0.128	0.215	-0.025 (0.980)

* The test statistic does not change significantly when using the natural log of total assets instead of the total assets as proxy for firm size

RESULTS

Efficient Choice Perspective

Regarding the univariate approach, table 2 contains some descriptive measures (mean, standard deviation, and the 1st, 2nd and 3rd quartiles) for each of the defined groups (ERP and non-ERP firms) and the results of the paired samples t tests for the difference of means.

It is remarkable that the mean size of adopting firms is significantly higher than that of non-

adopting companies ($p < 0.05$). This lends support to hypothesis H_2. Another interesting finding is that ROI appears to be somewhat higher for ERP firms than for their non-ERP counterparts. This difference is only moderately significant ($0.05 < p < 0.10$). So, there is slight evidence that H_3 does not hold. These results suggest that the availability of financial resources, that is, those large and financially healthy firms, is the main reason for the implementation of an ERP.

For the variables used to test the other hypotheses (EXPORTS, STOCKS and EFFIC), the t-tests

Figure 1. Quinlan's See5 decision tree

```
SIZE > 1515.1:⇒ ERP (12 cases, 2 of them misclassified)
SIZE ≤ 1515.1
:...SIZE > 188.1: ⇒ Non-ERP (22 cases, 4 of them misclassified)
    SIZE ≤ 188.1
    :...EXPORTS ≤ 0.266 ⇒ Non-ERP (5 cases, 2 of them misclassified)
        EXPORTS > 0.266 ⇒ ERP (7 cases, 0 of them misclassified)
```

Table 3. Classification errors of Quinlan's See5 decision tree

Global percentage of correct classifications: 82.6%		Forecasted class		
		Non-ERP	ERP	Total
Actual class	Non-ERP	21 (91.31%)	2 (08.69%)	23 (100%)
	ERP	6 (26.09%)	17 (73.91%)	23 (100%)

reveal that there are no significant differences between adopting and non-adopting firms. So, the efficiency of the company, the inventory level and the importance of the exports do not seem to be factors that influence the decision of adopting an ERP model.

However, as certain combinations of two or more variables can be associated with a high probability of adopting an ERP system, this decision must also be modelled using multivariate techniques. First of all, and in order to explore the data, we inducted a decision tree using Quinlan's See5 algorithm. This tree is represented in figure 1, and table 3 contains a summary of its classification errors.

It is noticeable that the majority of the biggest firms (10 out of 12) implemented an ERP system. Among the companies of an intermediate size the prevailing decision was not to adopt this innovation. For the smallest firms of the sample, the decision depended on the percentage of the sales that are exports (EXPORT variable). All the small and exporting firms decided to adopt an ERP, while for small and non-exporting firms the evidence is mixed (2 adopting and 3 non-adopting).

These findings confirm the importance of company size in the decision of implementing an ERP, and suggest that the influence of this factor might be nonlinear. However, the other variable that was significant in the univariate tests (ROI) does not appear in the inducted classification tree. As the correlation between ROI and the other variables is not significant in any case (results not shown due to space limitations), this indicates that in a multivariate context the classification power of profitability could be low. The tree also

suggests that the interaction between SIZE and EXPORT might be an influential factor in respect of the ERP decision.

Once the data were explored through the induction of a classification tree, the final step of the multivariate analysis was the application of an inferential statistical technique. As mentioned earlier, we estimated a backwards stepwise logistic regression model where the dependent variable was a dummy which equals one in the case of a firm implementing an ERP system and zero otherwise. As the set of dependent variables we used the indicators previously considered in the univariate analysis and three interaction terms:

a. The interaction between the size and the percentage of the sales that are exports (SIZE×EXPORTS). The tree inducted in the exploratory stage of the analysis using See5 algorithm suggests that the combined effect of these two variables could be significant.

b. The interaction between size and profitability (SIZE×ROI) and the interaction between size and efficiency (SIZE×EFFIC). According to Hayes *et al.* (2001) and Hunton *et al.* (2003), expected performance gains due to ERP adoption for large and healthy firms are less than those for a relatively unhealthy counterpart, as the latter have greater potential for improvement. The same authors also state that small and unhealthy firms may not fully benefit from the implementation of the ERP systems as they may be forced to undertake partial implementations, due to financial constraints. On the other hand,

Table 4. Logistic regression study[1]

	First model	Last model
Intercept term	-4.09077	-1.50214**
EXPORTS	1.80345	-
SIZE	0.00550	0.00054*
ROI	5.02448	5.78952*
EFFIC	1.61580	-
INVENTORY	3.80421	-
EXPORTS×SIZE	-0.00128	-
ROI×SIZE	0.00095	-
EFFIC×SIZE	-0.00502	-
χ^2	10.490	6.660
p-value	0.232	0.036
Cox and Snell's R^2	0.204	0.135
Percentage of correct classifications	67.4	63.0

* Significant at the 0.10 level.
** Significant at the 0.05 level.
[1]Cook's D tests (Cook, 1977) revealed no influential observations in any of the models. The statistical significance of the coefficients and the overall inferences remain unchanged when replacing the total assets by their natural logs.

small and healthy firms can probably acquire resources for a full integration. So, the profitability and the efficiency of the firm could play a different role depending on firm size.

The results from this estimation process are shown on table 4. We have only included the first and the last models estimated in the backwards stepwise regression, as in all models but the last one, the χ^2 test did not have statistically significant results.

The results from the logit estimation are similar to those obtained in the univariate analysis. We identify the variables ROI and SIZE as the only ones that seem to affect the probability of a firm implementing an ERP system. The rest of the variables, that is, the percentage of the sales that are exports, the importance of the inventory, the efficiency, and all the interaction terms do not

seem to have a significant influence on the probability of the adoption of this innovation.

The coefficients obtained for ROI and SIZE are positive and moderately significant (0.05<p<0.10). This finding is quite similar to the results obtained in the univariate analysis. It suggests that the availability of financial resources is a key factor in the decision of adopting the ERP innovation. The large and the financially healthy companies can obtain the funds for the implementation easier than their small and/or unhealthy counterparts.

Imitation Perspective

The results of the contrast of hypotheses H_{6a} and H_{6b} are summarized in table 5. Additionally, figure 2 displays a normal curve fitted to the data considered for the analysis.

A look at figure 2 and panels A and B of table 5 reveals that the adopters distribution follows

Table 5. Year of implementation of the ERP system

PANEL A—OBSERVED FREQUENCIES			
Year	Firms	Percentage	Cumulative Perc.
1991	1	3.6	3.6
1992	1	3.6	7.1
1993	1	3.6	10.7
1994	0	0.0	10.7
1995	1	3.6	14.3
1996	2	7.1	21.4
1997	1	3.6	25.0
1998	4	14.3	39.3
1999	7	25.0	64.3
2000	5	17.9	82.1
2001	2	7.1	89.3
2002	2	7.1	96.4
2003	1	3.6	100.0
TOTAL	28	100.0	100.0
PANEL B—DESCRIPTIVE MEASURES			
Mean		1998.36	
Median		1999	
Standard Deviation		2.896	
Skewness		-1.015	
Kurtosis		0.932	
PANEL C—TESTS			
95% Confidence Interval for Mean		(1997.23, 1999.48)	
99% Confidence Interval for Mean		(1996.84, 1999.87)	
Shapiro and Wilk's Normality Test		0.911 (p=0.021)	

approximately a bell-shaped curve, the derivative of the S-shaped diffusion curve. However, the distribution is negatively skewed. This finding suggests that the introduction of the euro and the Y2K effect had an influence on the decision of adopting an ERP system, forcing some companies to bring forward the implementation, in order to make all the changes in their information systems at one time. So, the results displayed in panel A show that only 3 out of the 28 firms considered for the test of H_{6a} and H_{6b} completed the implementation of the ERP after the end of the period for the introduction of the euro (31 december 2001).

These factors cause the fit to the normal curve to be only partial. As panel C shows, this is evidenced by the Shapiro and Wilk test ($0.01 < p < 0.05$). It is also noticeable that none of the upper limits of the confidence intervals for mean exceed the deadline for making the changes to cope with Y2K effect (31/12/1999). So, we can conclude that the data support hypothesis H_{6b}, lends only partial support to H_{6a}, due to the two factors (Y2K effect and the introduction of the euro) that accelerated the diffusion of the ERP innovation.

With regard to the test of H_{7a}, table 6 contains the crosstabulation of the dummy variables in-

Figure 2. ERP adopting firms by year

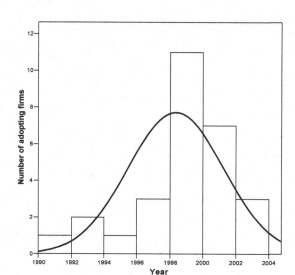

Table 6. ERP adoptions by sector

	Services	Manufacturing	Total
Non ERP firms	3 (21.40%)	11 (78.80%)	14 (100%)
ERP firms	14 (50.00%)	14 (50.00%)	28 (100%)
Total	17 (40.50%)	25 (59.50%)	42 (100%)

Table 7. Regression analysis

	Coefficient	Std. Error	t	Sig.
c_0	1999.27155	0.89366	2237.172	0.000
c_1	-2.34814	3.72737	-0.629	0.535
c_2	0.00018	0.00025	0.724	0.476
Adjusted R^2				-0.039
F-statistic				0.539 (p=0.590)
White's test for heteroskedasticity				1.344 (p=0.288)
Jarque-Bera's test for normality of residuals				0.253 (p=0.881)

dicating, respectively, ERP adoption and sector of activity.

It is noticeable that the companies which decided not to adopt an ERP were mainly manufacturers. However, the ERP group contains the same number of service and manufacturing firms.

Cramer's Φ statistic equals 0.274, which means p=0.075[g]. So, the hypothesis that sectoral assignation influences the decision of adopting the ERP innovation (H_{7a}) is only partially supported. In this respect, it is noticeable that Stedman (1999) found sectoral differences in the ERP implementation rate studying a sample of American firms. Nevertheless, he found a higher implementation rate in the manufacturing sector.

Regarding H_{7b}, and as mentioned earlier, we regressed the year of implementation for the 28 ERP firms the year of implementation on the indicators related to the efficient choice perspective. As the tests of hypotheses H_1 to H_5 revealed that only firm size and financial health have influence on the ERP decision, we considered these two indicators as the independent variables of the regression. So, the estimated model was the following:

$$Year = c_0 + c_1 \times ROI + c_2 \times SIZE + \varepsilon$$

Table 7, which contains the main results of this regression analysis, indicates that size and financial health are not factors with significant influence on the year the ERP was implemented. So, there is no evidence to support H_{7b}, and we cannot conclude that only firms with a later implementation were influenced by the fad while early adopters took the decision on the basis of size and financial health factors.

To ensure the robustness of this result, apart from White's test for heteroskedasticity and Jarque-Bera's test for normality of residuals, we conducted a Cook's D test, which revealed no influential observations. We also tested for multicollinearity using multicollinearity diagnostics (Belsley *et al.*, 1980) and variance inflation factors (Netter *et al.*, 1990). Both methods proved that multicollinearity was not significant. We repeated the analysis considering the natural log of total assets as the proxy for firm size. The statistical significance of the coefficients remained unchanged. Finally, we also conducted a stepwise regression analysis considering all the variables used in the logistic regression analysis, finding no significant factors.

CONCLUDING REMARKS

In the present research we have tried to determine the reasons that move a company to adopt an ERP system. We considered data from Spanish listed companies, because Spain is a country that is not at the highest level of technological development. As the bulk of the prior research on this issue has focused on ERP diffusion in the USA and other countries where technological awareness is higher, our results can be extrapolated to other similar economies.

We considered two approaches for the study of the diffusion of ERP systems: the efficient choice approach and the imitation perspective. The efficient choice approach postulates that the innovation decision is made using a cost-benefit analysis. The imitation perspective assumes conditions of uncertainty. It states that in order to reduce this uncertainty, organizations imitate other companies, basing the adoption decision on the decisions made by their competitors. In relation to both approaches, we formulated the hypotheses and considered a set of indicators to test them.

Regarding the hypotheses stemming from the efficient-choice perspective, firm size seems to have an influence in the decision of adopting an ERP, as the size of ERP adopters appears to be significantly bigger than that of non-adopters. ROI has a moderate influence, with low ROI firms being more averse to ERP adoption. In contrast, inventory levels, firm efficiency and the percentage of export sales do not seem to be influential factors. These results suggest that the availability of financial resources is the main reason for the implementation of an ERP, as large and financially healthy firms are more likely to adopt this innovation.

Another interesting conclusion is that the adopters distribution follows approximately a bell-shaped curve, the derivative of the S-shaped diffusion curve. However, the distribution is negatively skewed. This finding suggests that the introduction of the euro and the Y2K effect had an influence on the decision of adopting an ERP system.

Therefore, it can be concluded that in the decision of implanting an ERP system by the Spanish listed companies, the necessity to make changes in the computer systems due to the introduction of the euro and the Y2K effect had an important effect. The hypotheses that sectoral assignation influences the decision of adopting the ERP innovation was partially supported. These findings allow us to postulate a certain influence of the imitation effect.

These results are in accordance with what we expected, taking into account the special features of Spanish national culture. Due to their lack of technical skills, managers did not seem to have a clear perception of the advantages of the ERP systems and they considered them as only a solution to the euro and the Y2K problems. In addition, the tendency towards imitation that we observed reflects the significant uncertainty avoidance that characterizes Spanish management.

The above results could provide an indication of the reasons for ERP implementations in countries whose culture is similar to Spain's, as much in the case of the EU (for example, Italy, Greece or Portugal) as in Latin America (as for example Uruguay, Peru, Argentina, Chile, Colombia or Brasil).

Finally, it is necessary to indicate that the present work does not complete this research approach to the ERP systems adoption. A feasible extension of the present work is to determine whether the companies that decided to implement this innovation experimented significant variations in their profitability and efficiency in the years subsequent to the adoption (Poston and Grabski, 2001; Hunton, et al., 2003).

REFERENCES

Abrahamson, E. (1991). Managerial facts and fashions: The diffusion and rejection of innovation. *Academy of Management Review, 16*(3), 586-612.

Alpar, P., Kim, M. (1990). A microeconomic approach to the measurement of information technology value. *Journal of Management Information Systems, 7*(2)55-69.

Appleton, E. L. (1997). How to survive ERP. *Datamation, 43*(3), 50-3.

Balakrishnan, R., Linsmeier, T. J., Venkatachalam, M. (1996). Financial benefits from JIT adoption: effects of customer concentration and cost structure. *The Accounting Review, 71*(2), 183-205.

Barber, B. M., Lyon, J. D. (1996). Detecting abnormal operating performance: The empirical power and specification of test statistics. *Journal of Financial Economics, 41*(3), 359-99.

Belsley, D. A., Kuh, E., Welsch, R. E. (1980). *Regression Diagnostics: Identifying Influential Data and Sources of Collinearity.* New York: John Wiley & Sons.

Benders, J., & Van Veen, K. (2001). What's in a fashion? Interpretative viabililty and management fashions. *Organization, 8*(1), 33-53.

Bendoly, E., Jacobs, F. R. (2004). ERP architectural/operational alignment for order-processing performance. *International Journal of Operations & Product Management, 24*(1), 99-117.

Boldy, D., Jain, S., Northey, K. (1993). What makes an effective European manager? A case study of Sweden, Belgium, Germany, and Spain. *Management International Review, 33* (2), 157-69.

Brakely, H. H. (1999). What makes ERP effective?. *Manufacturinf Systems, 17*(3), 120.

Brown, C. V., Vessey, I., & Powell, A. (2000). The ERP purchase decision: Influential business and IT factors. *6th Americas Conference on Information Systems*, USA.

Cook, R. D. (1977). Detection of influential observations in linear regression. *Technometrics*, (19), 15-8.

Damanpour, F. (1992). Organizational Size and Innovation. *Organization Studies, 13*(3), 375-402.

Davenport, T. H., Harris, J., & Cantrell, S. (2002). *The Return of Enterprise Solutions: The Director's Cut.* Accenture. Available http://www.accenture.com/Global/

Research_and_Insights/Institute_For_High_Performance_Business/By_Subject/Innovation/TheCut.htm

Deloitte Consulting (1999). ERP's Second wave: Maximizing the value of ERP-enabled processes. New York: Deloitte Consulting.

DiMaggio, P., Powell, W. (1983). The iron cage revisited: institutional isomorphism and collective rationality in organization fields. *American Sociological Review, 48*, 147-60.

Eckhouse, J. (1999). ERP vendors plot a comeback. *Information Week,* (718), 126-28.

European Business School (2004). *ERP in Banking 2005-An Empirical Survey.* European Business School, Oestrich-Winkel, Germany.

European Commission (2005). *The European E-Business Report.* European Commision-e-business W@tch, Luxembourg.

Gorzalczany, M. B., & Piasta, Z. (1999). Neuro-fuzzy approach versus rough set inspired methodology for intelligent decisión support. *Information Sciences, 120*(1-4), 45-68.

Grandori, A. (1987). *Perspectives on organizational theory.* Ballinger Publishing Company, Cambridge, MA

Granlund, M., & Malmi, T. (2000). The liberations and limitations of ERP-systems for management accounting. *Communication presented in the 23rd Annual Congress of the European Accounting Association*, Munich, Germany.

Granlund, M., Malmi, T. (2002). Moderate impact of ERPS on management accounting: A lag or permanent outcome?. *Management Accounting Research, 13*(3), 299-321.

Grupo Penteo (2003). *Aplicaciones corporativas, situación en España y tendencias futuras -Año 2002, Grupo Penteo in colaboration with the E-Business Center PwC&IESE*, Madrid.

Hawking, P., Stein, A., & Foster, S. (2004). Revisiting ERP systems: Benefit realisation. *Proceedings of the 37th Hawaii International Conference on System Sciences*, Hawaii.

Hayes, D. C., Hunton, J. E., & Reck, J. L. (2001). Market reaction to ERP implementation announcements. *Journal of Information Systems, 15*(1), 3-18.

Hofstede, G. (1983). The cultural relativity of organizational practices and theories. *Journal of International Business Studies, 14*(2), 75-89.

Hunton, J. E., Lippincott, B., & Reck, J. L. (2003). Enterprise resource planning systems: Comparing firm performance of adopters and nonadopters. *International Journal of Accounting Information Systems*, (4), 165-84.

Hyvönen, T. (2003). Management accounting and information systems: ERP versus BoB. *European Accounting Review, 12*(1), 155-73.

Kimberly, J. R. (1981). Management innovation. In P. Nystrom and W.H. Starbuck (Eds.), *Handbook of organizational design.* Oxford University Press, New York, (pp. 84-104).

Kimberly, J. R., & Evanisko, M. J. (1981). Organizational innovation: the influence of individual, organizational, and contextual factors on hospital adoption of technology and administrative innovations. *Academy of Management Journal, 24*(4), 689-713.

Knapp, C. A., & Shin, N. (2001). Impacts of Enterprise Resource Planning systems selection and implementation. *7th Americas Conference on Information Systems,* USA.

Liang, T. P., Chandler, J. S., Han, I., & Roan, J. (1992). An empirical investigation of some data effects on the classification accuracy of probit, ID3 and neural networks. *Contemporary Accounting Research, 9*(1), 306-328.

Mabert, V. A., Soni, A., & Venkataraman, M. A. (2003a). The impact of organization size on enterprise resource planning (ERP) implementations in the US manufacturing sector. *Omega, 31*(3), 235-46.

Mabert, V. A., Soni, A., & Venkataraman, M. A. (2003b). Enterprise resource planning: Managing the implementation process. *European Journal of Operational Research, 146* (2), 302-14.

March, J. G. (1978). Bounded rationality, ambiguity and the engineering of choice. *Bell Journal of Economics, 9(*2), 587-608.

Marsh, R. M., & Mannari, H. (1989). The size imperative? Longitudinal tests. *Organizational Studies, 10*(1), 83-95.

McAdam, R., & Galloway, A. (2005). Enterprise resource planning and organisational innovation: a management perspective. *Industrial Management & Data Systems, 105*(3), 280-90.

McKee, T. E. (1995). Predicting bankruptcy via induction. *Journal of Information Technology,* (10), 26-36.

Mitra, S., & Chaya, A. K. (1996). Analyzing Cost-Effectiveness of Organizations: The Impact of Information Technology Spending. *Journal of Management Information Systems, 13* (2), 29-57.

Netter, J., Wasserman, W., & Kutner, M. H. (1990). *Applied Linear Statistical Models.* third ed., Irwin, Inc., Boston, MA.

O'Leary, D. (2000). *Enterprise resource planning: systems, life cicle, electronic commerce, and risk.* New York: Cambridge University Press.

O'Neill, H.M.; Pouder, R.W., Buchholtz, A.K. (1998). Patterns in the diffusion of strategies across organizations: insights from the innovation diffusion literature. *Academy of Management Review, 23*(1), 98-114.

Poole, M. S., & Van de Ven, A. H. (1989). Toward a general theory of innovation processes. in Van de Ven, A. H., Angle, H. L., Poole, M. S. (Eds.), *Research on the Management of Information: The Minnesota Studies.* Harper & Row, New York, (pp. 637-62).

Porter, M.E. (1987). From competitive advantage to corporate strategy. *Harvard Business Review, 65*(3), 43-59.

Poston, R., Grabski, S. (2001). Financial impacts of enterprise resource planning implementations. *International Journal of Accounting Information Systems, 2*(4), 271-94.

Quinlan, J.R. (1979). Discovering rules by induction from large collections of examples. In Michie, D. (Ed.), *Expert systems in the microelectronic age.*

Quinlan, J. R. (1993). *C4.5: Programs for machine learning.* Morgan Kaufmann Publishers, Inc., California.

Quinlan, J. R. (2004). *Data Mining Tools See5 & C5.0.* Available http://www.rulequest.com/see5-info.html

Rogers, E. M. (1962). *Diffusion of innovations.* New York: The Free Press, (4th ed. 1995).

Ross, J. W., & Vitale, M. R. (2000). The ERP revolution: surviving vs. thriving. *Information Systems Frontiers, 2*(2), 233-41.

Shapiro, S. S., & Wilk, M. B. (1965). An analysis of variance test for normality (complete samples). *Biometrika, 52*(3-4), 591-611.

Shin, N. (1999). Does information technology improve coordination? An empirical analysis. *Logistics Information Management, 12*(1/2), 138-44.

Stedman, C. (1999, August). What's next for ERP?. *Computerworld, 33*, 48-9.

Tornatzky, L. G., Eveland, J. D., Boylan, M. G., Hetzner, W. A., Johnson, E. C., Roitman, D., &Schneider, J. (1983). The spread of technology and Government policy and innovation. *The Process of Technological Innovation: Reviewing the Literature, National Science Foundation*, Washington, (pp. 155-216).

Wolfe, R. A. (1994). Organizational innovation: Review, critique and suggested research directions. *Journal of Management Studies, 31*(3), 405-31.

ENDNOTES

[a]   Other possible proxies, such as, for example, the number of overseas subsidiaries or the amount of the physical assets located abroad, were not available in the database used to gather the financial information of the analysed companies.

[b]   However, it must be taken into account that organizational complexity may produce a negative effect on implementation.

[c]   The t-test for independent samples and the U Mann-Whitney test were used.

[d]   The design implies that the same company can be both in the ERP and in the non-ERP group. For example, if a certain company implemented the ERP system in 1999, their 1997 financial data could be matched with those of a firm adopting the ERP in 1997, and their 1999 data with those of a firm that by 1999 had not implemented this innovation.

[e]   Financial services subsections were excluded because companies belonging to these present a different behaviour in respect of ERP implementation (European Business School, 2004).

[f]   The complete development and the source code of Quinlan's See5 can be found in Quinlan (1993, 2004).

[g]   The results obtained using a Monte Carlo approach, exact tests and the χ^2 test are not significantly different.

Chapter XI
Emerging Topics and Technologies in Information Systems

Jaakko Ikävalko
Helsinki University of Technology, Finland

Seppo J. Hänninen
Helsinki University of Technology, Finland

Ari Serkkola
Helsinki University of Technology, Finland

Ilkka Kauranen
Helsinki University of Technology, Finland

ABSTRACT

Technology programs are a means to facilitate the development and commercialization process of new innovative technologies. They are forums for the exchange of information and for networking between companies and research institutes. The programs provide opportunities and financial support to carry out ambitious research and development projects and to build business expertise. The core of technology programs are joint research projects between companies and research institutes. The objective of the study is to increase understanding of how such joint research projects within technology programs evolve in practice. The emphasis is on identifying factors that enhance the commercialization of new technologies and on finding barriers of commercialization. Based on the findings, practical recommendations are given on how the concept of technology programs can be further developed to utilize the unused potential in such programs. The empirical sample of companies in the study represents information technology. In the study, the microanalysis approach is used. The dominant approach in corresponding innovation research has been the macro perspective approach. The research data was gathered via personal interviews with key informants of joint research projects within a technology program. All the projects were new product development projects which the companies taking part in the technology program were conducting together with research institutes.

INTRODUCTION

Technology programs are a means to facilitate the development and commercialization process of new innovative technologies. They are forums for the exchange of information and for networking between companies and research institutes. (Hänninen, 2007) The programs provide opportunities and financial support to carry out ambitious research and development projects and to build business expertise. The essence of technology programs are joint research projects between companies and research institutes. The objective of the present study is to increase understanding of how such joint research projects within technology programs evolve in practice. The emphasis is on identifying factors that enhance the commercialization of new technologies and on finding barriers of commercialization. It is a top priority for the society that resources invested in technology programs enhance, in practice, the commercialization processes of companies as effectively as possible (Balthasarin et alii, 2000).

A dominant approach in innovation research has been the macro perspective approach. Earlier innovation research has typically been based on macro perspective innovation models (Cooper, 1990). Macro economic cluster analyses and general economic factors have been central for the macro perspective approach in innovation research. The macro perspective approach has focused on strategic factors defined by a company's market position and other organizational relationships (Johnson et alii, 2003).

On the other hand, the microanalysis approach is a more novel approach in the context of innovation research (Serkkola et alii, 2009). In it, detailed analyses of the organization's internal processes, for example, of the daily tasks, work practices, work conventions, work flows, decision making, chosen solutions, and organizational processes, are conducted in order to obtain a deeper understanding of the phenomena under investigation (Brown et alii 2000). The micro analysis approach is especially helpful in understanding the initial creation processes of innovations and the forces driving new product development.

In the present study, technology programs are analyzed using the microanalysis approach. This is done using in-depth analyses of individual joint research projects initiated and supported by a technology program (Hänninen et alii, 2007). Such joint research projects between companies and research institutes constitute the core of a technology program and, thus, attaining a deeper understanding of individual research projects will help to understand the essence of technology programs in general.

The research method was qualitative. In order to facilitate rich analyses of the technology project concept, as much information as possible was gathered from each individual joint research project. Generalization of the conceptual results attained in this activity-oriented multi-case study will be done by further studies applying quantitative research methods (Yin, 1994). Another direction for future research is the parallel use of the macro perspective approach and the microanalysis approach as Nieto (2002) recommends.

The research data was gathered via personal interviews with key informants of joint research projects within a technology program in the field of information technology. Because of the unpredictable character of the new product development, experts and other actors working in the organization and collaboration processes' interface are important key informants of the joint research projects (Johnson et alii, 1997).

All the projects were new product development projects which the companies taking part in the technology program were conducting together with research institutes. The sample includes 10 projects where each had one or more companies and research institutes participating. The interviews were conducted in 2004. Both successful and unsuccessful cases of commercialization were included in the sample. The companies in the technology program developed new products based on the Internet, telecommunications, GPS navigation systems, and other cutting-edge information technologies.

The technology program focused on user-orientated information technology applications. In user-orientated information technology application, innovations are based on the recognition of end-users' contextual expectations, and then the necessary applications for the needs are provided. In the present study, the development of these socio-technical applications was observed and general conclusions were drawn.

POSITIONING OF THE PARTNERS IN THE JOINT RESEARCH PROJECTS

New product development of an information technology application is a very complex and demanding process. No single company can master all the skills and knowledge needed for the development and launch of a new innovative product. Technology programs are a strategic option for a company to gain access to the latest technological knowledge required for new

product development. Partners in such technology programs negotiate and agree on mutual goals. Then, with the support of the organizer of the technology program, an individual joint research project is launched. The technology program offers support in the form of expertise and, often, financing.

In the technology program under investigation, most of the companies were interested in utilizing the latest cutting-edge technological research in their product development. Respectively, the participating research institutes were mainly interested in learning which new technologies could have commercial potential in the future. Even though the partners had agreed on the aims in advance, in some cases conflicts emerged between a company's short-term market-orientated goals and its partnering research institute's longer-term scientific-orientated interests.

Joint research projects can be organized as a one-to-one cooperation or as a multilateral cooperation. In the sample, small sized single technology companies and startup companies seemed to prefer one-to-one contracts in their joint research projects. One reason for this was that these companies were cautious of losing full control of the technology which their competitive advantage was based on. With their limited knowledge about immaterial property rights, selecting only a single research partner seemed safer.

One of the important contributions of technology programs is that in them, a company and a research institute share the financial risk of research and development. In addition, the technology program usually allocates financial support to the joint research projects done within the program. In radical or early stage technology development, potential rewards can be particularly high, but at the same time there are high risks of both technological and commercial failure. In the sample companies, most of these kinds of development projects would not have been launched without the help of the technology program offering potentially high financial rewards and limited financial risks for the companies.

In some of the case companies, the interest in benchmarking competitive new product development projects defined the companies' position in their joint research projects. One driver in this—often at least partially hidden—position was also a possibility to network with some specific technology experts as potential recruits. This position was especially tempting if the company could participate in several joint research projects at the same time or in related fields.

Some companies adopted a very passive strategy for their acquisition of the latest technological knowledge. They obtained access to research results with very little resource allocation from their own end. The downside of this position is that these companies had very little influence on decisions concerning the joint research project, which considerably lowered the value added they received themselves.

An interesting observation which has implications for the organization of technology programs was that the goals and the corresponding positioning of the participating companies and research institutes were not at all static but typically evolved during the joint research programs. For example, in some cases a company was a very active contributor to the joint research project at the beginning, but when the company did not seem to benefit in its own new product development as it had expected its position changed to one of being a passive spectator.

HOW THE JOINT RESEARCH PROJECTS IN THE TECHNOLOGY PROGRAM EVOLVED

Technology programs are aimed at supporting high-risk technology development projects. In the joint research projects, it was in reality easier for the companies to accept the relatively high risk related to technology development. However, when the companies applied the research results, the new products tended to be incremental—not radical—in character. The joint research helped to minimize technology development-related risks, but the risks related to the commercialization process were still perceived as very high by the companies. To mitigate the commercial risks, companies applied the new technologies only to commercially safer incremental product upgrades.

Although technology programs aim to support market orientated research and development projects, many of the joint research projects in the present study were more technology oriented than genuinely end-user orientated. A typical situation was that the joint research project started as a technology-driven project, and only in the later phases was the technology adapted to meet the end-user needs. Had the end-user needs been emphasized earlier in the project, the research efforts would have harmonized better with the company's market orientation.

The smaller sized companies were generally more interested in directly commercializing the research results, while the larger companies had more opportunities to take advantage of the longer-term benefits of knowledge building. Some of the larger companies just wanted to follow the latest developments in their field of research in order to be better prepared for future developments in their fields.

The companies in the present study often had unreasonably high expectations about the maturity level of the technologies developed during the technology program. Turning the research results into commercial applications required a company to have the necessary capabilities, motivation, and commitment for its own development efforts after the technology program had ended. In some cases, after the end of the joint research project, the company was still considerably dependent on the outside technological expertise. In such cases, these companies succeeded in continuing the development process to reach the desired commercial applications only with the continuing consultancy from the experts of joint research projects.

In many cases, the expertise provided during the technology program to the companies was not sufficient for the application development of the companies as much of the knowledge transfer was limited only to the narrow area of each specific development project. As a result, the companies themselves needed to have a wide range of skills to be able to transfer the new technologies to their commercial applications. Some of the companies realized rather late in their joint projects that the expertise provided by research institutes would not be sufficient and ended in difficulties in finding the missing expertise.

There was often some discontinuity between the joint research project and the company's new product development process, especially with the larger sized companies. In these cases, there was not much interaction and iterative feedback between the organizations, and thus the research institute was not thoroughly aware of the end-user needs.

Experts in the research institutes proved to be, as expected, very research orientated, and did not necessarily recognize limitations set by the commercialization process. Some consequences of this were that the research experts sometimes neglected factors such as production cost, market competitiveness, and immaterial property right issues.

The different organizational cultures and work methods in companies and research institutes created problems. However, in none of the participating companies did this hinder the possibility for cooperation. Mutual commitment and trust were a prerequisite for successful cooperation, and they were strengthened in longer-term contacts and collaborations.

Many of the participating companies deemed the administrative management and formal reporting requirements of the technology program as being too heavy. This derailed attention from the real essence of the cooperative projects and consumed resources.

The small sized companies tended to collaborate with regional research institutes, while the geographical distance was not as important for larger companies. The small companies were not aware of opportunities provided by research institutes located in areas that are more distant.

Many joint research projects emerged from previous contacts, while some came from unintended random connections between individual people. In addition, it was easier to collaborate with research institutes with whom the company had had cooperation before.

In the companies of the sample, it was felt that especially the informal communication about the research results and related issues enhanced the mutual learning process. This was emphasized by the fact that an incidental observation from the research process in several cases provided more value added to the companies than the final end results of the whole research project. By means of informal communication, companies were also able to gain deeper understanding of the new technologies. On the other hand, formal communication was more related to the negotiations and documentation of the decisions and results of the joint research projects.

An important aim of technology programs is to create new innovations. However, in the technology program under investigation, many benefits were achieved even without the emergence of new products. The participants acknowledged that valuable indirect benefits were attained purely by the partners actively exchanging essential knowledge. It was suggested that the technology programs should arrange more forums in which experiences of research cooperation could be shared and discussed in an informal manner.

FACTORS ENHANCING THE COMMERCIALIZATION PROCESS AND BARRIERS TO COMMERCIALIZATION

Based on the present research study, general conclusions on the commercialization of the results of joint research projects within technology programs were drawn. New factors that enhance the commercialization process were identified, along with new barriers for commercialization.

Factors enhancing the commercialization process were:

Involving the marketing function of the company already in the product development stage. In the successful innovation processes, the marketing function of the companies typically took part in the early stages of product conceptualization. Potential target groups were identified and the corresponding expected sales volumes estimated. A large existing network of partners was very helpful. The contacts could be used for testing the product ideas and getting other market related feedback.

Utilizing complementary expertise. In most cases it was impossible for the companies to internally develop all the expertise necessary for a successful commercialization process. Expanding the technology partnership beyond the technology program partners was often necessary. In successful innovations, partnerships in marketing were typical, especially for the smaller companies.

Correct choice of an alliance network. Most companies did not exercise refined thinking in choosing the alliance network needed in the commercialization process. An example of such refined questions is the choice between a narrow-based alliance and a broad alliance. A narrow-based alliance may mean access only to a small group of clientele, but can offer a dominant position within the network, whereas a broad alliance may offer access to an innovation for a wider group of potential users, but only as one alternative among many. There are usually several competing networks operating on the market place, and a crucial decision is therefore the choice of the best network in terms of optimizing business impact. There is no general answer to the choice of the correct alliance network. However, the successful companies had given more thought to this question and had made a choice more suitable to their specific needs.

Developing a derivative product in advance. In many cases the original product idea, against expectations and best wishes, failed. Many of the companies who were successful in the commercialization process had prepared themselves for this. They had already anticipated possibilities for derivative products based on the same product platform in their new product development stage. For them, the launch of the first product was a learning experience, the results of which were swiftly taken into use in the further derivative product development. With derivative products in mind at the new product development, the companies were better prepared for the inevitable development of their product becoming obsolete.

Conclusions concerning barriers to commercialization were:

'Perfect technology syndrome'. Some companies seemed to concentrate their resources on attempting to maximize the performance of the technology and to achieve unrivalled technical capacities. They seemed to believe that unrivalled technological solutions would create a situation of absence of competition and, thus, generate unlimited demand. As a result, insufficient resources were diverted to the investigation of the market, end-users, or substitute solutions to the same end-user needs. Skipping many preparatory investigations of the best practices of product development did not in reality support rapid commercial implementation. Instead, this over-focus on technological solutions actually delayed the products' access to the market. All the companies which could be deemed to show symptoms of the perfect technology syndrome not only had poor results in their commercialization processes under investigation, but also eventually found themselves in financial trouble in general.

Uncertainty in intellectual property rights. Intellectual property rights were not always addressed at the early stages of the joint research projects. This was particularly true in the case of collaboration between the companies and universities. When confusion emerged concerning these questions at later stages of the joint research projects, it caused wasted energy, personnel resources, and capital. Problems in intellectual property rights can be disastrous to cooperation, but in the sample of the present study, no project was endangered because of these issues. By nature, the different parties in technology programs have different objectives and interests and this makes intellectual property rights more difficult to address. Intellectual property rights questions were particularly prone to cause problems in the case of non-material innovations.

Delayed input of end-user needs. None of the companies denied the need for input concerning customer needs. However, the imbedded mode of operation was to start to seek this information at later stages of the development project. A consequence of this was that when the knowledge of end-user needs was available, changes needed in the product were profound, time consuming, and expensive.

Unclear value added to the customers. Often the technological solution was carefully thought out and cultivated, but its projection as value added to the end-users remained unclear. Even if the end-users attain new opportunities by means of the new product, the fact remained: The less clear the benefits of the new product were for the end-user, the greater the resistance to its acquisition was. Clearly defining the value added to the end-users is an important part of the commercialization process and cannot be left to the marketing channels.

Scant emphasis in building up a brand. All companies acknowledged that building a brand is necessary but, in practice, the actions taken by a few of the smaller companies in particular showed that they had not adequately understood the importance of brand capital. Typical was that in the graphic design of the products, priority was given to low production costs, neglecting the attractiveness of the design and the possibility to convey the high quality of the product by means of the design and brand. Another consequence of giving too little emphasis to brand issues was that the companies ended up spreading resources too widely as a result of trying to maintain several parallel brands at the same time.

Unintentional diversification. Every new technological innovation leads to diversification in the business logic required in the commercialization of the new product. In most of the companies, this happened unintentionally. In some cases the situation was so severe that it nearly resulted in the collapse of the company's previous business logic knowledge base. In other cases, when the commercialization process was successful, it was very difficult to trace and understand the diversification, even though it may have been hindering greater success.

PRACTICAL RECOMMENDATIONS

The study clearly confirmed that, in general, technology programs do enhance cooperation between companies and research institutes in a manner that positively contributes to new product development and to the commercialization of research-based inventions. The new findings, however, show that there is much unused potential in developing the concept of technology programs.

The observations of the companies revealed that ordinary companies still are not very aware of the various opportunities that cooperation with research institutes could offer to them. Technology programs offer a possibility to bridge this gap. Contact forums in which companies and for research institutes could share experiences and plan for cooperation could be arranged. Technology programs should be more pro-active and perhaps should not be restricted to one field of technology in order to target a larger number of companies. Marketing should not be neglected to get the message across.

A typical problem in innovative new product development projects was that the assessment of the specific end-user needs was often conducted at a very late stage of the project. This often led to the situation that the product did not meet the market needs. Even identified end-user needs had to be neglected because, at a later stage of the product development, it was too costly to alter the product specifications. Thus, in the structure of technology programs, mechanisms to secure early market input should be developed. From the early research and development stage there should be an active contact to the potential end-users in the market place.

The natural aim of companies to minimize their risks in new product development was seen in the companies investigated. A common way of doing so was to try to spread the risk by building a portfolio of parallel development projects, each with a different risk level. While the technology programs provided the companies with a tempting opportunity to join together with research institutes in technologically challenging new product development projects, the companies at the same time implemented more incremental, low risk in-house projects. As the commercial reward was clearly in sight in the in-house projects and the risk seemed high in the joint projects with the research institutes, the companies' attention seemed to shift towards the low risk projects. A consequence was that the development projects within the technology programs that were started as strategic projects in reality were not in the strategic focus of the companies. The joint projects, which were deemed risky, started to live their own lives. A solution to keep the joint projects initiated within the technology program in the strategic focus of companies needs to be found. One option would be to extend the support offered by the technology program further. It should cover later stages of the commercialization process in order to lower the perceived risk of continuing the projects.

The technology programs were very much focused on establishing formal collaboration between the different partners. However, the observations reconfirmed that informal communication and open interaction between people is conducive to creativity and the development of new inventions. Technology programs should pay constant attention to utilizing various means of enhancing informal contacts between companies and research institutes. Attention should not be limited to building contact between organizations: Person-to-person interaction is an important means of transferring tacit knowledge.

Immaterial property rights are a potential source of conflict in collaborative research projects. Especially in projects where small companies and large companies are collaborating with each other, large companies can dominate in immaterial property rights issues by means of their higher level of legal knowledge, their longer cumulative experience, and their stronger negotiation power. In the present study, some small and medium sized companies expressed a fear that in the cooperation with their larger partners they can end up losing their immaterial property rights to the larger and stronger companies. Technology programs should provide knowledge and training related to immaterial property rights issues to all participating companies. In some cases support to small and medium sized companies might be in place when the smaller companies have to negotiate on immaterial property rights questions related to their research projects. The structure of technology programs should guide the participants to negotiate and agree on immaterial property rights during the initial stages of the program.

A clear individual success factor for the collaborative projects in the study could be identified. The companies that had previous collaborative projects with research institutes were on an average more successful in their cooperation. It seemed to be easier for the partners who had previous experience in research cooperation to start with more realistic expectations, to build mutual commitment, and be more willing to work together. This observation can be utilized in many ways. The potential for enhancing company cooperation between companies and research institutes should be seen beyond the perspective of the technology program in question. A technology program should promote cooperation possibilities in future programs as well. The ultimate aim should be the establishment of continuous cooperative arrangements without the need for technology programs.

In the study, there were several new inventions that were successfully developed into new products which gained the acceptance of end-users. However, not all of these attained market success. It seemed that a large number of good ideas having market potential were not fully exploited. An idea to help overcome the obvious problems in the final commercialization process is to combine technology programs with innovation commercialization programs. Innovation commercialization programs would be based on the concerted joint effort of both traditional technology development organizations and risk financiers. Private venture capitalists as well as public financing organizations should work together. Overall, a global perspective in the commercialization should be adopted from the very beginning.

REFERENCES

Balthasar, A., Bättig, C., Thierstein, A., & Wilhelm, B. (2000). Developers: Key actors of the innovation process. Types of developers and their contacts to institutions involved in research and development, continuing education and training, and the transfer of technology. *Technovation, 20,* 523-538.

Brown, J. S. & Duguid, P. (2000). *The social life of information.* Boston, Illinois, USA: Harvard Business School Press.

Cooper, R. (1990). Stage-gate systems: a new tool for managing new products. *Business Horizons,* May-June 1990.

Hänninen, S. (2007). *Innovation commercialisation process from the 'four knowledge bases' perspective.* Doctoral Dissertation Series, Development and Management in Industry 2007/1, Espoo, Finland: Helsinki University of Technology.

Hänninen, S., Kauranen, I., Serkkola, A., & Ikävalko, J. (2007). Barriers to commercialisation from the 'four knowledge bases' perspective: A study of innovation in the software development sector. *International Journal of Management Practice,* 2:3, 197-213.

Johnson, G., Melin, L. & Whittington, R. (2003). Guest editor's introduction; micro Strategy and strategizing: Towards an activity-based view. *Journal of Management Studies, 40*(1), 3–22.

Johnson, G. & Huff, A. (1997). Everyday innovation/everyday strategy. In Hamel, G. Prahalad, C. K., Thomas, H. & O'Neill, D. (Ed.) *Strategy flexibility*. London, United Kingdom: Wiley.

Nieto, M. (2003). From R&D management to knowledge management: An overview of studies of innovation management. *Technological Forecasting and Social Change*, 70, 135–161.

Serkkola, A., Ikävalko, J. Hänninen, S., & Kauranen, I. (2009). Microanalysis in the identification and research of the product and service innovations: A conceptual framework, *International Journal of Entrepreneurial Venturing* (forthcoming).

Yin, R. K. (1994). *Case Study Research*. Thousand Oaks, California, USA: Sage Publications.

Chapter XII
Technology–Related Privacy Concerns:
An Emerging Challenge

Cliona McParland
Dublin City University, Ireland

Regina Connolly
Dublin City University, Ireland

ABSTRACT

While Internet-based technologies have the potential to empower users immensely, individuals are becoming increasingly aware of the ways in which those technologies can be employed to monitor their computer-based interactions. In the past, much attention has focused on the impact of technology-related privacy concerns from a transactional perspective. However, privacy concerns regarding communication monitoring are now emerging as a significant issue with the potential to negatively impact both productivity and morale within the computer-mediated work environment. This chapter outlines the evolution of technology-related privacy concerns. The lack of definitional consensus and the resulting conceptual and operational confusion that surrounds the privacy construct is described. Furthermore, the significant deficit of rigorous academic studies on this topic is highlighted. The current state of privacy legislation in Europe is addressed and some of the key challenges that face researchers who may wish to conduct research on this phenomenon are outlined.

INTRODUCTION

Privacy has been a contentious issue throughout the ages as individuals have sought to protect their personal information from misuse by others. The advent of the Internet and the increasing proliferation of technologies into our daily lives has only managed to heighten these concerns. The importance of individuals' privacy concerns is widely acknowledged in the literature. For example, in the social science literature researchers (e.g Konvitz, 1966; Powers, 1996; Froomkin, 2000; Rule, 2004; Cassidy and Chae, 2006) describe it as a dynamic issue that has the potential to impact attitudes, perceptions, and even the environment and future technology developments (Crompton, 2001). However, despite growing interest in the topic, empirical research on technology-related privacy concerns from an information systems perspective remains at an embryonic stage and the limited number of studies on the construct that do exist tend to be limited in size and nature (Gefen and Straub, 2000; Cockcroft and Heales, 2005). Compounding the problem is the fact that some of these studies are beset by conflicting conceptualisations of the construct, as well as a lack of agreement regarding the factors that predict the perceptions, attitudes and behaviours of the individuals themselves. Consequently, it is difficult for privacy researchers within the information systems field to compare and contrast the results of previous studies in their efforts to progress understanding in this area.

In general, the limited studies that do exist within the field of information systems tend to focus on the technology-related privacy issues that exist in the online marketplace and the fact that consumers are becoming increasingly aware of the ways in which online vendors can collect and use potentially sensitive information regarding them and their actions without their express permission. From a vendor perspective the ability to collate such data allows them to provide customers with specifically custom- ised information thus conferring the benefits of a personalised shopping experience. From a consumer perspective however, the price of this personalised shopping experience may outweigh any customisation benefits, particularly when vendors have been known to sell information on consumers to third parties without their knowledge or consent. More recently however, researchers within the information systems discipline are moving beyond the context of

the marketplace and are focusing their efforts towards the privacy concerns emerging within the organisational framework. Researchers such as Nord *et al.,* (2006) note how the increas- ing proliferation of technologies into working environments has resulted in numerous situa- tions whereby the right to invade the privacy of the employee is being taken for granted by management. As a result, information systems researchers have begun to focus attention on the factors that influence technology-related privacy concerns in that specific context and the behavioural outcomes of such concerns.

The aim of this chapter therefore is to thoroughly describe the factors that influence technology-related privacy concerns and the emerging challenges that face the issue, particu- larly within the computer-mediated work envi- ronment. The current state of privacy legislation within Europe will be addressed and compared with the privacy laws and legal codes practiced in the US. Before doing so however, it is important to first discuss the conceptual confusion that surrounds the privacy construct itself as well as identifying the changing pattern and shifts of privacy concerns over the years.

THE PRIVACY CONSTRUCT

Privacy is a complex construct that has received attention from researchers within a broad spectrum of disciplines including ethics (Platt, 1995), economics (Rust *et al.,* 2002), marketing (Graeff and Harmon, 2002), management (Robey, 1979) as well as from the legal discipline even as far back as 1860 (e.g. Warren and Brandeis). However, despite such interest, the construct remains beset by conceptual and operational confusion. For example, Tavani (1999) remarks that privacy is neither clearly understood nor clearly defined while Introna (1996) comments that for every definition of privacy, it is also pos- sible to find a counterexample in the literature.

Understandably therefore, many researchers choose to define privacy specific to the focus of their study or the lens of their discipline in an attempt to evade this problem (Smith, 2001) but consequently the conceptual confusion that surrounds the construct remains undiminished. Unsurprisingly, these differing conceptualisations have manifested in similarly differing views regarding how the construct should be examined and measured. For example, privacy researchers within the legal discipline argue that privacy should be measured in terms of the rights of the individual whilst ethics researchers contend that the morality of privacy protection mechanisms for the individual should be the focus of research attention. Interestingly, and perhaps more sensibly, some economics researchers (Parker, 1974; Acquisti, 2002; Rust *et al.*, 2002) argue that in order to gain a full understanding of the privacy construct it is necessary to examine it from a multiplicity of viewpoints. Consequently, Parker (1974) maintains that privacy can be examined as a psychological state, a form of power, an inherent right or an aspect of freedom. More recently, Acquisti (2004) has emphasised the multi-dimensional nature of the construct and posited that privacy should no longer be viewed as a single unambiguous concept, but instead become a class of multifaceted interests.

One aspect of privacy on which many researchers concur is that central to our understanding of the construct is the issue of control, specifically the individual's need to have control over their personal information. Practitioner reports also confirm the importance that individuals attribute to being able to control their personal information (e.g. Harris, 2004). Control has been defined as *"the power of directing command, the power of restraining"* (Oxford, 1996: 291) and is consistently proposed in the literature as a key factor in relation to understanding individual privacy concerns. For example, Westin (1967) argues that privacy is the claim of individuals, groups, or institutions to decipher for themselves when, how

and to what extent their personal information is conveyed to others. This issue of personal control is supported by many researchers such as Fried (1968: 482) who defines privacy as the *"control we have over information about ourselves"* and Parker (1974: 281) who defines privacy in terms of the *"control over who can sense us"*. Personal control is important as it relates to the interest of individuals to control or significantly influence the handling of personal data (Clarke, 1988).

However, some researchers dispute the relevance of control in understanding privacy concerns. They argue that to define privacy in terms of control can yield a narrow perspective as not every loss or gain of control over information constitutes a loss or gain of privacy (Parker, 1974). For example, all online users who voluntarily provide personal information in the course of their transactions do not necessarily view that as a loss of control and consequently a loss of privacy. Even the knowledge that each of their online interactions is providing the vendor with a potential trail of information regarding who they are, their buying habits and other personal details does not necessarily constitute a lack of control or a loss or privacy in the eyes of such individuals. With that in mind, some researchers (Moor 1990, 1997; Schoeman 1984) suggest that it would be better to focus on the issue of restricted access rather than on the individual's need for control when trying to understand technology-related privacy issues. However, agreement as to the relevance of control in relation to understanding privacy remains a disputed issue in the literature.

In summary, privacy has been defined in the literature from a multiplicity of viewpoints, which has resulted in definitional and operational confusion regarding the construct, and consequently hindered our progress in gaining insight into the phenomena. As we enter the third millennium we have turned the corner into a place where technology pervades our day-to-day lives, and many things that would previously have been considered flights of imagination, are as a result of technology, becoming part of our reality (Kostakos *et al.,* 2005, Galanxhi and Fui-Hoon 2004). The increasing proliferation of technologies into both our work and leisure environments has resulted in a shift in our privacy concerns whereby the need for an improved understanding of the nature of technology-related privacy construct has increased rather than diminished.

Changing Patterns of Privacy Concerns

There is a general consensus that the advent of the electronic age has made the art of communication significantly easier. However, as previously noted, the influx and increased adoption of technology has also made it significantly easier for third parties to intercept and collate communications by others (Ghosh, 1998). In fact the adoption of the Internet for both business and recreational purposes simply fuels the privacy debate as the potential for individuals to gain unauthorised access to electronic networks poses as a significant threat (Laudon and Laudon, 2002). Furthermore it is apparent that any abuse that does occur will potentially have a vast, widespread effect for all parties involved Consequently, researchers such as Langheinrich (2001) note how emerging technological developments have therefore altered our understanding and views of privacy.

Laudon and Laudon (2002) further describe how the balance between the risks and rewards involved for an individual in adopting online procedures has shifted and changed over the years. They point to the effects of Moore's Law, noting how users are becoming more dependent on technologies, thereby becoming more susceptible and vulnerable to system errors and consequently heightening public concerns. Advances in data storage and data mining techniques have made privacy violations cheap, simple and effective whereby third parties can drill down through

data storage, generating extremely detailed personal profiles (Laudon and Laudon, 2002). Furthermore the very nature of the Internet allows individuals to transmit sensitive data and information at a click of a button thus resulting in significant invasions of privacy.

The bursting of the dot-com bubble in early 2000 represents another shift on the privacy scale. Many of the failed dot-com ventures were acquired by major or leading companies during the technological slow-down and in many cases this resulted in the transfer of customer lists and other sensitive information to the purchasing company, a fact which generated significant privacy concerns among the general public (Greenstein and Vasarhelyi, 2002). Similarly, the introduction of the Federal Bureau of Investigation's (FBI) Internet sniffing software known as 'Carnivore' shortly after the dot-com era in April 2000 was met with considerable resistance further indicating the rising level of privacy concerns amongst individuals. This software package was designed to monitor and track data passing through an ISP network but the significant anxieties that it generated once again points to a shifting level of privacy concerns in the technology-mediated interaction domain.

Privacy concerns are likely to continue to increase in tandem with the evolution of the ubiquitous and pervasive era. In fact, researchers such as Galanxhi and Fui-Hoon (2004: 748) note how *"privacy is threatened in a world where everything will have eyes and memory"*. In order to combat the escalation of privacy concerns they posit that emerging threats to privacy must be revisited with each new technology. Hong *et al.,* (2005) concur suggesting that it is the invisibility or translucent factor that applies to these technologies that constitutes the greatest privacy concern. The consistent increase in privacy concerns has been evidenced in many practitioner reports such as the Harris Interactive Poll which reported an increase in the number of privacy pragmatists from 54% in 1999 to 64%

in 2003 and a decline in the number of privacy unconcerned from 22% in 1999 to 10% in 2003 (Galanxhi and Fui-Hoon, 2006).

This uncertainty and lack of control related to all of the technologies mentioned reflects the significant asymmetry that exists in terms of what the Internet means to individuals versus companies. For example, Prakhaber (2000) rightly points out that while the technology has created better, faster and cheaper ways for businesses to meet the needs of their customers and better faster and cheaper ways for customers to satisfy their needs, the capability to leverage this technology is far higher for companies than for individual consumers. Because unequal forces, leading to asymmetric information availability, tilt the playing field significantly in favour of industry, such technologies do not create market benefit to all parties in an equitable manner. This imbalance of power also applies in a computer-mediated work environment. With this in mind, the emerging privacy issues within the organisational perspective will now be discussed and balance of interests in the specific context of an organisation between the employer and employee will be further explained.

MONITORING AND SURVEILLANCE IN THE WORKPLACE

The increasingly pervasive nature of modern technologies has opened up a spectrum of unregulated behaviour whereby previously accepted distinctions regarding correct and immoral behaviour are no longer always clear (Turban, 2006). For example, many questions surround the issue of surveillance—and in particular electronic surveillance in the workplace—which according to Clarke (1988) is the systematic monitoring of the actions or communication of individuals. In some cases individuals may be conscious that they are being monitored, they are just not sure of the extent and detail of that

monitoring. Neither are they aware of how that collated information is being employed by the monitoring body. Researchers such as Safire (2002) note how extreme pervasive surveillance tends to result in a 'creepy feeling' among those being monitored despite the fact that they may have done nothing wrong to merit such scrutiny.

The negative impact of surveillance techniques were first highlighted in Foucault's (1977) study of Jeremy Bentham's Panopticon. The idea behind this observation unit was to obtain the power of mind over mind allowing a prison warden to observe inmates undetected turning visibility into a trap (Foucault, 1977). Examples of modern day surveillance techniques are increasingly apparent within computer-mediated work environments. As a result the need to protect employees' privacy rights has become critical as modern technologies provide the opportunity for constant observation and continuous data collection. In fact, the monitoring of employees' computer-related interactions has previously been described as an 'electronic whip' used unfairly by management (Tavani, 2004). Consequently employees are now facing an electronic form of panopticism whereby they can be observed by an electronic boss who never leaves the office (Wen *et al.*, 2007).

An Industry Perspective

As previously mentioned much of the past literature has focused on the impact of technology-related privacy concerns from a transactional perspective, with views of the online consumer paramount to the discussion. However, recent practitioner reports confirm that these privacy concerns are equally salient in the computer-mediated work environment. For example, in 2001 it was estimated that over three quarters of all major US firms monitored and recorded employees' activities in the workplace, a figure which has doubled since 1997 (AMA, 2001). This figure has remained constant over the years with researchers such as D'Urso in 2006 estimating the figure to now stand at 80% of all organisations. Forms of surveillance in the workplace can include anything from the monitoring of email and Internet usage, to the taping of phone conversations and use of video surveillance or in some cases GPS tracking devises. A recent survey carried out by The American Management Association (2005) revealed that 76% of organisations monitor an employee's Internet usage, 65% of which block certain Websites thus indicating inappropriate Web surfing as a primary concern. The use of email within organisations has quickly become a fundamental part of the communication structure of many organisations (Jackson *et al.,* 2001). In fact researchers such as Muckle (2003) note how access to email facilities within the workplace is now an expected practice. While the speed and productivity benefits of email are immense from an organisational perspective, the placing of stringent controls by management on the use of email systems may also jeopardise an employee's privacy (Van der Lee and Zwenne, 2002). It is now estimated that as many as 55% of the 526 US firms surveyed retain and review employee's email messages, a figure which has risen 8% since 2001 (AMA, 2005). While such reports give some indication of the growing problem within US industry, as far as it is possible to ascertain no practitioner studies have yet been conducted from a European perspective and consequently our understanding in how to diminish these growing concerns remains limited.

It is reasonable to assume that in some instances management may have legitimate reasons to monitor their employee's actions. For example researchers such as Laudon and Laudon (2001) emphasise the risk of adverse publicity for the company resulting from offensive or explicit material circulating within the organisation. In addition the Internet has increased the possible threat of hostile work environment claims by

providing access to inappropriate jokes or images that can be transmitted internally or externally at the click of a button (Lane, 2003). In fact, a study carried out in 2000 concluded that 70% of the traffic on pornographic Websites occurs during office hours, with ComScore networks reporting 37% of such visits actually taking place in the office environment (Alder *et al.,* 2006). Moreover, the risks to organisations stretch also to the abuse of the email system, with virtually all the respondents in an AMA (2003) survey reporting some sort of disruption resulting from employee's email use. For example, 33% of the respondents experienced a computer virus, 34% reporting business interruptions and 38% of which had a computer system disabled for some time as the result of a bogus email. In a similar vein, Jackson *et al.,* (2003) conducted a study to investigate the costs incurred by management as a result of such email interruption. The study indicated that it took the average employee between 1 and 44 seconds to respond to a new email when the icon or pop up box appeared on their screen. 70% of these mails were reacted to within 6 seconds of them appearing and a further 15% were reacted to within a 2 minute time period. Overall the study found that it took on average 64 seconds for an employee to return to a productive state of work for every one new mail sent. Other practitioner reports also identify the potential cost of email usage with as many as 76% reporting a loss of business time due to email problems, 24% of which estimating a significant two day loss of company time (AMA, 2003). These statistics are not so surprising given the amount of time the average employee today spends online. The survey further reported that the average employee spends 25% of his or her working day solely on their emails, with a further 90% admitting to sending and receiving personal mails during company time.

Whilst the need to improve productivity is a common rationale for employee monitoring, other motivations such as minimising theft and preventing workplace litigation are considered equally justifiable in the eyes of management seeking to protect the interests of the organisation. The former motivation is particularly understandable as research shows that employees stole over 15 billion dollars in inventory from their employers in the year 2001 alone (Lane, 2003). In addition, the seamless integration of technology into the workplace has increased the threat of internal attacks with Lane (2003) noting the ease at which sensitive corporate data and trade secrets can be downloaded, transmitted, copied or posted onto a Web page by an aggrieved employee. Internal attacks typically target specific exploitable information, causing significant amounts of damage to an organisation (IBM, 2006). Management need to ensure that their employees use their working time productively and are therefore benefiting the organisation as a whole (Nord *et al.*, 2006). It is apparent however, that tensions will remain constant between both parties unless some form of harmony or balance between the interests of both the employer and employee is achieved.

In order to balance this conflict of interests it is vital that clearly defined rules and communication regarding what constitutes disciplinary offences in relation to the use of technology are implemented into the workplace (Craver, 2006). The need for structure becomes all the more apparent with researchers such as Selmi (2006) emphasising the differing views and tolerance levels certain managers may hold. For example, if an employee is hired to work, then technically they should refrain from sending personal emails or shopping online during working hours. However, as a general rule, most management will overlook these misdemeanours as good practice or in order to boost worker morale. The situation becomes more serious however when the abuse of Internet privileges threatens to affect the company itself, be it through loss of profits or adverse publicity for the company. Evans (2007) notes how the problem increases

as boundaries in the modern workplace begin to blur and confusion between formal and informal working conditions arise. She argues for example that allowing an employee to take a company laptop into the privacy of their own home could send out a message that the computer can be used for personal use which may lead to the employee storing personal data on management's property. Legally, the employer would have claims over all of the data stored on the computer and could use it to discipline or even terminate an employee (Evans, 2007). Godfrey (2001) concludes that the apparent lack of natural limit in regards what is acceptable or indeed unacceptable relating to email privacy makes the task of defining appropriate principles all the more difficult for a researcher to contend.

Despite growing interest in communication-monitoring practices from an industry perspective, the number of empirical studies emerging in academic literature is remarkably limited (Boehele, 2000). The few studies that do exist provide interesting insights into the importance of this issue and its potential for future research. For example, Stanton and Weiss' (2000) study examined the issue of electronic monitoring from both the employer and employee perspective. A three-part survey was derived from a longer semi-structured research instrument used by the authors in a previous study. A surveillance-related question deliberately worded with both positive and negative connotations acted as the focal point of the survey. The respondents exhibited a mixed view of attitudes in response towards electronic surveillance. Surprisingly, only a minority of those actually subjected to monitoring found it to be invasive or negative in any way. Other employees actually displayed positive attitudes towards high levels of surveillance in that it provided them with a deep sense of security and ensured that the line of command was set in place. In this way the results presented go against that of popular culture and the negative hype surrounding electronic surveillance. However, the authors note that a number of limitations in relation to their study, particularly in relation to sample size, restrict its generalisability and point to the need for more detailed research on this issue.

Alder *et al.,* (2006) contend that a critical task facing organisations and researchers is to identify the factors that improve employees' attitude and behavioural reactions to internet monitoring. These authors developed a causal model to explain the impact Internet monitoring has on advanced notification, justification and perceived organisational support in relation to organisational trust in the workplace. Following an initial survey, the respondents were unknowingly subjected to an Internet monitoring and filtering system implemented in their company. Afterwards they were informed that this monitoring activity was taking place. After a set time period, the sample group was sent a second survey to which only 63% of the original sample responded. When the level of employee trust and their attitude towards their specific job was examined, the results indicated that frequent users' of the Internet were more affected by the implementation of internet monitoring than those who used it on an irregular basis. Table 1 outlines literature representing employee concerns.

Despite the limited nature of the above studies, some comparisons can be drawn. Firstly, in both studies the research instrument was adapted from a previous study and reused in a way specific to the study itself. A closer look at the studies presented reveals that both researchers employed a basic survey approach administering questionnaires and surveys to the respondents. Given the sensitive nature of the research undertaken, it is not surprising to see both paper and Web surveys utilised between the two. For example, Alder *at al.,* (2006) opted for a traditional paper and pencil survey in their study to alleviate any concerns the employee might have in regards leaving an electronic paper trail which could be monitored by the employer. The authors of both studies acknowledge their studies' limitations particularly in relation to sample size. It is clear that if understanding in this area is to be progressed, the need for researchers to employ extensive and rigorous surveys that contain large samples that can provide generalisable findings is mandated.

Another relatively new stream of research in the literature aims to control the growing fears surrounding this issue of intense surveillance by turning the tables on the issue. According to Mann (2004: 620) sousveillance or *"to watch from below"* offers a possible solution to the many challenges of monitoring technologies. Mann (2004) suggests an approach whereby the observer becomes the observed, in effect

Table 1. Employee dataveillance concerns

Study	Context	Research Method		
		Participants	**Sample**	**Methodology**
Stanton and Weiss (2000)	Identifies which attitudes, perceptions, beliefs were influenced by electronic monitoring	Employee	49 respondents from approx 25 different organisations.	Online survey
Alder *et al.,* (2006)	Examines the effects of Internet monitoring on job attitudes	Employee	62 employees from a heavy service sales and equipment sales and service centre	Two paper services were administered

transferring the balance of power in favour of the consumer or employee for a period. In this way monitoring techniques are not diminished but simply extended to consider the view of the opposite party, whereby a mutual respect will be achieved between both parties. While the question as to whether this can be realistically achieved by employees remains uncertain, the issue of sousveillance persists as a relatively new concept in the literature and certainly represents an interesting avenue for future research.

PRIVACY LEGISLATION FROM A EUROPEAN PERSPECTIVE

Little progress can be made to curb any privacy violations unless the relevant privacy legislation is taken into account. Currently, employment legislation within the United States does not sufficiently regulate and control managements' collection and use of employee data and consequently researchers such as Evans (2007) are looking towards their European counterparts for the solution. Any country that is a member state of the European Union [EU] must comply with the legislation that is passed by any one of its major institutions as well as any national laws or regulations set in place. Furthermore, under the Directive 95/46/EC and Article 29 WP55 all monitoring in the organisation must pass a number of specified criteria before being implemented into the workplace in order to curb growing concerns.

Under current EU legislation, the employer must prove that electronic observation is a necessary course of action for a specific purpose before engaging in it. In this way, management are encouraged to consider traditional and less intrusive measures of observation before resorting to electronic means (Directive 95/46/EC). For the purpose of Internet or indeed email surveillance, it is likely that some form of electronic monitoring would be enlisted, however in such

instances the employer by law can only keep the data in question no longer than necessary for the specific monitoring action. In a similar vein, the second principal of finality denotes that any data collected, must be used for an explicit purpose and therefore cannot be processed or used for any other purpose than initially intended (Directive 95/46/EC).

Under EU law, management must also be clear and open regarding the surveillance practices of the organisation and are therefore obliged to provide employees with information regarding organisational monitoring policies. In this way employees are advised of improper procedures and disciplinary offences that justify the scope of invasive monitoring techniques (Directive 95/46/EC). Furthermore details of the surveillance measures undertaken are also provided so as the employee will know who is monitoring them, how they are being monitored as well as when these actions are taking place. This principal of transparency also provides individuals with access rights to personal data processed or collated by management, allowing them to request its rectification or deletion where appropriate (Directive 95/46/EC).

The fourth criterion, legitimacy is similar to that of necessity in so far as data can only be obtained for a justifiable purpose and must not contravene an employee's fundamental or inherent right to privacy. Under this element of the legislation however, data of a very sensitive nature can be deemed too personal to collect and collection therefore must be specifically authorised by a national law in extreme circumstances (Directive 95/46/EC). Organisations must also comply with the notion of proportionality, using the most non-intrusive or least excessive action in order to obtain the desired information. For example the monitoring of emails should if possible focus on the general information such as the time and transmission as opposed to the content if the situation permits. If however viewing of the email content is deemed necessary then the law presides that the privacy of those outside of the organisation should also be taken into account and that reasonable efforts be made to inform the outside world of any monitoring practices (Directive 95/46/EC).

Any data that is collated on an employee must only be retained for as long as is necessary under this European law and data that is no longer needed should then be deleted. Management should specify a particular retention period based on their business needs so as employees are constantly aware of the ongoing process (Directive 95/46/EC). Furthermore, provisions should be set in place to ensure that any data that is held by the employer will remain secure and safe from any form of intrusion or disturbance. The employer is also required to protect the technological medium from the threat of virus as a further means of protecting the personal data (Directive 95/46/EC).

Researchers such as Laudon and Laudon (2001) suggest that the information privacy laws within the European Union are considerably more focused than the Fair Information Practices [FIP] eminent in the United States. While both Europe and the United States define privacy in a similar way, it is the fundamental objective of their information privacy laws that signifies the major difference between the two. The Fair Information Practices are a set of principals that govern the use and collection of data whereas the European equivalent lends itself more to the protection of data by allowing individuals to pursue complaints with the support of state bodies such as the data commissioners and data protection agencies (Laudon and Laudon, 2001). As a result researchers such as Evans (2007) note how the existence of these European laws that favour the employee are consequently putting considerable pressure on the United States to adopt similar laws. It is important to note however that while the issues of privacy are by and large well defined in European law—and in particular in Irish law, some smaller firms may

not be fully aware what their legal obligations entail (D'Arcy and O'Dea, 2008) and therefore future research would need to reflect this.

CONCLUSION

The primary objective of this chapter was to provide a concise and consolidated overview of the technology-related privacy construct with particular focus on emerging concerns regarding the use of employee dataveillance technologies within an organisational context. In general, studies on technology-related privacy concerns are few and the construct is characterised by a lack of conceptual consensus that further compounds our lack of understanding. While current European privacy legislation tends to favor the rights of the employee, the acuteness of employees' privacy concerns remains undiminished due to an increasing awareness of the ability of employers to use technology to gather, store and analyse sensitive information on employees on a continuously updated basis and without their knowledge.

Despite growing practitioner interest in internet-mediated communication monitoring within the workplace, this issue has received surprisingly little attention from academic researchers to date. This is particularly surprising considering the potential influence of such practices on employee productivity and morale. The critical tasks that organizations will need to consider in order to improve employees' attitudes and behavioural reactions to the practice of electronic surveillance techniques remain undetermined. In conclusion, the emerging privacy challenges that relate to living and working in a computer-mediated environment are significant and likely to increase in importance over the coming years. They highlight the need for rigorous research on technology-mediated privacy concerns in general, for definitional and conceptual consensus to progress our understanding of the construct, and the need to apply a focus that encapsulates the social, technical and legal issues that surround this phenomenon.

REFERENCES

Acquisti, A. (2002). Protecting Privacy with Economics: Economic Incentives for Preventive Technologies in Ubiquitous Computing Environment. *Workshop on Socially-informed Design of Privacy-enhancing Solutions in Ubiquitous Computing: Ubicomp.*

Acquisti, A. (2004). Privacy in Electronic Commerce and the Economics of Immediate Gratification. *Proceedings of ACM Electronic Commerce Conference [EC04]*, New York, NY: ACM Press, (pp. 21-29).

Alder, G. S., Noel, T. W., & Ambrose, M. L. (2006). Clarifying the effects of Internet Monitoring on Job Attitudes: The Mediating Role of Employee Trust. *Information and Management, 43(*7), 894-903.

AMA Survey (2001). *Workplace Monitoring and Surveillance* [online]. Available from: http://www.amanet.org/research/pdfs/ems_short2001.pdf

AMA Survey (2003). *Email Rules, Policies and Practices Survey* [online]. Available from: http://www.amanet.org/research/pdfs/email_policies_practices.pdf

AMA Survey (2005). *Electronic Monitoring and Surveillance Survey* [online]. Available from: http://www.amanet.org/research/pdfs/ems_summary05.pdf

Boehle, S. (2000). They're Watching You. *Training, 37*(8), 68-72.

Cassidy, C. M. & Chae, B. (2006). Consumer Information Use and Misuse in Electronic Business: An Alternative to Privacy Regulation. *Information Systems Management, 23*(3), 75-87.

Clarke, R. A. (1988). Information Technology and Dataveillance. *Communication of the ACM, 31*(5), 498-512.

Cockcroft, S., & Heales, J. (2005). National Culture, Trust and Internet Privacy Concerns. *16th Australasian Conference on Information Systems*, Sydney.

Concise Oxford Dictionary of Current English, Oxford University Press, England, 1996.

Craver, C. B. (2006). Privacy Issues Affecting Employers, Employees and Labour Organizations. *Louisiana Law Review, 66*, 1057-1078.

Crompton, M. (2001). What is Privacy? *Privacy and Security in the Information Age* Conference, Melbourne.

Directive 95/46/EC: Article 29 WP55 2002. [online]. Available from: http://ec.europa.eu/justice_home/fsj/privacy/docs/wpdocs/2002/wpss_en.pdf

D'Arcy, D., & O'Dea, A. (2008). Privacy Affairs. Marketing Age. *Marketing Institute of Ireland March/April, 2*(2), 20-26.

D'Urso, S. C. (2006). Who's Watching Us at Work? Toward a Structural-Perceptual Model of Electronic Monitoring and Surveillance in Organisations. *Communication Theory, 16*, 281-303.

Evans, L. (2007). Monitoring Technology in the American Workplace: Would Adopting English Privacy Standards Better Balance Employee Privacy and Productivity? *California Law Review, 95*, 1115-1149.

Foucault, M. (1977). *Discipline and Punish: The Birth of the Prison*. Great Britain: Penguin Books.

Fried, C. (1968). Privacy. *Yale Law Journal, 77(*1), 475-493.

Froomkin, A. M. (2000). The Death of Privacy? *Standford Law Review, 52*(146), 1461-1543.

Galanxhi-Janaqi, H., & Fui-Hoon Nah, F. (2004). U-commerce: Emerging Trends and Research Issues. *Industrial Management & Data System, 104*(9), 744-755.

Galanxhi-Janaqi, H., & Fui-Hoon Nah, F. (2006). Privacy Issues in the Era of Ubiquitous Commerce. *Electronic Market, 16*(3), 222-232.

Gefen, D., & Straub, D. (2000). The Relative Importance of Perceived Ease of Use in IS Adoption: A Study of E-Commerce Adoption. *Journal of the Association for Information Systems, 1*(8).

Ghosh, A.P. (1998). E-Commerce Security—Weak Links, Best Defenses. New York: John Wiley and Sons, Inc.

Godfrey, B. (2001). Electronic Work Monitoring: An Ethical Model. *Australian Computer Society,* 18-21.

Graeff, T. R., & Harmon, S. (2002). Collecting and Using Personal Data: Consumers' Awareness and Concerns. *Journal of Consumer Marketing, 19*(4), 302-318.

Greenstein, M., & Vasarhelyi, M. (2002). *Electronic Commerce: Security, Risk Management and Control.* Boston: McGraw-Hill.

Harris Poll (2004). *Privacy and American Business Press Release* [online]. Available from: http://www.epic.org/privacy/survey/

Hong, D., Yuan, M., & Shen, V.Y. (2005). Dynamic Privacy Management: A Plug-In Service for the Middleware in Pervasive Computing. In *Mobile-HCI, ACM International Conference Proceeding Series; 111, Proceedings of the 7th international conference on Human computer interaction with mobile devices & services.*

Introna, L.D. (1996). Privacy and the Computer: Why we need Privacy in the Information Society. *Ethicomp e-Journal, 1.*

IBM (2006). *Stopping Insider Attacks: How Organizations can Protect their Sensitive Information* [online]. Available from: http://www-935.ibm.com/services/us/imc/pdf/gsw00316-usen-00-insider-threats-wp.pdf

Jackson, T., Dawson, R., & Wilson, D. (2001). *The Cost of Email Interruption.* Loughborough University Institutional Repository: Item 2134/495 [online]. Available at: http://km.lboro.ac.uk/iii/pdf/JOSIT%202001.pdf

Konvitz, M. R. (1966). Privacy and the Law: A Philosophical Prelude. *Law and Contemporary Problems, 31*(2), 272-280.

Kostakos, V., O'Neill, E., Little, L., & Sillence, E. (2005). The Social Implications of Emerging Technologies. *Editorial/ Interacting with Computers, 17,* 475-483.

Lane, F.S. (2003). The Naked Employee: How Technology is Compromising Workplace Privacy. New York: AMACOM, American Management Association.

Langheinrich, M. (2001). Privacy by Design—Principles of Privacy—Aware Ubiquitous Systems. In *Proceedings of the 3rd International Conference on Ubiquitous Computing.* Springer-Verlag LCNS 2201, 273-291.

Laudon, K. C., & Laudon, J. P. (2001). Essentials of Management Information Systems. *Organisation and Technology in the Networked Enterprise.* New Jersey: Prentice Hall, 4th Edition.

Laudon, K. C., & Laudon, J. P. (2002). *Management Information Systems: Managing the Digital Firm.* New Jersey: Prentice Hall International, 7th Edition.

Mann, S. (2004). Sousveillance: Inverse Surveillance in Multimedia Imaging. *MM'04, ACM,* 620-627.

Moor, J. H. (1990). Ethics of Privacy Protection. *Library Trends, 39*(1&2), 69-82.

Moor, J. H. (1997). Towards a Theory of Privacy in the Information Age. *Computers and Society, 27*(3), 27-32.

Muckle. R. (2003, July). *Email Monitoring in the Workplace: A Simple Guide to Employers.* Waterford Technologies.

Nord, G. D., McCubbins, T. F., & Horn Nord, J. (2006). Email Monitoring in the Workplace: Privacy, Legislation, and Surveillance Software. *Communications of the ACM, 49*(8), 73-77.

Parker, R. B. (1974). A Definition of Privacy. *Rutgers Law Review, 27*(1), 275.

Platt, R. G. (1995). Ethical and Social Implications of the Internet. *The Ethicomp E-Journal, 1.*

Powers, M. (1996). A Cognitive Access Definition of Privacy. *Law and Philosophy, 15*(4), 369-386.

Prakhaber P.R. (2000). Who owns the Online Consumer? *Journal of Consumer Marketing, 17*(2), 158-171.

Robey, D. (1979). User Attitudes and Management Information System Use. *Academy of Management Journal, 22*(3), 527-538.

Rule, J.B. (2004). Towards Strong Privacy: Values, Markets, Mechanisms, and Institutions. *University of Toronto Law Journal, 54*(2), 183-225.

Rust, R. T., Kannan, P. K. & Peng, Na. (2002). The Customer Economics of Internet Privacy. *Journal of the Academy of Marketing Science, 30*(4), 455-464.

Safire, W. (2002). The Great Unwatched. *New York Times.* Available at http://query.nytimes.com/gst/fullpage.html?res=9A03E7DB1E3FF93BA25751C0A9649C8B63

Schoeman F. (1984). Privacy: Philosophical Dimensions of the Literature. In *Philosophical Dimensions of Privacy: An Anthology,* (F. Schoeman, ed., 1984).

Selmi, M. (2006). Privacy for the Working Class: Public Work and Private Lives. *Louisiana Law Review, 66,* 1035-1056.

Smith, H. J. (2001). Information Privacy and Marketing: What the U.S Should (and Shouldn't) Learn from Europe. *California Management Review Reprint Series, 43*(2), 8-33.

Stanton, J. M. & Weiss, E. M. (2000). Electronic Monitoring in their Own Words: An Exploratory Study of Employees' Experiences with New Types of Surveillance. *Computers in Human Behavior, 16*(4), 423-440.

Tavani, H. T. (1999). Internet Privacy: Some Distinctions between Internet Specific and Internet-Enhanced Privacy Concerns. *The ETHICOMP E-Journal, 1.*

Tavani, H. T. (2004). *Ethics and Technology: Ethical Issues in an Age of Information and Communication Technology.* New Jersey: John Wiley and Sons, Wiley International Edition.

Turban, E., Leidner, D., McClean, E., & Wetherbe, J. (2006). *Information Technology for Management—Transforming Organisations in the Digital Economy.* USA: John Wiley & Sons Inc, 5th Edition.

Van der Lee, J., & Zweene, G. J. (2002). Email and Internet Monitoring at Work. *MTA* January/February, 36-37.

Warren, S., & Brandeis, L. D. (1860). The Right to Privacy. *Harvard Law Review, 4*(193).

Wen, H. J., Schwieger, D., & Gershuny, P. (2007). Internet Usage Monitoring in the Workplace: Its Legal Challenges and Implementation Strategies. *Information Systems Management, 24,* 185-196.

Westin, A. (1967). *Privacy and Freedom.* New York: Ateneum.

Chapter XIII
Fear of Flying and Virtual Environments:
An Introductory Review

Giovanni Vincenti
Gruppo Vincenti S.r.l., Italy

ABSTRACT

Fear of flying is a common problem that many people have to face. As varied as the causes may be, all kinds of fears have many aspects in common. Much is known to us about fear, and the fields of psychology and psychiatry teach us that many times we can conquer fears simply by exposing the subject to the dreaded object. Human-Computer Interaction has branched even in this direction, including the treatment of phobias. With the help of Virtual Reality researchers around the world have recreated using a computer the way that psychologists and psychiatrists cure fears, adding a twist. Many times patients are supposed to go the extra mile and expose themselves, little by little, to what they are afraid of. Virtual Reality brings this type of exposure directly to the patient, with the comfort that such fear can be stopped at any time, since it is only a computer simulation. The most successful studies have been performed on arachnophobia, or the fear of spiders. There are also studies that deal with the fear of heights and the fear of public speaking. Some studies have also been performed on addressing the fear of flying using a virtual environment. This work is a review of such methods, and an explanation of the principles behind the motivation for these studies.

INTRODUCTION

Computers play a significant role in most aspects of our lives nowadays. We use computers when we drive to work, they help us perform our jobs better and more accurately, and sometimes they even help us fall in love by letting us talk to old friends and make new ones through chat programs. Some people share their whole lives on a computer, recording nearly every move they make on a web log, an on-line diary (Wijnia, 2005).

As this invention takes more of a dominant part in our lives, we adapt more and more to having this powerful tool around. Especially, children are growing up using computers as their teachers, playgrounds and friends (Subrahmanyam et al., 2000). The same computers help our lives not only in health, but also when we are sick. Computers help hospitals keep track of patients, but they are also used as a diagnostic tool, allowing doctors to reach conclusions on tough cases or request the help of colleagues located on the other side of the world (Shortliffe et al., 2001). In these cases, computers serve as passive tools that increase the quality of work.

Human-Computer Interaction

The field of Human-Computer Interaction (HCI) is a rather new addition to the world of computer science. The potential that HCI has is great, when we explore in a bit more detail all the applications and repercussions that these concepts bring to the world of computing (Shneiderman, 1998). The branch of HCI that deals with "Direct Manipulation and Virtual Environments', as discussed in Shneiderman (1998), is most relevant to this discussion. Virtual Environments (VE) and Virtual Reality (VR) are closely tied with informatics applied to the fields of medicine and psychology. Hodges et al. (2001) report that some of the applications of VR that are more widely used are the ones that interact with "humans' cognitive and physical (manipulation) aspects",

besides its application to entertainment. If we apply these concepts to medical informatics, the role of computers towards patients becomes more active.

Hodges et al. (2001) explore the application of VR to curing psychological and physical disorders, such as fears. This team of researchers applied concepts of HCI to the treatment of patients who suffer of many types of phobias, such as fear of height, or acrophobia, fear of spiders, or arachnophobia, and fear of public speaking. In this chapter we will explore a few, but we will concentrate especially on the fear of flying.

VIRTUAL REALITY AND VIRTUAL ENVIRONMENTS

Anyone who has created a program to supply the demands of a customer knows about scope creep. When the project starts, the future users usually list an endless sequence of features they would like to see included in their new work tool. As they test the application, they say that it would be nice if this program could also do this or if it could do that. Scope creep does not only mean that users are asking for more, it also means that programmers will have to provide greater functionality. This very concept is the driving motor that pushed developers to create programs that users could not only observe, but could interact with at multiple levels.

Although the distinction between VR and VE is not well agreed-upon, most resources seem to point to the idea that VR is the field that addresses the creation of VEs that make users believe they are immersed in real environments. Shneiderman (1998) introduces the concepts of VR and VE using an example that is extremely effective. As a team of people start the creation of a building, the people who are commissioning such work will get a good idea of what things will look like from the sketches and diagrams. Should the same drawings be reproduced on a computer screen, they will get a much more vivid representation of what is going to be built.

An even more realistic representation would come from substituting a projector to the computer monitor. Such projector would display the image of the new building onto a wall, giving to the observers a much more impressive display. The next step is the creation of controls that allows the commissioners to zoom in, move the point of view around the building, and perhaps even change the height of the observation point.

This level of exploration is not that far from connecting the controls to a treadmill, where observers can actually walk around the scene, which is now projected through a head-mounted display, instead of a projector. What the commissioners are now experiencing is a virtual environment.

"Looking at" vs "Being in"

Many fields and applications are sufficiently satisfied by letting users "look at" something, as explained in Shneiderman (1998), but some may benefit greatly from allowing them to "be in" the situation that they would otherwise have to imagine. Some of the most common simulators replicate the behaviors of airplanes (Shneiderman, 1998). These simulations are built using the same components that are also used to build the real airplanes, giving them a realistic feel. The pilots are exposed to scenarios from all around the world, thanks to high quality displays that replace the windows. They are also given a sense of motion through elaborate hydraulic systems.

The cost of such simulators can be quite high, but their value is far greater than anything else (Shneiderman, 1998). A pilot can train for any type of occurrence using one of these simulators, while staying safe within a confined environment. These pilots can fail certain maneuvers over and over, until they finally understand the dynamics of the situation. They will not have destroyed any planes, but, more importantly, they will be

alive and they will walk away from the simulator with the knowledge of what to do in those emergencies.

A Recipe for Success

In order to create a successful VE, Shneiderman (1998) says that it is important to integrate multiple technologies. These technologies include visual displays, head-position and hand-position sensing devices, force feedback, sound input and output, if possible, the recreation of other sensations, and finally the use of cooperative and competitive VR. All these aspects enhance the realism that the VE brings to the users, submerging their senses even deeper.

WHAT IS FEAR

As we will see shortly, such immersion of the senses is necessary to bring healing to the person who has a hard time at dealing with phobic episodes. Before we get any deeper into the adaptation of VR to clinical purposes, we should review briefly the beast that we are trying to eradicate.

Fear is a debilitating factor that many people have to confront over and over, sometimes on a daily basis. Whatever the fear may be, the person who is victim to this dormant enemy can be truly impaired from functioning properly. For this reason, fears need to be addressed to their core. Taking care of the symptoms may not be enough.

Fear belongs to the group of Obsessive-Compulsive Disorders (OCD), as described in Jenike (2001). Even though fear is well documented in the reactions that the body encompasses, there is no one source where all fears come from (Jenike, 2001).

We can distinguish between two categories of reactions (Richmond, 2005). The first deals with the body, and a person may show any of the following symptoms: muscle tension, tremors, heavy breathing, heart palpitations, sweating, weakness and dizziness among the most common (Richmond, 2005). The second category of reactions deals with psychological responses. The symptoms that accompany a fear attack are: impaired memory, narrowed perceptions, poor judgment, negative expectancies and perseverative thinking (Richmond, 2005). In this particular work we will observe the fear of flying a bit more closely, but all fears have these common symptoms.

One Output from Many Inputs

Every fear addresses multiple weak points of the person that may lead to the reactions that we just presented. Fear of flying, for example, can be triggered by a single factor, or a combination of multiple reasons. Usually fear of flying can be associated with any of these problems: fear of heights, enclosed spaces, crowded conditions, not feeling in control, being in a machine which functions in ways that the subject ignores (Richmond, 2005).

Exposure Therapy

The most common remedy for all types of fear is well agreed upon, and that is exposure therapy (Jenike, 2001; Richmond, 2005; Hodges et al., 2001). Such exposure can be sudden, but in most cases, when the treatment to a phobia is coordinated by a specialist, it is administered in increasing doses. Curing fear of flying usually starts from meetings with a psychologist to learn how to deal with anxiety, and then slowly the person is introduced to the object of fear (Hodges et al., 2001). The first exposures may be limited to just a trip to the airport, seeing and hearing planes take off and land, eventually the patient will then be able to enter a stationary airplane. The most effective part of the cure would be a flight after such slow habituation to this feared environment (Hodges et al., 2001).

Exposure is then the silver bullet that may destroy fears. But can a computer really replace the exposure to the real thing, the object, or the situation, that is feared? We will explore some well-known phobias, and the changes that can be seen in a person after they take part in sessions where they were treated using computers.

VIRTUAL ENVIRONMENTS APPLIED TO CLINICAL SETTINGS

As the power of computers increases and people ask that programs do more and more, the market now has a wide variety of applications that perform every function imaginable and some that can't even be imagined possible. Medicine is one of the fields that benefit the most from these technological advancements. The field of medical informatics is deeply involved with the field of computer science to bring to doctors and patients the best possible applications. Many times doctors and patients turn to a computer screen to compromise between the highly technical jargon that every caregiver is used to and the poor medical vocabulary that the average person possesses. As the doctor explains the images that both see, the patient may feel relieved by understanding better the matters discussed.

Computers as Passive or Active Tools

The visualization aspect of medical informatics is just one side of a diamond that is extremely multifaceted. Szekely and Satava (1999) give a brief introduction to the role that VR has come to play in daily practices in hospitals around the world. VR has dramatically changed the way many doctors prepare for surgery. Surgeons used to review anatomy books and operating procedures before VR took over with tools that allow the user to walk through a complete surgery. Such tools are not used only to perform preparations for surgeries, but they are also used by students as a learning ground for anatomical, physiological and pathological notions. Diagnosis is, of course, another aspect of medicine that benefits greatly from these advancements (Shortliffe et al., 2001).

The uses that Szekely and Satava (1999) list in their article are primarily passive uses, the computer serves as a tool, and not as an active element of a therapy. This is where VR shows all its strengths. Hodges et al. (2001) describe three applications that were deeply affected by VR. These three clinical applications are the treatment of anxiety disorders, such as phobias, pain distraction and ankle rehabilitation. We will explore in depth only the first application.

Defining Metrics

Conducting a scientific experiment to find a clear physiological correlation between the pre-exposure and the post-exposure anxiety conditions of a patient who undergoes exposure therapy is hard, as Hellstrom and Ost (1996) report. Their study investigated the physiological changes that a subject experiences before coming into contact with the object feared. They were monitoring the diastolic blood pressure of the subject before exposure to VR treatment and then they compared it with the post-exposure reading.

The subjects analyzed were tested for a variety of fears, as to establish a common denominator that could be used as a baseline for further studies. There were four tests in this experiment, two related to phobia of spiders, one related to blood phobia, and the fourth related to phobia of needles. The results were inconclusive about the hypothesis that diastolic blood pressure can be used as a metric when analyzing the effect of VR exposure treatment. For this reason, the majority of researchers base their findings on subjective reports coming from the patient, or the observation of the modification of the person's behavior when facing the feared object.

The First Experiments

The mid to late '90s are the years that are most prolific for studies on VR applied to the treatment of phobias. We can see through the work of various groups that this alternate approach to exposure therapy is actually worthy of notice.

The first study, a classic that is mentioned in various sources, is the work of Hodges et al. (1995) that worked on acrophobia, or the fear of heights. Participants were exposed to virtual footbridges, balconies and glass elevators. Results from this experiment laid the ground for what was coming next. The researchers were actually able to note that the changes made in the participants were not just an effect of short-term habituation, but it changed how they felt about heights perhaps permanently. Seven out of 10 subjects exposed themselves to what was the dreaded situation in real-life, without being prompted to do so (Hodges et al., 1995).

A second publication that is worthy of notice is the one that reports the case study on a single subject about the treatment of claustrophobia, or the fear of enclosed spaces (Botella et al., 1998). In this work, the patient was exposed to a graded exposure method by means of a VE. At every step the perception of the VE was getting smaller around the subject. The patient was originally scheduled to receive only six exposures. After the final exposure, she had to undergo a medical test unrelated to the study that placed her in a small enclosed environment. She reported a little stress, but overall she was extremely satisfied with the outcome. At that point, the researchers decided to administer two more exposure sessions to achieve overlearning (Botella et al., 1998).

Attacking Arachnophobia at Multiple Levels

An extremely successful study was conducted by Hoffman et al. (2003). As we stated earlier,

Shneiderman (1998) says that an effective VE must include simulations of several aspects of an environment.

Most studies only report of exposing the person to a VE with a head-mounted display and perhaps with sound. This takes care of only two of the senses. Hoffman et al. (2003) take this matter further and decide to simulate tactile cues. They investigated different exposure therapies where subjects were exposed to no treatment, subjects were exposed to a standard VE (without tactile cues) and finally subjects exposed to VE and tactile cues. This study concluded that both VE exposure therapies are more effective than no therapy, showing that their VE is suitable for exposure therapy. Moreover, they linked a higher decrease in the symptoms of phobia displayed by the subjects that received exposure therapy with tactile cues (Hoffman et al, 2003).

Post-Traumatic Stress Disorders

Fear does not come only from an object or a situation, but also from memories, as explained in Foa and Kozak (1986). Such phobias can be classified under the name of Post-Traumatic Stress Disorders (PTSD). Consequently, studies were conducted to investigate if VE approaches to exposure therapy can help in the habituation of a person to memories of a harmful situation. Especially two teams of researchers stress such aspect.

Weiss et al. (1992) led a study on patients with PTSD from the Vietnam War. This study does not show VE as an effective exposure therapy for curing PTSD in post-war patients, but it is reported that this tool is a very effective one when a psychologist is walking the subject through memories.

The second team of researchers investigated the usefulness of VE for exposure therapy in a PTSD patient after a terroristic attack, the attack to the Twin Towers on September 11th, 2001 (Difede and Hoffman, 2002). The subject already sought help with traditional image exposure therapy, but

this approach was ineffective. Difede and Hoffman (2002) created a VE where the patient was exposed to planes flying over the towers, planes crashing, sounds imitating explosions, and the images of people falling from the windows. Such exposure therapy was reported by the subject to be effective. As specified by the researchers, this report analyzes only one subject and it should not be generalized. The outcome though seems promising for a larger scale testing.

FEAR OF FLYING AND VIRTUAL ENVIRONMENTS

So far we have analyzed many aspects that relate to the field of HCI: psychology, physiology and perhaps even medicine. We have explored what VR is with Shneiderman's work (1998). We have also explored a bit what fear is, and some of the responses that we get from being afraid of something (Jenike, 2001). We have merged the fields of HCI and cognitive psychology by reviewing some work that was done in this direction (Hellstrom and Ost, 1996, Hodges et al, 1995, Botella et al., 1998, Hoffman et al., 2003, Weiss et al., 1992, Difede and Hoffman, 2002). We can now focus on the analysis of the fear of flying.

Quantifying the Fear of Flying

Hodges et al. (1996a) say that, as an estimate, 10 to 25 percent of the population suffers from a fear of flying. Moreover, they report of a survey that was conducted by the Boeing Airplane Company that affirms that "25 million adults in the United States are fearful about flying" (Hodges et al., 1996a). It was not specified if any of these people do fly, it was clearly stated though that "20 percent of those who do fly depend on alcohol or sedatives during flight" to mitigate the symptoms of their phobia (Hodges et al., 1996a). In this article the authors cite the work of Roberts (1989), which affirms that in 1989 the airline industry had an estimated annual revenue loss of $1.6 billion dollars because of people's fear of flying. Although more recent estimates are not available, Osborne (2001) speculates about the cost of a higher fear of flying after the episodes of September 11th, 2001.

Steps to Recovery (That Become Obstacles)

Just like every other phobia we have analyzed so far, exposure is one of the best ways to break down the physical and psychological responses. Hodges et al. (1996a) outline the steps to recovery: therapists, sessions that describe accurately the functioning of a plane, and an actual plane for exposure therapy. They also outline some of the reasons why people do not want to go through a program that would help them. Therapists take time, and meeting a therapist may be expensive. Most people won't push themselves to do something unless they really have to, and the fear of being on an airplane keeps them from flying, but

also from seeking help. They also feel that they put themselves at risk. There are also expenses associated with the final stages of the exposure therapy, which will, most likely, involve a round trip flight.

Fear of Flying: A Case Study

For these many reasons, Hodges et al. (1996b) proposed the solution of using VR to manage some of the issues that may lead people to desist from taking action against their fears. In their article they write about the VE that they developed, and that they feel would replace in vivo (in real life) exposure therapy. They created a VE that matched the scale of a real Boeing 747 airplane. They modeled the interior of the cabin as well as the outside of the airplane because the key to a stationary simulator is making the person feel as if they were inside the real environment. In order to fully do so, the investigators also created all the items that a person would see through the window, such as runways, airports and clouds.

Figure 1. State diagram (Hodges et al., 1996b)

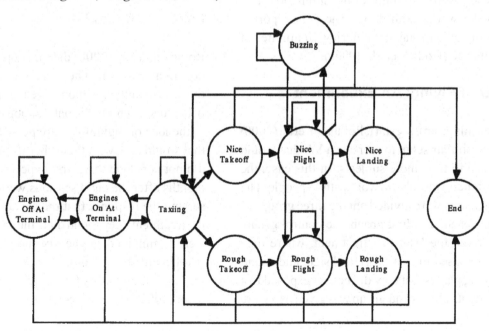

Figure 1 shows the state diagram representing an airplane. Such diagram outlines the possibilities that were explored during the simulation within Hodges et al. (1996b). The subject was not only exposed to a head-mounted display, but sound was also accompanying the experience. The subject was exposed to this therapy for six sessions. Each time the simulation was composed of a different series of events, based on the state diagram in Figure 1. The researchers were trying to recreate an environment that would be as similar to the real environment as possible. As there is no metric that assesses such gap, they were not able to verify this aspect.

Upon completing the six exposures, the subject was then able to complete a round trip flight on a real airplane. The subject reported that she was much less afraid after VR exposure therapy. She took questionnaires that classified her fears on a scale from 1 to 10, where a 1 indicates calm when flying and 10 indicated a debilitating effect of the phobia. Before exposure her score was 8, and after the treatment her level lowered to 4. Clinically, her tests showed a great improvement as well. She said that she still felt some of the physical and psychological symptoms of fear, but she just had to think of the simulation, and then she would calm down. She even reported of being able to stay calm during 10 minutes of turbulence (Hodges et al., 1996b).

Fear of Flying: An Experiment

Given this promising start, Rothbaum et al. (2000) used a similar setup to recreate a VE that would be used to treat more subjects. In this case, the researchers were able to work with 45 people. The participants were divided among three groups of fifteen each. The first group, the control group, was given the Wait List treatment, where they were exposed to an airport, and sight and sound of flying planes, but they did not get exposed to a real flight. The second group was given exposure to a real airplane and real flights. Finally, the third group was given the VE exposure treatment. All groups were to undergo an 8-session procedure. The first four sessions were the same for everyone, and it consisted of counseling sessions with a therapist. Then each of the groups took their own route.

The results this time left no doubt in the matter of VE exposure accommodating only one person's fears, or if it would also help others. Rothbaum et al. (2000) write:

"In this controlled trial comparing [VR exposure] therapy, [in-vivo exposure] therapy, and a [wait-list] control for treatment of FOF, VRE and SE were shown to be equally effective both in decreases in symptoms as measured by standardized questionnaires and by the number of participants to actually fly on a real airplane following treatment."

Moreover, they report that "[anxiety] ratings during the actual flight indicated that [VR exposure]-treated patients were as comfortable as [in-vivo exposure]-treated patients" (Rothbaum et al., 2000). These results are in line with the hypothesis that was proposed by this team of researchers and many others before them.

Lasting Effects?

Rothbaum et al. (2000) did not stop at a post-exposure assessment. They wanted to ensure that the effects of this method were not only to be attributed to a temporary habituation of the person to the idea of flight, but were persistent changes that would stay with them. For this reason, they did not conclude their first experiment until six months after the eight sessions were over. In assessing the response that the participants had to the treatment, they found that "the gains observed were maintained at the six month follow-up" (Rothbaum et al., 2000).

In addition to this first follow-up, Rothbaum et al. (2002) also performed a second follow-up with the participants that were assigned to the VR exposure group as well as the ones assigned to the standard exposure. Although the researchers were not able to get in touch with everyone, they were able to base their observations on 24 people. As a further affirmation that this method does have lasting effects, it was reported that 92% of VR exposed participants and 91% of standard exposure participants had flown on a plane since the end of the sessions described in Rothbaum et al. (2000). These findings show that not only VR exposure is as effective as standard exposure therapy in the short term, but they also have lasting effects.

CONCLUSION

The world of Virtual Reality is a branch of computer science, and especially Human-Computer Interaction, that is undergoing constant development and improvement. Applications range from simple interfaces that allow children to play games more interactively to curing fears that a person may have carried within for years.

We explored many different phobias and their treatments, both with in-vivo exposure and exposure by means of a virtual environment. We put special emphasis on the cure of fear of flying, reviewing not only a case study that seemed promising, but also a full experiment with three groups of subjects. The outcomes of these experiments were very clear when we compare the effects of exposure to a virtual environment with those of a standard exposure therapy. Moreover, the fact that a virtual reality exposure has lasting effects comparable to the ones of standard exposure therapy suggest that this approach leverages on the same inputs that make the in-vivo exposure so successful, leaving us with a cheaper and safer alternative for curing phobias.

REFERENCES

Botella, C., Banos, R., Perpina, C., Villa, H., Alcaniz, M. & Rey, A. (1998). Virtual Reality Treatment of Claustrophobia: a Case Report. *Behaviour Research and Therapy*, 36(2), 239-246.

Difede J. & Hoffman, H. (2002). Virtual Reality Exposure Therapy for World Trade Center Post-traumatic Stress Disorder: A Case Report. *CyberPsychology and Behavior*, 5(6), 529-535.

Foa, E. & Kozak, M. (1986). Emotional Processing of Fear: Exposure to Corrective Information. *Psychological Bulletin*, 99(1), 20-35.

Hellstrom, K. & Ost, L. (1996). Prediction of Outcome in the Treatment of Specific Phobia. A Cross-Validation Study. *Behaviour Research and Therapy*, 34(5), 403-411.

Hodges, L., Kooper, R., Meyer, T., Rothbaum, B., Opdyke, D., deGraaff, J., Williford, J. & North, M. (1995). Virtual Environments for Treating the Fear of Heights. *IEEE Computer*, 28(7), 27-34.

Hodges, L., Watson, B., Kessler, G., Rothbaum, B. & Opdyke, D. (1996a). Virtually Conquering Fear of Flying. *IEEE Computer Graphics and Applications*, 16 (6), 42-49.

Hodges, L., Rothbaum, B., Watson, B., Kessler, G. & Opdyke, D. (1996b). A Virtual Airplane for Fear of Flying Therapy. *Proc. VRAIS '96, IEEE Virtual Reality Annual Symposium*, 86-93.

Hodges, L., Anderson, P, Burdea, G., Hoffman, H. & Rothbaum, B. (2001). Treating Psychological and Physical Disorders with VR. *IEEE Computer Graphics and Applications*, 21(6), 25-33.

Hoffman, H., Garcia-Palacios, A., Carlin, A., Furness III, T. & Botella-Arbona, C. (2003). Interfaces that Heal: Coupling Real and Virtual Objects to Treat Spider Phobia. *International Journal of Human-Computer Interaction*, 16(2), 283-300.

Jenike, M. (2001). An Update on Obsessive Compulsive Disorder. *Bulletin of the Menninger Clinic*, 65(1), 4-25.

Osborne, A. (2001). *Fear of Flying 'will Cost Airlines Billions'*. Money.Telegraph. Retrieved on April 10th, 2005, from http://www.news.telegraph.co.uk/money/main.jhtml?xml=/money/2001/09/12/cnair12.xml

Richmond, R. (2005). Fear *of Flying: Symptoms, Medical Issues, and Treatment*. Retrieved on April 10th, 2005, from http://www.guidetopsychology.com/fearfly.htm

Roberts, R. (1989). Passenger Fear of Flying: Behavioural Treatment with Extensive In Vivo Exposure and Group Support. *Aviation, Space, and Environmental Medicine*, 60, 342-348.

Rothbaum, B., Hodges, L., Smith, S., Lee, J. & Price, L. (2000). A Controlled Study of Virtual Reality Exposure Therapy for the Fear of Flying. *Journal of Consulting and Clinical Psychology*, 68(6), 1020-1026.

Rothbaum, B., Hodges, L., Anderson, P., Price, L. & Smith, S. (2002). Twelve-Month Follow-up of Virtual Reality and Standard Exposure Therapies for the Fear of Flying. *Journal of Consulting and Clinical Psychology*, 70(2), 428-432.

Shortliffe, E., Perreault, L, Wiederhold G. and Fagan, L. (2001). *Medical Informatics*. New York, NY: Springer-Verlag Publishers.

Shneiderman, B. (1998). *Designing the User Interface*. Reading, MA: Addison Wesley Longman Publisher.

Subrahmanyam, K., Kraut, R., Greenfield, P. & Gross, E. (2000). The Impact of Home Computer Use on Children's Activities and Development. *The Future of Children*, 10(2), 123-144.

Szekely, G. & Satava, R. (1999). Virtual Reality in Medicine. *British Medical Journal*, 319, 1305-1308.

Weiss, D., Marmar, C., Fairbank, J., Schlenger, W., Kulka, R., Hough, R. & Jordan, B. (1992). The Prevalence of Lifetime and Partial Post-Traumatic Stress Disorder in Vietnam Veterans. *Journal of Traumatic Stress*, 5, 365-376.

Wijnia, E. (2005). *Understanding Weblogs: a Communicative Perspective*. Retrieved on April 10th, 2005, from http://elmine.wijnia.com/weblog/

Chapter XIV
A Context–Based Approach for Supporting Knowledge Work with Semantic Portals

Thomas Hädrich
Martin-Luther-University Halle-Wittenberg, Germany

Torsten Priebe
University of Regensburg, Germany

ABSTRACT

Knowledge work can be characterized by a high degree of variety and exceptions, strong communication needs, weakly structured processes, networks and communities, and as requiring a high level of skill and expertise as well as a number of specific practices. Process-oriented knowledge management suggests to focus on enhancing efficiency of knowledge work in the context of business processes. Portals are an enabling technology for knowledge management by providing users with a consolidated, personalized interface that allows accessing various types of structured and unstructured information. However, the design of portals still needs concepts and frameworks to guide their alignment with the context of persons consigned with knowledge-intensive tasks. In this context the concept of knowledge stance is a promising starting point. This paper discusses how knowledge stances can be applied and detailed to model knowledge work and support to support it with semantic context-based portals. We present the results from implementing a portal prototype that deploys Semantic Web technologies to integrate various information sources and applications on a semantic level and discuss extensions to this portal for the support of knowledge stances.

INTRODUCTION

Knowledge work can be characterized by a high degree of variety and exceptions, strong communication needs, weakly structured processes, networks and communities, and as requiring a high level of skill and expertise as well as a number of specific practices (Schulze, 2003). Process-oriented knowledge management (KM) suggests to focus on enhancing efficiency of knowledge work in the context of business processes and by this way to link KM efforts the value chains of organizations (Edwards & Kidd, 2003; Maier & Remus, 2003). Various types of information and communication technologies (ICT) are deployed to support knowledge work, ideally forming an enterprise-wide knowledge infrastructure (EKI) (Maier, Hädrich, & Peinl, 2005). Portals are an important part of the EKI since they provide users with a consolidated, personalized interface that allows accessing various types of structured and unstructured information as well as applications simultaneously.

Models are a foundation to design supporting ICT in general and portals in particular. However, process-oriented KM lacks ways to model knowledge work in the context of business processes, especially the knowledge-oriented actions connected to the tasks accomplished in business processes. Here, the concept of knowledge stance can be seen as a promising starting point (Hädrich & Maier, 2004). This paper has the goals to (a) discuss how knowledge stances can be applied and detailed to model knowledge work and to support it with semantic portals, (b) present results from implementing a portal prototype that deploys Semantic Web technologies to integrate various information sources on a semantic level (Priebe, 2004; Priebe & Pernul, 2003), and (c) discuss extensions to this portal to support knowledge stances.

The remainder of this paper is organized as follows: The concept of knowledge stance is outlined in section 2 together with its conceptual foundations. Section 3 provides a framework for context information and relates knowledge stances to it. Section 4 presents the INWISS knowledge portal prototype and how it applies Semantic Web technologies to provide a context-based portlet integration. Section 5 proposes extensions to the portal based on knowledge stances and discusses how these can be implemented. Section 6 concludes the paper and gives an outlook on future research.

MODELING KNOWLEDGE WORK

Modeling approaches applied in KM can be classified according to the concepts that they primarily emphasize into four categories: (1) person (e.g., communication relationships and structural organization), (2) process (e.g., business processes and tasks), (3) topic (e.g., knowledge structure defined by an ontology) and (4) tool (e.g., software architecture and interaction of components) (Maier, 2004). From the view of KM, particularly the interconnections between concepts in these categories are of interest, e.g., "Markus Schmidt" (person) is experienced in "project management" (topic). When choosing a process-oriented KM approach, the relationships between the categories process and topic are of primary interest, i.e. the link between functions and tasks accomplished in business processes and the knowledge applied and created in this context. This section describes two perspectives on knowledge work that correspond to these two categories: a process-oriented and an activity-oriented perspective. The concept of knowledge stance is one possible way to connect these perspectives.

Process Modeling vs. Activity Modeling

Examples for traditional process modeling approaches are ADONIS (Junginger, Kühn, Strobl, & Karagiannis, 2000), ARIS (Scheer, 2001), IEM

(Spur, Mertins, & Jochem, 1996), MEMO (Frank, 2002), PROMET (Österle, 1995), SOM (Ferstl & Sinz, 1994), UML-based process modeling (Oestereich, Weiss, Schröder, Weilkiens, & Lenhard, 2003) and IDEF. Examples for approaches that extend process modeling for KM are ARIS with extensions (Allweyer, 1998), PROMET®I-NET (Bach & Österle, 2000), GPO WM (Heisig, 2002), KMDL (Gronau, 2003), Knowledge MEMO (Schauer, 2004) and PROMOTE (Karagiannis & Woitsch, 2003). The main extensions are the introduction of additional object types like knowledge object, i.e. topics of interest, documented knowledge, individual employee, and skill as well as the introduction of model types like knowledge structure diagram and communication diagram. Even though the added concepts describe a portion of the context of knowledge work, they are not suited to model the often unstructured and creative learning and knowledge practices in knowledge work and particularly their link to business processes.

Activity theory has been proposed to guide the analysis of knowledge work (Blackler, 1995) and the design of information systems (Clases & Wehner, 2002; Kuutti, 1997; Sachs, 1995). The underlying thesis is that knowledge is not an object, a passive unit. Rather, the processes of knowing and doing take place in so-called activity systems (Blackler, 1995) which are the basic unit of analysis (not to be confused with activities in Porter's value chain and activities in UML). The core idea of activity theory is that human activity is a dialectic relationship between individuals (called agents or subjects) and objects (the purpose of human activity) that is mediated (a) by tools and instruments like cultural signs, language and technologies and (b) by communities of people that are involved within the transformation process of the activity (see Figure 1). The relation between subject and community is determined by implicit or explicit social rules. A division of labor (e.g., role system) defines the relation of the

community to the object of the activity system. The outcomes of the activities' transformation process are intended or unintended results.

Another important feature of activity theory is that activities have a hierarchical structure: (1) The activity is driven by a common motive which reflects a collective need and the reason why the activity exists (Engeström, 1999). (2) It is accomplished by actions directed to goals coupled to the motive of the activity. Actions consist of an orientation and an execution phase: the first comprises the planning for action, the latter its execution by a chain of operations (Kuutti, 1997). Repeated exercise leads to better planning of the action that then can be conducted more successfully. Due to learning and reutilization, the planning phase can become obsolete and actions collapse into operations. (3) Operations are executed under certain conditions. They are clearly structured and easy to automate. These levels are characterized by a dynamic relationship: Elements of higher levels collapse to constructs of lower levels if learning takes place. They unfold to higher levels if changes occur and learning is necessary. Activity modeling comprises identification of activity systems together with their context and history. It emphasizes analysis of the mediating relationships and tensions between their constituting components and other activity systems.

Figure 1. Socially-distributed activity system (Blackler, 1995; Kuutti, 1997)

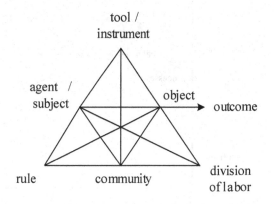

Compared to process modeling, activity theory contributes the concept of mediation, consideration of individual and group motives, the notion of communities and ways to conceptualize learning by routinization. The concepts provided by activity theory are well suited to analyze the creative, unstructured and learning-oriented practices of knowledge work. However, activities primarily aim at the joint creation of knowledge (exploration of knowledge). They lack integration with the value chain and it is not ensured that they are oriented towards creating customer value (exploitation of knowledge). Therefore, concepts of process and of activity modeling have to be combined in order to get a more comprehensive picture of knowledge work in a business context.

The Concept of Knowledge Stance

As we have seen, activity modeling differentiates between the levels motives, goals and conditions. Approaches for process modeling distinguish be-

tween three corresponding levels of granularity: (1) Value chains arrange value-adding activities (Porter, 1985), (2) business processes connect functions and (3) workflows orchestrate tasks. Figure 2 contrasts both perspectives. An important difference is that in the process-oriented perspective, a change from a higher to a lower level corresponds to refinement whereas in the activity-oriented perspective this is associated with routinization. We propose to connect both perspectives on the level of goals by the concept of knowledge stance.

A knowledge stance is a class of recurring situations in knowledge work defined by occasion, context, and mode resulting in knowledge-oriented actions (Hädrich & Maier, 2004). It describes a situation in which a person can, should, or must switch from a business-oriented function to a knowledge-oriented action. In a process-oriented perspective, an employee accomplishes functions on the level of goals that belong to a value chain on the level of motives by fulfilling a sequence of tasks on the level of conditions. Simultane-

Figure 2. Concept of knowledge stance

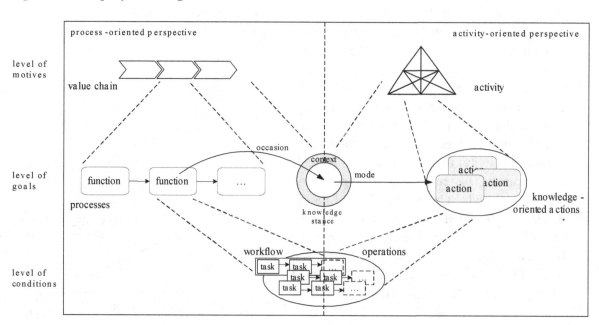

Table 1. Components of the knowledge stance

Component	Description
Occasion	is a type of opportunity to learn and to generate knowledge related to the (core) competencies of the organization within the function of a business process.
Context	describes the current work situation, i.e. process context, activity context, and person-related information.
Mode	classifies knowledge-oriented actions into expressing, monitoring, translating and networking.
Action	refers to an unstructured knowledge-oriented action and is specified by occasion, context and mode.

ously, she can be involved in an activity framing knowledge-oriented actions and corresponding operations. It can (a) be focused on the business process or (b) pursue a motive not related to the business process (e.g., an effort to build competencies) and thus may make a direct or indirect contribution to the process goal.

A business process offers several *occasions* to learn and to generate knowledge related to the core competencies of the organization. Occasions trigger knowledge stances and are associated with the functions of the business process by offering the opportunity or the need for knowledge-related actions. A knowledge stance is not limited to the generation of knowledge, but may also include the translation and application of knowledge created outside the knowledge stance.

The *context* includes all dimensions suitable to describe the current situation of the person. It comprises the process context consisting of elements such as involved organizational units, roles, and resources as well as elements of the activity context, e.g., contacts to persons that are member of a community dealing with creation of related knowledge. We will discuss types and dimensions of context information in detail in section 3.1.

The *mode* classifies what actions can be performed and refers to four informing practices (Schulze, 2000; Schulze, 2003): (a) expressing is the practice of self-reflexive conversion of individual knowledge and subjective insights into informational objects that are independent of the person, (b) monitoring describes continuous non-focused scanning of the environment and gathering of useful "just in case"-information, (c) translating involves creation of information by ferrying it across different contexts until a coherent meaning emerges, and (d) networking is the practice of building and maintaining relationships with people inside and outside the organization.

During the process pf modeling, context, mode and occasion are means to specify a set of available, allowed or required knowledge-oriented actions. Examples for actions are evaluate source, indicate level of certitude, compare sources, link content, relate to prior information, add metadata, notify and alert, ask questions, and offer interaction (Eppler, 2003). In contrast to the clearly defined sequences of functions in the process-oriented perspective, there is no predetermined flow of actions. They are accomplished by executing operations suited to serve the goals of the action. Table 1 summarizes the components of a knowledge stance.

An example for a knowledge stance is "learning about product features", which is related by the occasion "product introduced by vendor" to the procurement process of a company that sells home electronics. It is linked to an activity that aims at gathering knowledge about relevant products and their features and thus strongly related to the core competency "offering the right product at superior prices to the customer".

Shop assistants involved in the sales process and consigned with the tasks to consult customers are part of this activity. The knowledge stance thus links multiple processes, activities and people in support of learning and generation of new knowledge. Examples for knowledge-related actions triggered by the knowledge stance are "contact a shop assistant" and "look-up information about product features".

CONTEXT-BASED SUPPORT

Knowledge comprises observations that have been meaningfully organized and embedded in a context through experience, communication, or inference that an actor uses to interpret situations and to accomplish tasks (Maier, 2004). It is tightly coupled to and embedded in its context of creation and application. In a broad definition, context is "any information that can be used to characterize the situation of an entity; an entity is a person, place or object that is considered relevant to the interaction between a user and an application, including the user and applications themselves" (Dey & Abowd, 1999). Note that our idea of a user context is different from the notion of context in work on context mediation and interchange for data integration (Tan, Madnick, & Tan, 2004) which rather considers a user-independent application context.

To effectively support knowledge work, it is crucial to provide specifically those functions and knowledge artifacts that the user needs in his current context. Main challenges are to identify and model the relevant context dimensions, to automatically recognize the user's current context, to detect transitions between contexts, to keep context models up-to-date and last but not least to (dynamically) decide which functions and elements are suited best to support users in a certain context. Another challenge is that users may not apply a system because context-based filtering

mechanisms are experienced as being too rigid by hiding information that may be relevant (Dey & Abowd, 1999; Klemke, 2000).

In the last years, many approaches and prototypes for context-based support of system users were introduced, particularly in the area of knowledge management and information retrieval, but also in computer supported co-operative work (CSCW), workflow, and more recently in mobile computing. For example, the PreBIS approach (Böhm & Härtwig, 2005) provides a situated information delivery by attuning a so-called contextualized information system to an organization in a pre-build (modeling) phase. Similarly, the KnowMore project (Abecker, Bernardi, Maus, Sintek, & Wenzel, 2000; Maus, 2001) proposes the use of the context information that can be derived from a workflow management system. Information on the current task context is taken from the workflow and organizational model and transferred into a query on a document base. The DECOR project (Abecker et al., 2001) tries to extend the ideas form the KnowMore project, that were originally developed for strongly structured processes, to weakly structured processes. Finally, Henrich & Morgenroth (2002) (see also below) propose a high-level architecture for retrieving documents relevant to the current user context by including plug-ins in client applications that communicate the context to a search engine. In more recent publications the authors have concentrated on the particular use within the software development environment (Henrich & Morgenroth, 2003).

Context Types and Dimensions

In the following, we present a framework suited to structure relevant context dimensions. We distinguish two general categories of context types: (a) The context of a person dealing with a concrete task in a specific situations and (b) the context of knowledge elements (to be) stored in a system (see Figure 3).

Figure 3. Context types and corresponding dimensions

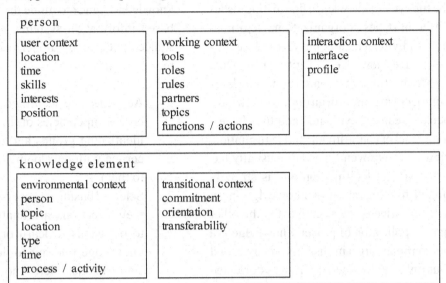

The situation of a person can be described by the following types of contexts (Henrich & Morgenroth, 2003):

- The *user context* represents the physical context (location, time) of the user, her personal profile including her interests and skills in selected topics as well as the organizational position (leading e.g., to specific user privileges).

- The *working context* characterizes the current tasks and actions a user needs to accomplish in a process-oriented *and* in an activity-oriented perspective (see section 2.1) with regard to available material or immaterial tools (e.g., information systems, methods, language), roles (e.g., role of the user in a business process, role in a community), rules (e.g., access rights, organizational and social rules), partners (e.g., communication partner, external contact persons, experts in a specific domain), topics (e.g., information and knowledge relevant for completion of a task) and related functions or knowledge-oriented actions (e.g., functions of another business process that applies the results of the current function).

- The user's *interaction context* reflects past and current interactions with the application system, e.g., selected menus or dialogues and protocols about the systems usage.

The context of knowledge elements can be described by an *environmental context* consisting of the six dimensions person (e.g., author, target group, expert), related topics (e.g., knowledge domains), geographical location (e.g., of organizational unit, of creation), type of knowledge (e.g., technical format, conceptual structure), time (e.g., creation time, modified date) and processes/activities where the knowledge element is applied or was created (Maier & Sametinger, 2002). These dimensions render the static part of the context directly related to the content of the knowledge element.

Additionally, the *transitional context* links the knowledge element to the processes of creation and application of knowledge:

- The dimension *level of commitment* refers to the life cycle of knowledge that distinguishes different stages of organizational legitimation. Individual ideas, opinions and suggestions have a low level of legitimation while good or best practices shared between a large number of members of an organization have been repeatedly evaluated and thus have a high level of commitment and legitimation. New and unproven knowledge usually has low levels of legitimation and is strongly linked to exploration of knowledge in an activity-oriented perspective. On the other hand, application of proven knowledge is a predominant target in business processes and thus links knowledge to the process-oriented perspective.

- *Orientation* refers to whether the context reflects the circumstances of creation, e.g., author's name, creation date and assumptions or purpose of creation, or whether it relates to retrieval and application of knowledge, e.g., by categorizing knowledge, relating it to other knowledge elements or domains, describing access rights, usage restrictions and circumstances as well as feedback from its re-use (Barry & Schamber, 1998; Eppler, 2003).

- The *level of transferability* indicates whether the knowledge element represents generalized knowledge that can be more or less easily be transferred to other contexts (e.g., guidelines applicable in multiple different processes) or reflects a particular case (e.g., experience about a particular product configuration in a special setting).

Applying Knowledge Stances for Context-Based Support

Compared to previous approaches of context-based support, our conceptualization of context is broader as it includes elements related to knowledge creation and thus to learning. This section clarifies how to apply the concept of knowledge stance to guide the design of context-based information systems. Firstly, knowledge stances need to be modeled by accomplishing the following steps:

1. Activities are identified by analyzing the core competencies of the organization and identifying groups and communities concerned with developing knowledge related to them.

2. Selected business processes are detailed and their functions are analyzed with regard to occasions to learn or to generate new knowledge relevant to develop these core competencies. Here, knowledge stances are linked to the process.

3. The context of each knowledge stance is defined based on elements of the working context elements for both, the process-oriented and activity-oriented perspective.

4. Knowledge-oriented actions suited to accomplish the function are defined and linked to the knowledge stance.

Knowledge stances are defined on type-level during build-time. At this stage, only those elements can be assigned that are valid for all instances of related processes and activities. Examples are guidelines, checklists and good or best practices (Goesmann & Herrmann, 2001). During run-time, the context of a knowledge stance can also comprise instance-level information, e.g., documents or functions used for the last execution of the function, contact information about employees that recently answered questions about a related topic or entries about new documented experiences. These elements will be part of the interaction context. Additionally, the user context can be combined with the working and interaction context to further filter the system's output.

Knowledge stances can be supported at different levels and by different means, e.g., by portals or workspaces that bundle KM functions and filter contents for knowledge stances, by user agents that guide through an action, by workflows that routinize parts of actions, by functions that enable for communication and collaboration between individuals that is triggered by the knowledge stance.

Ideally, an enterprise knowledge portal provides a platform with advanced knowledge services for publication, discovery, collaboration and learning, which brings together the various heterogeneous data and information sources and applications of the organization (Priebe & Pernul, 2003). Semantic Web technologies aim at structuring, describing, translating, reasoning about and securely accessing metadata and provide promising starting points for developing and implementing systems that support knowledge stances. Ontologies help to organize and link knowledge elements from multiple systems on a semantic level, represent the semantics of the organizational knowledge base and to structure the context of the knowledge elements. We will now turn to a prototypical implementation of a portal that deploys Semantic Web technologies and discuss extensions to it for supporting knowledge stances.

INWISS—AN INTEGRATIVE ENTERPRISE KNOWLEDGE PORTAL

Using Web-based technologies, knowledge portals are an emerging approach to provide a single point of access to various information sources and applications. Today's portal systems allow combining different portal components, so-called portlets, side by side on a single portal webpage (Wege, 2002). However, there is only little interaction between those portlets, which means that the user needs to manually transfer the context. Earlier, we presented an approach for integrative knowledge portals, communicating the user context among portlets using Semantic

Web technologies (Priebe & Pernul, 2003). For example, the query context of a reporting portlet, i.e. the information shown within a certain Online Analytical Processing (OLAP) report (Chaudhuri & Dayal, 1997), can be used by a search portlet to automatically provide the user with related intranet articles or documents. The approach is implemented within the INWISS knowledge portal prototype[a] (Priebe, 2004).

The use of Semantic Web technologies within knowledge portals has also been proposed in other works such as OntoViews (Mäkelä, Hyvönen, Saarela, & Viljanen, 2004), ODESeW (Corcho, Gómez-Pérez, López-Cima, López-García, & Suárez-Figueroa), and SEAL (Stojanovic, Maedche, Staab, Studer, & Sure, 2001). There however, metadata and ontologies are mainly used for content management and searching. Within INWISS we use a semantic representation of the user context to allow portlets to communicate with each other.

Context-Based Portlet Integration and Retrieval

Current portal systems provide only limited inter-portlet communication capabilities. If they are offered at all, they require extensive individual programming and are not suitable for portlets that are supposed to be deployed as standard software components. The IBM WebSphere Portal[b] provides a concept called Click-to-Action (C2A) and Cooperative Portlets which add advanced capabilities for managing portlet messaging. The communication paths between portlets no longer have to be explicitly coded but can be bound dynamically, i.e. the communication targets do not need to be known when the portlets are developed. However, the interpretation of messages and back-end integration are not addressed. The SAP Enterprise Portal[c] provides a technology called Drag&Relate. It allows dragging objects from a portlet onto a navigation panel invoking certain navigation actions. Drag&Relate only works for special Unifier iViews (portlets), which can be used to access (and combine) information from structured data sources such as relational databases or legacy systems. It handles the backend integration by means of a Unification Server. However, it can not be used to integrate third party portlets.

Our generic portlet integration approach within INWISS is based on communicating the user context among portlets, utilizing Semantic Web technologies for the context representation and back-end integration. Usually portlets only provide their portlet content for rendering the user interface (Wege, 2002). In addition, we introduce a context management service, where portlets can publish their current context, i.e. a semantic representation of what the user sees. Other portlets can pick that context up and use it to display related information. Figure 4 shows the overall architecture of our context-based portlet integration.

In order to be able to map the semantics of context elements between portlets, we base our approach on Semantic Web standards and technologies. The main idea is to use the Resource Description Framework (RDF) (W3C, 2004) to represent the context, i.e. portlets should annotate their content with RDF metadata. For example, if a user displays an OLAP report, the context can be represented as the set of elements such as product categories shown on the report (see Figure 5), or a portlet representing a customer relationship management (CRM) system displaying information about a certain customer can point to a customer object to represent its context.

The anonymous RDF description of the context represents the elements shown on the report by identifying them with URIs. Web Ontology Language (OWL) subclassing and concept mapping (W3C, 2004) (e.g., "owl:equivalentClass" and "owl:sameAs") and an inference engine can be used to map these to business objects from an enterprise ontology (see below). Hence, the portlets can use their own "language" to represent and interpret the context. The advantage of using the Semantic Web standards RDF and OWL over other logic languages is the already large (and emerging) support by standard software tools for storage and reasoning (e.g. Sesame[d] and Jena[e]).

We have identified different context integration scenarios, distinguished by the dimensions shown in the morphological box in Figure 6.

The first dimension is the *communication paradigm*. Context integration can follow a push or a pull principle. An example for a context pull is a search engine that uses the context of the other

Figure 4. Architecture for context integration

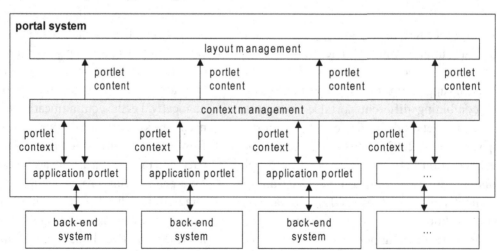

Figure 5. Sample portlet context

```
<?xml version="1.0"?>
<rdf:RDF xmlns:rdf="http://www.w3.org/1999/02/22-rdf-syntax-ns#"
  xmlns:mstr="http://www.microstrategy.com/terms/">

<rdf:Description>
  <mstr:metric rdf:resource="http://www.microstrategy.com/metrics/DollarSales"/>
  <mstr:element rdf:resource=
    "http://www.microstrategy.com/elements/Quarter_199801"/>
  <mstr:element rdf:resource=
    "http://www.microstrategy.com/elements/Quarter_199802"/>
  <mstr:element rdf:resource=
    "http://www.microstrategy.com/elements/Quarter_199803"/>
  <mstr:element rdf:resource=
    "http://www.microstrategy.com/elements/Quarter_199804"/>
  <mstr:element rdf:resource=
    "http://www.microstrategy.com/elements/Subcategory_1"/>
  <mstr:element rdf:resource=
    "http://www.microstrategy.com/elements/Subcategory_7"/>
  <mstr:element rdf:resource=
    "http://www.microstrategy.com/elements/Subcategory_9"/>
</rdf:Description>

</rdf:RDF>
```

Figure 6. Morphological box of context integration scenarios

communication paradigm	context push		context pull	
triggering event	explicit		implicit	
transmission method	unicast	multicast	broadcast	
published context	full		selective	

portlets to enhance the precision of the search results. For context pushes, the *triggering event* can be explicit or implicit. Explicit context pushes require the user to explicitly invoke the event, e.g. by clicking a "find related" button. Implicit context pushes are triggered automatically by other events, e.g., by user navigation within a portlet. An example for an implicit context push would be a topic navigation portlet that publishes the selected topic after every browsing event. Context push messages can be transmitted as *unicast* with a single portlet as the destination, as *multicast* with a set of target portlets, or as *broadcast* to all other portlets. Finally, the context published with a context push can be *full* (i.e. cover all information that is shown within the portlet) or *selective*.

A selective context push can only be explicit, as it requires the user to select the part of the context that should be published. An example for a selective context push would be a "find related" button next to a customer name in a customer list that triggers a CRM portlet to display related customer information.

Note that not all combinations of all characteristics are possible. The INWISS prototype realizes different context integration scenarios. A major application is to provide implicit searches based on the current user context. A "find related" button is provided in reporting and content portlets that triggers a search portlet to search for related documents by means of an *explicit unicast context push*. In order to be able to perform context-based searches and due to semantics that can be used, we use metadata queries rather than full-text searches by utilizing an enterprise ontology. For example, Figure 7 shows the Dublin Core[f] metadata for two documents: a product experience report (linked to the Freeplay Solar Radio product) and a procurement guidelines document. In addition to ontology elements a simple topic taxonomy is used for the annotation.

A search initiated by the portlet context shown in Figure 5 should also find the above experience report as being related if the described product belongs to one of the subcategories in the context. Firstly, the concepts used by the context provider (in this case a business intelligence system) need to be mapped to the ones used by the search engine. For example, the product category identified by the URI "http://www.microstrategy.com/elements/ Subcategory_1" needs be mapped to something like "http://www.inwiss.org/ontology#Audio".

Secondly, inference rules need to be used to provide that documents annotated with products belonging to "audio" are also annotated with the category. Finally, the property "mstr:element" needs to be considered as semantically identical with "dc:coverage". Note that this can be achieved by means of OWL or a similar ontology language, combined with an inference engine, requiring no modification of the portlets themselves.

Besides ontological concept mapping, such implicit queries require a fuzzy retrieval approach. Current metadata querying techniques, however, do not support vague queries. Hence, we developed a metadata-based information retrieval approach similar to classical retrieval models like the Vector Space Model (VSM) (Baeza-Yates & Ribeiro-Neto, 1999). It is based on the similarity of RDF descriptions: Both, the query and the resources are represented as RDF descriptions and the ranking of the search results is done

Figure 7. Sample document metadata

```
<?xml version="1.0"?>
<rdf:RDF xmlns:rdf="http://www.w3.org/1999/02/22-rdf-syntax-ns#"
  xmlns:dc="http://purl.org/dc/elements/1.1/">

<rdf:Description rdf:about=
  "http://www.inwiss.org/documents/FreeplaySolarRadio.pdf">

  <dc:type rdf:resource="http://www.inwiss.org/ontology#ExperienceReport"/>
  <dc:title>Freeplay Solar Radio Experience Report</dc:title>
  <dc:creator rdf:resource="ldap://cn=Tina Techwriter,ou=Sales,o=MyCompany"/>
  <dc:date>1998-04-05</dc:date>
  <dc:format>application/pdf</dc:format>
  <dc:description>The Freeplay(TM) Solar Radio never needs batteries -- the
    crank-up radio that runs for an hour on a single crank up. Solar power
    provides additional play time.</dc:description>
  <dc:subject rdf:resource="http://www.inwiss.org/topics/Sales"/>
  <dc:coverage rdf:resource="http://www.inwiss.org/ontology#FreeplaySolarRadio"/>
</rdf:Description>

<rdf:Description rdf:about=
  "http://www.inwiss.org/documents/ProcurementGuidelines.pdf">

  <dc:type rdf:resource="http://www.inwiss.org/ontology#Guideline"/>
  <dc:title>Procurement Guidelines</dc:title>
  ...
  <dc:subject rdf:resource="http://www.inwiss.org/topics/Procurement"/>
</rdf:Description>

</rdf:RDF>
```

using a similarity measure (Priebe, Schläger, & Pernul, 2004).

Such a metadata-based search engine will of course only work if the documents are properly annotated. This requires a certain critical mass of metadata-enriched documents. Users will only manually annotate documents, if they see a significant benefit from it. An extension to INWISS approaches the problem of metadata creation by means of text mining and (semi) automated annotation (Priebe, Kiss, & Kolter, 2005).

Prototype

Figure 8 shows a screenshot of the INWISS prototype (Priebe, 2004). At this point we provide four portlets: One is responsible for displaying intranet articles. A second one provides reporting access to a data warehouse. The navigation portlet represents a taxonomy-based topic browser.

Finally, a fourth portlet is responsible for metadata-based searches.

As mentioned above, INWISS demonstrates different context integration scenarios. The navigation portlet publishes its topic to the other portlets, triggered implicitly by browse events (*context push*). The search portlet accepts context messages from the content and the OLAP portlet. In this case the context push is triggered explicitly when the user clicks a "find related" control in the portlet title bar. Finally, when checking to use the portal context in the search portlet, the search engine will query the context of the other portlets and add it to the user query (*context pull*).

The context management is implemented as an extension to the Apache Jetspeed Portal platform[g]. For the data warehouse access we use the MicroStrategy 7i business intelligence system[h]. The open source Sesame RDF Framework[i] (Broekstra, Kampman, & van Harmelen, 2002)

Figure 8. Screenshot of the INWISS prototype

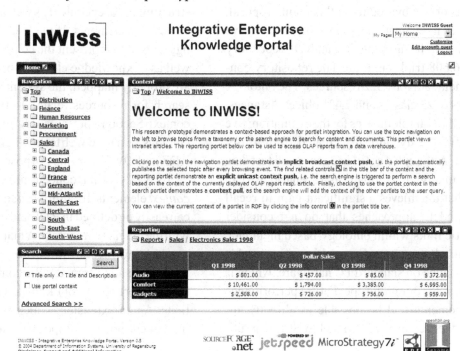

is used as a repository for resource metadata, a taxonomy, and an ontology.

Evaluation

The main contribution of INWISS is the proposal for a context-based portlet integration in enterprise portals. It enables the portal to allow implicit searches for unstructured documents (based on their metadata) using the context of an external application with access to structured database data. As an example we use a business intelligence system that views OLAP reports. The approach can, however, also be generalized to other scenarios.

The results are very promising. A major—although hardly measurable—success is the generic practicability of the context integration approach. The mentioned reporting portlet has been built completely independently, i.e. it contains no specific code that considers the existence of any of the other portlets. This ensures an applicability of the approach also for portlets that are provided as third party software components.

The semantic search engine (Priebe et al., 2004) is only a byproduct of this main proposal. However, its evaluation is more tangible. We have run the search engine against an RDF repository with 46.608 triples in total. The repository contains metadata for 1.322 resources. The ontology consists of 23 classes and 2.421 object instances. We used 10 sample queries for the evaluation; five of them were dynamically created from a user context. Although we still use generated test data and an imaginary company as a scenario, we can state that it achieves a significant gain in recall compared to approaches that do not consider semantic links within ontology-based metadata. In terms of query speed, we achieved acceptable performance on standard PC hardware, which is sufficient for our prototype. Future performance improvements will be possible by directly applying the Vector Space Model (VSM), e.g. utilizing the Jakarta Lucene information retrieval framework[j].

SUPPORTING KNOWLEDGE STANCES

User actions can be supported by various functions and services of the ICT infrastructure presented within the portlets of the portal. This comprises services for operative tasks and specifically those services part of a knowledge portal targeting support of knowledge-related actions and learning connected to the current function of the business process. These are (a) publication services to create, store and edit documents and to complement them with metadata, (b) discovery services to navigate the system, retrieve documented knowledge and discover subject matter experts, (c) collaboration services that allow for knowledge exchange over various media and cooperation between users, and (d) learning services that facilitate creation and use of electronic courses or evaluations (Maier, 2004; Maier et al., 2005).

In section 3 we have discussed dimensions to structure the user context as well as the context of knowledge elements. If one and the same ontology is used to represent the context of the user as well as of knowledge elements or if the concepts are properly mapped, the system can proactively search for resources related to the current user context. Section 4 presented INWISS, a portal that employs Semantic Web technologies (in particular RDF and OWL) for this purpose.

INWISS so far concentrates on *interaction context* elements. In addition, a static *user context* can easily be defined in RDF and queried together with the interaction context. A major improvement would be to regard the *working context* within the portal and to transfer this context to services that support (parts of) knowledge-oriented actions. As an extension, which we are currently implementing, we propose to add the idea of knowledge stances explicitly to the system, i.e. a knowledge stance model is used to represent the working context.

Representing Knowledge Stances

Figure 9 shows the schema of the knowledge stance and context model on which we base our extensions to INWISS (which represents a subset of the dimensions discussed in section 3.1). The part that already existed in the prototype before is the knowledge element perspective. Knowledge elements (*resources*, e.g., documents) are annotated with Dublin Core metadata pointing to a *type*, taxonomy *topics*, and ontology *objects* (e.g., products). Recall the examples from Figure 7 in section 4.1.

In addition, we introduce a person perspective, i.e. *persons* can also be described by metadata. The main concept that us used for annotation is

role, which will also be used to define responsibilities in the knowledge stance model. For example, Figure 10 shows the metadata for the employee "Michael Bates" who has the role "shop assistant" and is involved in the "sales" process. Annotating persons (and roles) with other context elements (topics and ontology objects) may also provide a *user context* that can be used together with the interaction context for contest pulls as sketched above. In addition, persons may also be considered as elements that are found by a semantic search engine as they may be contacted for collaboration purposes.

We capture the working context by means of a knowledge stance model, represented by the elements explained in section 2.2: *process, occasion, activity, action,* and *task*. The link between the process- and activity-oriented perspectives is realized by associating occasions with activities. The knowledge stance elements can be annotated

Figure 9. Schema of the knowledge stance model and context elements

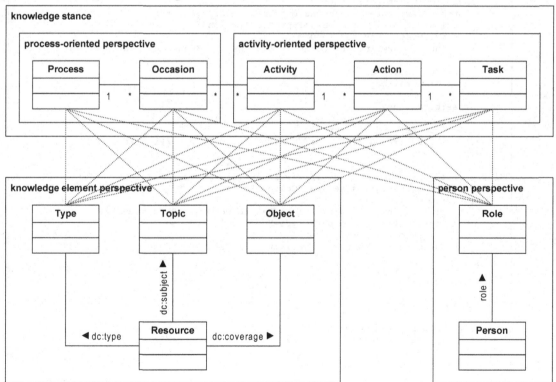

with the same concepts as the knowledge elements (depicted by the dotted lines in Figure 9), i.e. an activity can, for example, be related to a certain topic, as well as roles to define responsibilities.

Figure 11 and Figure 12 show an example of a knowledge stance model in RDF. Figure 11 defines two occasions "new product introduced by vendor" and "new product demand by customer"

Figure 10. Example of person-related metadata[k]

```
<?xml version="1.0"?>
<rdf:RDF xmlns:rdf="http://www.w3.org/1999/02/22-rdf-syntax-ns#"
  xmlns:foaf="http://xmlns.com/foaf/0.1/"
  xmlns:inwiss="http://www.inwiss.org/schema#">

<foaf:Person rdf:about="ldap://cn=Michael Bates,ou=Sales,o=MyCompany">
  <foaf:name>Michael Bates</foaf:name>
  <inwiss:role rdf:resource="http://www.inwiss.org/roles/ShopAssistant">
</rdf:Description>

</rdf:RDF>
```

Figure 11. Process-oriented part of a knowledge stance model in RDF

```
<?xml version="1.0"?>
<rdf:RDF xmlns:rdf="http://www.w3.org/1999/02/22-rdf-syntax-ns#"
  xmlns:inwiss="http://www.inwiss.org/schema#"
  xmlns:dc="http://purl.org/dc/elements/1.1/">

<inwiss:Process rdf:about="http://www.inwiss.org/processes/Procurement">
  <inwiss:occasions rdf:parseType="Collection">
    <inwiss:Occasion rdf:about=
      "http://www.inwiss.org/occasions/NewProductByVendor">
      <inwiss:activities rdf:parseType="Collection">
        <inwiss:Activity rdf:about=
          "http://www.inwiss.org/activities/DevelopKnowledgeAboutProducts">
        ...
      <inwiss:activities/>
    </inwiss:Occasion>
    ...
  </inwiss:occasions>

  <!-- Process-related context -->
  <dc:subject rdf:resource="http://www.inwiss.org/topics/Procurement"/>
</inwiss:Process>

<inwiss:Process rdf:about="http://www.inwiss.org/processes/Sales">
  <inwiss:occasions rdf:parseType="Collection">
    <inwiss:Occasion rdf:about=
      "http://www.inwiss.org/occasions/NewProductDemandByCustomer">
      <inwiss:activities rdf:parseType="Collection">
        <inwiss:Activity rdf:about=
          "http://www.inwiss.org/activities/DevelopKnowledgeAboutProducts">
        ...
      <inwiss:activities/>
    </inwiss:Occasion>
    ...
  </inwiss:occasions>

  <!-- Process-related context -->
  <dc:subject rdf:resource="http://www.inwiss.org/topics/Sales"/>
</inwiss:Process>

</rdf:RDF>
```

linked to the procurement and sales process respectively. These occasions link the process to the shared activity "develop knowledge about products". This activity is defined in Figure 12 by a set of actions and corresponding tasks. On each level, context information can be incorporated into the definition. For example, the processes are related to the corresponding topics of the organization's taxonomy. The action "lookup experiences with related products" relates to documents of the product experience report type. Additionally, persons of the role "purchaser" or "shop assistant" are related to the action (i.e. they might be worth being contacted). Activity and process-related contexts thus represent parts of the working contexts defining situations that are triggered by the two occasions.

Utilizing the Working Context

Ideally, the portal would automatically recognize occasions by processing information of the current interaction context. It could then notify the user about occasions and present supportive contents and functions. Challenges are whether the portal contains enough information to conclude to the user's working context and to define rules that allow concluding from interaction context to working context elements. Since users are only confronted with a manageable number of occasions (usually five to ten, depending on their tasks), a straightforward way is to let the user manually choose from a list of occasions.

It is desirable to guide or even automate the operations that execute knowledge-oriented

Figure 12. Activity-oriented part of the knowledge stance model

```xml
<?xml version="1.0"?>
<rdf:RDF xmlns:rdf="http://www.w3.org/1999/02/22-rdf-syntax-ns#"
  xmlns:inwiss="http://www.inwiss.org/schema#"
  xmlns:dc="http://purl.org/dc/elements/1.1/">

<inwiss:Activity rdf:resource=
  "http://www.inwiss.org/activities/DevelopKnowledgeAboutProducts">
  <inwiss:actions rdf:parseType="Collection">
    <inwiss:Action rdf:resource=
      "http://www.inwiss.org/actions/LookupRelatedProductExperiences">
    ...
  </inwiss:actions>

  <!-- Activity-related context -->
  <inwiss:role rdf:resource="http://www.inwiss.org/roles/Purchaser"/>
  <inwiss:role rdf:resource="http://www.inwiss.org/roles/ShopAssistant"/>
</inwiss:Activity>

<inwiss:Action rdf:resource=
    "http://www.inwiss.org/actions/LookupRelatedProductExperiences">
  <inwiss:tasks rdf:parseType="Collection">
    <inwiss:Task rdf:resource=
      "http://www.inwiss.org/tasks/SearchForRelatedDocuments"/>
    ...
  </inwiss:tasks>

  <!-- Action-related context -->
  <dc:type rdf:resource="http://www.inwiss.org/ontology#ExperienceReport"/>
</inwiss:Action>

...

</rdf:RDF>
```

actions. Hence, an expedient extension to the INWISS portal would be a "My Work" portlet as shown in Figure 13. Current process, occasion, and activity are presented in this portlet and may be changed by the user. Depending on his choices, appropriate actions are shown in the list below. If a corresponding workflow is defined, the user can select from the available workflow tasks and is taken to a supporting portlet, activating the desired application function and presenting appropriate content based on the current context. The workflows are modeled in advance at the time when knowledge stances and corresponding actions are defined. Knowledge elements (e.g., topics, objects, roles) related to the knowledge stance can be linked to them.

Figure 14 shows a possible working context as provided by the "My Work" portlet. The working context comprises knowledge stance elements as well as context elements that can be inferred from the knowledge stance model in Figure 11 and

Figure 13. Screen design of a "My Work" portlet

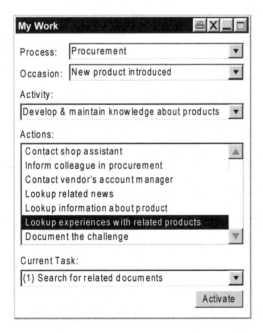

Figure 12. Everything with the subject "procurement" is considered as possibly relevant to the current knowledge stance. In addition, the activity definition includes a link to the "purchaser" and "shop assistant" roles which might guide the user to find other persons that are worth being contacted. Finally, the current action reveals that documents of type "experience report" might be of interest. The inclusion of these context elements can be achieved automatically by means of the "owl:TransitiveProperty" directive when using an OWL reasoner. This inference is depicted by the arrows in Figure 14.

The definition of the "search for related documents" task is assumed to specify the search portlet as the corresponding target application. Hence, when the user clicks the "Activate" button, the system will guide him to this portlet in order to search for related documents. As a result from the context-based search, the procurement guidelines document from Figure 7 will be found as relevant as it is annotated with the procurement topic. Also in combination with an explicit user query, it can be expected that the inclusion of the context information in the query will be significantly improve the search performance.

While the working context (from the knowledge stance model) is mainly defined on a type-level, the inclusion of interaction context elements (from the user's interaction with other portlets during previous tasks) will also reveal instance information. Assume a newly introduced product is the "Shower Companion" within the "audio" product category and this information has found its way into the interaction context by browsing the product database. As a consequence, the search engine will also find the product experience report from Figure 7 with a particularly high score as it has the type "experience report" and deals with a product of the same product category.

Now, consider the next task of the "lookup related product experiences" action, which might be "contact experts for their opinion". The task might point to a messaging portlet. By using the

Figure 14. Example of a working context

```xml
<?xml version="1.0"?>
<rdf:RDF xmlns:rdf="http://www.w3.org/1999/02/22-rdf-syntax-ns#"
   xmlns:inwiss=http://www.inwiss.org/schema#
xmlns:dc="http://purl.org/dc/elements/1.1/">

<rdf:Description>
   <inwiss:process rdf:resource="http://www.inwiss.org/processes/Procurement"/>
   <inwiss:occasion rdf:resource=
     "http://www.inwiss.org/occasions/NewProductByVendor"/>
   <inwiss:activity rdf:resource=
     "http://www.inwiss.org/activities/DevelopKnowledgeAboutProducts"/>
   <inwiss:action rdf:resource=
     "http://www.inwiss.org/actions/LookupRelatedProductExperiences"/>
   <inwiss:task rdf:resource=
     "http://www.inwiss.org/tasks/SearchForRelatedDocuments"/>

   <!-- Inferred working context -->
   <dc:type rdf:resource="http://www.inwiss.org/ontology#ExperienceReport"/>
   <inwiss:role rdf:resource="http://www.inwiss.org/roles/Purchaser"/>
   <inwiss:role rdf:resource="http://www.inwiss.org/roles/ShopAssistant"/>
   <dc:subject rdf:resource="http://www.inwiss.org/topics/Procurement"/>
</rdf:Description>

</rdf:RDF>
```

working context information, the system can look for persons of the "purchaser" and "salesperson" roles. Note that Michael Bates (from Figure 10) will be found even though he works in a different department on a different process. The link exists solely through the "develop knowledge about products" activity.

So far, the interaction context has so far been volatile and bound to a user session in INWISS. As an extension we propose to bind it to a workflow instance. This way the context will persist for the lifetime of the workflow instance and can even be transported from one user to the other if different responsibilities are defined. Also when using collaboration technology sending the context along with the user messages seems promising as the message can automatically be enriched with and carry the current context. The recipient can thus easily use the portal to find information related to the message received.

CONCLUSION AND FUTURE WORK

This paper discussed how the concept of knowledge stance can be applied to portals which are an important technology to support knowledge work in the context of business processes. We presented the experiences from developing a prototype that applies Semantic Web technologies, proposed extensions and discussed how they can be implemented. A semantic description of information resources and therefore Semantic Web standards and technologies are constitutional for the implementation. The next steps are to develop the portal further based on our proposals. The open source workflow engine jBpm[l] and the workflow editor JaWE[m] may serve as a basis, however they need to be enhanced to support the activity-oriented perspective of knowledge stances. A modeling notation to model knowledge stances also needs to be defined.

So far, we considered the working context as statically resulting from modeling. As future work the context arising from occasions should not be considered statically defined but rather evolving so that knowledge stances can continuously evolve by gathering knowledge related to specific instances of processes, activities, and user actions. In addition, the context could also flow between users by means of knowledge-related actions and workflows. By this way, we provide means to communicate practices linked to a knowledge stance between multiple persons (e.g., that fulfill similar functions within a process) and to generalize proven practices and knowledge connected to a knowledge stance. This idea of communicating the context among users of course raises security and privacy issues. Finally, ways for automatic detection of occasions need to be studied, which could be based on detection of identifying patterns in the history of the interaction context.

Altogether, knowledge stance-oriented portals can be seen as a step towards making knowledge work in business processes more efficient by supporting integrated and context-oriented access to heterogeneous systems.

REFERENCES

Abecker, A., Bernardi, A., Maus, H., Sintek, M., & Wenzel, C. (2000). Information Supply for Business Processes: Coupling Workflow with Document Analysis and Information Retrieval. *Knowledge Based Systems, 13*(5), 271-284.

Abecker, A., Bernardi, A., Ntioudis, S., Herterich, R., Houy, C., Legal, M., et al. (2001). *The DECOR Toolbox for Workflow-Embedded Organizational Memory Access*. Paper presented at the 3rd International Conference on Enterprise Information Systems (ICEIS 2001), Setubal, Portugal.

Allweyer, T. (1998). Modellbasiertes Wissensmanagement. *Information Management, 13*(1), 37-45.

Bach, V., & Österle, H. (Eds.). (2000). *Customer Relationship Management in der Praxis. Erfolgreiche Wege zu kundenzentrierten Lösungen.* Berlin: Springer.

Baeza-Yates, R., & Ribeiro-Neto, B. (Eds.). (1999). *Modern Information Retrieval.*Essex: Addison Wesley Longman Limited.

Barry, C. L., & Schamber, L. (1998). Users' Criteria for Relevance Evaluation: A Cross-Situational Comparison. *Information Processing & Management, 34*(2-3), 219-236.

Blackler, F. (1995). Knowledge, Knowledge Work and Organizations: An Overview and Interpretation. *Organization Studies, 16*(6), 1021-1046.

Böhm, K., & Härtwig, J. (2005). *Prozessorientiertes Wissensmanagement durch kontextualisierte*

Informationsversorgung aus Geschäftsprozessen. Paper presented at the 6. Internationale Tagung Wirtschaftsinformatik (WI 2005), Bamberg, Germany.

Broekstra, J., Kampman, A., & van Harmelen, F. (2002). *Sesame: A Generic Architecture for Storing and Querying RDF and RDF Schema.* Paper presented at the First International Semantic Web Conference (ISWC 2002), Sardinia, Italy.

Chaudhuri, S., & Dayal, U. (1997). An Overview of Data Warehousing and OLAP Technology. *ACM SIGMOD Record, 26*(1).

Clases, C., & Wehner, T. (2002). Steps Across the Border—Cooperation, Knowledge Production and Systems Design. *Computer Supported Cooperative Work, 11*(1), 39-54.

Corcho, Ó., Gómez-Pérez, A., López-Cima, A., López-García, V., & Suárez-Figueroa, M. d. C.*ODESeW—Automatic Generation of Knowledge Portals for Intranets and Extranets.* Paper presented at the 2nd International Semantic Web Conference (ISWC 2003), Sanibel Island, Florida, USA.

Dey, A. K., & Abowd, G. D. (1999). *Towards a Better Understanding of Context and Context-Awareness* (No. GIT-GVU-99-32): College of Computing, Georgia Institute of Technology.

Edwards, J. S., & Kidd, J. B. (2003). Bridging the Gap from the General to the Specific by Linking Knowldge Management to Business Processes. In V. Hlupic (Ed.), *Knowledge and Business Process Management* (pp. 118-136). Hershey: Idea Group Publishing.

Engeström, Y. (1999). Expansive Visibilization of Work: An Activity-theoretical Perspective. *Computer Supported Cooperative Work, 8*(1), 63-93.

Eppler, M. J. (2003). *Managing Information Quality: Increasing the Value of Information in Knowledge-intensive Products and Processes.* Berlin: Springer.

Ferstl, O. K., & Sinz, E. J. (1994). *From Business Process Modeling to the Specification of Distributed Business Application Systems—An Object-Oriented Approach* (Research Paper): Dept. of Business Information Systems, University of Bamberg.

Frank, U. (2002). Multi-Perspective Enterprise Modeling (MEMO)—Conceptual Framework and Modeling Languages. In *Proceedings of the 35th Hawaii International Conference on System Sciences (HICSS-35).*Honolulu.

Goesmann, T., & Herrmann, T. (2001). Wissensmanagement und Geschäftsprozessunterstützung—am Beispiel des Workflow Memory Information System WoMIS. In T. Herrmann, A.-W. Scheer & H. Weber (Eds.), *Verbesserung von Geschäftsprozessen mit flexiblen Workflow-Management-Systemen 4* (pp. 83-101). Heidelberg: Physica-Verlag.

Gronau, N. (2003). Modellierung von wissensintensiven Geschäftsprozessen mit der Beschreibungssprache K-Modeler. In N. Gronau

(Ed.), *Wissensmanagement: Potenziale—Konzepte—Werkzeuge, Proceedings of the 4th Oldenburg Conference on Knowledge Management, University of Oldenburg, June 2003* (pp. 3-29). Berlin: Gito.

Hädrich, T., & Maier, R. (2004). *Modeling Knowledge Work.* Paper presented at the Multikonferenz Wirtschaftsinformatik (MKWI 2004), Essen, Germany.

Heisig, P. (2002). GPO-WM: Methoden und Werkzeuge zum geschäftsprozessorientierten Wissensmanagement. In A. Abecker, K. Hinkelmann & M. Heiko (Eds.), *Geschäftsprozessorientiertes Wissensmanagement* (pp. 47-64). Berlin: Springer.

Henrich, A., & Morgenroth, K. (2002). *Integration von kontextunterstütztem Information Retrieval in Portalsysteme.* Paper presented at the Teilkonferenz Management der Mitarbeiter-Expertise in IT-Beratungsunternehmen, MKWI 2002, Nürnberg, Germany.

Henrich, A., & Morgenroth, K. (2003). *Supporting Collaborative Software Development by Context-Aware Information Retrieval Facilities.* Paper presented at the DEXA 2003 Workshop on Web Based Collaboration (WBC 2003), Prague, Czech Republic.

Junginger, S., Kühn, H., Strobl, R., & Karagiannis, D. (2000). Ein Geschäftsprozessmanagement-Werkzeug der nächsten Generation—ADONIS: Konzeption und Anwendungen. *Wirtschaftsinformatik, 42*(5), 392-401.

Karagiannis, D., & Woitsch, R. (2003). The PROMOTE Approach: Modelling Knowledge Management Processes to Describe Knowledge Management Systems. In N. Gronau (Ed.), *Wissensmanagement: Potenziale—Konzepte—Werkzeuge, Proceedings of the 4th Oldenburg Conference on Knowledge Management, University of Oldenburg, June 2003* (pp. 35-52). Berlin: Gito.

Klemke, R. (2000). *Context Framework—an Open Approach to Enhance Organisational Memory Systems with Context Modeling Techniques.* Paper presented at the th-31th October 2000, Basel, Switzerland.

Kuutti, K. (1997). Activity Theory as a Potential Framework for Human-Computer Interaction Research. In B. A. Nardi (Ed.), *Context and Consciousness: Activity Theory and Human-Computer Interaction* (pp. 17-44). Cambridge, Mass.: MIT Press.

Maier, R. (2004). *Knowledge Management Systems: Information and Communication Technologies for Knowledge Management* (2nd ed.). Berlin et al.: Springer.

Maier, R., Hädrich, T., & Peinl, R. (2005). *Enterprise Knowledge Infrastructures (forthcoming).* Berlin: Springer.

Maier, R., & Remus, U. (2003). Implementing Process-oriented Knowledge Management Strategies. *Journal of Knowledge Management, 7*(4), 62-74.

Maier, R., & Sametinger, J. (2002). *Infotop—An Information and Communication Infrastructure for Knowledge Work.* Paper presented at the 3rd European Conference on Knowledge Management, Trinity College Dublin, Ireland.

Mäkelä, E., Hyvönen, E., Saarela, S., & Viljanen, K. (2004). *OntoViews—A Tool for Creating Semantic Web Portals.* Paper presented at the 3rd International Semantic Web Conference (ISWC 2004), Hiroshima, Japan.

Maus, H. (2001). *Workflow Context as a Means for Intelligent Information Support.* Paper presented at the 3rd Intl. Conf. on Modeling and Using Context (CONTEXT 2001).

Oestereich, B., Weiss, C., Schröder, C., Weilkiens, T., & Lenhard, A. (2003). *Objektorientierte Geschäftsprozessmodellierung mit der UML.* Heidelberg: dpunkt.

Österle, H. (1995). *Business Engineering. Prozeß- und Systementwicklung. Band 1: Entwurfstechniken.* Berlin: Springer.

Porter, M. E. (1985). *Competitive Advantage: Creating and Sustaining Superior Performance.* New York, London: Free Press.

Priebe, T. (2004). *INWISS—Integrative Enterprise Knowledge Portal.* Paper presented at the 3rd International Semantic Web Conference (ISWC 2004), Hiroshima, Japan.

Priebe, T., Kiss, C., & Kolter, J. (2005). *Semiautomatische Annotation von Textdokumenten mit semantischen Metadaten.* Paper presented at the 6. Internationale Tagung Wirtschaftsinformatik (WI 2005), Bamberg, Germany.

Priebe, T., & Pernul, G. (2003). *Towards Integrative Enterprise Knowledge Portals.* Paper presented at the Twelfth International Conference on Information and Knowledge Management (CIKM 2003), New Orleans, LA, USA.

Priebe, T., Schläger, C., & Pernul, G. (2004). *A Search Engine for RDF Metadata.* Paper presented at the DEXA 2004 Workshop on Web Semantics (WebS 2004), Zaragoza, Spain.

Sachs, P. (1995). Transforming Work: Collaboration, Learning, and Design. *Communications of the ACM, 38*(9), 36-44.

Schauer, H. (2004). *Knowledge MEMO: Eine Methode zur Planung, Steuerung und Kontrolle ganzheitlichen betrieblichen Wissensmanagements.* Unpublished PhD thesis, University of Koblenz, Koblenz.

Scheer, A.-W. (2001). *ARIS—Modellierungsmethoden, Metamodelle, Anwendungen.* Berlin: Springer.

Schulze, U. (2000). A Confessional Account of an Ethnography About Knowledge Work. *MIS Quarterly, 24*(1), 3-41.

Schulze, U. (2003). On Knowledge Work. In C. W. Holsapple (Ed.), *Handbook on Knowledge Management—Volume 1: Knowledge Matters* (pp. 43-58). Berlin: Springer.

Spur, G., Mertins, K., & Jochem, R. (1996). *Integrated Enterprise Modelling.*Berlin: Beuth.

Stojanovic, N., Maedche, A., Staab, S., Studer, R., & Sure, Y. (2001). *SEAL—A Framework for Developing SEmantic PortALs*. Paper presented at the First International Conference on Knowledge Capture (K-CAP 2001), Victoria, BC, Canada.

Tan, P., Madnick, S. E., & Tan, K.-L. (2004). *Context Mediation in the Semantic Web: Handling OWL Ontology and Data Disparity through Context Interchange* (MIT Sloan Working Paper No. 4496-04; CISL Working Paper No. 2004-13).

W3C. (2004). OWL Web Ontology Language Overview. W3C Recommendation. Retrieved April 1, 2005, from http://www.w3.org/TR/2004/REC-owl-features-20040210/

W3C. (2004). Resource Description Framework (RDF): Concepts and Abstract Syntax. W3C Recommendation. Retrieved April 1, 2005, from http://www.w3.org/TR/2004/REC-rdf-concepts-20040210/

Wege, C. (2002). Portal Server Technology. *IEEE Internet Computing, 6*(3), 73-77.

ENDNOTES

[a] http://www.inwiss.org, last accessed April 1, 2005

[b] http://www.ibm.com/software/genservers/portal/, last accessed April 1, 2005

[c] http://www.sap.com/solutions/netweaver/enterpriseportal/, last accessed April 1, 2005

[d] http://www.openrdf.org, last accessed April 1, 2005

[e] http://jena.sourceforge.net, last accessed April 1, 2005

[f] http://www.dublincore.org, last accessed April 1, 2005

[g] http://portals.apache.org/jetspeed-1/, last accessed April 1, 2005

[h] http://www.microstrategy.com, last accessed April 1, 2005

[i] http://www.openrdf.org, last accessed April 1, 2005

[j] http://jakarta.apache.org/lucene/, last accessed April 1, 2005

[k] The concepts "Person" and "name" are borrowed from the Friend of a Friend (FOAF) project; http://www.foaf-project.org, last accessed April 1, 2005

[l] http://www.jbpm.org

[m] http://jawe.objectweb.org, last accessed April 1, 2005

This work was previously published in Int. Journal on Semantic Web & Information Systems, Vol 1, Issue 3, edited by A. Sheth and M. Lytras, pp. 64-88, copyright 2005 by IGI Publishing (an imprint of IGI Global).

Chapter XV
A Survey of Web Service Discovery Systems

Le Duy Ngan
Nanyang Technological University, Singapore

Angela Goh
Nanyang Technological University, Singapore

Cao Hoang Tru
Ho Chi Minh City University of Technology, Viet Nam

ABSTRACT

Web services form the core of e-business and hence, have experienced a rapid development in the past few years. This has led to a demand for a discovery mechanism for web services. Discovery is the most important task in the web service model because web services are useless if they cannot be discovered. A large number of web service discovery systems have been developed. Universal Description, Discovery and Integration (UDDI) is a typical mechanism that stores indexes to web services but it does not support semantics. Semantic web service discovery systems that have been developed include systems that support matching web services using the same ontology, systems that support matching web services using different ontologies, and systems that support limitations of UDDI. This paper presents a survey of web service discovery systems, focusing on systems that support semantics. The paper also elaborates on open issues relating to such discovery systems.

INTRODUCTION

Web service technology enables e-business and e-commerce to become a reality. It has become a competitive tool of companies by reducing cost through fast, effective, and reliable services to customers, suppliers, and partners over the internet. It enables more efficient business operations via the web and enhances business opportunities to companies. These are achieved through its support of *discovery, composition, invocation, monitoring* and so on. A web service is a software component representing a specific business function that can be described, published, and invoked over the network (typically Internet) using open-standards.

A Web service based on Web Service Description Language (WSDL) (Walsh, 2002) can be termed "non-semantic web services". However, using WSDL to describe the services only allows them to be accessed by keyword. This limitation prevents fully automatic *discovery, composition, invocation*, and *monitoring*. The reason for this shortcoming is the lack of semantic understanding. To overcome this problem, web services require a method to incorporate semantics. Just as the Semantic Web is an extension of the current World Wide Web, a semantic web service is an extension of web services. It overcomes web service limitations by using knowledge representation technology from the semantic web. Specifically, it uses ontologies to describe its service instead of using WSDL. Such ontologies can be understood by machines and can be reasoned upon. This allows a fully automatic *discovery, composition, invocation*, and *monitoring* in web services.

In a web service model, a *service provider* offers web services which provide functions or business operations which can be deployed over the Internet, in the hope that they will be invoked by partners or customers; a web *service requester* describes requirements in order to locate *service providers*. Publishing, binding, and discovering web services are three major tasks in the model.

Discovery is the process of finding web services provider locations which satisfy specific requirements. Web services are useless if they cannot be discovered. So, discovery is the most important task in the web service model.

The greatest difficulty in a web service discovery mechanism is *heterogeneity* between services (Garofalakis *et al.*, 2004). Heterogeneities include different platforms, different data formats as well as heterogeneities of ontologies. Regarding ontology heterogeneities, semantic web services may use different ontologies or different ontologies description language such as OWL, DAML, RDF etc to describe the services. There is also heterogeneity between semantic web services and non-semantic web services. Therefore, when developing a discovery system, these heterogeneities should be borne in mind.

A survey of web service discovery system is needed to explore existing techniques and to highlight the advantages and disadvantages of each system. (Garofalakis *et al.*, 2004) presented a survey on these systems but their work mainly focused on aspects and approaches of web service architecture and has not paid adequate attention to the usage of semantics. In semantic web services, the usage of semantics is the most important factor. This paper presents a survey of web service discovery systems which focuses mainly on the use of semantics. In this paper, we use the term "non-semantic web services" to refer to web services without semantics, whereas the term "web services" is used in a generic manner to cover both semantic web services and non-semantic web services.

The rest of the paper is as follows. Section 2 introduces the background of web service description languages and the web services model. Section 3 introduces a taxonomy of web services discovery systems. In this section, advantages and disadvantages of each system are highlighted. Section 4 presents the issues related to web services discovery, followed by the conclusion in section 5.

WEB SERVICES DISCOVERY

Web service discovery is widely used in work-flow, e-learning, and e-business systems such as e-supply chain, e-manufacturing, etc. Non-semantic web services can be discovered using UDDI (Walsh, 2002). UDDI is an industry specification for describing, publishing, and finding web services. It allows developers to describe and classify their services, and the technical details about the interfaces of the web services which are exposed. UDDI also enables developers to consistently discover services, or interfaces of a particular type, classification, or function. It also defines a set of Application Programming Interfaces (APIs) that developers can use in order to interact with UDDI data directly. The UDDI scheme uses *White, Yellow,* and *Green pages* as data categories. *White pages* store basic contact information about an advertised company. *Yellow pages* store industry classification. *Green pages* provide technical information on the behavior and supported functions of a business service hosted by a business.

Semantic web service discovery systems have been developed to discover semantic web services. To be discovered, web services must be described by web service description languages. This section introduces web service description languages, followed by the web service model and several categories of discovery systems.

Web Service Description Languages

WSDL is used to describe non-semantic web services. Ontologies and features such as service name, service description in text, etc. are used to describe semantic web service. The following is an introduction to WSDL and semantic web description languages.

WSDL—A Non Semantic Web Description Language

Web Service Description Language (WSDL) (Walsh, 2002) is a standard to describe how to access a non-web service and what operations (methods) it performs. It is also used to locate web services when a service requester and provider use WSDL to describe the service. A WSDL document defines a web service using four major elements, namely, port, message, types, and binding. An elaboration of these elements is as follows:

1. *WSDL Ports*: The <portType> is the most important element in WSDL. It defines a web service with operations that can be performed and messages that are involved. The <portType> element is similar to a function library (or a module, or a class) in a traditional programming language.
2. *WSDL Messages*: The <message> element defines an abstract, typed definition of the data being communicated. Each message can consist of one or more logical parts like parameters of a function call in a traditional programming language.
3. *WSDL Types*: The <types> element defines a container for data type definitions that are relevant for the exchanged messages. For maximum interoperability and platform neutrality, WSDL uses XML Schema syntax to define data types.
4. *WSDL Bindings*: The <binding> element defines a concrete protocol and data format specification for a particular port type.

Semantic Web Service Description Languages

Semantic web services use ontologies to describe their services. OWL-S, DAML-S, and RDFS are examples of semantic web services description languages which use OWL, DAML, and RDF ontology respectively to describe their services.

Figure 1. Top level of the service ontology

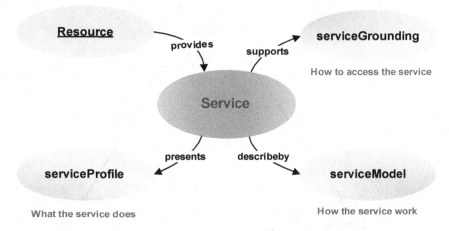

DAML-S and OWL-S which are widely used web service description languages include *Service* class and three sub-classes, namely, *serviceProfile*, *serviceModel*, and *serviceGrounding* (figure 1).

Matching uses only *ServiceProfile* because it contains the description of the service to be discovered. The *ServiceProfile* represents the service through class *Profile*. A class *Profile* has three basic types of information, namely, contact information, functional description of the service, and additional properties.

The contact information is meant for human users. It includes *serviceName* which is the name of the service, and *contactInformation* which shows the address, telephone number, etc. of the owner of the service. The *textDescription* provides a brief description of the service. It summarizes what the service offers, or describes what service is requested. In discovery, *textDescription* of the web service provider and requester is checked to determine if two services have a common description. If such a commonality exists, it implies that the provider is able to meet the requester's need.

The functional description of the service is the most important declaration in the *Profile* that is used for matching. It specifies the parameters

comprising the *inputs, outputs, preconditions,* and *effects* of the service. The *inputs* are parameters required by the service and the *outputs* are the parameters which are generated by the service. The *precondition* indicates the condition necessary before execution of the service and the *effect* is the condition after execution of the service. For example, to invoke a web service to buy a computer and pay via credit card, the input is price, the output is the computer configuration, the precondition is that the credit card must be valid, and the effect is that the credit card must be charged. Additional properties which describe features of the service are *serviceParameter, qualityRating, serviceCategory,* etc. The Profile also declares an operation of the web service.

Web Service Model

The web service model in figure 2 shows the interaction between a service requester, service providers, and a service discovery system.

- The service providers offer web services which provide functions or business operations. They are created by companies or organizations. In order to be invoked, the web services must be described. This will

Figure 2. Web service model

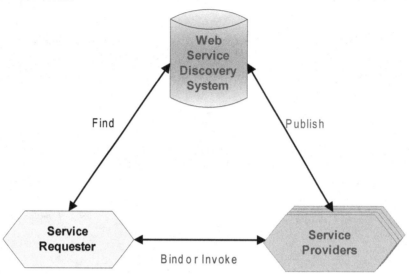

facilitate discovery and composition. WSDL or service profile of semantic web service is used to carry out this function.

- The web service requester describes requirements in order to locate service providers. Service requesters usually contain a description of the web service, though it is not a web service which can run on the internet. The requirements are usually described by WSDL, service template or service profile.
- The web service discovery or service registry is a broker that provides registry and search functions. The service providers advertise their service information in the discovery system. This information will be stored in the registry and will be searched when there is a request from service requester. UDDI is used as a registry standard for non-semantic web service. Semantic web service discovery systems are developed for semantic web services.

The above three components interact with each other via publishing, discovery, and bind-

ing operations. These operations are elaborated upon as follows:

1. *Publish*: the web service providers publish their service information through the discovery system for requesters to discover. Through the publishing operation, the web service provider stores the service description in the discovery system.

2. *Discovery*: the web service requesters retrieve service providers from the service registry. Based on service descriptions, which describes the requirements of the web service requesters, the discovery system will output a list of web service providers which satisfy the requirements.

3. *Bind*: After discovering, the discovery system provides a number of web service providers. The web service requester invokes these web service providers. The binding occurs at runtime. The web service requesters and web service providers will communicate via SOAP protocol (W3C, ; Walsh, 2002) which is an XML based protocol for web service exchange information.

Category of Web Service Discovery Systems

There are many ways to categorize web services discovery systems. Depending on various view points, we can category them as follows: distributed systems, supporting QoS systems, or applying fuzzy logic to the systems. Details of each category are given in the following subsections.

Distributed Discovery Systems

While web services have provided distributed operation execution, most discovery systems are still based on centralized registries. However, as the number of web services grows rapidly, a single point failure and performance bottleneck result in centralized registries becoming impractical. To overcome the disadvantages of the centralized systems, a large number of decentralized solutions based on P2P technologies have been proposed. Most of the systems build on P2P network use ontologies to publish and discover the web services descriptions. Some typical systems are found in (Gagnes *et al.*, 2006; Y. Li *et al.*, 2006; Wu *et al.*, 2005; Yu *et al.*, 2004a, 2004b). These systems present approaches for distributed web services organization by combining the capabilities of semantic web services with the dynamics and real-time search capabilities of peer to peer (P2P) networks. They use category ontology to organize services based on semantic classification of domains.

QoS Discovery Systems

Web service discovery can be divided into two phases. The first phase is matching functional aspects of the web service such as input, output, precondition, effect, operation … etc. The output of the first phase may be many advertised web service that satisfy the requirement. To reduce the number of advertised web service providers and to find the most appropriate service, the second phase uses QoS. QoS refers to *Quality of Service* which considers availability, accessibility, integrity, performance, reliability, regulatory, and security. Several discovery systems supporting QoS have been developed such as (Frolund & Koistinen, 1998; Hondo & Kaler, 2002; Ludwig, 2003; Sahai *et al.*, 2002; Zhou *et al.*, 2005a, 2005b; Zinky *et al.*, 1997).

Applying Fuzzy Logic to Discovery

Since the model-theoretic semantics of the languages used in the Semantic Web are crisp, the need to extend them to represent fuzzy data arises, (Chao *et al.*, 2005; Huang *et al.*, 2005; Recuerda & Robertson, 2005) (Mazzieri & Dragoni, 2005; Stoilos *et al.*, 2005). As ontology languages are based on Description Logics which lack the ability to encode and reason with imprecise knowledge, (Stoilos *et al.*, 2005) extended the DL language with fuzzy set theory and provided sound and complete reasoning algorithms for the extended language.

In semantic web service, the method of using semantics is the most important factor. Therefore, our survey of discovery systems focuses on the use of semantics in web service discovery systems.

A TAXONOMY OF WEB SERVICES DISCOVERY SYSTEMS

This section contains a survey of web service discovery systems which focuses on methods using semantics. A taxonomy of web service discovery systems is introduced. The survey also compares different systems to highlight the advantages and disadvantages of each system.

Introduction to the Taxonomy

Figure 3 presents a taxonomy of web service discovery systems, which can be divided into systems for matching semantic web services and systems

Figure 3. Taxonomy of web service discovery systems

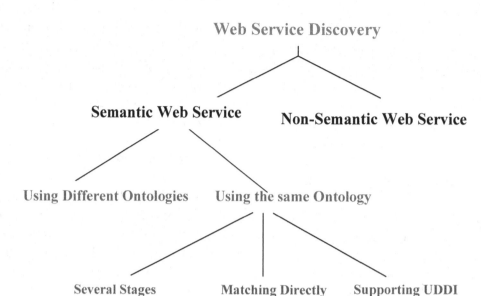

for matching non-semantic web services. The semantic web service discovery systems include systems that support matching web services using different ontologies and systems that support matching web services using the same ontology. There are three main approaches for matching semantic web services using the same ontology, namely, dividing matching process into several stages, matching two profiles directly and supporting UDDI.

The system described by (Liang *et al.*) is an example of non-semantic web service discovery system. The authors introduced a system that can provide semi-automatic discovery and composition by indexing service advertisements. Currently, most systems use UDDI for discovering such services which are usually described in WSDL. Furthermore, these services use WSDL to register in UDDI. UDDI finds the service providers based on WSDL. The shortcoming of this system is a lack of semantic understanding. This shortcoming has been explained in earlier sections.

Semantic web services overcome the mismatch of web services. This is done by adding more information to the web service descriptions.

Discovery of Semantic Web Services Using the Same Ontology

Almost all web service discovery systems that support matching web services assume the same ontology is used. Some systems divide the matching into several stages; others match two service profiles directly, while some support UDDI.

Direct Matching

This category of semantic web services discovery systems matches two service description "profiles" directly instead of dividing the matching into several stages. As mentioned in section 2, the service profile consists of information about the services for matching purpose. In these systems, users are not permitted to manage the degree of similarity of matching. Direct matching systems are accurate but are time-consuming. Furthermore, they do not allow users to manage the trade-off between performance and quality of matching which is the most important characteristic of internet application.

InfoSleuth (Bayardo *et al.*, 1997; Helal, 1997) is one of the earliest matching agent system. The matching agent enables the querying agent to locate all available agents that provide appropriate services. It supports syntactic and semantic matchmaking. In InfoSleuth, the service capability information is written in LDL++ (Hsu & Zaniolo, 1993; Shaw *et al.*, 1993), a logic deduction language. Agents use a set of LDL++ deductive rules to support inferences about whether an expression of requirements matches a set of advertised capabilities. The system provides syntactic and semantic matching. However, LDL++ is outdated and limited in its expressivity. LDL++ is not a standard supported by W3C. At the point of its development, OWL-S and DAML-S which are currently emergent web services description language were unavailable. Therefore, InfoSleuth does not support matching web services using OWL-S and DAML-S.

Similarly, (Trastour *et al.*, 2001) did not use DAML-S or OWL-S for describing web services because their work was carried out before the existence of these languages. Therefore, they developed their own specification for web services description by converting services to RDF graph. Services are nodes of the graph. Two nodes are considered matched if one node is a subtype of the other. Trastour et al extended this work by using DAML+OIL as the web description language (Castillo *et al.*, 2001). The matching is based on the subsumption relationship to find matches between concepts. DL (Description Logic) reasoner is used to determine the similarity between concepts. The system has the drawback that it only considers the relationship between direct sub-concepts and super-concepts. It does not consider the relationship between concepts that are more distantly related.

(Benatallah *et al.*, 2005) present an approach for web service discovery based on Description Logic. They formalized service discovery based on rewriting concepts using terminologies. This is called the *best covering problem*. They presented a formalization of the *best covering problem* in the framework of DL-based ontologies and proposed a hypergraph-based algorithm to effectively compute best covers of a given request. In this system, matchmaking is based on DAML-S. Similarly, Li and Horrocks (L. Li & Horrocks, 2003) developed a framework for matching web service based on DAML-S. Their Matchmaker uses Racer (Haarslev & Möller, 2001) as DL (Description Logic) reasoner to determine the semantic match between services. It tries to match two profiles of the requested service and advertised service, instead of dividing the matching into several stages. As mentioned in section 2.1, the service profile is part of any web service description language and includes information such as input, output, precondition, effect, user information etc. Therefore, without dividing the matching into several stages, it will be difficult for these systems to automate reasoning techniques to compute semantic matching and the matching will be inefficient.

Web Service Modeling Ontology (WSMO) provides a conceptual model for service discovery that exploits WSMO formal descriptions of goals and web services. WSMO Discovery Engine (Roman *et al.*, 2004) can match WSMO goals, and hence, web services requester description against web service provider's description. The advantages are that WSMO can be described semantically. However, WSMO is not a standard of W3C and the current version only supports goal matching.

Dividing the Matching Process into Several Stages

The challenge of dynamic matchmaking in the Internet is to optimize the trade-off between performance and quality of matching. Complex matching has to be restricted to allow meaningful semantic matches of requests and advertisements in a reasonable time. Direct matching systems are accurate but time-consuming. They do not allow users to manage the trade-off between performance and quality of matching. To overcome this, some systems divide the matching process into several stages. Systems that divide the matching process into stages include TU-Berlin (Jaeger *et al.*), LARKS (Sycara *et al.*, 1999a, 1999b; Sycara *et al.*, 2002), and the Matchmaker from the collaboration between Toshiba and Carnegie Mellon University (Kawamura *et al.*, 2003, 2004).

As heterogeneous web services use different description languages to describe the services and do not understand each other across distributed networks, the LARKS (Language for Advertisement and Request for Knowledge Sharing) project (Sycara *et al.*, 1999a, 1999b; Sycara *et al.*, 2002) defined an expressive common language called ACDL (Agent Capability Description Language). The LARKS matching agent uses this language to match web services requesters with web service providers. It includes five different filters, namely, context matching, word frequency profile comparison, similarity matching, signature matching, and constraint matching. Each filter has different functions. LARKS is expressive and capable of supporting inferences. Its knowledge is specified as local ontologies in the concept language ITL. It supports matching syntactical and semantic similarity among web services by using techniques from information retrieval and AI. It also allows users to restrict the result of matching. However, all services in LARKS must be described in ACDL which is not a standard and is quite difficult to write. Furthermore, LARKS does not support other commonly used web service description languages such as DAML-S and OWL-S.

(Paolucci *et al.*, 2002) have developed an algorithm for matching semantic web services using DAML-S. Their work considers only input and output matching. Input and output are concepts

based on an ontology. Therefore, the similarity of input, output matching is treated as the similarity of concepts from the same ontology. Paolucci et al. defined four levels of similarity: exact, plug in, subsumes, and fail. This definition is based on concepts that have a direct relationship: sub-concept or super-concept. Matching two concepts should also include the properties of the two concepts. It should consider general and specific concepts when these concepts are not related directly as sub-concept or super-concept. It also should consider syntactic matching which is based on service name and description of the service.

The semantic web service matching system from the collaboration between Toshiba and Carnegie Mellon University (Kawamura *et al.*, 2003, 2004) is based on LARKS and the algorithm from (Paolucci *et al.*, 2002). To overcome the drawback that requires ADCL, the system supports semantic web services which are described in RDFS, DAML-S, and OWL-S. Similar to LARKS, the system provides a set of filters and allows users to configure these filters to achieve the desired tradeoff between performance and matching quality. There are four filters which are independent of each other. These are Namespace Filter, Text Filter, I/O Type Filter, and Constraint Filter. The system can be installed as an add-on to UDDI; therefore, it supports matching of both semantic web services and non-semantic web services. When it receives a request for a service, it performs the matching process. If it receives a non-semantic web service request, it redirects the request to UDDI to perform the matching process.

The Matchmaker from TU-Berlin (Jaeger *et al.*) is a good example of a matching algorithm which is divided into four stages. The four stages are input matching, output matching, profile matching, and user-defined matching. By dividing the matching algorithm, the Matchmaker not only avoids the drawback in the system by (L. Li & Horrocks, 2003) but also helps users to choose the degree of matching from each stage in order to control the number of results and accuracy. An earlier version supported matching DAML-S semantic web services while the current version supports matching OWL-S semantic web services. The user-defined matching stage allows users to describe more constraints to restrict the number of results and to increase the accuracy of the results. However, the system is too simplistic. It only presents a demonstration of matching two web services; it is not really a discovery system since it does not store the advertisement into a database. It is also very difficult for users to utilize user-defined matching. With user-defined matching, the user must define their rules and constraints without user-friendly graphical user-interfaces.

Supporting UDDI

Using UDDI for discovery has limitations. UDDI uses XML to describe its data model. XML's lack of explicit semantics proves to be an additional barrier to the UDDI's discovery mechanism. To overcome this problem, some projects add semantics to UDDI, for example, by including semantic web service profile. The project from Carnegie Mellon (Srinivasan et al., 2004) is a typical example. It has added OWL-S profile to UDDI. Kawamura et al. (Kawamura et al., 2003, 2004) added advertising WSDL to UDDI and advertising DAML-S profile to its Matchmaker. If the requested web services use WSDL, the discovery system will access UDDI to look for suitable service providers. Otherwise, the discovery system will revert to the Matchmaker. By combining the Matchmaker and UDDI, the system can support matching both semantic and non-semantic web services, but in a separate manner. In other words, the two types of web services are not considered as alternatives to each other. Matches are to either semantic or non-semantic web services. Another example is from (Sivashanmugam et al., 2003) who have added semantics to WSDL using DAML+OIL ontologies. It also uses UDDI to store these semantics and searches for web services based on these semantics. By adding semantics to WSDL

and UDDI, the project in (Sivashanmugam et al., 2003) achieves sufficient expressiveness to automate the discovery process.

The registration and discovery with UDDI is based on a centralized design whereas web service providers developed their own stores called private registries. As web services support distributed operation execution, this has led to a demand to combine UDDI registry with private registeries. (Thaden et al., 2003) have developed a distributed peer-to-peer infrastructure. They created a virtual global registry by connecting all private registries in a P2P network. Furthermore, they also used DAML-S to enhance semantic search capabilities.

The advantages and disadvantages of the three methods that use the same ontology are summarised in table 1:

Discovery of Web Services Using Different Ontologies

The above mentioned web service discovery systems only support matching web services requesters and web services providers who use the same ontology. This assumption implies that if different ontologies are used, matching cannot be carried out. This is a major limitation since web services are heterogeneous, autonomous, and developed independently. It is necessary to discover web services that are based on different ontologies.

Cardoso and Sheth in "Semantic e-Workflow Composition" (Cardoso & Sheth, 2003) have addressed this problem. The system supports syntactic matching, quality of service (QoS) matching, and semantic matching. Syntactic matching involves computing the syntactic similarity of web services requesters and web services providers based on their service names and service descriptions. They use "string-matching" as a way to calculate how closely service names and service descriptions of the two semantic web services resemble each other. QoS is used to match web

Table 1. Advantages and disadvantages of three approaches to semantic web discovery based on the same ontology

Systems	Advantages	Disadvantages
Matching Directly	+ Matches all information of the two web services	- Consumes much time to match all information of the two web services. - Does not support user-definition in each part of matching (e.g. input, output matching, etc)
Divide the matching process into several stages	+ Can specify the degree of the similarity + Can define more constraints to enhance the result.	- Some information of web service may not be matched; therefore, the accuracy may be lower than direct matching.
Supporting UDDI	+ Can support both semantic matching and non-semantic matching	- Enhancing semantics to UDDI but not to a full extent.

services requesters and web services providers based on three important QoS factors, namely, time, cost and reliability. Semantic matching is computed relying on concepts and their properties. Property matching is based on domain, name, and range of properties.

However, the system is a part of a work-flow project (Cardoso & Sheth, 2003). Therefore, this discovery system has been developed mainly to support the project. So, it is limited as a discovery system. It supports user defined degree of similarity but it does not allow users to declare more rules or constraints to restrict the matching result. Semantic matching based on only concepts, and their properties is insufficient. It must also include the sub-concept, super-concept and properties of these concepts. The context of concepts also should be considered. Moreover, it is unclear how to determine whether two ontologies are the same or different.

(Oundhankar *et al.*, 2005) presented an extension of the algorithm in (Cardoso & Sheth, 2003) with two new measures: context and coverage similarity. The discovery technique is based on METEOR-S (Patil et al., 2004) which is a web service discovery infrastructure. This infrastructure provides a facility to access registries that are divided based on business domains and grouped into federations. The discovery algorithm used input, output of web services for matching. The matching is divided into *syntactic* and *semantic* matching. The syntactic matching is similar to Cardoso's work which uses n-gram (Angell & Freund, 1983; Salton, 1988; Zamora et al., 1981) technology. But in semantic matching, the algorithm improved Cardoso's work by considering the context and the coverage information of concepts.

By considering the concept and the coverage information of the matched concepts, the algorithm is able to find good matches and eliminate false matches. Moreover, based on METEOR-S, indexing and retrieving information in the registries is facilitated. However, the system does not allow users to intervene during the matching process. It also does not allow users to define more rules or constraints to restrict the matching result. This will be a significant problem since the number of web services from matching arising is huge. Furthermore, the approach to measure coverage similarity is incomplete since it is only based on similarity and disjointness relationship.

Similarly, (Le & Goh, 2005; Le *et al.*, 2005; Le *et al.*, 2006) proposed an algorithm to support matching web services that use both the same ontology as well as different ontologies. The system improves previous work by checking the relationship between ontologies before the matching process. If the two ontologies are related, the concept similarity is computed as they are in the same ontology. The two ontologies are related if they are formed from an original ontology. Otherwise, they are computed as in different ontologies. For different ontologies, the concept similarity is computed based on five similarity dimensions, namely, syntactic, properties, neighborhood, domain, and equivalent similarity. With the five dimensions, the system improves matching and avoids mismatch.

WEB SERVICES DISCOVERY ISSUES

This section introduces three web service discovery issues. They are: matching semantic web services against non-semantic web services, matching semantic web services using different description languages, and matching semantic web services using different ontologies.

Matching Semantic Web Services Against Non-Semantic Web Services

As mentioned in earlier sections, UDDI and some systems have been developed for matching non-semantic web services. They support searching by service names and service categories. They also support matching by inputs and outputs but are not based on semantics. The development of semantic web services has led to discovery mechanisms for semantic web services. Some semantic web services discovery systems have been developed to meet this need. However, these systems only search for semantic web services, and not non-

semantic web services. In short, we lack systems which can support matching both semantic web services and non-semantic web services.

For example, a company A developed web services to sell computers online. At that time, semantic web service technology was not available. Hence, WSDL was employed to describe the services. Another company B, which is interested in purchasing computers, started recently. It developed an ontology in OWL and uses OWL-S to describe their request services. Company A is able to provide services to company B. However, with the current web service discovery, company A cannot be found to match the requirement of the company B because they use different web service discovery languages: company A uses non-semantic web services description language while company B uses semantic web services description language.

Matching Semantic Web Services that Use Different Description Languages

Semantic web services have developed very rapidly because of their contribution to e-business and e-commerce applications. There are a large number of semantic web services based on different description languages, including DAML-S, OWL-S, WSMO etc. Existing semantic web services discovery mechanisms support matching based on specific description languages but they cannot perform matching on different description languages.

Suppose a web service uses OWL-S to describe the service. Another service uses DAML-S to describe the service. OWL-S uses OWLJessKB as a reasoner while DAML-S uses DAMLJessKB as a reasoner. The service provider which is described by OWL-S can meet the requirements of a web service requester which is described by DAML-S. However, these two services cannot be matched using current semantic web services discovery systems because the two different reasoners do not interact with each other.

Matching Web Services Using Different Ontologies

Current discovery systems are adequate when the web service requester and provider use the same ontology and reasoner to determine the relationship between two services. Unfortunately, most of them do not support the situation where a web service requester and provider use different ontologies. Only one group from University of Georgia (Cardoso & Sheth, 2003; Oundhankar et al., 2005) has addressed this problem. However, there are short-comings which were mentioned in section 3.3. These drawbacks should be addressed. In the real world where the web service requester and provider operate independently, each defines their own ontologies to describe their services. However, a web service provider can provide an exact service to the requester even though both services use different ontologies. Therefore, a discovery system that supports web services using distinct ontologies is necessary. This is an emergent research issue that has yet to be addressed.

Consider the following scenario: Some companies in Singapore provide computer solution services. They define their own ontology in the computer domain to describe their services. A company in Vietnam wishes to buy a computer and it defines its own ontology in the same computer domain to describe its services. There are no global ontologies in the domain and the provider and the requester do not know each other. So, though the two ontologies are within the same domain, they are basically different. Current discovery systems are unable to match the web service requester and provider in such a situation, but obviously, the providers can provide an exact fit to the requester's demands.

CONCLUSION

The paper presented a survey of web services discovery systems which focuses on methods of using semantics. A taxonomy of discovery systems was introduced. The advantages and disadvantages of various systems were highlight. There are two categories of the discovery systems that cater to semantic web services and non-semantic web services respectively. UDDI is a typical registry and discovery system for non-semantic web services. For semantic web services, the systems can be categorized as systems that support matching based on the same ontology or on different ontolgies. In systems supporting the same ontology, we can further classify them as systems that divide matching process into several stages, matching directly two web service profiles, or supporting UDDI.

We have introduced three open issues arising from current web service discovery systems, namely, matching semantic web services against non-semantic web services, matching semantic web services using different description languages, and matching semantic web services using distinct ontologies. A new web services discovery mechanism is required to overcome the three shortcomings. When designing a web service discovery system, the main problem of dynamic matchmaking in the Internet, namely the trade-off between performance and quality of matching should be borne in mind. The heterogeneities of web service also should be considered.

REFERENCES

Angell, R., & Freund, G. (1983). Automatic spelling correction using a trigram similarity measure. *Information Processing and Management, 19*(4), 255-161

Bayardo, R., W, B., R, B., A, C., G, F., A, H., et al. (1997). *Semantic integration of informa-*

tion in open and dynamic environments. Paper presented at the Proceedings of the 1997 ACM International Conference on the Management of Data (SIGMOD).

Benatallah, B., Hacid, M.-S., Leger, A., Rey, C., & Toumani, F. (2005). On automating Web services discovery. *The VLDB Journal — The International Journal on Very Large Data Bases, 14*(1), 84—96.Springer-Verlag New York

Cardoso, J., & Sheth, A. (2003). Semantic e-Workflow Composition. *Journal of Intelligent Information Systems, 21*(3), 191—225.Kluwer Academic Publishers

Castillo, J. G., Trastour, D., & Bartolini, C. (2001). *Desctiption Logics for Matchmaking of Services.* Paper presented at the Paper presented at the Workshop on Application of Description Logic.

Chao, K.-M., Younas, M., Lo, C.-C., & Tan, T.-H. (2005). *Fuzzy Matchmaking for Web Services.* Paper presented at the WAMIS Workshop, Tamkang University, Taiwan.

Frolund, S., & Koistinen, J. (1998). QML: A Language for Quality of Service Specification. *Technical report HPL on HP Laboratories*

Gagnes, T., Plagemann, T., & Munthe-Kaas, E. (2006). *A Conceptual Service Discovery Architecture for Semantic Web Services in Dynamic Environments.* Paper presented at the The 22nd International Conference on Data Engineering, Georgia, USA.

Garofalakis, J., Panagis, Y., Sakkopoulos, E., & Tsakalidis, A. (2004). *Web Service Discovery Mechanisms: Looking for a Needle in a Haystack?* Paper presented at the International Workshop on Web Engineering.

Haarslev, V., & Möller, R. (2001). *RACER System Description.* Paper presented at the the First International Joint Conference on Automated Reasoning.

Helal, A. (1997). InfoSleuth: Agent-based Semantic Integration of Information in Open and Dynamic Environments. In M. Huhns & M. Singh (Eds.), *Readings in Agents*: Morgan Kaufman.

Hondo, M., & Kaler, C. (2002). Web Services Policy Framework (WSPolicy) Version 1.0. *Availabel at http://www.verisign.com/wss/WS-Policy.pdf*

Hsu, P.-Y., & Zaniolo, C. (1993). *A new User's Impressions on LDL++ and CORAL.* Paper presented at the Workshop on Programming with Logic Databases (Informal Proceedings).

Huang, C.-L., Chao, K.-M., & Lo, C.-C. (2005). *A Moderated Fuzzy Matchmaking for Web Services.* Paper presented at the The 5th International Conference on Computer and Information Technology (CIT2005), Shanghai, China.

Jaeger, M. C., Tang, S., & Liebetruth, C., *The TUB OWL-S Matcher.*

Kawamura, T., Blasio, J. D., Hasegawa, T., Paolucci, M., & Sycara, K. (2003). *Preliminary Report of Public Experiment of Semantic Service Matchmaker with UDDI Business Register.* Paper presented at the 1st International Conference on Service Oriented Computing (ICSOC 2003), Trento, Italy.

Kawamura, T., Blasio, J. D., Hasegawa, T., Paolucci, M., & Sycara, K. (2004). *Public Deployment of Semantic Service Matchmaker with UDDI Business Registry.* Paper presented at the 3rd International Semantic Web Conference (ISWC 2004).

Le, D. N., & Goh, A. (2005). *Matching Semantic Web Services Using Different Ontologies.* Paper presented at the ICWE 2005, Sydney, Australia.

Le, D. N., Goh, A., & Tru, C. H. (2005). *Multi-Ontology Matchmaker*. Paper presented at the 7th International conference on Information Integration and Web Based Applications and Services (iiWAS2005), Malaysia.

Le, D. N., Hang, T. M., & Goh, A. (2006). *MOD- A Multi Ontology Discovery system*. Paper presented at the International Workshop on Semantic Matchmaking and Resource Retrieval, Seoul, Korean.

Li, L., & Horrocks, I. (2003). *A software framework for matchmaking based on semantic web technology*. Paper presented at the 12th International World Wide Web Conference, Budapest, Hungary.

Li, Y., Su, S., & Yang, F. (2006). *A Peer-to-Peer Approach to Semantic Web Services Discovery*. Paper presented at the Computational Science—ICCS 2006: 6th International Conference, Reading, UK.

Liang, Q., Chakarapani, L. N., Su, S. Y. W., Chikkamagalur, R. N., & Lamr, H. (2004). A Semi-automatic approach to composite web services discovery, description and invocation,. *International Journal of Web Services Research, 1*(4), 64–89.Idea Group Publishing

Ludwig, H. (2003). Web Service Level Agreement (WSLA) Language Specification Version 1.0. *Techincal report in IBM*

Mazzieri, M., & Dragoni, A. F. (2005). *A Fuzzy Semantics for Semantic Web Languages*. Paper presented at the Proceedings of the ISWC Workshop on Uncertainty Reasoning for the Semantic Web, Galway, Ireland.

Oundhankar, S., Verma, K., Sivashanugam, K., Sheth, A., & Miller, J. (2005). Discovery of web serivces in a Muti-Ontologies and Federated Registry Environment. *International Journal of Web Services Research, 1*(3)

Paolucci, M., Kawamura, T., Payne, T. R., & Sycara, K. (2002). *Semantic Matching of Web services Capabilities*. Paper presented at the 1st International Semantic Web Conference (ISWC 2002), Sardinia, Italy.

Patil, A., Oundhakar, S., Sheth, A., & Verma, K. (2004). *METEOR-S Web service Annotation Framework*. Paper presented at the Proceeding of the World Wide Web Conference.

Recuerda, F. M., & Robertson, D. (2005). *Discovery and Uncertainty in Semantic Web Services*. Paper presented at the Proceedings of the International Semantic Web Conference (ISWC 2005), Workshop 3: Uncertainty Reasoning for the Semantic Web, Galway, Ireland.

Roman, D., Lausen, H., & Keller, U. (2004). *Web Service Modeling Ontology—Standard (WSMO—Standard), WSMO deliverable D2 version 1.1*.

Sahai, A., Durante, A., & Machiraju, V. (2002). Towards Automated SLA Management for Web Services. *Technical report HPL-2001-310 (R.1) on HP Laboratories*

Salton, G. (1988). *Automatic Text Processing: The Transformation, Analysis and Retrieval of Information by Computer*: Massachusetts.

Shaw, S., Foggiato-Bish, L., Garcia, I., Tillman, G., Tryon, D., Wood, W., *et al*. (1993). *Improving Data Quality Via LDL++*. Paper presented at the Workshop on Programming with Logic Databases (Informal Proceedings).

Sivashanmugam, K., Verma, K., Sheth, A., & Miller, J. (2003). *Adding Semantics to Web Services Standards*. Paper presented at the The 2003 International Conference on Web Services (ICWS'03), Erfurt, Germany.

Srinivasan, N., Paolucci, M., & Sycara, K. (2004, 6-9). *Adding OWL-S to UDDI, implementation and throughput*. Paper presented at the First International Workshop on Semantic Web Services and Web Process Composition (SWSWPC 2004), San Diego, California, USA.

Stoilos, G., Stamou, G., Tzouvaras, V., Pan, J., & Horrocks, I. (2005). *The Fuzzy Description Logic f-SHIN*. Paper presented at the Proceedings of the ISWC Workshop on Uncertainty Reasoning for the Semantic Web, Galway, Ireland.

Sycara, K., J. Lu, M. K., & Widoff, S. (1999a). Dynamic service matchmaking among agents in open information environments. *ACM SIGMOD Record (Special Issue on Semantic Interoperability in Global Information Systems),, 28*(No.1), 47-53

Sycara, K., J. Lu, M. K., & Widoff, S. (1999b). *Matchmaking among heterogeneous agents on the internet*. Paper presented at the AAAI Spring Symposium on Intelligent Agents in Cyberspace.

Sycara, K., Widoff, S., & M. Klusch, J. L. (2002). *LARKS: Dynamic Matchmaking Among Heterogeneous Software Agents in Cyberspace*. Paper presented at the Autonomous Agents and Multi- Agent Systems.

Thaden, U., Siberski, W., & Nejdl, W. (2003). *A Semantic Web based Peer-to-Peer Service Registry Network* (Technical Report): Learning Lab Lower Saxony.

Trastour, D., Bartolini, C., & Gonzalez-Castillo, J. (2001). *A Semantic Web Approach to Service Description for Matchmaking of Service*. Paper presented at the 1st Semantic Web Working Symposium, CA.

W3C. Organization, *SOAP—Simple Object Access Protocol*.

Walsh, A. E. (2002). *UDDI, SOAP, and WSDL: The Web Services Specification Reference Book* (1st edition ed.) 0130857262: Pearson Education.

Wu, H., Jin, H., Li, Y., & Chen, H. (2005). *An Approach for Service Discovery Based on Semantic Peer-to-Peer*. Paper presented at the Advances in Computer Science—ASIAN 2005: 10th Asian Computing Science Conference, Kunming, China.

Yu, S., Liu, J., & Le, J. (2004a). *Decentralized Web Service Organization Combining Semantic Web and Peer to Peer Computing*. Paper presented at the Web Services: European Conference, ECOWS 2004, Erfurt, Germany.

Yu, S., Liu, J., & Le, J. (2004b). *Intelligent Web Service Discovery in Large Distributed System*. Paper presented at the Intelligent Data Engineering and Automated Learning—IDEAL 2004, Exeter, UK.

Zamora, E., Pollock, J., & al, e. (1981). The Use of Trigram Analysis for Spelling Error Detection. *Information Processing and Management, 6*(17), 305-316

Zhou, C., Chia, L.-T., & Lee, B.-S. (2005a). Semantics in Service Discovery and QoS Measurement. *IEEE IT Professional Magazine, 7*(2), 29-34

Zhou, C., Chia, L.-T., & Lee, B.-S. (2005b). Web Services Discovery with DAML-QoS Ontology. *International Journal of Web Services Research(JWSR), 2*(2), 44-67

Zinky, J. A., Bakken, D. E., & Schantz, R. E. (1997). Architectural Support for Quality of Service for CORBA Objects. *Theory and Practice of Object Systems, 3*(1).

This work was previously published in Int. Journal of Information Technology and Web Engineering, Vol 2, Issue 2, edited by G. Alkhatib and D. Rine, pp. 65-80, copyright 2005 by IGI Publishing (an imprint of IGI Global).

Chapter XVI
User Relevance Feedback in Semantic Information Retrieval

Antonio Picariello
Università di Napoli Federico II, Italy

Antonio M. Rinaldi
Università di Napoli Federico II, Italy

ABSTRACT

The user dimension is a crucial component in the information retrieval process and for this reason it must be taken into account in planning and technique implementation in information retrieval systems. In this paper we present a technique based on relevance feedback to improve the accuracy in an ontology based information retrieval system. Our proposed method combines the semantic information in a general knowledge base with statistical information using relevance feedback. Several experiments and results are presented using a test set constituted of Web pages.

INTRODUCTION

A user is a fundamental component in the information retrieval process and we can affirm that the goal of an information retrieval system is to satisfy a user's information needs. In several contexts, with the Web it can be very hard to satisfy completely the request of a user, given the great amount of information and the high heterogeneity in the information structure. On the other hand, users find it difficult to define their information needs, either because of the inability to express information need or just insufficient knowledge about the domain of interest hence they use just a few keywords. In this context, it is very useful to define the concept of *relevance information*. We can divide relevance into two main classes (Harter, 1992; Saracevic, 1975; Swanson, 1986) called *objective* (system-based) and *subjective* (human (user)-based) relevance respectively. The objective relevance can be viewed as a topicality measure, i.e. a direct match of the topic of the retrieved document and the one defined by the query. Several studies on the human relevance show that many other criteria are involved in the evaluation of the IR process output (Barry, 1998; Park, 1993; Vakkari & Hakala, 2000). In particular the subjective relevance refers to the intellectual interpretations carried out by users and it is related to the concepts of *aboutness* and *appropriateness* of retrieved information. According to Saracevic (1996) five types of relevance exist: an *algorithmic relevance* between the query and the set of retrieved information objects; a *topicality-like type*, associated with the concept of aboutness; *cognitive relevance*, related to the user information need; *situational relevance*, depending on the task interpretation; and *motivational and affective relevance*, which is goal-oriented. Furthermore, we can say that relevance has two main features defined at a general level: *multidimensional relevance*, which refers to how relevance can be perceived and assessed differently by different users; *dynamic relevance*, which instead refers to how this perception can change over time for the same user. These features have great impact on information retrieval systems which generally have not a user model and are not adaptive to individual users. It is generally acknowledged that some techniques can help the user in information retrieval tasks with more awareness, such as *Relevance Feedback* (RF). Relevance feedback is a means of providing additional information to an information retrieval system by using a set of results provided by a classical system by means of a query (Salton & Buckley, 1990). In the RF context, the user feeds some judgment back to the system to improve the initial search results.

The system can use this information to retrieve other documents similar to the relevant ones or rank the documents on the basis of user clues. In this paper we use the second approach. A user may provide the system with relevance information in several ways. He may perform an *explicit feedback* task, directly selecting documents from list results, or an *implicit feedback* task, where the system tries to estimate the user interests using the relevant documents in the collection. Another well known technique is the *pseudo-relevance feedback* where the system chooses the top-ranked documents as the relevant ones. This paper is organized as follows: in section 2 some related work about relevance feedback techniques and different methods and contexts are presented; section 3 briefly summarizes the fundamental theoretical background used in this work; several novel similarity metrics are then introduced in section 4; in section 5 we describe our Web information retrieval system based on ontologies and user feedback, while evaluations, experiments and conclusions are described in section 6 and 7 respectively.

RELATED WORKS

Relevance feedback techniques have been investigated for more then 30 years (Spink & Losee, 1996) and several papers show that they are effective for improving retrieval performance (Harman, 1992; Rocchio, 1971). From a general point of view RF techniques refer to the measure of relevance. In this context an end-user bases his judgment on the expected contribution of the analyzed document to his task. In Resnick et al. (1994) is presented GroupLens, a collaborative filter-based system which ranks the documents on the basis of numeric ratings explicitly assigned by the user. The basic idea is that people who agreed with the evaluation of past articles are likely to agree again in the future. Moreover the system tries to predict user's agreement using the ratings from similar users. SIFT's (Yan & Garcia-Molina, 1995) approach requires the user to explicitly submit his profile and update it using relevance feedback. The SIFT engine uses profiles to filter documents and notifies them according to user-specified parameters. AntWorld (Kantor et al., 2000) pursues the ant metaphor allowing internet users to get information about other users' quests. The users have to give a judgment about the visited pages. The judgment is expressed using textual annotation and numeric value. The quests are stored in the system and the similarity between them and the documents is computed as the sum of a *tf/idf* (term frequency/inverse document frequency) score and user relevance feedbacks. Powerize Server (Kim, Oard & Romanik, 2000) is a content-based system which builds a model to take into account user's information needs. This model is constructed explicitly by the user or implicitly inferring user behaviour. The proposed system is based on parameters to define the user behaviour and starting from them and their correlations the user model. In White, Ruthven & Jose (2002) a system for relevance feedback in Web retrieval is presented. The authors follow two types of approaches based on explicit and implicit feedback. They investigate on the degree of substitution between the two types of evidence. Using relevance feedback the system displays new documents and in particular documents that have been retrieved but not yet considered. Relevance feedback techniques are also used in other contexts, such as multimedia retrieval; e.g. in Zhang, Chai & Jin (2005) where a text-based image retrieval system is described.

THE USER NEEDS REPRESENTATION

In past years, the ontological aspects of information have acquired a strategic value. These aspects are intrinsically independent from information codification, so the information itself may be isolated, recovered, organized, and integrated with respect to its content. A formal definition of ontology is proposed in Gruber (1993) according to whom "an ontology is an explicit specification of a conceptualization"; *conceptualization* is referred to as an abstract model of a specified domain in which the component concepts are identified; *explicit* means that the type of concepts used and the constraints on them are well defined; *formal* is referred to as the ontology propriety of being "machine-readable"; *shared* is about the propriety that an ontology captures consensual knowledge, accepted by a group of person, not only by individuals. We also consider other definitions of ontology; in Neches et al. (1991) "an ontology defines the basic terms and relations comprising the vocabulary of a topic area, as well as the rules for combining terms and relations to define extensions to the vocabulary". This definition indicates the way to proceed in order to build an ontology: i) identification of the basic terms and their relations; ii) agreeing on the rules that arrange them; iii) definition of terms and relations among concepts. From this perspective, an ontology doesn't include just the terms that explicitly are defined in it, but also those that can be derived by means of well defined rules and properties. In our work, the ontology can be seen as the set of "terms" and "relations" among them, denoting the concepts that are used in a domain. We use ontologies to represent the user interest domain.

Dynamic Semantic Network

In the proposed system, the implementation of the ontology is obtained by means of a Semantic Network (i.e. DSN), dynamically built using a dictionary based on WordNet (Miller, 1995). WordNet organizes several terms using their linguistic proprieties. Moreover, every domain keyword may have various meanings (senses) due to the polysemy property, so a user can choose its proper sense of interest. In WordNet these senses

Figure 1. An example of DSN: (A) Music, sense 1; (B) Car, Sense 1

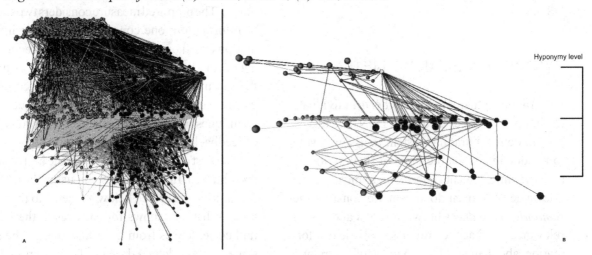

are organized in synsets composed of synonyms; therefore, once chosen the sense is chosen (i.e. the appropriate synset), it is possible to take into account all the possible terms (synonyms) that are in the synset. Beyond the synonymy, we consider other linguistic properties applied to typology of the considered terms in order to have a strongly connected network. The DSN is built starting from the domain keyword that represents the context of interest for the user. We then consider all the component synsets and construct a hierarchy based on the hyponymy property; the last level of our hierarchy corresponds to the last level of WordNet's hierarchy. After this first step, we enrich our hierarchy by exploiting all the other kinds of relationships in WordNet. Based on these relations we can add other terms to the hierarchy obtaining an highly connected semantic network.

Figure 1 shows an example of DSN. Figure 1 (A) represents the music domain; we can see the high complexity of the network, due to the generality of the chosen term. On the other hand, figure 1 (B) shows a semantic network about the concept car; in this figure we can see better the

network structure organized around the hyperonymy/hyponymy hierarchy.

The arcs between the nodes of the DSN are assigned a weight σ_i, in order to express the strength of the relation. The weights are real numbers in the [0,1] interval and their values are defined experimentally. To calculate the relevance of a term in a given domain we assign a weight to each one in the DSN considering the polysemy property (that can be considered as a measure of the ambiguity in the use of a word, when it can assume several senses). Thus we define the *centrality* of the term *i* as:

$$\varpi(i) = \frac{1}{poly(i)} \qquad (1)$$

where *poly(i)* is the polysemy (number of senses) of *i*. For example, the word *music* has five senses in WordNet, so the probability that it is used to express a specific meaning is equal to 1/5. Therefore, we build a representation of the retrieved Web pages using the DSN; each word in the page which matches any of the terms in the DSN is a component of the document representation and the links between them are the relations in the DSN.

SYNTACTIC-SEMANTIC METRIC

Given a conceptual domain, in order to individuate the interesting pages by using a DSN, it is necessary to define a grading system to assign a vote to the documents on the basis of their syntactic and semantic content. Therefore, to measure the relevance of a given document we consider the *semantic relatedness* between terms and, using relevance feedback techniques, statistical information about them. The concept of "semantic relatedness" refers to the perceived relations between words and concepts. Several metrics have been defined in the literature in order to measure the semantic relatedness of two words. These metrics can be grouped in the following categories:

- **Dictionary-based.** Dictionaries are a natural linguistic information source for people knowledge about the world; they form a knowledge base in which the headwords are defined by other headwords and/or their derivatives;
- **Thesaurus-based.** These metrics use a thesaurus in which words are related to concepts; each word is related to a category by means of an index structure;
- **Semantic network-based.** These metrics use semantic networks, i.e. graphs in which the nodes are the concepts and the arcs represent relations between concepts;
- **Integrated approach.** This approach takes into account additional knowledge sources to enrich the information already present in the network.

An exhaustive overview of the metrics based on these approaches can be found in Budanitsky (1999) and a new approach for measuring semantic similarity is proposed in Li, Bandar & Mclean (2003). The proposed measure considers two types of information; one concerning syntactic information based on the concepts of word frequency and term centrality and another one concerning the semantic component calculated on each set of words in the document. The Relevance Feedback techniques we used take into account two types of feedback: explicit and blind feedback.

The first one is performed after the first results presentation. In fact, the system, using the metric for ranking described below, presents to the user a result list and shows for each result the top 2 ranked sentences from the related page. The top sentences are detected using the system metric on each sentence in the document and ordering them. With this information the user can manually choose relevant documents or he can open the whole page. With the blind approach the user can allow the system to automatically perform the relevance feedback on a defined number of documents. The first contribution is called the syntactic-semantic grade (SSG). In this paper we propose a new approach to calculate the SSG and compare it with the one proposed in Albanese, Picariello & Rinaldi (2004); the metric proposed there represents our standard metric. We can define the relevance of a word in a given conceptual domain and, if the feedback functions are chosen, in the set of selected documents. Therefore we use an hybrid approach exploiting both statistical and semantic information. The statistical information is obtained by applying the relevance feedback technique described in Weiss, Vélez & Sheldon (1996), and it is enriched with the semantic information provided by computing the centrality of the terms (equation 1). In this way we divide the terms into classes, on the basis of their centrality:

$$SSG_{i,k} = \frac{\left(0.5 + 0.5\left(TF_{i,k} \middle/ TF_{\max,k}\right)\right)\varpi_i}{\sqrt{\sum_{i \in k}\left(0.5 + 0.5\left(TF_{i,k} \middle/ TF_{\max,k}\right)\right)^2 (\varpi_i)^2}}$$

$$(2)$$

where k is the k-th document, i is the i-th term, $TF_{i,k}$ is the term frequency of i in k, $TF_{max,k}$ is the maximum term frequency in k, ϖ_i is the centrality of i.

We use this approach to improve the precision of the model of the domain of interest and to overcome the lack of very specific terms in Wordnet (e.g. computer science specific terminology). Thus, the use of relevance feedback re-weighs and expands the semantic network by adding new terms—not present in the DSN—from the relevant documents. After the relevance feedback step, the system assigns a $\varpi_i = 1$ to the new terms thus considering them as important in the context. The other contribution is based on a combination of the path length (l) between pairs of terms and the depth (d) of their subsumer (i.e. the first common ancestor), expressed as the number of hops. The correlation between terms constitutes the semantic relatedness and it is computed through a nonlinear function. The choice of a nonlinear function to express the semantic relatedness between terms derives from several considerations. The value of the length and the depth of a path, based on how they are defined, may vary from 0 to infinity, while relatedness between two terms should be expressed as a number in the [0,1] interval. In particular, when the path length decreases to 0 the relatedness should monotonically increase to 1, while it should monotonically decrease to 0 when path length goes to infinity. Also we need a scaling effect on the depth, because words in the upper levels of a semantic hierarchy express more general concepts than the words in a lower level. We use a non linear function for scaling down the contribution of subsumers in an upper level and scaling up those in a lower one. Given two words w_1 and w_2, the length l of the path between w_1 and w_2 is computed using the DSN and it is defined as:

$$l(w_1, w_2) = \min_j \sum_{i=1}^{h_j(w_1, w_2)} \frac{1}{\sigma_i} \cdot$$

$$(3)$$

where j spans over all the paths between w_1 and w_2, $h_j(w_1, w_2)$ is the number of hops in the j-th path and σ_i is the weight assigned to the i-th hop in the j-th path in respect to the hop linguistic property. As an example, let us consider three concepts X, Y and Z and some possible f paths between them. The paths, represented by arcs, are labelled with their linguistic properties σ and the concepts have a common subsumer S having a distance of 8 levels from the WordNet root. Now suppose that $\sigma_i = \sigma_j = 0.8$ and $\sigma_t = 0.3$, where σ_i is the path between X and Z, σ_j is the one between Y and Z and σ_t is the path between X and Y. In this case the best path is the one traversing Z with a value of l=1.58. The depth d of the subsumer of w_1 and w_2 is also computed using WordNet. To this aim only the hyponymy and hyperonymy relations (i.e. the IS-A hierarchy) are considered; $d(w_1, w_2)$ is computed as the number of hops from the subsumer of w_1 and w_2 to the root of the hierarchy. Given the above considerations, we selected an exponential function that satisfies the previously discussed constraints; our choice is also supported by the studies of Shepard (1987), who demonstrated that exponential-decay functions are a universal law in psychological science. We can now introduce the definition of Semantic Grade (SeG), which extends a metric proposed in Li, Bandar & Mclean (2003):

$$SeG(v) = \sum_{(w_i, w_j)} e^{-\alpha \cdot l(w_i, w_j)} \frac{e^{\beta \cdot d(w_i, w_j)} - e^{-\beta \cdot d(w_i, w_j)}}{e^{\beta \cdot d(w_i, w_j)} + e^{-\beta \cdot d(w_i, w_j)}}$$

$$(4)$$

where v is the considered document, (w_i, w_j) are the pairs of words in pre-processed document and $\alpha \geq 0$ and $\beta > 0$ are two scaling parameters whose values are experimentally defined. This formula has been used in our previous work (Albanese, Picariello & Rinaldi, 2004) with good results and its fine performance is highlighted in Varelas et al. (2005).

Both grades are computed for each Web page element considering them as composed of four elementary document elements, namely the *title*, the *keywords*, the *description* and the *body*. Both metric components are computed for each of these elements.

WEB RETRIEVAL SYSTEM

The proposed method and technique have been implemented and evaluated by an IR system running on the Web. We propose a Web search engine that takes into account relevance feedback to improve the precision of information retrieval systems based on general ontologies. The information used to build the domain ontology is dynamically extracted from WordNet. For this reason the query structure is constituted as a *list of terms* to retrieve (i.e. subject keywords) and a *domain of interest* (i.e. domain keyword) provided by the user using the system interface. For example, if a user wants to get information about the famous jazzman Miles Davis, we have: *subject keywords*:=*"Davis"*, and *domain keyword*:=*"music"*. We want to be able to retrieve the interesting pages from the user perspective, without considering the ones related to tennis' Davis Cup, that pertains to the Sport Domain. Our system must be able to retrieve and rank results, taking into account the semantics of the pages and the interaction with the user. In other words, this system performs the following tasks:

- **Fetching.** Fetching consists of searching Web documents containing the keywords specified in the query. This task can be accomplished using traditional search engines.
- **Preprocessing.** This task is needed to remove from Web documents all those elements that do not represent useful information (HTML tags, scripts, applets, etc.).

- **Mining.** Mining consists of analyzing the content of the documents from a semantic point of view, assigning them a score with respect to the query.
- **Reporting.** This task consists in ranking and returning the documents relevant to the query allowing some functionality for relevance feedback.

We use external search engines in the fetching step.

The system implementation is based on several services. In this context each software module performs one of the actions previously described.

Figure 2 presents a complete architectural view of the proposed system. The user interface allows the insertion of keywords and it also enables the setting of a certain number of parameters, namely: the search engines to be used in the syntactic search and their relative weights, the number of links to be returned by the underlying search engines, the relative weights of title, description,

Figure 2. System architecture

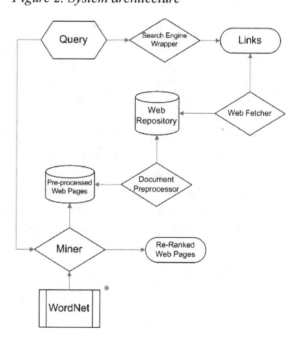

Figure 3. An example of sense selection

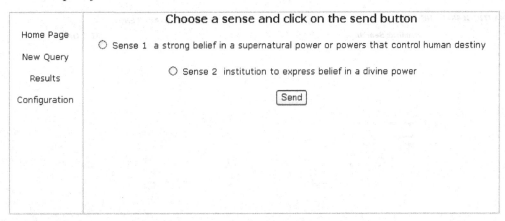

keywords and body tags, the relative weights of Syntactic Grade, Syntactic-Semantic Grade and Semantic Grade.

Let us consider the case of a user interested in finding some pages about the *Madonna*, in the religion domain. He can submit a query specifying "madonna" as the *subject keyword* and "religion" as the *domain keyword* (see figure 4). If the domain keyword has more than a single sense, the user is asked to choose one of them; in this case the system shows the WordNet the descriptions of all the senses related to the word *religion* as shown in figure 3.

The user can perform three different types of search:

- **Standard searching.** The system ranks the results without relevance feedback;
- **Explicit feedback.** The results interface allows choosing relevance documents as feedback;
- **Blind feedback.** The search interface allows choosing relevance documents by the system.

RESULTS AND EVALUATION

The need for a suitable evaluation of information retrieval systems imposes the adoption of meth-

odologies to give answers about *why*, *what* and *how-to* evaluate. Several authors give answers to these questions (Cleverdon, Mills & Keen, 1996; Vakkari & Hakala, 2000). The techniques used to measure the effectiveness are often affected by the used retrieval strategy and the results presentation. We use a *test set collection* to evaluate our system. A test collection is a set of documents, queries and a list of relevant document in the collection. We use it to compare the results of our system using the ranking strategies described previously. It is important to have standard parameters for IR system evaluation. For this reason we use *precision* and *recall* curves. Recall is the fraction of all relevant material that is returned by a search; precision is a measure of the number of relevant documents in the set of all documents returned by a search. We built the test set from the directory service of the search engine yahoo (search. yahoo.com/dir). The directory service supplies the category referred to each Web page. In this way we have a *relevance assessment* useful to compare our results. The test collection is more then 800 pages retrieved using words with a high polysemic value so that the documents belong to different categories. We choose keywords about both general and specific subjects. This class distinction is useful to measure the performance differences between the rank strategies using a

Figure 4. Search page and results

general knowledge base and adding relevance feedback.

In Ruthven & Lalmas (2003) there are some important considerations derived from the analysis of references, criticising the use of the precision-recall measure for RF (Chang, Cirillo & Razon, 1971; Borlund & Ingwersen, 1997; Frei, Meienberg & Schauble, 1991). In fact, using relevance feedback the documents marked as relevant are pushed to the top of the result list improving *artificially* the Recall-Precision curve (*ranking effect*) rather then taking into account the *feedback effect*, that is liable to push to the top of the ranked list the unseen relevant documents. The proposed alternatives to consider the feedback on the unseen relevant documents are:

- **Residual Ranking.** This strategy removes from the collection those items which were assessed for relevance for feedback purposes, and it evaluates two runs (with or without feed- back) on the reduced collection.
- **Freezing** the documents, examined for relevance before feedback, are retained as the top-ranking documents in the feedback run.

- **Test and Control Groups.** The collection is randomly split into two collections: the *test group* and the *control group*. Relevance Feedback information are taken from the test group but the Recall-Precision is performed only on the control group, so there is no ranking effect.

In our approach we use the last strategy to perform our experiments. The document collection is split randomly in order to consider documents from all topics. The random function is calculated on each single category. The used test set simulates a "real" search on the Web because we analyze the pages that are fetched from a standard search engine and we consider also problems such as "page not found", "redirecting" and so on.

In figure 5 the trend of the experimental results is shown: for low recall values, the precision is high with all strategies. This is a suitable effect in IR retrieval systems because the real relevant documents are immediately presented to the user; moreover RF techniques improve the results accuracy with respect our standard strategy (without RF) because by increasing the recall the precision also improves. We note that the blind RF strategy gives an initial improvement but it is lower than

Figure 5. Experimental results

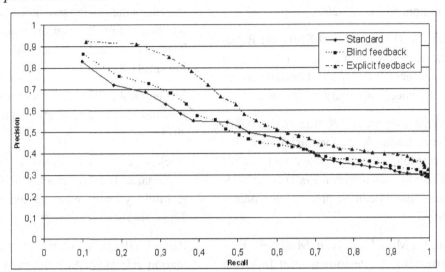

the standard one because the system considers false positives in the feedback step.

CONCLUSION AND FUTURE WORKS

In this paper we have presented a system and a novel metric to improve ranking accuracy in IR on the Web, using relevance feedback techniques. We have proposed an hybrid approach that take into account both syntactic, semantic and statistical information and we have used a general knowledge base in order to dynamically extract a semantic network for representing user information needs. We have evaluated the proposed system and the algorithms on a test set built to consider the *feedback effect* and we have used a relevance feedback test strategy. The experiments have shown a performance improvement using our approach compared with previously presented search strategies.

Our work is preliminary research on the use of relevance feedback techniques in an ontology based systems. Many other topics could be inves-

tigated such as: (1) using of implicit feedback and user characteristics; (2) adding relevance terms to user query refinement to consider new documents after the first interaction; (3) considering multimedia information to perform RF on other features different to textual ones; (4) inferring relevant documents and related terms in order to have specialized ontologies merged with the proposed DSN.

REFERENCES

Albanese, M., Picariello, A., & Rinaldi A. M. (2004). A Semantic Search Engine for WEB Information Retrieval: an Approach Based on Dynamic Semantic Networks. Semantic Web Workshop, ACM SIGIR 2004, 25-29.

Barry, C.L. (1998). Document representations and clues to document relevance. Journal of the American Society for Information Science, 49(14), 1293-1303.

Borlund, P., & Ingwersen, P. (1997). The Development of a Method for the Evaluation of Interactive Information Retrieval Systems. Journal of Documentation. 53(3), 225-250.

Budanitsky, A. (1999). Lexical Semantic Relatedness and Its Application in Natural Language Processing. Technical report. Department of Computer Science, University of Toronto.

Chang, Y. K., Cirillo, C. & Razon, J. (1971). Evaluation of feedback retrieval using modified freezing, residual collection & test and control groups. The SMART retrieval system—experiments in automatic document processing, Chapter 17, 355-370.

Cleverdon, C., Mills J., & Keen, M. (1966). Factors Determining the Performance of Indexing Systems. Technical report. ASLIB Cranfield Research Project, Cranfield.

Frei, H.P., Meienberg, S., & Schauble, P. (1991). The Perils of Interpreting Recall and Precision Values. In Proceedings of GI/GMD-Workshop Information Retrieval, 1-10.

Gruber, T. R. (1993). A translation approach to portable ontology specifications. Knowledge Acquisition, 5(2), 199-220.

Harman, D. (1992) Relevance feedback revisited. In Proceedings of the 15th annual international ACM SIGIR conference on Research and development in information, 1-10.

Harter, S.P. (1992). Psychological relevance and information science. Journal of the American Society for Information Science, 43(9), 602-615.

Kantor, P., Boros, E., Melamed, B., Menkov, V., Shapira, B., & Neu, D. (2000). Capturing human intelligence in the net. Communications of the ACM , 43(8), 112-115.

Kim, J., Oard, D., & Romanik, K. (2000). Using implicit feedback for user modeling in Internet and Intranet searching. Technical Report, College of Library and Information Services, University of Maryland at College Park.

Li, Y., Bandar Z.A., & Mclean D. (2003). An approach for measuring semantic similarity between words using multiple information sources. IEEE Transactions on Knowledge and Data Engineering, 15(4), 871-882.

Miller, G. A. 1995. WordNet: a lexical database for English. Communication of the ACM, 38(11), 39-41.

Neches, R., Fikes R., Finin, T., Gruber, T., Patil, R., Senator, T., & Swartout, W.R. (1991), Enabling technology for knowledge sharing, AI Magazine, 12(3), 36-56.

Park, T. (1993).The nature of relevance in information retrieval: An empirical study. Library Quarterly, 63, 318-351.

Resnick, P., Iacovou, N., Suchak, M., Bergstrom, P., & Riedl, J. (1994). GroupLens: an open architecture for collaborative filtering of netnews. In Proceedings of the 1994 ACM Conference on Computer Supported Cooperative Work, 175-186.

Rocchio, J.J. (1971). Relevance feedback in information retrieval. The SMART Retrieval System, 313–323

Ruthven, I., & Lalmas, M. (2003). A survey on the use of relevance feedback for information access systems. Knowledge Engineering Review, 18(2), 95-145.

Salton, G., & Buckley, C. (1990). Improving retrieval performance by relevance feedback. Journal of the American Society for Information Science, 41(4), 288-97.

Saracevic, T. (1975). Relevance: A review of and framework for the thinking on the notion in information science. Journal of the American Society for Information Science, 26(6), 321-343.

Saracevic, T. (1996). Relevance reconsidered. In Proceedings of the Second Conference on Conceptions of Library and Information Science (CoLIS 2), 201-218.

Shepard, R.N.(1987). Towards a Universal Law of Generalisation for Psychological Science. Science, 237,1317-1323.

Spink, A., & Losee, R.M. (1996). Feedback in information retrieval. Review of Information Science and Technology, 31, 33-78.

Swanson, D.R. (1986). Subjective versus objective relevance in bibliographic retrieval systems. Library Quarterly 56(4), 389-398

Vakkari, P. & Hakala, N. (2000). Changes in Relevance Criteria and Problem Stages in Task Performance. Journal of Documentation, 56(5), 540-562.

Varelas, G., Voutsakis, E., Raftopoulou, P., Petrakis, E. G., & Milios, E. E. (2005). Semantic similarity methods in WordNet and their application to information retrieval on the web. In Proceedings of the 7th Annual ACM international Workshop on Web information and Data Management—WIDM '05, 10-16.

VanRijsbergen, C.J., (1979). Information Retrieval. Butterworth-Heinemann. Newton, MA, USA.

Weiss, R., Vélez, B., & Sheldon, M. A. (1996). HyPursuit: a hierarchical network search engine that exploits content-link hypertext clustering. In Proceedings of the the Seventh ACM Conference on Hypertext, 180-193.

White, R.W., Ruthven, I. & Jose, J.M. (2002). The use of implicit evidence for relevance feedback in web retrieval. In Proceedings of 24th BCS-IRSG European Colloquium on IR Research. Lecture notes in Computer Science 2291, 93-109.

Yan, T., & Garcia-Molina, H. (1995). SIFT—A tool for wide-area information dissemination. Proceedings of USENIX Winter 1995 Technical Conference, 177-186

Zhang, C., Chai, J. Y., & Jin, R. (2005). User term feedback in interactive text-based image retrieval. In Proceedings of the 28th Annual international ACM SIGIR Conference on Research and Development in information Retrieval, 51-58.

This work was previously published in Int. Journal of Intelligent Information Technologies, Vol 3, Issue 2, edited by V. Sugumaran, pp. 36-50, copyright 2007 by IGI Publishing (an imprint of IGI Global).

Chapter XVII
A Preliminary Study toward Wireless Integration of Patient Information System

Abdul-Rahman Al-Ali
American University of Sharjah, UAE

Tarik Ozkul
American University of Sharjah, UAE

Taha Landolsi
American University of Sharjah, UAE

ABSTRACT

This paper presents the results of a study toward generating a wireless environment to provide real-time mobile accessibility to patient information system. A trial system is set up where database, internet, and wireless personal digital assistants (PDAs) are integrated in such a way that the medical professionals like physicians, nurses and lab assistants can create, access and update medical records using wireless PDAs from any location in the hospital which is covered by wireless LAN. The same services which can be carried out via fixed terminals with internet connectivity can be carried out using wireless PDAs. The implementation has used and integrated many technologies like Active Server Pages (ASP), Visual Basic®, Structured Query Language (SQL) Server, ActiveSync®, IEEE802.11 Wireless Local Area Network (WLAN) technology and wireless security concepts. The paper details the architectural aspects of technology integration and the methodology used for setting up the end-to-end system. The proposed architecture, its performance data and the common implementation barriers are reported.

INTRODUCTION

Medical professionals have already recognized the importance of keeping patient information (medical records) in an electronic format rather than paper-based format because of the sheer size of records generated daily. Due to the extensive size and costly storage requirements, keeping paper-based records became more expensive than keeping records electronically. A study conducted in a 500-bed hospital indicated that a 7-inch stack of paper based laboratory reports must be filed daily. The informal survey was conducted with medical professionals among the American University of Sharjah medical center staff and a neighboring local hospital in which receptionists, laboratory and X-ray technicians, nurses and physicians participated. Most of them liked the idea of using electronic patient record (EPR) technology. Some of them expressed some concerns about the screen size and the resolution limitation of the personal digital assistants (PDAs) used in the trial. Others worried that if such ubiquitous systems are deployed, then medical staff will have to be available all the time even during vacations days. They stated that if such technology is available, they will be liable if they do not answer even during their breaks. "It is a matter of life and death" one of the nurses stated, "I should answer calls anywhere, anytime".

The cost of maintaining paper based records and filing them in an ordered fashion to keep them accessible is over US$10 per record (Safran, Goldberg, 2000). Keeping records electronically also presented the opportunity of being able to access records over the internet from anywhere, anytime. Together with the powerful PDAs and wireless connectivity tools it became feasible to access EPR remotely without being tied to workstations. There are several records in the literature which mention successful implementations of web-based access to patient databases (Liu, et. al., 2001; Garcia, et. al. 2002). Others have reported wireless healthcare using wireless local area networks (WLAN) and discussed the electronics home healthcare concepts and challenges (Wang, Hongwei, 2005; Wickramasighe, Misra, 2004). A trial study conducted recently among medical professionals in real hospital settings indicated that medical professionals regard mobile access to the following data highly useful (Ammenwerth, et al., 2000):

- Medical knowledge like drug data,
- Medical coding references like ICD-10 codes (International Classification of Diseases) and literature databases,
- Patient database and administrative patient data,
- General information like telephone numbers and medical databases.

After using the system for a week, the respondents indicated that mobile communication and mobile information processing power offered by PDAs are very valuable. However, the respondents also reported that they were not satisfied with the 9600 baud rate communication speed offered by the early versions of PDAs and the mobile phones based on the Global System for Mobile (GSM) standard used in the study. During the study it also became apparent that the messaging ability offered by PDAs was much superior to personal accessibility provided by pagers and mobile phones (Ammenwerth, et al., 2000). Since then, the rapid change in the technology provided better connection methods, more durable and faster handheld mobile computing devices. The wireless accessibility provided by nowadays existing WLAN standards such as IEEE802.11g can support 54 Mbits/s data rate and the soon to come IEEE802.11n standard will support 540 Mbits/s data rate. This will clearly satisfy the need to higher access bandwidth required by healthcare providers. Along with the other contemporary software and database tools, this new connectivity method promised better EPR system and motivated many researchers in the healthcare industry to develop integrated wireless applications for use on pocket PC, smart-phone PDAs and other portable device platforms (Lu et. al., 2005).

In this study, we will design a prototype electronic medical database system and evaluate its performance in near-realistic settings. Another aspect of the research conducted is the design of a web-based database for hospital environment which could be equally accessed by wireline and wireless networks.

TECHNOLOGY IMPLEMENTATION BARRIERS

As is the case for many newly-introduced technologies, even with uncontested technological and economical benefits of the proposed architecture are tremendous however, the implementation may be impeded by the perceived steep learning curve for potential users. This fact is especially true for medical professionals who are in general uncomfortable introducing new technology due to the risks involved and required "protected time" to integrate it in their work environment (Van Ginneken, 2002). The flexibility and adaptability to change are regarded as the key factors for medical applications. Standardized and open-vendor systems are also important factors for getting new technology accepted by the user community. Acceptance of EPR by the medical community has improved after an initial hesitation. The technology to access patients' information varies. Literature search indicated that there are several techniques that are currently being used:

- Hybrid architecture using PDAs and wireless GSM modems
- IEEE802.11 WLAN standard
- IEEE802.15 known as Bluetooth standard

Software applications were based on Wireless Application Protocol (WAP). The hybrid system using PDA and GSM modems combination was used in a trial study conducted in real hospital settings (Van Ginneken, 2002). This valuable study was aimed at determining expectations of medical professionals from potential wireless enabled hospital settings. The study indicated many points which are regarded important by medical professionals. But the study also indicated that the data rate offered by the hybrid solution is far lower than expected to be considered useful. Another connectivity method used in some studies was WAP connectivity which is used by mobile phones to transfer web contents to mobile devices. In a successful WAP-based system, patient data was sent successfully from patients monitored to WAP-enabled phone. Information like Electro-Cardiogram (ECG) signal was displayed graphically on the medical professionals WAP enabled phone (Hung, Zhang, 2003). Although the project was successful, the authors reported that the data transfer rate was low. Another major drawback of the system is the limited screen size of the WAP phone. Another similar study used WAP services for connectivity to biological databases (Riikonen, et al., 2002). The Mobile and PDA phones successfully queried the databases and displayed the contents in a browser page on the mobile device. PDA-based client-server architecture is preferred for flexible telemedicine systems (Nazeran, et al., 2004). The client uses a Pocket PC client because of its processing capabilities, low cost and compact size. The system could be used to transmit audio, still images and vital signs from a remote site to a clinic or a hospital web-server that implements standard Internet protocols.

Adoption of wireless solutions in the healthcare sector has many advantages and but also poses some challenges (Lu, et. all, 2005; Demiris, 2004). Time and cost saving, mobility and real-time access, reducing medical errors, enhancing productivity and quality of care are major advantages of using PDA in healthcare (Lu, et. all, 2005). However, speed, screen size, data entry, maintenance, interoperability issues, patient privacy issues, interference with medical equipment, data security issue, negative patient perception of delicate devices are notable challenges (Lin, Vassar, 2004; Lu, et al., 2005).

DESIGN CONSIDERATIONS FOR THE TRIAL SYSTEM

Literature and informal surveys of medical professionals showed that the designed system should have the following requirements:

*   The system should have an EPR database which is user friendly, robust and web-enabled.
*   The system should be secure. Several layers of security should be established at different levels.
*   Access speed to the system, data access and update speed should be high; PDA used for

the system should have reasonable size and weight.
*   The system should use off-the-shelf components and the cost should be reasonable.
*   The system should be accessible at any time. Hence architecture should be robust to provide the needed high availability.

To achieve the above requirements a client-sever model is designed and constructed. Figure 1 shows the system hardware architecture. A database is designed and managed by SQL-sever, website and wireless connectivity via PDA are developed. Figure 2 shows the system software tiers.

Database Design

A database system is designed to serve the requirements of the overall system. Entity Relationship

Figure 1. System hardware architecture

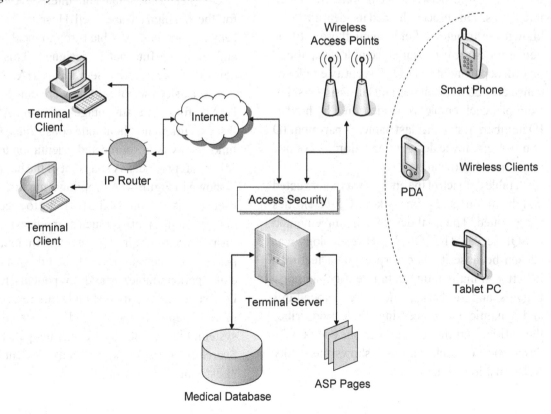

Figure 2. System software tiers

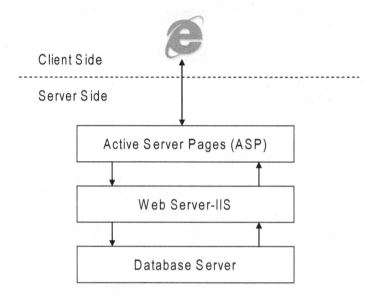

Diagram (ERD) is used to describe the objects in the hospital database. The objects or entities and the relationship between them were translated into tables. This process helped us identify facts, known as attributes or fields, about these entities. Four entities are used namely; employee, patient, record, department and test. The entity employee consists of doctors, nurses and lab assistants. For example, each employee is identified by his/her ID number, first name, last name, department ID number, employee designation, address, contact number and nationality.

A table for each of the entities was constructed and the unique and primary keys for the entities were issued. The final design was implemented in SQL server. The SQL Server technology was chosen because it has enterprise data features, is better in maintaining data integrity, supports triggers and rollbacks, and stores procedures and dynamic data processing. Table 1 describes the entities and the attributes along with a brief description of each. Figure 3 shows the Entity Relationship Diagram.

WEBSITE DESIGN

A complete functional and interactive website for the hospital "Care Well Hospital" medical centre which is accessible through local intranet and from the Internet is designed. This site is developed using Active Server Pages (ASP®) and Visual Basic® scripting that were embedded in HTML files. The advantages of using ASP are fast execution, no client-side constraints, ODBC links to any data source and orientation towards Microsoft products. A snapshot of the home page is shown in Figure 4. A dropdown menu helps the users to activate one of the hotlinks to access any of the system functions such as medical services, visiting hours, login, logout, etc. An authorized person can access personal records, patient records, patients table and add new patients' records. For example, the patients' table link returns a list of all patients who are already registered in the system. Figure 5 shows the existing patients list. Search by a specific key such as "Patient ID" or "Last Name". Figure 6 shows that a patient search

Table 1. Database fileds corresponding to the system entities

Sr. No	Entity	Attribute	Description
1	**Employee**	ID	Unique identification number of the employee
		FName	First name of the employee
		LName	Last name of the employee
		Dept_ID	Unique department to which the employee belongs
		Designation	Post of the employee in his/her respective department
		Address	Mailing address of the employee
		Contact_no	Contact information
		nationality	Nationality of the employee
2	**Patient**	P_ID1	Unique identification number(patient id) of the patient
		FName	First name of the patient
		LName	Last name of the patient
		DOB	Date of birth of the patient
		Height	Height of the patient
		Weight	Weight of the patient
		Blood	Blood group of the patient
		Address	Mailing address of the employee
		Contact_no	Contact information
		Nationality	Nationality of the employee
3	**Record**	Record_ID	Unique identification of the record along with the P_ID
		CDate	System Date when the record is stored
		Dr_ID	Doctor id
		Diagnosis	Diagnosis of the medical problem
		Medication	Medication prescribed
		Comments	Further comments regarding the record
		References	References to other doctors, medical staff, etc.
4	**Department**	Dept_ID	Unique identification of the department
		Name	Name of the department
5	**Test**	Test_ID	Unique identification of the test in combination with the record id and patient id
		Type	The type of the test
		Result	The results of the test
		CDate	System Date when the record is stored

Figure 3. Entity relationship diagram

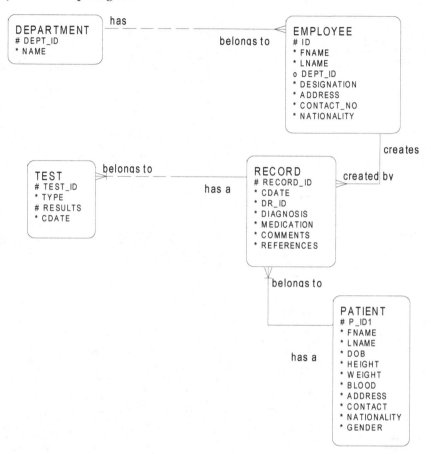

Figure 4. Homepage of "Care Well Hospital" website designed for the study

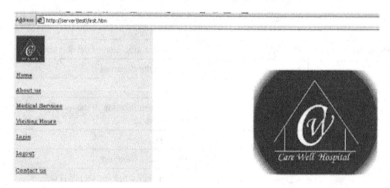

Figure 5. Patients record table

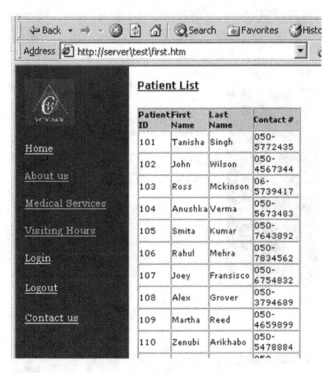

by last name "Kumar" returns a list of patients records with matching last name.

PDA INTERFACE AND CONNECTIVITY

System Hardware and Software Description

To access the website that contains the patient information system via PDA, combination of hardware devices and software drivers are needed. As shown in Figure 1, the hardware requirements are:

- A web server along with internet connection to the service provider,
- PDA with WLAN access interface card,
- Wireless access points.

The software drivers used a set of protocols that provide client utilities such as client manager, link status, wireless client login, and encryption manager. The USB connection between the server and the PDA is used to install the above-mentioned software utilities on the PDAs. The USB cable is later removed and the wireless connection became available between the PDA and the LAN via the wireless access point.

The system provides two modes of connectivity, namely; server-client model and wireless model. The server-client model uses standard access method to the LAN of the hospitable where doctors, nurses and lab assistant can create, modify and access the patient's information system via the Internet Service Provider (ISP) wired conductivity.

In the wireless model, the study used an off-the-shelf Compaq-200 PDA with the following specifications:

Figure 6. Search by last name output

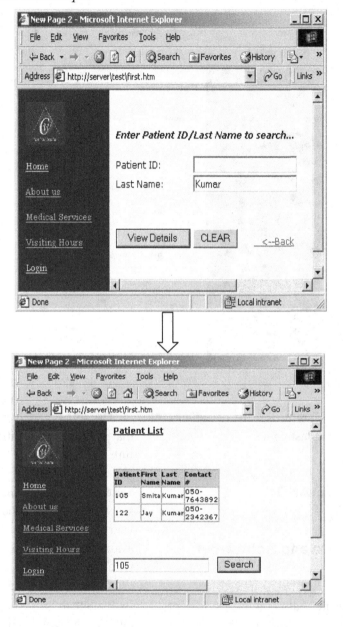

- 400MHz processor, Windows CE for Pocket PC operating system, 64-MB SDRAM & 32-MB Flash ROM memory.
- Interfaces: WLAN (IEEE802.11b) and Bluetooth (IEEE802.15) compliant. The distance range of the PDA was 100 meters (class-2 radio).

- TFT liquid crystal display with viewable 64K color image size 2.25 inch wide by 3.02 inch tall.

For wireless access purposes, commercially available wireless access points are used in the study. The access point provides 40-bit and 128-bit wired-equivalent privacy (WEP) encryption security over the 100m coverage area. It is IEEE 802.11b compliant and works at self-adjusted data rates of 11, 5.5, 2 and 1 Megabits/s (Mbps) (3COM, 2004).

Wireless Access Client-Server Synchronization

Synchronizing the wireless access between the Server and the Client is done in two ways:

- Configuration of the wireless access through the Server being connected to the Internet: This was accomplished using a hub through which the server was connected to another network, which was connected to the Internet. The PDA accessed this server through the wireless access point and was able to access sites on the Internet as well.
- Configuration of the wireless access through Terminal Services on LAN: Wireless access through terminal services was introduced as a safety procedure in case Internet access is not available. Terminal services are implemented using Windows 2000® Advanced Server.

SECURITY ISSUES

Two levels of security were implemented, one for the advanced server and the other for the SQL server:

Windows Advanced Server Security

Using the Administrative tools, privileges are granted to users and groups. Privileges include restarting the server, modifying certain settings, accessing databases etc. This is done by creating different profiles for the users and then granting the required privilege. For instance, if an employee is registered under the group "Lab Assistant", upon logging-on to the Windows 2000® system as a Lab Assistant, he/she is given those privileges assigned to the group 'Lab Assistant'. The privilege denies the lab assistant to reboot the system.

Microsoft SQL Server Security

The SQL Server authentication mode used is "Windows Authentication Only". In other words, SQL Server automatically authenticates users based on their Windows user account names or their group membership. If you've granted the user or the user's group access to a database, the user is automatically granted access to that database.

The SQL Server security model controls access to the database using the server login, permissions and roles.

IMPLEMENTATION AND TESTING

Trial System Implementation

One of the problems encountered during implementation was due to the mismatch of screen resolution of PDA and the web page. The problem occurred because the contents were being directly viewed from the server's default browser. The problem was solved by using a built-in browser of the PDA. Setting of wireless configurations presented another problem. Initially, a personal LAN was set up using the 3COM wireless access points. Following this, the wireless network card was registered with the Information Technology department of the American University of Sharjah (AUS), so that the PDAs could access the AUS network. Problems such as conflicting devices and security issues had to be dealt with. The solution was to select the auto channel setting when configuring the access point.

Trial System Testing

The designed system has been implemented using AUS infrastructure and tested by doctors, nurses and lab assistants of AUS health care center. AUS infrastructure provided large number of workstations and wireless points distributed throughout the campus. Two wireless PDAs with wireless jackets are used for testing wireless functions.

Each one of the users logs on to network with his/her unique ID and password. The system first validates the ID and password, and then gives access based on the assigned privileges. The following instance shows how the SQL Server database is accessed to retrieve or modify data.

Doctors have the following options and privileges:

- View Personal Records
- Update Address and Contact Number
- Search for a Patient using Patient's last name or ID
- Search for the general record details of a patient using the unique patient ID.
- View the specific record details for a particular record given the record number and Patient ID.
- Create new records for the patient. View a list of all those patients who are under him.

Figure 7. System output using patient's ID key search

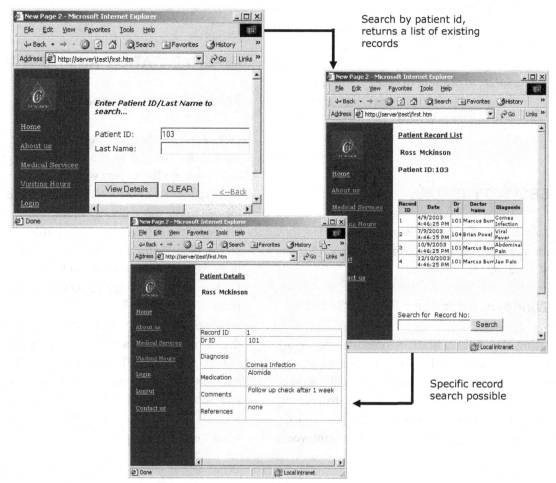

292

- Can add a new patient to the Patient Database.

The options given to nurses are:

- Update, Create Personal Records.
- Update, Create Patient Records.
- View Patient Table.
- Add New Patient.

The authorized privileges for lab assistants are:

- View Personal Records
- Can update Address and Contact Number
- Register Test Results for a patient by entering the patient ID number and the record number view the test results for a patient by entering the patient ID number and the record number.

When the nurse chooses to view the patient table, a list of all the patients is generated. This list contains the Patient ID, First Name, Last Name and Contact Number of the patient. Figure 7 shows the system response for such a query. It shows the number of record for the patient, data of the visit, visited physician ID and Name and the diagnosis by each physician.

The ASP Code accesses the database from the SQL Server because the nurse has been authenticated by the login process. Following this, a selected set of columns is retrieved from the database and is displayed to the end user. All of the above activities are tested using wireless PDAs. Also, it is found that they can be carried out and viewed just as it can be done using wired servers.

The ASP Script appends the entered data into the Record Table of the Hospital Database. Furthermore, the ASP Script also stores the Doctor ID (which is a session variable) and the System date into the Record Table. It is worth mentioning that once a patient record is accessed for editing, the database locks the file and it can not be updated by the another user until the current session is finished. However, the stored version of record can be viewed while the update session in progress.

Figure 8. Simultaneous access times through web-based database using wired and wireless PDA combinations

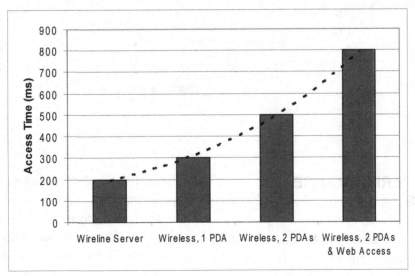

Figure 9. Impact of concurrent Internet access on the access times through web-based database

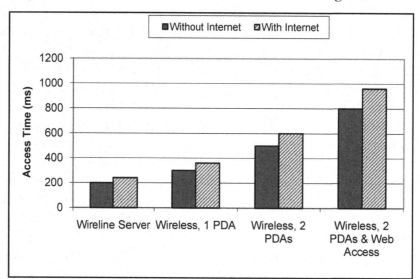

Figure 10. System access failure rate as a function of distance for different numbers of mobile users

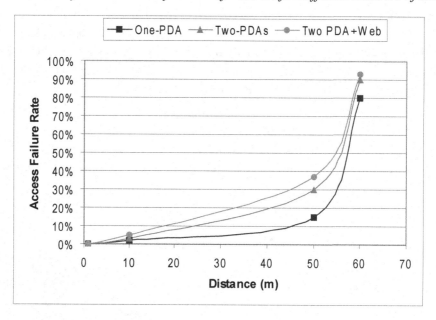

SYSTEM PERFORMANCE ANALYSIS

The system is implemented on AUS network which covers the entire campus with wired and wireless links. Two wireless PDAs are used for measuring performance of the system. Figure 8 indicates the access time performance values measured during the trial. The access time values were measured while the PDAs were trying to access the server simultaneously. Even though the manufacturer specifications indicate that wireless devices should work with up to 100 meter distance from wireless access points, our tests indicated that the maximum reliable distance from wireless points are around 60 meters.

Our tests also indicated that network traffic over the intranet which is not related to electronic patient record database increased the above mentioned access times about 20% as shown in Figure 9.

System access failure rate was studied as a function of PDA-access point separation. The results are shown is Figure 10. As it can be seen, the success rate drops drastically as the distance approaches 60 meters.

CONCLUSION

A wireless PDA-based patient's information system was designed, implemented and tested. Hospital personnel can access, create and update the patient's record using standard internet browsing method through wireless mobile devices. The system gives the health personnel the mobility feature where they can check their patient's record from anywhere in the hospital using the wireless PDA or using internet browser from any other location. Limited system performance tests indicated satisfactory performances as long as the hospital's environment is well covered with wireless access points with access distance not exceeding 60 meters. Although it is not implemented in the test system, the users indicated that the inclusion of a practical messaging system similar to pagers will make the system even more useful.

REFERENCES

Alan, T., Lefor, MD, Lefor, MK. (2003), 'Wireless Computing in Health Care' Current Surgery, Vol. 60, No. 4, pp. 477-479.

Ammenwerth, E., Buchauer, A., Bludau, B., Haux, R. (2000) 'Mobile information and communication tools in the hospital', International Journal of Medical Informatics, vol. 57, pp. 21-40.

Cisco (2003) 'Aironet 230 series wireless jacket user manual'.

Compaq, (2002) 'IPAQ 3950 reference manual'.

Demiris, G., (2004) 'Electronic home healthcare: concepts and challenges', Int. J. Electronic Healthcare", Vol. 1, No. 1, pp. 4–16.

Garcia, J., Martinez, I., Sornmo, L., Olmos, S., Mur, A., Laguna, P. (2002) 'Remote processing server for ECG based clinical diagnosis support," IEEE Transactions on Information Technology in Medicine, vol. 6, No.4, pp. 277-284.

Hung, K. Zhang, Y. (2003) 'Implementation of a WAP-Based telemedicine system for patient monitoring," IEEE Transactions on Information Technology in Medicine, Vol. 7, No.2, pp. 101-107.

Lin, B., Vassar, J.A. (2004) 'Mobile healthcare computing devices for enterprise-wide patient data delivery', Int. J. Mobile Communications, Vol. 2, No. 4, pp.343–353.

Liu, C., long, A., Li, Y., Tsai, K., Kuo, H. (2001) 'Sharing patient care records over the World Wide Web', International Journal of Medical Informatics, Vol. 61, pp. 189-205.

Lu, Y, Xiao, Y., Sears, A., Jacko, J. (2005), 'A review and a framework of handheld computer adoption in healthcare', International Journal of Medical Informatics Vol. 74, pp. 409—422.

Metaxiotis, K., (2005) 'E-health versus KM-based health: a dilemma in researchers' minds', International J. of Electronics Healthcare- Vol. 1, No. 3, pp. 303-315.

Nazeran, H.; Setty, S.; Haltiwanger, E.; Gonzalez, V. 'A PDA-based flexible telecommunication system for telemedicine applications', Proceeding of the IEEE Engineering in Medicine and Biology Society Conference, EMBC 2004. pp.2200-2203.

Riikonen, P. Boberg, J., Slakoski, T., Vihinen, M. (2002) 'Mobile access to biological databases on the internet," IEEE Transactions on Biomedical Engineering, vol. 49, No. 12, pp. 1477-1479.

Safran, C., Goldberg, H. "Electronic patient records and the impact of the internet," Int. Journal of Medical Informatics, vol. 60, pp. 77-83, 2000.

Van Ginneken, A. M. (2002) 'the computerized patient record: balancing effort and benefit' International Journal of Medical Informatics, vol. 65, pp. 97-119.

Wang, J., Hongwei, D. (2005) 'Setting up a Wireless Local Area Network (WLAN) for a healthcare system', Int. J. Electronic Healthcare Vol. 1, No. 3 pp. 335-348.

Wickramasinghe, N., Misra, S.K. (2004) 'A wireless trust model for healthcare', Int. J. Electronic Healthcare, Vol. 1, No. 1, pp.60–77.

3COM (2002) 'Access point reference manual'.

This work was previously published in Int. Journal of Healthcare Information Systems and Informatics, Vol 1, Issue 4, edited by J. Tan, pp. 1-14, copyright 2006 by IGI Publishing (an imprint of IGI Global).

Compilation of References

Abdul-Nour, G., Drolet, J., & Lambert, S. (1999). Mixed Production, Flexibility, and SME. *Computers and Industrial Engineering, 37*(1-2), 429-432.

Abecker, A., Bernardi, A., Maus, H., Sintek, M., & Wenzel, C. (2000). Information Supply for Business Processes: Coupling Workflow with Document Analysis and Information Retrieval. *Knowledge Based Systems, 13*(5), 271-284.

Abecker, A., Bernardi, A., Ntioudis, S., Herterich, R., Houy, C., Legal, M., et al. (2001). *The DECOR Toolbox for Workflow-Embedded Organizational Memory Access.* Paper presented at the 3rd International Conference on Enterprise Information Systems (ICEIS 2001), Setubal, Portugal.

Aboba, B., & Dixon, W. (2004). *IPsec-Network Address Translation (NAT) Compatibility Requirements.* Tech. rep., IETF.

Aboba, B., Blunk, L., Vollbrecht, J., Carlson, J., & Levkowetz, H. (2004). Extensible Authentication Protocol (EAP). *IETF RFC 3748.*

Abrahamson, E. (1991). Managerial facts and fashions: The diffusion and rejection of innovation. *Academy of Management Review, 16*(3), 586-612.

ACM (2005). *The ACM Computing Classification System.* 1998 Version. Available at http://www.acm.org/class/1998/, 07.01.2005.

Acquisti, A. (2002). Protecting Privacy with Economics: Economic Incentives for Preventive Technologies in Ubiquitous Computing Environment. *Workshop on Socially-informed Design of Privacy-enhancing Solutions in Ubiquitous Computing: Ubicomp.*

Acquisti, A. (2004). Privacy in Electronic Commerce and the Economics of Immediate Gratification. *Proceedings of ACM Electronic Commerce Conference [EC04],* New York, NY: ACM Press, (pp. 21-29).

Alan, T., Lefor, MD, Lefor, MK. (2003), 'Wireless Computing in Health Care' Current Surgery, Vol. 60, No. 4, pp. 477-479.

Albanese, M., Picariello, A., & Rinaldi A. M. (2004). A Semantic Search Engine for WEB Information Retrieval: an Approach Based on Dynamic Semantic Networks. Semantic Web Workshop, ACM SIGIR 2004, 25-29.

Albarracin, D., & Wyer, R. S., Jr. (2000). The cognitive impact of past behaviour: Influences on beliefs, attitudes, and future behavioural decisions. *Journal of Personality and Social Psychology 79,* 5-22.

Alder, G. S., Noel, T. W., & Ambrose, M. L. (2006). Clarifying the effects of Internet Monitoring on Job Attitudes: The Mediating Role of Employee Trust. *Information and Management, 43*(7), 894-903.

Allen, B. R., & Boynton, A. C. (1991). Information Infrastructure: In Search of Efficient Flexibility. *MIS Quarterly, 15*(5), 435-445.

Allweyer, T. (1998). Modellbasiertes Wissensmanagement. *Information Management, 13*(1), 37-45.

Alpar, P., Kim, M. (1990). A microeconomic approach to the measurement of information technology value. *Journal of Management Information Systems, 7*(2)55-69.

AMA Survey (2001). *Workplace Monitoring and Surveillance* [online]. Available from: http://www.amanet.org/research/pdfs/ems_short2001.pdf

AMA Survey (2003). *Email Rules, Policies and Practices Survey* [online]. Available from: http://www.amanet.org/research/pdfs/email_policies_practices.pdf

AMA Survey (2005). *Electronic Monitoring and Surveillance Survey* [online]. Available from: http://www.amanet.org/research/pdfs/ems_summary05.pdf

Amazon (2005). *Amazon start page.* http://www.amazon.com/gp/homepage.html/103-4263439-7624613, 06.01.2005.

Amit, R., & Schoemaker, P. J. (1993). Strategic assets and organizational rent. *Strategic Management Journal, 14*, 33-46.

Ammenwerth, E., Buchauer, A., Bludau, B., Haux, R. (2000) 'Mobile information and communication tools in the hospital', International Journal of Medical Informatics, vol. 57, pp. 21-40.

Angell, R., & Freund, G. (1983). Automatic spelling correction using a trigram similarity measure. *Information Processing and Management, 19*(4), 255-161

Anonymous. (2006). Real-time Computing. *Wikipedia.* Retrieved June 06, 2006, from http://en.wikipedia.org/wiki/Real-time_computing

Apache Struts. http://struts.apache.org/, 20.01.06.

Appadurai, A. (1991). In A. D. King, (ed.), *Culture Globalisation and the World-System.* Macmillan Press Ltd, SUNY-Binghampton.

Appleton, E. L. (1997). How to survive ERP. *Datamation, 43*(3), 50-3.

Argyris, C. (1977). Double loop learning in organizations. *Harvard Business Review*, September-October.

Argyris, C. (1992). *On Organizational Learning.* Cambridge MA: Blackwell.

Argyris, C. A., & Schön, D. (1978). *Organizational Learning: A Theory of Action Perspective.* Reading, MA: Addison-Wesley.

Arkko, J., & Haverinen, H. (2004). *Extensible Authentication Protocol Method for 3rd Generation Authentication and Key Agreement (EAPAKA).* Internet draft, IETF.

Arkko, J., Kempf, J., Sommerfeld, B., Zill, B., & Nikander, P. (2004). *Secure Neighbor Discovery (SEND).* Internet draft, IETF.

Asnicar, F., & Tasso, C. (1997). ifWeb: A Prototype of User-Model-Based Intelligent Agent for Document Filtering and Navigation in the World Wide Web. In *Proceedings of the Workshop Adaptive Systems and User Modelling on the World Wide Web.* User Modelling Conference 97.

Baader, F., Calvanese, D., McGuinness, D. L., Nardi, D., Patel-Schneider, P. F. (2003). *The description logic handbook: theory, implementation, and applications.* Cambridge University Press.

Bach, V., & Österle, H. (Eds.). (2000). *Customer Relationship Management in der Praxis. Erfolgreiche Wege zu kundenzentrierten Lösungen.*Berlin: Springer.

Backhouse, C. J., & Burns, N. D. (1999). Agile Value Chains for Manufacturing—Implications for Performance Measures. *International Journal of Agile Management Systems, 1*(2), 76-82.

Baeza-Yates, R., & Ribeiro-Neto, B. (Eds.). (1999). *Modern Information Retrieval.*Essex: Addison Wesley Longman Limited.

Bal, J., Wilding, R., & Gundry, J. (1999). Virtual Teaming in the Agile Supply Chain. *The International Journal of Logistics Management, 10*(2), 71-82.

Balakrishnan, R., Linsmeier, T. J., Venkatachalam, M. (1996). Financial benefits from JIT adoption: effects of customer concentration and cost structure. *The Accounting Review, 71*(2), 183-205.

Balthasar, A., Bättig, C., Thierstein, A., & Wilhelm, B. (2000). Developers: Key actors of the innovation process. Types of developers and their contacts to institutions involved in research and development, continuing education and training, and the transfer of technology. *Technovation, 20*, 523-538.

Bandura, A. (1977). *Social Learning Theory.* Englewood Cliffs, NJ: Prentice-Hall.

Bankinter (2000). *Annual Report 2000.*

Barber, B. M., Lyon, J. D. (1996). Detecting abnormal operating performance: The empirical power and specification of test statistics. *Journal of Financial Economics, 41*(3), 359-99.

Barber, W., & Badre, A. (1998). Culturability: The Merging of Culture and Usability. Retrieved from http://www.research.att.com/conf/hfweb/.

Barnes S. J. (2002). Wireless digital advertising: nature and implications. *International Journal of Advertising, 21*(3), 399-419.

Barney, J. (1991). Firm resources and sustained competitive advantage. *Journal of Management, 17*(1), 99-120.

Barney, J. B. (1992). Integrating organizational behaviour and strategy formulation research: A resource-based analysis. In P. Shrivastava, A. Huff and J. Dutton (Eds.), *Advances in strategic management, 8*, 39-61.

Barney, J. B. (2001). Is the resource-based view a useful perspective for strategic management research? Yes. *Academy of Management Review, 26*(1), 41-56.

Barry, C. L., & Schamber, L. (1998). Users' Criteria for Relevance Evaluation: A Cross-Situational Comparison. *Information Processing & Management, 34*(2-3), 219-236.

Barry, C. L. (1998). Document representations and clues to document relevance. *Journal of the American Society for Information Science, 49*(14), 1293-1303.

Bauer, R., & Greyser, S. (1968). *Advertising in America: The Consumer View.* Graduate School of Business Administration, Division of Research, Harvard University, Boston, MA.

Baumgartner, R. Flesca, S., & Gottlob, G. (2001, September). Visual Web Information Extraction with Lixto. In *Proceedings of the 27th International Conference on Very Large Data Bases*, S. 119-128.

Bayardo, R., W, B., R, B., A, C., G, F., A, H., *et al.* (1997). *Semantic integration of information in open and dynamic environments.* Paper presented at the Proceedings of the 1997 ACM International Conference on the Management of Data (SIGMOD).

BBVA (1999). *Annual Report 1999.*

Belew, R. K. (1986). *Adaptive Information Retrieval: Machine Learning in Associative Networks.* Ph.D. dissertation, Computer Science Dept., University of Michigan. Ann Arbor. Michigan.

Bellifemine, F. L., Caire, G., & Greenwood, D. (2007). *Developing Multi-Agent Systems with JADE.* Wiley

Belsley, D. A., Kuh, E., Welsch, R. E. (1980). *Regression Diagnostics: Identifying Influential Data and Sources of Collinearity.* New York: John Wiley & Sons.

Benatallah, B., Hacid, M.-S., Leger, A., Rey, C., & Toumani, F. (2005). On automating Web services discovery. *The VLDB Journal — The International Journal on Very Large Data Bases, 14*(1), 84—96.Springer-Verlag New York

Benders, J., & Van Veen, K. (2001). What's in a fashion? Interpretative viabilility and management fashions. *Organization, 8*(1), 33-53.

Bendoly, E., Jacobs, F. R. (2004). ERP architectural/operational alignment for order-processing performance. *International Journal of Operations & Product Management, 24*(1), 99-117.

Berners-Lee, T., Hendler, J., & Lassila, O. (2001). The Semantic Web. *Scientific American, 284*(5), 34-43.

Bernstein, D. (2004) *DJBDNS: Domain Name System tools. BIND9.NET. DNS, BIND, DHCP, LDAP* and Directory Services.

Bessant, J., Francis, D., Meredith, S., & Kalinsky, R. (2001). Developing Manufacturing Agility in SMEs.

International Journal of Technology Management, 22(1, 2, 3), 28-54.

Bigelow, L., (2002). A Brand in Your Hand. *Admap, 426,* 47-50.

Billings, R. S., Milburn, T. W., & Schaalman, M. L. (1980). A Model for Crisis Perception: A Theatrical and Empirical Analysis. *Administrative Science Quarterly, 25*(2), 300-316.

Bin, Q., Chen, S., & Sun, S. (2003). Cultural Differences in E-Commerce. *Journal of Global Information Technology Management, 11*(2), 48-55.

Bititci, U. S., Turner, T. J., & Ball, P. D. (1999). The Viable Business Structure for Managing Agility. *International Journal of Agile Management Systems, 1*(3), 190-202.

Blackler, F. (1995). Knowledge, Knowledge Work and Organizations: An Overview and Interpretation. *Organization Studies, 16*(6), 1021-1046.

Bodine, W. E. (1998). Making Agile Assembly Profitable. *Manufacturing Engineering, 121*(4), 60-68.

Boehle, S. (2000). They're Watching You. *Training, 37*(8), 68-72.

Böhm, K., & Härtwig, J. (2005). *Prozessorientiertes Wissensmanagement durch kontextualisierte*

Boisot, M. (2002). The creation and sharing of knowledge. In C. W. Choo. and N. Bontis (Eds.), *The Strategic Management of Intellectual Capital and Organizational Learning.* Oxford University Press.

Boldy, D., Jain, S., Northey, K. (1993). What makes an effective European manager? A case study of Sweden, Belgium, Germany, and Spain. *Management International Review, 33* (2), 157-69.

Bonfield, P. (1995). Building International Agility. *Chief Executive, January/February,* 50-53.

Bonoma, T. V. (1985). Case Research in Marketing: Opportunities, Problems, and a Process. *Journal of Marketing Research, 22*(2), 199-208.

Bontis, N. (1999). Managing organizational knowledge by diagnosing intellectual capital: framing and advancing the state of the field. *International Journal of Technology Management, 18,* 433-462.

Borlund, P., & Ingwersen, P. (1997). The Development of a Method for the Evaluation of Interactive Information Retrieval Systems. Journal of Documentation. 53(3), 225-250.

Borsboom, D., Mellenbergh, G. J., & Heerden, J. V. (2003). The Theoretical Status of Latent Variables. *Psychological Review, 110*(2), 203-219.

Bosse, T., & Treur, J. (2006). Formal interpretation of a multi-agent society as a single agent. *Journal of Artificial Societies and Social Simulation, 9*(2).

Botella, C., Banos, R., Perpina, C., Villa, H., Alcaniz, M. & Rey, A. (1998). Virtual Reality Treatment of Claustrophobia: a Case Report. *Behaviour Research and Therapy*, 36(2), 239-246.

Bouchet, S. (1995). Marketing and the Redefinition of Ethnicity. In J. Costa, & G. Balmossy, (eds.), *Marketing in a Multicultural World*. London: Sage Publications.

Brachman, F. J., & Schmolze, J. G. (1985). An overview of the KL-ONE knowledge representation system. *Cognitive Sci., 9.2.* S. 171-216.

Brackett, L. K., & Carr, B. N. (2001). Cyberspace Advertising vs. Other Media: Consumer vs. Mature Student Attitudes. *Journal of Advertising Research, 41*(5), 23-32.

Brakely, H. H. (1999). What makes ERP effective?. *Manufacturinf Systems, 17*(3), 120.

Brancheau, J. C., Janz, B. D., & Wetherbe, J. C. (1996). Key Issues in Information Systems Management: 1995 SIM Delphi Results. *MIS Quarterly, 20*(2), 225-242.

Bresciani, P., Perini, A., Giorgini, P., Giunchiglia, F., & Mylopoulos, J. (2004). Tropos: An agent-oriented software development methodology. *Autonomous Agents and Multi-Agent Systems, 8*(3), 203-236.

Bristol, T., & Fern, E. F. (1996). Exploring the Atmosphere Created in Focus Group Interviews: Comparing Consumers' Feelings Across Qualitative Techniques. *Journal of the Market Research Society, 38*(2), 185-195.

Brock, D. L., & Schuster, E. W. (2006). *On the Semantic Web of things.* Semantic Days 2006. Norway, April 26, 2006.

Broekstra, J. (2005, July). *Storage, Querying and Inferencing for Semantic Web Languages.* PhD Thesis. Vrije Universiteit Amsterdam. SIKS Dissertation Series 2005-09. ISBN 90-9019-236-0.

Broekstra, J., Ehrig, M., Haase, P., van Harmelen, F., Menken, M., Mika, P., Schnizler, B., & Siebes, R. (2004). Bibster—A semantics-based bibliographic peer-to-peer system. In *Proceedings of the WWW'04 Workshop on Semantics in Peer-to-Peer and Grid Computing.*

Broekstra, J., Kampman, A., & van Harmelen, F. (2002). *Sesame: A Generic Architecture for Storing and Querying RDF and RDF Schema.* Paper presented at the First International Semantic Web Conference (ISWC 2002), Sardinia, Italy.

Browless (2001). Wireless Internet Revolution: Anywhere, Anything, Anytime.—Hull: Butler Group.

Brown, C. V., Vessey, I., & Powell, A. (2000). The ERP purchase decision: Influential business and IT factors. *6th Americas Conference on Information Systems*, USA.

Brown, J. L., & Agnew, M. (1982). Corporate Agility. *Business Horizons, 25*(2), 29-33.

Brown, J. S. & Duguid, P. (2000). *The social life of information.* Boston, Illinois, USA: Harvard Business School Press.

Bruner II, G. C., & Kumar, A. (2000). Web Commercials and Advertising Hierarchy of Effects. *Journal of Advertising Research, 40*(1/2), 35-44.

Brunner, J. A., Chan, C. S., & Zhou, N. (1989). The role of guanxi in negotiation in the Pacific Basin. *Journal of Global Marketing*, 3(2), 58-72.

Brusilovsky, P. (1996). Methods and Techniques of Adaptive Hypermedia. In *Proceedings of User Modelling and User-Adapted Interaction, 6*, S. 87–129. Kluwer academic publishers.

Brusilovsky, P., & Cooper, D. W. (2001). Domain, task, and user models for an adaptive hypermedia performance support system. In *Proceedings of the 7th international conference on intelligent user interfaces.* San Francisco, California, USA. S. 23-30.

Bryman, A., & Bell E. (2003). Business Research Methods. Oxford University Press, Oxford.

BSCH (2000). *Annual Report 2000.*

Buckley, J. (2006). *From RFID to the Internet of Things: Pervasive Networked Systems*, Final Report on the Conference organized by DG Information Society and Media, Networks and Communication Technologies Directorate, CCAB, Brussels (available in: http://www.rfidconsultation.eu/docs/ficheiros/WS_1_Final_report_27_Mar.pdf).

Budanitsky, A. (1999). Lexical Semantic Relatedness and Its Application in Natural Language Processing. Technical report. Department of Computer Science, University of Toronto.

Buddhikot, M., Hari, A., Singh, K., & Miller, S. (2003). MobileNAT: A New Technique for Mobility across Heterogeneous Address Spaces. *In Proceedings of the 1st ACM international workshop on Wireless mobile applications and services on WLAN hotspots.* ACM Press. (pp. 75- 84).

Byrd, T. A., & Turner, D. E. (2000). Measuring the Flexibility of Information Technology Infrastructure. *Journal of Management Information Systems, 17*(1), 167-208.

Calhoun, P., Loughney, J., Guttman, E., Zorn, G., & Arkko, J. (2003). *Diameter Base Protocol.* RFC RFC3588, IETF.

Cannataro, M., & Pugliese, A. (2001, August). A flexible architecture for adaptive hypermedia systems. In proceedings of the IJCAI's Workshop on Intelligent Techniques for Web Personalization.

Canter, J. (2000). An Agility Based OODA Model for the E-Commerce/E-Business Enterprise. Retrieved Dec 28, 2000, from http://www.belisarius.com/canter.htm

Cardoso, J., & Sheth, A. (2003). Semantic e-Workflow Composition. *Journal of Intelligent Information Systems, 21*(3), 191—225. Kluwer Academic Publishers

Cassidy, C. M. & Chae, B. (2006). Consumer Information Use and Misuse in Electronic Business: An Alternative to Privacy Regulation. *Information Systems Management, 23*(3), 75-87.

Castillo, J. G., Trastour, D., & Bartolini, C. (2001). *Desctiption Logics for Matchmaking of Services.* Paper presented at the Paper presented at the Workshop on Application of Description Logic.

Cavnar, W., & Trenkle, J. (1994). N-Gram-Based Text Categorization. In *Proceedings of the 3rd Annual Symposium on Document Analysis and Information Retrieval (SDAIR 94),* S. 161-175, Las Vegas, NV, USA, April 11-13.

Chaffey, D. (2003). *E-Business and E-Commerce Management.* London: Prentice Hall.

Chang, S. F. (2000). *A Study of Cultural Influences on Singapore-Chinese Use of E-Commerce.* Major Thesis, RMIT.

Chang, Y. K., Cirillo, C. & Razon, J. (1971). Evaluation of feedback retrieval using modified freezing, residual collection & test and control groups. The SMART retrieval system—experiments in automatic document processing, Chapter 17, 355-370.

Chao, K.-M., Younas, M., Lo, C.-C., & Tan, T.-H. (2005). *Fuzzy Matchmaking for Web Services.* Paper presented at the WAMIS Workshop, Tamkang University, Taiwan.

Chaudhuri, S., & Dayal, U. (1997). An Overview of Data Warehousing and OLAP Technology. *ACM SIGMOD Record, 26*(1).

Chen, L., & Sycara, K. (1998). Webmate: A Personal Agent for Browsing and Searching. In *Proceedings of AGENTS '98,* S. 132–139. ACM.

Chen, Y., Wu, J., & Chung, Y. (2008). Cultural impact on Trust. *Journal of Global Information Technology Management, 11*(1), 28-48.

Chen, Z., Meng, X., Zhu, B., & Fowler, R. (2000). WebSail: From On-Line Learning to Web Search. In *Proceedings of the 2000 International Conference on Web Information Systems Engineering.*

Cheshire, S., & Krochmal, M. (2004). *Multicast DNS.* Internet draft, Apple Computer, Inc. http://files.multicastdns.org/draft-cheshire-dnsext-multicastdns.txt.

Cheshire, S., Aboba, B., & Guttman, E. (2004). *Dynamic Configuration of IPv4 Link-Local Addresses.* Internet draft, IETF.

Cho, H., Jung, M., & Kim, M. (1996). Enabling Technologies of Agile Manufacturing and its Related Activities in Korea. *Computers and Industrial Engineering, 30*(3), 323-335.

Christian, P. H., Govande, V., Staehle, W., & Jr., E. W. Z. (1999). Advantage Through Agility. *IEEE Solutions, 31*(11), 26-33.

Christian, W., & Frederick, K. (1996). Why Isn't Your Company Agile? *Manufacturing Engineering, 116*(6), 104-105.

Christopher, M. (2000). The Agile Supply Chain: Competing in Volatile Markets. *Industrial Marketing Management, 29*(1), 37-44.

Cisco (2003) 'Aironet 230 series wireless jacket user manual'.

Clarke, R. A. (1988). Information Technology and Dataveillance. *Communication of the ACM, 31*(5), 498-512.

Clases, C., & Wehner, T. (2002). Steps Across the Border—Cooperation, Knowledge Production and Systems Design. *Computer Supported Cooperative Work, 11*(1), 39-54.

Cleverdon, C., Mills J., & Keen, M. (1966). Factors Determining the Performance of Indexing Systems. Technical report. ASLIB Cranfield Research Project, Cranfield.

CNNIC (2001, 2000). Semi-Annual China Internet Report, 2000.

Cockcroft, S., & Heales, J. (2005). National Culture, Trust and Internet Privacy Concerns. *16th Australasian Conference on Information Systems*, Sydney.

Collier, R., Ross, R., & O'Hare, G. M. P. (2005). Realising reusable agent behaviours with ALPHA. In *Proc. 3rd Conference on Multi-Agent System Technologies (MATES-05), LNCS 3550*, 210–215.

Collis, D. J., & Montgomery, C. A. (1995). Competing on resources: Strategy in the 1990s. *Harvard Business Review*, July-August, 118-128.

Compaq, (2002) 'IPAQ 3950 reference manual'.

Concise Oxford Dictionary of Current English, Oxford University Press, England, 1996.

Conlan, O., Wade, V., Bruen, C., Gargan, M. (2002). *Multi-model, Metadata Driven Approach to Adaptive Hypermedia Services for Personalized eLearning*. Malaga, Spain, Mai 2002, S. 100–111.

Conta, A., & Deering, S. (1998). *Internet Control Message Protocol (ICMPv6) for the Internet Protocol version 6 (ipv6) specifications*. RFC 2463, IETF.

Cook, R. D. (1977). Detection of influential observations in linear regression. *Technometrics*, (19), 15-8.

Cook, S. D. N., & Yanow, D. (1993). Culture and organizational learning. *Journal of Management Inquiry, 2*(4), 373-390.

Cooper, R. (1990). Stage-gate systems: a new tool for managing new products. *Business Horizons*, May-June 1990.

Corcho, Ó., Gómez-Pérez, A., López-Cima, A., López-García, V., & Suárez-Figueroa, M. d. C.*ODESeW—Automatic Generation of Knowledge Portals for Intranets and Extranets*. Paper presented at the 2nd International Semantic Web Conference (ISWC 2003), Sanibel Island, Florida, USA.

Coronado, A. E., Sarhadi, M., & Millar, C. (2002). Defining a Framework for Information System Requirements for Agile Manufacturing. *International Journal of Production Economics, 75*(1-2), 57-68.

COWI (1999). *Intellectual Capital Report 1999.*

Craver, C. B. (2006). Privacy Issues Affecting Employers, Employees and Labour Organizations. *Louisiana Law Review, 66*, 1057-1078.

Crispin, M. (1996, December). Internet Message Access Protocol—Version 4rev1. RFC 2060, IETF.

Crompton, M. (2001). What is Privacy? *Privacy and Security in the Information Age* Conference, Melbourne.

Crossan, M. M., Lane, H. W., White, R. E., & Djurfeldt, L. (1995). Organizational learning: Dimensions for a theory. *The International Journal of Organizational Analysis, 3*(4), (October), 337-360.

Crossan, M., Lane, H., & White, R. (1999). An organizational learning framework: From intuition to institution. *Academy of Management Review, 24*(3), 522-537.

Cunningham, P., Bergmann, R., Schmitt, S., Traphoner, R., Breen, S. & Smyth, B. (2001). *WebSell: Intelligent Sales Assistants for the World Wide Web*. In E-2001.

D'Arcy, D., & O'Dea, A. (2008). Privacy Affairs. Marketing Age. *Marketing Institute of Ireland March/April, 2*(2), 20-26.

D'Urso, S. C. (2006). Who's Watching Us at Work? Toward a Structural-Perceptual Model of Electronic Monitoring and Surveillance in Organisations. *Communication Theory, 16*, 281-303.

Daft, R. L., & Weick, K. E. (1984). Toward a model of organizations as interpretation systems. *Academy of Management Review, 9*, 284-295.

Damanpour, F. (1992). Organizational Size and Innovation. *Organization Studies, 13*(3), 375-402.

Danish Agency for Development of Trade and Industry (2000). *Intellectual Capital Statement-Towards a Guidelines.*

Danish Agency for Development of Trade and Industry (2001). *A Guideline for Intellectual Capital Statements: A Key to Knowledge Management.*

Dastani, M., van Riemsdijk, B., Dignum, F., & Meyer, J.-J.Ch. (2003). A programming language for cognitive agents: Goal directed 3APL. *Proc. First International Workshop on Programming Multi-Agent Systems, LNCS 3067*, 111-130.

Davenport, T. H. (1993). *Process Innovation: Reengineering Work Through Information Technology*. Boston: Harvard Business School Press.

Davenport, T. H. (1998). Putting the Enterprise into the Enterprise Systems. *Harvard Business Review*, 121-135.

Davenport, T. H., Harris, J., & Cantrell, S. (2002). *The Return of Enterprise Solutions: The Director's Cut.* Accenture. Available http://www.accenture.com/Global/

Davies, H., & Howard, L. (1995). The Benefits of Guanxi. *Industrial Marketing Management, 24*, 207-213.

Davison, R. (2002, July). Cultural Complications of ERP. *Communications of the ACM, 45*(7), 109-110.

Day, M., Forrester, P., & Burnett, J. (2000). Agile Supply: Rethinking Systems Thinking, Systems Practice. *International Journal of Agile Management Systems, 2*(3), 178-186.

De Bra, P., Aroyo, L., Chepegin, V., (2005). The Next Big Thing: Adaptive Web-Based Systems. In *Journal of Digital Information, 5*, 247.

Deering, S. (1991, September). *ICMP Router Discovery Messages.* RFC 1256, IETF.

Deering, S., & Hinden, R. (1998, December). *Internet Protocol, Version 6 (IPv6) Specification.* RFC 2460, IETF.

Deloitte Consulting (1999). ERP's Second wave: Maximizing the value of ERP-enabled processes. New York: Deloitte Consulting.

Demeulemeester, E., Reyck, B. D., & Herroelen, W. (2000). The Discrete Time/Resource Trade-off Problem in Project Networks: A Branch-and-Bound Approach. *IIE Transactions, 32*(11), 1059-1069.

Demiris, G., (2004) 'Electronic home healthcare: concepts and challenges', Int. J. Electronic Healthcare", Vol. 1, No. 1, pp. 4–16.

Devor, R., Graves, R., & Miles, J. J. (1997). Agile Manufacturing Research: Accomplishments and Opportunities. *IIE Transactions, 29*(10), 813-823.

Dey, A. K., & Abowd, G. D. (1999). *Towards a Better Understanding of Context and Context-Awareness* (No. GIT-GVU-99-32): College of Computing, Georgia Institute of Technology.

Dickinger, A., Haghirian, P., Murphy, J., & Scharl, A.,(2004). An investigation and conceptual model of SMS marketing. *Proceedings of the 37ᵗʰ Hawaii International Conference on System Sciences,* Hawaii, January.

Dierickx, I., & Cool, K. (1989). Assets stock accumulation and sustainability of competitive advantage. *Management Science, 35*(12), 1504-1511.

Dierickx, I., & Cool, K. (1989). Assets stock accumulation and sustainability of competitive advantage: Reply. *Management Science, 35*(12), 1512-1513.

Difede J. & Hoffman, H. (2002). Virtual Reality Exposure Therapy for World Trade Center Post-traumatic Stress Disorder: A Case Report. *CyberPsychology and Behavior, 5*(6), 529-535.

DiMaggio, P., Powell, W. (1983). The iron cage revisited: institutional isomorphism and collective rationality in organization fields. *American Sociological Review, 48*, 147-60.

Directive 95/46/EC: Article 29 WP55 2002. [online]. Available from: http://ec.europa.eu/justice_home/fsj/privacy/docs/wpdocs/2002/wpss_en.pdf

Dixon, N. M. (1992). Organizational learning: A review of the literature with implication for HRD professionals. *Human Resource Development Quarterly, 3*(1), 29-49.

Dolog, P., Gavriloaie, R., Nejdl, W. & Brase, J. (2005). *Integrating Adaptive Hypermedia Techniques and Open RDF based Environments.* Available at www.kbs.uni-hannover.de/Arbeiten/Publikationen/2002/www2003-10.pdf.

Dolog, P., Henze, N., Nejdl, W., & Sintek, M. (2003). Towards the adaptive semantic web. In Proceedings *of the 1st Workshop on Principles and Practice of Semantic Web Reasoning.*

Dolog, P., Henze, N., Nejdl, W., & Sintek, M. (2004). *The personal reader: Personalizing and enriching learning resources using semantic web technologies.* Technical report, University of Hannover. Hannover, Germany.

Donovan, R. M. (n/d). *Why the controversy over ROI from ERP?* Accessed December 5, 2007. http://www.rmdonovan.com/pdf/perform.pdf

Dove, R. (1994). The meaning of Life & The meaning of Agile. *Production, 106*(11), 14-15.

Dove, R. (1995). Agile Cells and Agile Production. *Automotive Production*(October), 16-18.

Dove, R. (1995). Measuring Agility: The Toll of Turmoil. *Production, 107*(1), 12-14.

Dove, R. (1996). Building Agility Improvement Strategies. *Automotive Production, 108*(7), 16-17.

Dove, R. (1996). Critical Business Practices for Agility. *Automotive Production*(June), 16-17.

Dove, R. (1999). Agility = Knowledge Management + Response Ability. *Automotive Manufacturing & Production, 111*(3), 16-17.

Dr. Ecommerce (2001). What are the key cross cultural differences that will affect E-Commerce Web site development. Retrieved from http://www.jpb.com/drecommerce/answers/00340.html.

Ducoffe, R. H. (1995). How Consumers Assess the Value of Advertising. *Journal of Current Issues and Research in Advertising, 17*(1), 1-18.

Ducoffe, R. H. (1996). Advertising Value and Advertising on the Web. *Journal of Advertising Research, 36*(September/October), 21-36.

Duncan, N. B. (1995). Capturing Flexibility of Information Technology Infrastructure: A Study of Resource Characteristics and their Measure. *Journal of Management Information Systems, 12*(2), 37-57.

Easterby-Smith, M. (1997). Disciplines of organizational learning: Contributions and critiques. *Human Relations, 50*(9).

Eastlake, D. (1999, March). Domain Name System Security Extensions. RFC 2535, IETF.

Ebay (2005). *EBay start page.* http://www.ebay.com. 06.01.2005.

Eckhouse, J. (1999). ERP vendors plot a comeback. *Information Week,* (718), 126-28.

Edvinsson, L., & Malone, M. S. (1997). *Intellectual Capital. Realizing Your Company's True Value by Finding its Hidden Brainpower,* Harper Collins Publishers, Inc., 1ªed.

Edwards, H., & Humphries, L. (2005, Oct.-Dec.). Change Management of People & Technology in an ERP Implementation. *Journal of Cases on Information Technology, 7*(4), 144-160.

Edwards, J. S., & Kidd, J. B. (2003). Bridging the Gap from the General to the Specific by Linking Knowldge Management to Business Processes. In V. Hlupic (Ed.), *Knowledge and Business Process Management* (pp. 118-136). Hershey: Idea Group Publishing.

Efendioglu, A., Yip, V. (2004). Chinese Culture and E-Commerce. *Interacting with Computers, 16,* 45-62.

Engeström, Y. (1999). Expansive Visibilization of Work: An Activity-theoretical Perspective. *Computer Supported Cooperative Work, 8*(1), 63-93.

Epicor Software Corporation (2003). The ROI of ERP: Proven Implementation Methodology Is the Determining Factor. Accessed December 5, 2007. http://www.crm2day.com/library/EpZZpEFkpAPBNvjUTC.php

Eppler, M. J. (2003). *Managing Information Quality: Increasing the Value of Information in Knowledge-intensive Products and Processes.*Berlin: Springer.

European Business School (2004). *ERP in Banking 2005-An Empirical Survey.* European Business School, Oestrich-Winkel, Germany.

European Commission (2005). *The European E-Business Report.* European Commision-e-business W@tch, Luxembourg.

Evans, L. (2007). Monitoring Technology in the American Workplace: Would Adopting English Privacy Standards Better Balance Employee Privacy and Productivity? *California Law Review, 95,* 1115-1149.

Express Computer, (2003). *Tata Refractories: Another ERP Success Story.* Indian Express Group. Mumbai, India. Accessed December 5, 2007. http://www.express-computeronline.com

Fannin, R. (2003). The eBay of China, *Chief Executive,* Aug/Sep. 2003, 31-32.

Farinacci, D., Li, T., Hanks, S., Meyer, D., & Traina, P. (2000, March). *Generic Routing Encapsulation (GRE).* RFC 2784, IETF.

Ferstl, O. K., & Sinz, E. J. (1994). *From Business Process Modeling to the Specification of Distributed Business Application Systems—An Object-Oriented Approach* (Research Paper): Dept. of Business Information Systems, University of Bamberg.

Fikes, R., & Kehler, J. (1985, September). The role of frame-based representation in reasoning. *Comm. of the Assoc. for Computing Machinery, 28*(9).

Foa, E. & Kozak, M. (1986). Emotional Processing of Fear: Exposure to Corrective Information. *Psychological Bulletin, 99*(1), 20-35.

Foster, J. S., & Welch, L. D. (2000). *The Evolving Battlefield.* December 2000. Retrieved Sept, 15, 2001, from http://physicstoday.org/pt/vol-53/iss-12/p31.html

Foucault, M. (1977). *Discipline and Punish: The Birth of the Prison.* Great Britain: Penguin Books.

Frank, U. (2002). Multi-Perspective Enterprise Modeling (MEMO)—Conceptual Framework and Modeling Languages. In *Proceedings of the 35th Hawaii International Conference on System Sciences (HICSS-35).*Honolulu.

Frasincar, F., Houben, G. J., & Vdovjak, R. (2002). Specification framework for engineering adaptive web applications. In *The Eleventh International World Wide Web Conference, WWW.*

Frasincar, F., Houben, G., & Vdovjak, R. (2001). An RMM-Based Methodology for Hypermedia Presentation Design. In *Proceedings of the Fifth East-European Conference on Advances in Databases and Information Systems (ADBIS '01)*. Springer.

Freeman, P. A. (2006). *Statement before the Committee on Science of the U.S. House of Representatives,* Hearing on Innovation and Information Technology: The Government, University and Industry Roles in Information Technology Research and Commercialization, Austin, Texas (available in: http://www.house.gov/science/hearings/full06/May%205/ Freeman.pdf).

Frei, H.P., Meienberg, S., & Schauble, P. (1991). The Perils of Interpreting Recall and Precision Values. In Proceedings of GI/GMD-Workshop Information Retrieval, 1-10.

Fried, C. (1968). Privacy. *Yale Law Journal, 77(1)*, 475-493.

Friedlos, D. (2006). *Legacy IT systems a 'ticking time bomb'.* Retrieved May 24, 2006, from http://www.vnunet.com/articles/print/2155608

Frolund, S., & Koistinen, J. (1998). QML: A Language for Quality of Service Specification. *Technical report HPL on HP Laboratories*

Froomkin, A. M. (2000). The Death of Privacy? *Standford Law Review, 52(146)*, 1461-1543.

Fulla, S. (2007). Change Management: Ensuring Success in Your ERP Implementation. *Government Finance Review, 23(2)*, 34-40.

Gagnes, T., Plagemann, T., & Munthe-Kaas, E. (2006). *A Conceptual Service Discovery Architecture for Semantic Web Services in Dynamic Environments.* Paper presented at the The 22nd International Conference on Data Engineering, Georgia, USA.

Galal-Edeen, G. H. (2003). System Architecting: The Very Idea. *Logistics Information Management, 16(2)*, 101-105.

Galanxhi-Janaqi, H., & Fui-Hoon Nah, F. (2004). U-commerce: Emerging Trends and Research Issues. *Industrial Management & Data System, 104(9)*, 744-755.

Galanxhi-Janaqi, H., & Fui-Hoon Nah, F. (2006). Privacy Issues in the Era of Ubiquitous Commerce. *Electronic Market, 16(3)*, 222-232.

Galbraith, J. R. (1977). *Organization Design*. Reading, M.A: Addison-Wesley.

Gandossy, R. (2003). The Need for Speed. *The Journal for Business Strategy, 24(1)*, 29-33.

Garcia, J., Martinez, I., Sornmo, L., Olmos, S., Mur, A., Laguna, P. (2002) 'Remote processing server for ECG based clinical diagnosis support," IEEE Transactions on Information Technology in Medicine, vol. 6, No.4, pp. 277-284.

Garofalakis, J., Panagis, Y., Sakkopoulos, E., & Tsakalidis, A. (2004). *Web Service Discovery Mechanisms: Looking for a Needle in a Haystack?* Paper presented at the International Workshop on Web Engineering.

Garvin, D. A. (1993). Building a learning organization. *Harvard Business Review*, July—August, 78-91.

Gefen, D., & Straub, D. (2000). The Relative Importance of Perceived Ease of Use in IS Adoption: A Study of E-Commerce Adoption. *Journal of the Association for Information Systems, 1(8)*.

Gherardi, S., & Nicolini, D. (2002). The sociological foundations of organizational learning. in C. W. Choo and N. Bontis (eds.), *The Strategic Management of Intellectual Capital and Organizational Learning*. Oxford University Press.

Ghosh, A.P. (1998). E-Commerce Security—Weak Links, Best Defenses. New York: John Wiley and Sons, Inc.

Glenn, R., & Kent, S. (1998, November). *The NULL Encryption Algorithm and Its Use With IPsec*. RFC 2410, IETF.

Global Reach (2004). Global Statistics on World Online Populations by Languages. Retrieved from http://globalreach.biz/globstats/evol.htm.

Godfrey, B. (2001). Electronic Work Monitoring: An Ethical Model. *Australian Computer Society*, 18-21.

Goesmann, T., & Herrmann, T. (2001). Wissensmanagement und Geschäftsprozessunterstützung—am Beispiel des Workflow Memory Information System WoMIS. In T. Herrmann, A.-W. Scheer & H. Weber (Eds.), *Verbesserung von Geschäftsprozessen mit flexiblen Workflow-Management-Systemen 4* (pp. 83-101). Heidelberg: Physica-Verlag.

Goh, M., & Ling, C. (2002). Logistics Development in China. *International Journal of Physical Distribution and Logistics Management, 33(10)*, 886-917.

Goldman, S. L., Nagel, R. N., & Preiss, K. (1995). *Agile Competitors and Virtual Organizations: Strategies for Enriching the Customer* (First ed.). New York: Van Nostrand Reinhold.

Goldsmith, R. E., Lafferty, B. A., & Newell, S. J. (2000). The impact of corporate credibility and celebrity credibility on consumer reaction to advertisements and brands. *Journal of Advertising, 29*(3), 43-54.

Good, N., Schafer, J. B., Konstan, J. A., Borchers, A., Sarwar, B., Herlocker, J., & Riedl, J. (1999). Combining collaborative filtering with personal agents for better recommendations. In *Proceedings of the AAAI '99 Conference on Artificial Intelligence*, Orlando, FL, 1999, S. 439-446.

Gordon, W., & Langmaid, R. (1988). *Qualitative market research: a practitioner's and buyer's guide*. Gower, London.

Gorzalczany, M. B., & Piasta, Z. (1999). Neuro-fuzzy approach versus rough set inspired methodology for intelligent decisión support. *Information Sciences, 120*(1-4), 45-68.

Graeff, T. R., & Harmon, S. (2002). Collecting and Using Personal Data: Consumers' Awareness and Concerns. *Journal of Consumer Marketing, 19(*4), 302-318.

Grandori, A. (1987). *Perspectives on organizational theory*. Ballinger Publishing Company, Cambridge, MA

Granlund, M., & Malmi, T. (2000). The liberations and limitations of ERP-systems for management accounting. *Communication presented in the 23rd Annual Congress of the European Accounting Association*, Munich, Germany.

Granlund, M., Malmi, T. (2002). Moderate impact of ERPS on management accounting: A lag or permanent outcome?. *Management Accounting Research, 13*(3), 299-321.

Grant, R. (1991). A resource-based theory of competitive advantage: Implications for strategy formulation. *California Management Journal, 33*(3), 114-135.

Grant, R. (1996). Toward a knowledge-based theory of the firm. *Strategic Management Journal, 17*(Winter special issue), 109-122.

Grant, R. (1996). Prospering in dynamically competitive environments: Organizational capability as knowledge integration. *Organization Science, 7*(4), *375-388.*

Grant, R. (1997). The knowledge-based view of the firm: implication for management practice. *Long Range Planning, 30*(3), 450-454.

Greenstein, M., & Vasarhelyi, M. (2002). *Electronic Commerce: Security, Risk Management and Control*. Boston: McGraw-Hill.

Grenci, R., & Hull, B. (2004, Fall). New Dog, Old Tricks: ERP and the Systems Development Life Cycle. *Journal of Information Systems Education, 15*(3), 277-286.

Gronau, N. (2003). Modellierung von wissensintensiven Geschäftsprozessen mit der Beschreibungssprache K-Modeler. In N. Gronau (Ed.), *Wissensmanagement: Potenziale—Konzepte—Werkzeuge, Proceedings of the 4th Oldenburg Conference on Knowledge Management, University of Oldenburg, June 2003* (pp. 3-29). Berlin: Gito.

Grove, A. S. (1999). *Only the Paranoid Survive*. New York: Doubleday.

Gruber, T. R. (1993). A translation approach to portable ontology specifications. Knowledge Acquisition, 5(2), 199-220.

Grupo Penteo (2003). *Aplicaciones corporativas, situación en España y tendencias futuras -Año 2002, Grupo Penteo in colaboration with the E-Business Center PwC&IESE*, Madrid.

Gunson, J., & de Blasis, J. P. (2007). *The Place and Key Success Factors of Enterprise Resource Planning (ERP) in the New Paradigms of Business Management*. University of Geneva. Accessed December 5, 2007. http://www.crm2day.com/library/EpFlAAAkElDCUAUBZU.php

Gupta, A.F. (2001). Internet and the English Language, from http://www.fas.nus.edu.sg/staff/conf/poco.paper6.html.

Guttman, E., Perkins, C., Veizades, J., & Day, M. (1999, June). *Service Location Protocol, Version 2*. RFC 2608.

Haarslev, V., & Möller, R. (2001). *RACER System Description*. Paper presented at the the First International Joint Conference on Automated Reasoning.

Hädrich, T., & Maier, R. (2004). *Modeling Knowledge Work*. Paper presented at the Multikonferenz Wirtschaftsinformatik (MKWI 2004), Essen, Germany.

Haeckel, S. H., & Nolan, R. L. (1996). *Managing By Wire: Using I/T to Transform a Business From "Make-and-Sell" to "Sense-and-Respond"*. London, UK: Oxford University Press Inc.

Haghirian, P., & Inoue, A. (2007). An advanced model of consumer attitudes toward advertising on the mobile internet. *International Journal Mobile Communications, 5*(1), 48-67.

Haghirian, Parissa, & Madlberger, M. (2005). *Consumer attitude toward advertising via mobile devices—an em-*

pirical investigation among Austrian users. http://is.lse.ac.uk/asp/aspecis/20050038.pdf, 5th June 2005.

Hamel, G., & Prahalad, C. K. (1993). Strategy as strech and leverage. *Harvard Business Review,* March-April, 75-84/

Hamel, G., & Prahalad, C. K. (1994). *Competing for the Future.* Boston: Harvard Business School Press.

Hammer, M. (1997). *Beyond Reengineering: How the Process-Centered Organization Is Changing Our Work and Our Lives.* New York: Harper Collins.

Hammer, M., & Champy, J. (1993). *Reengineering the Cooperation.* New York: Harper Collins.

Handschuh, S., Staab, S., & Maedche, A. (2001). Cream—creating relational metadata with a component-based, ontology-driven annotation framework. In *Proceedings of 1st International Conference on Knowledge Capture,* (pp. 76-83). ACM Press.

Hänninen, S. (2007). *Innovation commercialisation process from the 'four knowledge bases' perspective.* Doctoral Dissertation Series, Development and Management in Industry 2007/1, Espoo, Finland: Helsinki University of Technology.

Hänninen, S., Kauranen, I., Serkkola, A., & Ikävalko, J. (2007). Barriers to commercialisation from the 'four knowledge bases' perspective: A study of innovation in the software development sector. *International Journal of Management Practice,* 2:3, 197-213.

Hardaker G., & Graham G. (2001). Wired marketing: energizing business for E-Commerce. London: Wiley.

Harkins, D., & Carrel, D. (1998, November). *The Internet Key Exchange (IKE).* RFC 2409, IETF.

Harman, D. (1992) Relevance feedback revisited. In Proceedings of the 15th annual international ACM SIGIR conference on Research and development in information, 1-10.

Harris Poll (2004). *Privacy and American Business Press Release* [online]. Available from: http://www.epic.org/privacy/survey/

Harter, S.P. (1992). Psychological relevance and information science. Journal of the American Society for Information Science, 43(9), 602-615.

Haverinen, H., & Salowey, J. (2004, October). *Extensible Authentication Protocol Method for GSM Subscriber Identity Modules (EAPSIM).* Internet draft, IETF.

Hawking, P., Stein, A., & Foster, S. (2004). Revisiting ERP systems: Benefit realisation. *Proceedings of the 37th Hawaii International Conference on System Sciences,* Hawaii.

Hawkins, D., Best, R. J., Coney, K. A. (2001). Consumer behavior: Building marketing strategy. 8th ed., Irwin McGraw-Hill, London.

Hawksworth, M. (2007). *Six Steps to ERP Implementation Success.* Accessed December 5, 2007. http://hosteddocs.ittoolbox.com/WP-2007-08-6StepstoERPImplementationSuccess.pdf

Hayes, D. C., Hunton, J. E., & Reck, J. L. (2001). Market reaction to ERP implementation announcements. *Journal of Information Systems, 15*(1), 3-18.

Hayes, R., Okonkwo, P., & Utecht, K. (2004). Enterprise Resource Planning and the Competitive Advantage: The Ease of Integrating Information between Corporate Headquarters in the United States and Factories in Mexico. *Competitiveness Review, 14*(1/2), 13-17.

Heckmann, D., & Krueger, A. (2004). *A User Modeling Markup Language (UserML) for Ubiquitous Computing, 2004.* Available at www.dfki.de/~krueger/PDF/UM2003.pdf.

Heckmann, D., Schwartz, T., Brandherm, B., & Schmitz, M. (2005). *Wilamowitz-Moellendorff, M., GUMO—the General User Model Ontology.* Available at w5.cs.uni-sb.de/~schmitz/publications/UM05_Gumo.pdf.

Hedberg, B. (1981). How organizations learn and unlearn. In P. C. Nystrom and W. H. Starbuck (eds.), *Handbook of Organizational Design,* New York: Oxford University Press, (pp. 3-27).

Hedlund, G. (1994). A model of knowledge management and the N-form corporation. *Strategic Management Journal, 15,* 73-90.

Heilala, J., & Voho, P. (2001). Modular Reconfigurable Flexible Final Assembly Systems. *Assembly Automation, 21*(1), 20-28.

Heisig, P. (2002). GPO-WM: Methoden und Werkzeuge zum geschäftsprozessorientierten Wissensmanagement. In A. Abecker, K. Hinkelmann & M. Heiko (Eds.), *Geschäftsprozessorientiertes Wissensmanagement* (pp. 47-64). Berlin: Springer.

Helal, A. (1997). InfoSleuth: Agent-based Semantic Integration of Information in Open and Dynamic Environments. In M. Huhns & M. Singh (Eds.), *Readings in Agents*: Morgan Kaufman.

Hellstrom, K. & Ost, L. (1996). Prediction of Outcome in the Treatment of Specific Phobia. A Cross-Validation Study. *Behaviour Research and Therapy*, 34(5), 403-411.

Helsinger, A., Thome, M., & Wright, T. (2004). Cougaar: A scalable, distributed multi-agent architecture. In *Proc. IEEE International Conference on Systems, Man and Cybernetics*, 2, 1910–1917.

Henrich, A., & Morgenroth, K. (2002). *Integration von kontextunterstütztem Information Retrieval in Portalsysteme*. Paper presented at the Teilkonferenz Management der Mitarbeiter-Expertise in IT-Beratungsunternehmen, MKWI 2002, Nürnberg, Germany.

Henrich, A., & Morgenroth, K. (2003). *Supporting Collaborative Software Development by Context-Aware Information Retrieval Facilities*. Paper presented at the DEXA 2003 Workshop on Web Based Collaboration (WBC 2003), Prague, Czech Republic.

Henze, N. (2000). *Adaptive Hyperbooks: Adaptation for Project-Based Learning Resources*. PhD thesis, University of Hannover.

Henze, N., & Nejdl, W. (1999). *Adaptivity in the KBS Hyperbook System. Workshop on Adaptivity and User Modeling on the WWW, International Conference on User Modeling UM'99*.

Henze, N., & Nejdl, W. (2002). Knowledge modeling for open adaptive hypermedia. In *Proccedings of the 2nd International Conference on Adaptive Hypermedia and Adaptive Web-Based Systems (AH 2002)*, Malaga, Spain.

Henze, N., Dolog, P., & Nejdl, W. (2004). Reasoning and Ontologies for Personalized E-Learning in the Semantic Web. *Educational Technology & Society*, 7(4), S. 82-97.

Hepner, G. F., Logan, T., Ritter, N., & Bryant, N. (1990). Artificial neural network classification using a minimal training set: comparison to conventional supervised classification. *Photogrammetric Engineering and Remote Sensing, 56*(4), S. 469-473.

Herlocker, J. L., Konstan, J. A., Borchers, A., & Riedl, J. (1999). An algorithmic framework for performing collaborative filtering. In *Proceedings of SIGIR '99 Conference on Research and Development in Information Retrieval*, ACM Press, New York, NY, 1999, S. 230-237.

Herlocker, J., Konstan, J. & Riedl, J. (2000). Explaining Collaborative Filtering Recommendations. In *Proceedings of ACM 2000 Conference on Computer Supported Cooperative Work*.

Hertzog, R. (2004, November). *Overview of zcip source package*. Referred: 26 Nov 2004.

Hibbert, L. (1999). Expecting the Unexpected. *Manufacturing, 12*(6), 39-40.

Hodges, L., Anderson, P, Burdea, G., Hoffman, H. & Rothbaum, B. (2001). Treating Psychological and Physical Disorders with VR. *IEEE Computer Graphics and Applications*, 21(6), 25-33.

Hodges, L., Kooper, R., Meyer, T., Rothbaum, B., Opdyke, D., deGraaff, J., Williford, J. & North, M. (1995). Virtual Environments for Treating the Fear of Heights. *IEEE Computer*, 28(7), 27-34.

Hodges, L., Rothbaum, B., Watson, B., Kessler, G. & Opdyke, D. (1996). A Virtual Airplane for Fear of Flying Therapy. *Proc. VRAIS '96, IEEE Virtual Reality Annual Symposium*, 86-93.

Hodges, L., Watson, B., Kessler, G., Rothbaum, B. & Opdyke, D. (1996). Virtually Conquering Fear of Flying. *IEEE Computer Graphics and Applications*, 16 (6), 42-49.

Hoek, R. I. V. (2000). The Thesis of Leagility Revisited. *International Journal of Agile Manufacturing Management Systems, 2*(3), 196-201.

Hoffman, H., Garcia-Palacios, A., Carlin, A., Furness III, T. & Botella-Arbona, C. (2003). Interfaces that Heal: Coupling Real and Virtual Objects to Treat Spider Phobia. *International Journal of Human-Computer Interaction*, 16(2), 283-300.

Hofstede, G. (1983). The cultural relativity of organizational practices and theories. *Journal of International Business Studies, 14*(2), 75-89.

Hofstede, G. (1997). *Cultures and Organizations: Software of the Mind*. McGraw-Hill.

Hofstede, G. (2001). *Culture's Consequences: Comparing Values, Behaviors, Institutions, and Organizations Across Nations*. 2nd ed., London: Sage

Hondo, M., & Kaler, C. (2002). Web Services Policy Framework (WSPolicy) Version 1.0. *Availabel at http://www.verisign.com/wss/WS-Policy.pdf*

Hong, D., Yuan, M., & Shen, V.Y. (2005). Dynamic Privacy Management: A Plug-In Service for the Middleware in Pervasive Computing. In *MobileHCI, ACM International Conference Proceeding Series; 111, Proceedings of the 7th international conference on Human computer interaction with mobile devices & services*.

Hopp, W. J., & Oyen, M. P. V. (2004). Agile Workforce Evaluation: A Framework for Cross-training and Coordination. *IIE Transactions, 36*(10), 919-940.

Houben, G. (2000). HERA: Automatically Generating Hypermedia Front-Ends for Ad Hoc Data from Heterogeneous and Legacy Information Systems. In *Proceedings of the Third International Workshop on Engineering Federated Information Systems*. Aka and IOS Press.

Houben, G., Barna, P., Frasincar, F., & Vdovjak, R. (2003). *Hera: Development of Semantic Web Information.* Available at SiteCeer http://citeseer.ist.psu.edu/cached-page/675475/1, 06.01.06.

Howcroft, B., Hamilton, R., & Hewer, P. (2002). Consumer attitude and the usage and the adoption of home-based banking in the United Kingdom. *International Journal of Marketing, 20*(3), 111-121.

Hsu, P.-Y., & Zaniolo, C. (1993). *A new User's Impressions on LDL++ and CORAL.* Paper presented at the Workshop on Programming with Logic Databases (Informal Proceedings).

Huang, C.-C. (1999). An Agile Approach to Logical Network Analysis in Decision Support Systems. *Decision Support Systems, 25*(1), 53-70.

Huang, C.-L., Chao, K.-M., & Lo, C.-C. (2005). *A Moderated Fuzzy Matchmaking for Web Services.* Paper presented at the The 5th International Conference on Computer and Information Technology (CIT2005), Shanghai, China.

Huang, C.-Y., & Nof, S. Y. (1999). Enterprise Agility: A View from the PRISM Lab. *International Journal of Agile Management Systems, 1*(1), 51-59.

Huang, C.-Y., Ceroni, J. A., & Nof, S. Y. (2000). Agility of Networked Enterprises—Parallelism, Error Recovery, and Conflict Resolution. *Computers in Industry, 42*(2,3), 275-287.

Huang, S., Chang, I., Li, S., & Lin, M. (2004). Assessing Risk in ERP Projects: Identify and Prioritize the Factors. *Industrial Management and Data Systems, 104*(8/9), 681-688.

Huff, A. S., & Jenkins, M. (2002). *Mapping Strategic Knowledge.* Sage Publications.

Hung, K. Zhang, Y. (2003) 'Implementation of a WAP-Based telemedicine system for patient monitoring," IEEE Transactions on Information Technology in Medicine, Vol. 7, No.2, pp. 101-107.

Hunton, J. E., Lippincott, B., & Reck, J. L. (2003). Enterprise resource planning systems: Comparing firm performance of adopters and nonadopters. *International Journal of Accounting Information Systems*, (4), 165-84.

Huttunen, A., Swander, B., Volpe, V., DiBurro, L., & Stenberg, M. (2004, May). *UDP Encapsulation of IPsec ESP Packets.* Internet draft, IETF.

Hyvönen, T. (2003). Management accounting and information systems: ERP versus BoB. *European Accounting Review, 12*(1), 155-73.

IBM (2006). *Stopping Insider Attacks: How Organizations can Protect their Sensitive Information* [online]. Available from: http://www-935.ibm.com/services/us/imc/pdf/gsw00316-usen-00-insider-threats-wp.pdf

IBM Corporation. *IBM Websphere Portal Server Product Architecture.* www.ibm.com/pvc/tech/whitepapers, 18.01.06.

IEEE P1484.2/D7, 2000-11-28. (2002). *Draft standard for learning technology. Public and private information (papi) for learners (papi learner).* Available at: http://ltsc.ieee.org/wg2/. Accessed on October 25, 2002.

IEEE. IEEE Std 802.11 1999, Part 11: Wireless LAN Medium Access Control (MAC) and Physical Layer (PHY) Specifications, IEEE Std 802.11 1999 ed. IEEE, 1999.

IEEE. IEEE Std 802.11b-1999, Part 11: Wireless LAN Medium Access Control (MAC) and Physical Layer (PHY) Specifications: Higher-Speed Physical Layer extension in the 2.4 GHz Band, IEEE Std 802.11b-1999 ed. IEEE, 1999.

IEEE. IEEE Std 802.11i-2004, Part 11: Wireless Medium Access Control (MAC) and Physical Layer (PHY) specifications—Amendment 6: Medium Access Control (MAC) Security Enhancements, IEEE Std 802.11i-2004 ed. IEEE, 2004.

IEEE. IEEE Std 802.1X-2001, Port-Based Network Access Control, IEEE Std 802.1X-2001 ed. IEEE, 2001.

IEEE. IEEE Std 802.3-2002, Part 3: Carrier sense multiple access with collision detection (CSMA/CD) access method and physical layer specifications, IEEE Std 802.3-2002 ed. IEEE, 2002.

IMS (2002). IMS learner information package specification. Available at: http://www.imsproject.org/profiles/index.cfm. Accessed on October 25, 2002.

Informationsversorgung aus Geschäftsprozessen. Paper presented at the 6. Internationale Tagung Wirtschaftsinformatik (WI 2005), Bamberg, Germany.

Introna, L.D. (1996). Privacy and the Computer: Why we need Privacy in the Information Society. *Ethicomp e-Journal, 1.*

ISO. Information technology- Open Systems Interconnection—Basic Reference Model: The Basic Model, ISO/IEC 7498-1:1994 ed., 1994.

Jackson, T., Dawson, R., & Wilson, D. (2001). *The Cost of Email Interruption.* Loughborough University Institutional Repository: Item 2134/495 [online]. Available at: http://km.lboro.ac.uk/iii/pdf/JOSIT%202001.pdf

Jacobs, F. R., & Whybark, D. C. (2000). *Why ERP?* Boston: McGraw-Hill.

Jaeger, M. C., Tang, S., & Liebetruth, C., *The TUB OWL-S Matcher.*

James, T. (2005). Stepping Back from Lean. *Manufacturing Engineering, 84*(1), 16-21.

Jameson A. (1998). *User Modeling: An Integrative Overview.* Tutorial ABIS98: Workshop on Adaptivitiy and User Modeling in Interactive Software Systems, FORWISS Report.

Jenike, M. (2001). An Update on Obsessive Compulsive Disorder. *Bulletin of the Menninger Clinic, 65*(1), 4-25.

Jennings, A. & Higuchi, H. (1993). A User Model Neural Network for a Personal News Service. *User Modeling and User-Adapted Interaction 3,* S. 1–25, 1993.

Jennings, N. R. (2000). On agent-based software engineering. *Artificial Intelligence 117*(2), 277-296.

Jennings, N. R. (2001). An agent-based approach for building complex software systems. *Communications of the ACM 44*(4), 35-41.

Jennings, N. R., Sycara K. P., & Wooldridge, M. (1998). A roadmap of agent research and development. *Autonomous Agents and Multi-Agent Systems 1*(1), 7-38.

Jensen, F. V. (1996). *An Introduction to Bayesian Networks.* New York: Springer.

Jesdanun, A. (2008). China Catching Up to US in Number of Web Surfers. *Associated Press/ECT News Network,* 1/21/08.

Jiang, B., & Prater, E. (2002). Distribution and logistics development in China. *International Journal of Physical Distribution and Logistics Management, 32,* 9, 783-798.

Jiao, L. M., Khoo, L. P., & Chen, C. H. (2004). An Intelligent Concurrent Design Task Planner for Manufacturing Systems. *International Journal of Advanced Manufacturing Technology, 23*(9/10), 672-681.

Jin, X., Zhou, Y., Mobasher, M. (2004). *A Unified Approach to Personalization Based on Probabilistic Latent Semantic Models of Web Usage and Content.* Available at Citeseer http://citeseer.ist.psu.edu/715309.html.

Jing, L. B. (1993, July 10). The influence of Chinese culture on marketing management, Economics Studies, *36.*

Johnson, G. & Huff, A. (1997). Everyday innovation/everyday strategy. In Hamel, G. Prahalad, C. K., Thomas, H. & O'Neill, D. (Ed.) *Strategy flexibility.* London, United Kingdom: Wiley.

Johnson, G., Melin, L. & Whittington, R. (2003). Guest editor's introduction; micro Strategy and strategizing: Towards an activity-based view. *Journal of Management Studies, 40*(1), 3–22.

Junginger, S., Kühn, H., Strobl, R., & Karagiannis, D. (2000). Ein Geschäftsprozessmanagement-Werkzeug der nächsten Generation—ADONIS: Konzeption und Anwendungen. *Wirtschaftsinformatik, 42*(5), 392-401.

Jutras, C. (October 2, 2006). *The Total Cost of ERP Ownership.* Aberdeen Group.

Kantor, P., Boros, E., Melamed, B., Menkov, V., Shapira, B., & Neu, D. (2000). Capturing human intelligence in the net. Communications of the ACM , 43(8), 112-115.

KAON—*Karlsruhe Ontology and Semantic Web framework,* http://kaon2.semanticweb.org/,20.02.2007.

Karagiannis, D., & Woitsch, R. (2003). The PROMOTE Approach: Modelling Knowledge Management Processes to Describe Knowledge Management Systems. In N. Gronau (Ed.), *Wissensmanagement: Potenziale—Konzepte—Werkzeuge, Proceedings of the 4th Oldenburg Conference on Knowledge Management, University of Oldenburg, June 2003* (pp. 35-52). Berlin: Gito.

Karjaluoto, H., Matilda, M., & Pento, T. (2002). Factors underlying attitude formation towards online banking in Finland. *International Journal of Bank Marketing, 20*(6), 261-272.

Kassim, N. M., & Zain, M. (2004). Assessing the Measurement of Organizational Agility. *Journal Of American Academy of Business, 4*(1/2), 174-177.

Katasonov, A. (2008). *UBIWARE Platform and Semantic Agent Programming Language* (S-APL): Developer's guide, Online: http://users.jyu.fi/~akataso/SAPLguide.pdf.

Katasonov, A., & Terziyan, V. (2007). SmartResource Platform and Semantic Agent Programming Language (S-APL). In *Proc. 5th Conf. Multi-Agent Technologies (MATES'07), LNAI, 4687*, 25-36.

Kaufman, C. (2004, September). *Internet Key Exchange (IKEv2) Protocol.* Internet draft, IETF.

Kawamura, T., Blasio, J. D., Hasegawa, T., Paolucci, M., & Sycara, K. (2003). *Preliminary Report of Public Experiment of Semantic Service Matchmaker with UDDI Business Register.* Paper presented at the 1st International Conference on Service Oriented Computing (ICSOC 2003), Trento, Italy.

Kawamura, T., Blasio, J. D., Hasegawa, T., Paolucci, M., & Sycara, K. (2004). *Public Deployment of Semantic Service Matchmaker with UDDI Business Registry.* Paper presented at the 3rd International Semantic Web Conference (ISWC 2004).

Kaykova O., Khriyenko O., Kovtun D., Naumenko A., Terziyan V., & Zharko A. (2005). General Adaption Framework: Enabling Interoperability for Industrial Web Resources. *International Journal on Semantic Web and Information Systems, 1*(3), 31-63. Idea Group.

Kaykova O., Khriyenko O., Naumenko A., Terziyan V., & Zharko A. (2005). RSCDF: A Dynamic and Context Sensitive Metadata Description Framework for Industrial Resources. *Eastern-European Journal of Enterprise Technologies, 3*(2), 55-78.

Kaykova O., Khriyenko O., Terziyan V., & Zharko A. (2005). RGBDF: Resource Goal and Behaviour Description Framework. In *Proc. 1st International Conference on Industrial Applications of Semantic Web, Springer, IFIP, 188*, 83-99.

Kent, S., & Atkinson, R. (1998, November). *IP Authentication Header.* RFC 2402, IETF

Kent, S., & Atkinson, R. (1998, November). *IP Encapsulating Security Payload (ESP).* RFC 2406, IETF.

Kephart J. O., & Chess D. M. (2003). The vision of autonomic computing. *IEEE Computer 36*(1), 41-50.

Khriyenko O., & Terziyan V. (2006). A Framework for Context-Sensitive Metadata Description. *International Journal of Metadata, Semantics and Ontologies, 1*(2), 154-164.

Kiesler, S., & Sproull, L. (1982). Managerial Response to Changing Environments: Perspectives on Problem Sensing from Social Cognition. *Administrative Science Quarterly, 27*(2), 548-570.

Kim, J., Oard, D., & Romanik, K. (2000). Using implicit feedback for user modeling in Internet and Intranet searching. Technical Report, College of Library and Information Services, University of Maryland at College Park.

Kimberly, J. R. (1981). Management innovation. In P. Nystrom and W.H. Starbuck (Eds.), *Handbook of organizational design.* Oxford University Press, New York, (pp. 84-104).

Kimberly, J. R., & Evanisko, M. J. (1981). Organizational innovation: the influence of individual, organizational, and contextual factors on hospital adoption of technology and administrative innovations. *Academy of Management Journal, 24*(4), 689-713.

King, A. D. (1991). (ed.) *Culture Globalisation and the World-System.* Macmillan Press Ltd, SUNY-Binghampton.

Kinsella, J. (1998, July). Open Automation: A Perspective on Connection. *Manufacturing Engineering, 121,* 94-95.

Kivinen, T., Huttunen, A., Swander, B., & Volpe, V. (2004, February). *Negotiation of NAT-Traversal in the IKE.* Internet draft, IETF.

Klemke, R. (2000). *Context Framework—an Open Approach to Enhance Organisational Memory Systems with Context Modeling Techniques.* Paper presented at the th-31th October 2000, Basel, Switzerland.

Klensin, J. (2001, April). *Simple Mail Transfer Protocol.* RFC 2821, IETF.

Knapp, C. A., & Shin, N. (2001). Impacts of Enterprise Resource Planning systems selection and implementation. *7th Americas Conference on Information Systems,* USA.

Koch, C. (2006). *ABC: An Introduction to ERP.* CIO. Available at http://ww.cio.com/article/print/40323

Koh, S. C. L., & Simpson, M. (2007). Could enterprise resource planning create a competitive advantage for small businesses? *Benchmarking, 14*(1), 59-76.

Konstan, J. A., Miller, B. N., Maltz, D., Herlocker, J. L., Gordon, L., & Riedl, J. (1997, March). GroupLens: Applying collaborative filtering to Usenet news. In *Communication of the ACM, 40*(3), S. 77-87.

Konvitz, M. R. (1966). Privacy and the Law: A Philosophical Prelude. *Law and Contemporary Problems, 31*(2), 272-280.

Kostakos, V., O'Neill, E., Little, L., & Sillence, E. (2005). The Social Implications of Emerging Technologies. *Editorial/ Interacting with Computers, 17*, 475-483.

Krasner, G. E., & Pope, S. T. (1988). A cookbook for using the model-view-controller user interface paradigm in Smalltalk-80. *Journal of Object-Oriented Programming, 1*(3), S. 26-49.

Krulwich, B. (1997). LifeStyle Finder: Intelligent User Profiling Using Large-Scale Demographic Data. *AI Magazine 18*(2), 37–45.

Krulwich, B., & Burkey, C. (1995). ContactFinder: Extracting Indications of Expertise and Answering Questions with Referrals. *Working Notes of the 1995 Fall Symposium on Intelligent Knowledge Navigation and Retrieval*, S. 85–91, Technical Report FS-95-03, The AAAI Press.

Krulwich, B., & Burkey, C. (1996). Learning User Information Interests through Extraction of Semantically Significant Phrases. In *Proceedings of the AAAI Spring Symposium on Machine Learning in Information Access*. Stanford, CA.

Krummenacher, R., & Strang, T. (2005). Ubiquitous Semantic Spaces, In *Conference Supplement to the 7th Intl. Conf on Ubiquitous Computing (UbiComp 2005)*, Tokyo.

Kuutti, K. (1997). Activity Theory as a Potential Framework for Human-Computer Interaction Research. In B. A. Nardi (Ed.), *Context and Consciousness: Activity Theory and Human-Computer Interaction* (pp. 17-44). Cambridge, Mass.: MIT Press.

Lai, J. (2001). *Marketing Web Sites in China*. Minor Thesis, RMIT.

Lane, F.S. (2003). The Naked Employee: How Technology is Compromising Workplace Privacy. New York: AMACOM, American Management Association.

Langer, G., & Alting, L. (2000). An Architecture for Agile Shop Floor Control Systems. *Journal of Manufacturing Systems, 19*(4), 267-281.

Langford, H. P., & Scheuermann, L. (1998). Cogeneration and Self-generation for Energy Agility. *Industrial Management + Data Systems, 98*(2), 44-47.

Langheinrich, M. (2001). Privacy by Design—Principles of Privacy—Aware Ubiquitous Systems. In *Proceedings of the 3rd International Conference on Ubiquitous Computing*. Springer-Verlag LCNS 2201, 273-291.

Lassila, O. (2005). Applying Semantic Web in Mobile and Ubiquitous Computing: Will Policy-Awareness Help? In *Proc. Semantic Web Policy Workshop, 4th International Semantic Web Conference*, Galway, Ireland. (pp. 6-11).

Lassila, O. (2005). Using the Semantic Web in Mobile and Ubiquitous Computing. In *Proc. 1st IFIP Conference on Industrial Applications of Semantic Web*, Springer IFIP. (pp. 19-25).

Lassila, O., & Adler, M. (2003). Semantic Gadgets: Ubiquitous Computing Meets the Semantic Web, In: D. Fensel et al. (eds.), *Spinning the Semantic Web,* MIT Press. (pp. 363-376).

Laudon, K. C., & Laudon, J. P. (2001). Essentials of Management Information Systems. *Organisation and Technology in the Networked Enterprise.* New Jersey: Prentice Hall, 4th Edition.

Laudon, K. C., & Laudon, J. P. (2002). *Management Information Systems: Managing the Digital Firm*. New Jersey: Prentice Hall International, 7th Edition.

Le, D. N., & Goh, A. (2005). *Matching Semantic Web Services Using Different Ontologies.* Paper presented at the ICWE 2005, Sydney, Australia.

Le, D. N., Goh, A., & Tru, C. H. (2005). *Multi-Ontology Matchmaker.* Paper presented at the 7th International conference on Information Integration and Web Based Applications and Services (iiWAS2005), Malaysia.

Le, D. N., Hang, T. M., & Goh, A. (2006). *MOD- A Multi Ontology Discovery system.* Paper presented at the International Workshop on Semantic Matchmaking and Resource Retrieval, Seoul, Korean.

Lederman, L. C. (1990). Accessing Educational Effectiveness: The Focus Group interview as techniques for data collection. *Communication Education, 39*(2), 117-127.

Lee, B., & Lee, R. S (1995). How and Why People Watch TV: Implications for the Future of Interactive Television. *Journal of Advertising Research* (November/December), 9-18.

Lee, S. M. (1986). *Spectrum of Chinese Culture*. Pelanduk Publications (M), Selangor Darul Ehsau.

Leech, M., Ganis, M., Lee, Y., Kuris, R., Koblas, D., & Jones, L. *SOCKS Protocol Version 5.* RFC 1928, IETF.

Lengnick-Hall, C. A.; Lengnick-Hall, M. and Abdinnour-Helm, S. (2004). The Role of Social and Intellectual Capital in Achieving Competitive Advantage Through

Enterprise Resource Planning (ERP) Systems. *Journal of Engineering and Technology Management, 21*(4), 307-330.

Levitt, D., & March, J. G. (1988). Organizational learning. *Annual Review of Sociology, 14*, 319-340.

Li, C. H. (1998). *China: The Consumer Revolution.* New York: Wiley.

Li, L., & Horrocks, I. (2003). *A software framework for matchmaking based on semantic web technology.* Paper presented at the 12th International World Wide Web Conference, Budapest, Hungary.

Li, Y., Bandar Z.A., & Mclean D. (2003). An approach for measuring semantic similarity between words using multiple information sources. IEEE Transactions on Knowledge and Data Engineering, 15(4), 871-882.

Li, Y., Su, S., & Yang, F. (2006). *A Peer-to-Peer Approach to Semantic Web Services Discovery.* Paper presented at the Computational Science—ICCS 2006: 6th International Conference, Reading, UK.

Liang, Q., Chakarapani, L. N., Su, S. Y. W., Chikkamagalur, R. N., & Lamr, H. (2004). A Semi-automatic approach to composite web services discovery, description and invocation,. *International Journal of Web Services Research, 1*(4), 64–89.Idea Group Publishing

Liang, T. P., Chandler, J. S., Han, I., & Roan, J. (1992). An empirical investigation of some data effects on the classification accuracy of probit, ID3 and neural networks. *Contemporary Accounting Research, 9*(1), 306-328.

Lin, B., Vassar, J.A. (2004) 'Mobile healthcare computing devices for enterprise-wide patient data delivery', Int. J. Mobile Communications, Vol. 2, No. 4, pp.343–353.

Ling, L., Calton, P., & Wei, H. XWRAP (2000). *An XMLEnabled Wrapper Construction System for Web Information Sources. In International Conference on Data Engineering ICDE*, S. 611- 621.

Linthicum, D. S. (1999). *Enterprise Application Integration.* Boston: Addison-Wesley.

Lippman, S., & Rumelt, R. P. (1982). Uncertain imitability: An analysis of interfirm differences in efficiency under competition. The *Bell Journal of Economics, 13*, 418-438.

Little, J., Geurts, & J. Hunter (2002, September). Dynamic Generation of Intelligent Multimedia Presentations through Semantic Inferencing. In *6th European Conference on Research and Advanced Technology for Digital Libraries*, S. 158-189. Springer.

Liu, C., long, A., Li, Y., Tsai, K., Kuo, H. (2001) 'Sharing patient care records over the World Wide Web', International Journal of Medical Informatics, Vol. 61, pp. 189-205.

Lo, W. N., & Gong, P. (2005). Cultural Impact of E-Commerce Web sites. *Issues in Information Systems, VI*(2), 182-188.

Lohse, G., Bellman, S., & Johnson, E. (2000). Consumer Buying Berhavior on the Internet. *Journal of Interactive Marketing, 14*(1), 15-29.

LOM (2001, April). *LOM, Draft Standard for Learning Object Metadata.* IEEE P1484.12/D6.1. 18.

Long, C. (2000). Measuring Your Strategic Agility. *Consulting Management, 11*(3), 25-28.

Lu, Y, Xiao, Y., Sears, A., Jacko, J. (2005), 'A review and a framework of handheld computer adoption in healthcare', International Journal of Medical Informatics Vol. 74, pp. 409—422.

Lucene Search Engine. http://lucene.apache.org/java/docs/, 16.01.2008

Ludwig, H. (2003). Web Service Level Agreement (WSLA) Language Specification Version 1.0. *Techincal report in IBM*

Luna, D., Peracchio, L., & de Juan, M. (2002). Cross-Cultural and Cognitive Aspects of Web Site Navigation. *Journal of the Academy of Management Science, 30*(4), 397-410.

Lund, D., Wolin, L. D., Kargaonkar P. (2002). Beliefs, Attitudes and Behaviour Towards Web Advertising. *International Journal of Advertising, 21*(1).

Lyles, M. A. (N/D). Learning among joint venture sophisticated firms. *Management International Review, 28*(Special Issue): 85-98.

Lytras, M. D., & Ordóñez de Pablos, P. (2007). The building of the intellectual capital statement in multinationals: challenges for the future. In K. O'Sullivan (Ed), *Strategic Knowledge Management in Multinational Organizations.* Idea Group Inc. (pp. 195-206).

Lytras, M. D., & Ordóñez de Pablos, P. (2009). Managing, measuring and reporting knowledge-based resources in hospitals. *International Journal of Technology Management, forthcoming.*

Mabert, V. A., Soni, A., & Venkataraman, M. A. (2003). The impact of organization size on enterprise resource planning (ERP) implementations in the US manufacturing sector. *Omega, 31*(3), 235-46.

Mabert, V. A., Soni, A., & Venkataraman, M. A. (2003). Enterprise resource planning: Managing the implementation process. *European Journal of Operational Research, 146* (2), 302-14.

MacKenzie, S. B., & Lutz, R. J. (1989). An empirical examination of the structural antecedents of attitude toward the ad in an advertising pre-testing context. *Journal of Marketing Research, 23*(2), 48-65.

Maier, R. (2004). *Knowledge Management Systems: Information and Communication Technologies for Knowledge Management* (2nd ed.). Berlin et al.: Springer.

Maier, R., & Remus, U. (2003). Implementing Process-oriented Knowledge Management Strategies. *Journal of Knowledge Management, 7*(4), 62-74.

Maier, R., & Sametinger, J. (2002). *Infotop—An Information and Communication Infrastructure for Knowledge Work.* Paper presented at the 3rd European Conference on Knowledge Management, Trinity College Dublin, Ireland.

Maier, R., Hädrich, T., & Peinl, R. (2005). *Enterprise Knowledge Infrastructures (forthcoming)*.Berlin: Springer.

Mäkelä, E., Hyvönen, E., Saarela, S., & Viljanen, K. (2004). *OntoViews—A Tool for Creating Semantic Web Portals.* Paper presented at the 3rd International Semantic Web Conference (ISWC 2004), Hiroshima, Japan.

Mann, S. (2004). Sousveillance: Inverse Surveillance in Multimedia Imaging. *MM'04, ACM,* 620-627.

March, J. G. (1978). Bounded rationality, ambiguity and the engineering of choice. *Bell Journal of Economics, 9*(2), 587-608.

Markus, K. (2006). What is a Good Definition? Retrieved March 12, 2006, from Structural Equation Modeling Discussion Group [SEMNET@BAMA.UA.EDU]

Markus, M. L., & Tanis, C. (2000). The Enterprise System Experience—From Adoption to Success. In R. W. Zmud (ed.), *Framing the Domains of IT Management: Projecting the Future through the Past.* Cincinnati, OH: Pinnaflex Education Resources, Inc. (pp. 173-203).

Marsh, R. M., & Mannari, H. (1989). The size imperative? Longitudinal tests. *Organizational Studies, 10*(1), 83-95.

Mason-Jones, R., & Towill, D. R. (1999). Total Cycle Time Compression and the Agile Supply Chain. *International Journal of Production Economics, 62*(1,2), 61-73.

Maus, H. (2001). *Workflow Context as a Means for Intelligent Information Support.* Paper presented at the 3rd Intl. Conf. on Modeling and Using Context (CONTEXT 2001).

Mazzieri, M., & Dragoni, A. F. (2005). *A Fuzzy Semantics for Semantic Web Languages.* Paper presented at the Proceedings of the ISWC Workshop on Uncertainty Reasoning for the Semantic Web, Galway, Ireland.

McAdam, R., & Galloway, A. (2005). Enterprise resource planning and organisational innovation: a management perspective. *Industrial Management & Data Systems, 105*(3), 280-90.

McCarthy, T. (2000). China's Internet Gold Rush, *TIME Magazine,* Feb 28 2000, 20-23.

McGaughey, R. E. (1999). Internet Technology: Contributing to Agility in the Twenty-First Century. *International Journal of Agile Management Systems, 1*(1), 7-13.

McKee, T. E. (1995). Predicting bankruptcy via induction. *Journal of Information Technology,* (10), 26-36.

Meehan, M. (2005). 2005: The year SOA broke big. Retrieved 01/16/2006, 2006

Meier, R. L., Humphreys, M. A., & Williams, M. R. (1998). The Role of Purchasing in the Agile Enterprises. *International Journal of Purchasing and Materials Management, 34*(4), 39-45.

Melarkode, A., From-Poulsen, M., & Warnakulsuriya, S. (2004). Delivering Agility through IT. *Business Strategy Review, 15*(3), 45-50.

Melcher, A. J., & Schwitter, J. P. (1967). *Designing an Empirical Research Project: Considerations and Guidelines.* Unpublished manuscript, Kent.

Meredith, S., & Francis, D. (2000). Journey Towards Agility: The Agile Wheel Explored. *The TQM Magazine, 12*(3), 137.

Metaxiotis, K., (2005) 'E-health versus KM-based health: a dilemma in researchers' minds', International J. of Electronics Healthcare- Vol. 1, No. 3, pp. 303-315.

Michelis, G. D., Dubois, E., Jarke, M., Matthes, F., Mylopoulos, J., Papazoglou, M., et al. (1998). A Three-Faceted View of Information Systems: The Challenge of Change. *Communications of the ACM, 41*(12), 64-70.

Milakov, S. (1995). *Asian Games.* Coolum Beach: Gull Publishing, 19.

Miles, M. B., & Huberman, M. (1994). *Qualitative Data Analysis: An Expanded Sourcebook* (2nd ed.). Thousand Oaks, CA: Sage Publication.

Miller, G. A. (1995). WordNet: A Lexical Database. *Communication of the ACM, 38*(11): S. 39-41.

Miller, G. A. 1995. WordNet: a lexical database for English. Communication of the ACM, 38(11), 39-41.

Mitra, S., & Chaya, A. K. (1996). Analyzing Cost-Effectiveness of Organizations: The Impact of Information Technology Spending. *Journal of Management Information Systems, 13* (2), 29-57.

Montaner, M., Lopez, B., & Dela, J. L. (2003). A taxonomy of recommender agents on the internet. *Artificial Intelligence Review 19(*2003), 285-330.

Mooij, M. (1998). *Global Marketing and Advertisin*g. California: Sage Publications.

Moor, J. H. (1990). Ethics of Privacy Protection. *Library Trends, 39*(1&2), 69-82.

Moor, J. H. (1997). Towards a Theory of Privacy in the Information Age. *Computers and Society, 27*(3), 27-32.

Morash, E. A. (2001). Supply Chain Strategies, Capabilities, and Performance. *Transportation Journal, 41*(1), 37-54.

Morgan, D. (1988). Focus groups as qualitative Research. London: Sage.

Motiwalla, L., & Thompson, J. (2008). Enterprise Systems Management: ERP Implementation in Organizations. New York: Prentice Hall Publications.

Motta, E., & Sabou, M. (2006). Next Generation Semantic Web Applications. In *Proc. 1st Asian Semantic Web Conference (ASWC)*, Beijing, China.

Muckle. R. (2003, July). *Email Monitoring in the Workplace: A Simple Guide to Employers.* Waterford Technologies.

Narasimhan, R. (1999). Manufacturing Agility and Supply Chain Management Practices. *Production and Inventory Management Journal, 40*(1), 4-10.

Nathan, A. (1998). *China's Transition.* New York: Columbia U. Press.

Nazeran, H.; Setty, S.; Haltiwanger, E.; Gonzalez, V. 'A PDA-based flexible telecommunication system for telemedicine applications', Proceeding of the IEEE Engineering in Medicine and Biology Society Conference, EMBC 2004. pp.2200-2203.

Neches, R., Fikes R., Finin, T., Gruber, T., Patil, R., Senator, T., & Swartout, W.R. (1991), Enabling technology for knowledge sharing, AI Magazine, 12(3), 36-56.

Neidl, W., Wolf, B., Qu, Ch., Decker, S., Sintek, M., Naeve, A., Nilsson, M., Palmer, M., & Risch, T (2002, May). Edutella—A P2P Networking Infrastructure Based on RDF. *Proceedings of the Semantic Web Workshop, 11th Intl. WWW Conference.*

Nelson, R., & Winter, S. (1982). *An Evolutionary Theory of Economic Change.* Harvard University Press.

Netter, J., Wasserman, W., & Kutner, M. H. (1990). *Applied Linear Statistical Models.* third ed., Irwin, Inc., Boston, MA.

Nicolini, D., & Meznar, M. B. (1995). The social construction of organizational learning. *Human Relations, 48,* 727-46.

Nieto, M. (2003). From R&D management to knowledge management: An overview of studies of innovation management. *Technological Forecasting and Social Change, 70,* 135–161.

Noaker, P. M. (1994). The Search for Agile Manufacturing. *Manufacturing Engineering, 113*(5), 5-11.

Nonaka, I. (1991). The knowledge-creating company. *Harvard Business Review,* noviembre-diciembre, (pp. 96-104).

Nonaka, I., & Takeuchi, H. (1995). *The Knowledge Creating Company: How Japanese Companies Create the Dynamics of Innovation.* Oxford University Press.

Nord, G. D., McCubbins, T. F., & Horn Nord, J. (2006). Email Monitoring in the Workplace: Privacy, Legislation, and Surveillance Software. *Communications of the ACM, 49*(8), 73-77.

O'Connor, L. (1994). Agile Manufacturing in a Responsive Factory. *Mechanical Engineering, 16*(7), 54-57.

O'Leary, D. (2000). *Enterprise resource planning: systems, life cicle, electronic commerce, and risk.* New York: Cambridge University Press.

O'Leary, D. E. (2000). Enterprise Resource Planning Systems. London: Cambridge University Press.

O'Neill, H.M.; Pouder, R.W., Buchholtz, A.K. (1998). Patterns in the diffusion of strategies across organizations: insights from the innovation diffusion literature. *Academy of Management Review, 23*(1), 98-114.

Oestereich, B., Weiss, C., Schröder, C., Weilkiens, T., & Lenhard, A. (2003). *Objektorientierte Geschäftsprozessmodellierung mit der UML.* Heidelberg: dpunkt.

Okazaki, S. (2004). How Do Japanese Consumers Perceive Wireless Ads? A Multivariate Analysis. *International Journal of Advertising, 23*(4), 429-454.

Orbell, S., Hodgkins, S., & Sheeran, P. (1997). Implementation intentions and the theory of planned behaviour. *Personality and Social Psychology Bulletin, 23,* 945-954.

Ordóñez de Pablos, P. (2004). A guideline for building the intellectual capital statement: the 3R Model. *International Journal of Learning and Intellectual Capital, 1*(1), 3-18.

Ordóñez de Pablos, P. (2005). Intellectual capital accounts: what pioneering firms from asia and europe are doing now. *International Journal of Knowledge and Learning, 1*(3), 249-268.

Ordóñez de Pablos, P., Edvinsson, L., & Lytras, M. D. (2008). The Intellectual Capital Statements: Evolution And How To Get Started. In M. Lytras, M. Russ, R. Maier, and A. Naeve, (Eds.), *Knowledge Management Strategies.* IGI, (pp. 64-91).

Ortolani, A. (2005). Chinese begin Paying by Cellphone. *Wall Street Journal,* Feb 2, p. 1.

Osborne, A. (2001). *Fear of Flying 'will Cost Airlines Billions'.* Money.Telegraph. Retrieved on April 10th, 2005, from http://www.news.telegraph.co.uk/money/main.jhtml?xml=/money/2001/09/12/cnair12.xml

Ossenbruggen, J. van, Geurts, J., Cornelissen, F., Rutledge, L., & Hardman., L. (2001, May). Towards Second and Third Generation Web-Based Multimedia. *In Proceedings of the Tenth International World Wide Web Conference (WWW10).* Hong Kong: ACM Press, S. 479-488.

Österle, H. (1995). *Business Engineering. Prozeß- und Systementwicklung. Band 1: Entwurfstechniken.* Berlin: Springer.

Ota, M. (2001). The Concepts of Production-Marketing Integration Towards Agile Manufacturing. *International Journal of Manufacturing Technology and Management, 3*(3), 225-237.

Oundhankar, S., Verma, K., Sivashanugam, K., Sheth, A., & Miller, J. (2005). Discovery of web serivces in a Muti-Ontologies and Federated Registry Environment. *International Journal of Web Services Research, 1*(3)

Oyen, M. P. V. (2001). Performance Opportunity for Workforce Agility in Collaborative and Non-Collaborative Work Systems. *IEEE Transactions, 33*(9), 761-777.

Paiva, A., & Self, J. (1995). TAGUS: A User and Learner Modeling Workbench. *International Journal of User Modeling and User-adapted Interaction, 5*(3), 197-224. Kluwer Academic Publishers.

Pankaj, & Hyde, M. (2003, 2003). *Organizations and the Necessity of Computer Based Information Systems.* Paper presented at the 9th Americas Conference on Information Systems, Tampa, FL.

Paolucci, M., Kawamura, T., Payne, T. R., & Sycara, K. (2002). *Semantic Matching of Web services Capabilities.* Paper presented at the 1st International Semantic Web Conference (ISWC 2002), Sardinia, Italy.

Park, T. (1993). The nature of relevance in information retrieval: An empirical study. Library Quarterly, 63, 318-351.

Parker, R. B. (1974). A Definition of Privacy. *Rutgers Law Review, 27*(1), 275.

Parr, A., & Shanks, G. (2000). A Taxonomy of ERP Implementation Approaches. *Proceedings of the 33rd Hawaii International Conference on System Sciences,* Monash University.

Patil, A., Oundhakar, S., Sheth, A., & Verma, K. (2004). *METEOR-S Web service Annotation Framework.* Paper presented at the Proceeding of the World Wide Web Conference.

Pazzani, M., Muramatsu, J., & Billsus, D. (1996). Syskill & Webert: Identifying Interesting Web Sites. In *Proceedings of the Thirteenth National Conference on Artificial Intelligence,* S. 54–61.

Pearlson, K., & Saunders, C. (2006). *Managing & Using Information Systems: A Strategic Approach,* 3rd Edition. Hoboken, New Jersey: Wiley & Sons, Inc.

Pedler, M., Boydell, T., & Burgoyne, J. (1991). *The Learning Company.* McGraw-Hill, Londres.

Pedler, M., Boydell, T., & Burgoyne, J. G. (1989). Towards the learning company. *Management Education and Development, 20*(1), 1-8.

Pemberton, D., Rodden, T., & Procter, R. (2000). Group-Mark: A WWW recommender system combining collaborative and information filtering. In *Proceedings of the 6th ERCIM Workshop,* Florence, Italy, Oct. 25-26.

Penazola, (1998). L. N. Immigrant Consumer Acculturation. In Srull, (ed.), *Advances in Consumer Research.* Provo, UT: Assn. For Consumer Research.

Penrose, E. T (1959). *The Theory of the Growth of the Firm.* New York: John Wiley & Sons.

Peteraf, M. A. (1993). The conerstones of competitive advantage: A resource-based view. *Strategic Management Journal, 14,* 179-191.

Pfohl, H.-C. (1997). Logistics: State of the Art. *Human Systems Management, 16*(3), 153-158.

Platt, R. G. (1995). Ethical and Social Implications of the Internet. *The Ethicomp E-Journal, 1.*

Polanyi, M. (1966). *The Tacit Dimension.* London: Routledge & Kegan Paul.

Pollay, R. W., & Mittal, B. (1993). Here's the Beef: Factors, Determinants, and Segments in Consumer Criticism of Advertising. *Journal of Marketing, 57*(July), 99-114.

Poole, M. S., & Van de Ven, A. H. (1989). Toward a general theory of innovation processes. in Van de Ven, A. H., Angle, H. L., Poole, M. S. (Eds.), *Research on the Management of Information: The Minnesota Studies.* Harper & Row, New York, (pp. 637-62).

Porter, M. E. (1985). *Competitive Advantage: Creating and Sustaining Superior Performance.* New York, London: Free Press.

Porter, M.E. (1987). From competitive advantage to corporate strategy. *Harvard Business Review, 65*(3), 43-59.

Poston, R., Grabski, S. (2001). Financial impacts of enterprise resource planning implementations. *International Journal of Accounting Information Systems, 2*(4), 271-94.

Powers, M. (1996). A Cognitive Access Definition of Privacy. *Law and Philosophy, 15*(4), 369-386.

Prakhaber P.R. (2000). Who owns the Online Consumer? *Journal of Consumer Marketing, 17*(2), 158-171.

Priebe, T. (2004). *INWISS—Integrative Enterprise Knowledge Portal.* Paper presented at the 3rd International Semantic Web Conference (ISWC 2004), Hiroshima, Japan.

Priebe, T., & Pernul, G. (2003). Towards Integrative Enterprise Knowledge Portals. In *Proc. of the Twelfth International Conference on Information and Knowledge Management (CIKM 2003).* New Orleans, USA.

Priebe, T., Kiss, C., & Kolter, J. (2005). *Semiautomatische Annotation von Textdokumenten mit semantischen Metadaten.* Paper presented at the 6. Internationale Tagung Wirtschaftsinformatik (WI 2005), Bamberg, Germany.

Priebe, T., Schläger, C., & Pernul, G. (2004). *A Search Engine for RDF Metadata.* Paper presented at the DEXA 2004 Workshop on Web Semantics (WebS 2004), Zaragoza, Spain.

Priem, R. L., & Butler, J. E. (2001). Is the resource-based "view" a useful perspective for strategic management research? *Academy of Management Review, 26,* 22-40.

Priem, R. L., & Butler, J. E. (2001). Tautology in the resource-based view and the implications of externally determined resource value: Further comments. *Academy of Management Review, 26,* 57-66.

Pullin, J. (2001). How Being Agile is the Best Way Up. *Professional Engineering, 14*(11), 32-33.

Qasem, A., Heflin J., & Mucoz-Avila H. (2004). Efficient Source Discovery and Service Composition for Ubiquitous Computing Environments. In: *Workshop on Semantic Web Technology for Mobile and Ubiquitous Applications,* ISWC 2004.

Quinlan, J. R. (1993). *C4.5: Programs for machine learning.* Morgan Kaufmann Publishers, Inc., California.

Quinlan, J. R. (2004). *Data Mining Tools See5 & C5.0.* Available http://www.rulequest.com/see5-info.html

Quinlan, J.R. (1979). Discovering rules by induction from large collections of examples. In Michie, D. (Ed.), *Expert systems in the microelectronic age.*

Quinn, J. B. (1980). Managing Strategic Change. *Sloan Management Review, 21*(4), 3-20.

Raman, N. V., & Leckenby, J. D. (1998). Factors affecting consumers' "Webad" visits. *European Journal of Marketing, 32*(7/8), 737-748.

Rao, A. S. (1996). AgentSpeak(L): BDI agents speak out in a logical computable language. *Proc. 7th European Workshop on Modelling Autonomous Agents in a Multi-Agent World, LNCS 1038,* 42-55.

Rao, A. S., & Georgeff, M. P. (1991). Modeling rational agents within a BDI architecture. *Proc. 2nd International Conference on Principles of Knowledge Representation and Reasoning* (KR'91), (pp. 473-484).

Recuerda, F. M., & Robertson, D. (2005). *Discovery and Uncertainty in Semantic Web Services.* Paper presented at the Proceedings of the International Semantic Web Conference (ISWC 2005), Workshop 3: Uncertainty Reasoning for the Semantic Web, Galway, Ireland.

Reddy, S. B., & Reddy, R. (2002). Competitive Agility and the Challenge of Legacy Information Systems. *Industrial Management + Data Systems, 102*(1/2), 5-16.

Reed, R., & Defillippi, R. (1990). Causal ambiguity, barriers to imitation and sustainable competitive advantage. *Academy of Management Review, 15*(1), 88-102.

Resnick, P., Iacovou, N., Suchak, M., Bergstrom, P., & Riedl, J. (1994). GroupLens: an open architecture for collaborative filtering of netnews. In Proceedings of the 1994 ACM Conference on Computer Supported Cooperative Work, 175-186.

Richards, C. W. (1996). Agile Manufacturing: Beyond Lean? *Production an Inventory Management Journal, 37*(2), 60-64.

Richmond, R. (2005). Fear *of Flying: Symptoms, Medical Issues, and Treatment.* Retrieved on April 10th, 2005, from http://www.guidetopsychology.com/fearfly.htm

Riikonen, P. Boberg, J., Slakoski, T., Vihinen, M. (2002) 'Mobile access to biological databases on the internet," IEEE Transactions on Biomedical Engineering, vol. 49, No. 12, pp. 1477-1479.

Roberts, R. (1989). Passenger Fear of Flying: Behavioural Treatment with Extensive In Vivo Exposure and Group Support. *Aviation, Space, and Environmental Medicine*, 60, 342-348.

Robey, D. (1979). User Attitudes and Management Information System Use. *Academy of Management Journal, 22*(3), 527-538.

Robins, F. (2003). The Marketing of 3G. *Marketing Intelligence & Planning, 21*(6), 370-378.

Rocchio, J.J. (1971). Relevance feedback in information retrieval. The SMART Retrieval System, 313–323

Rogers, E. M. (1962). *Diffusion of innovations.* New York: The Free Press, (4th ed. 1995).

Roman, D., Lausen, H., & Keller, U. (2004). *Web Service Modeling Ontology—Standard (WSMO—Standard), WSMO deliverable D2 version 1.1.*

Ross, J. W., & Vitale, M. R. (2000). The ERP revolution: surviving vs. thriving. *Information Systems Frontiers, 2*(2), 233-41.

Rossi, H. (2006). What is a Good Definition? Retrieved March 12, 2006, from Structural Equation Modeling Discussion Group [SEMNET@BAMA.UA.EDU]

Roth, A. V. (1996, March). Achieving Strategic Agility Through Economies of Knowledge. *Strategy & Leadership, 24,* 30-37.

Rothbaum, B., Hodges, L., Anderson, P., Price, L. & Smith, S. (2002). Twelve-Month Follow-up of Virtual Reality and Standard Exposure Therapies for the Fear of Flying. *Journal of Consulting and Clinical Psychology, 70*(2), 428-432.

Rothbaum, B., Hodges, L., Smith, S., Lee, J. & Price, L. (2000). A Controlled Study of Virtual Reality Exposure Therapy for the Fear of Flying. *Journal of Consulting and Clinical Psychology*, 68(6), 1020-1026.

Rule, J.B. (2004). Towards Strong Privacy: Values, Markets, Mechanisms, and Institutions. *University of Toronto Law Journal, 54*(2), 183-225.

Rumelt, R. P. (1984). Towards a strategic theory of the firm. In R. B. LAMB (ed.), *Competitive Strategic Management.* Englewood Cliffs, NJ: Prentice-Hall. (pp. 556-570).

Rust, R. T., Kannan, P. K. & Peng, Na. (2002). The Customer Economics of Internet Privacy. *Journal of the Academy of Marketing Science, 30*(4), 455-464.

Ruthven, I., & Lalmas, M. (2003). A survey on the use of relevance feedback for information access systems. Knowledge Engineering Review, 18(2), 95-145.

Sabou, M., Lopez, V., & Motta, E. (2006). Ontology Selection on the Real Semantic Web: How to Cover the Queens Birthday Dinner? In *Proceedings of EKAW*, Podebrady, Czech Republic.

Sachs, P. (1995). Transforming Work: Collaboration, Learning, and Design. *Communications of the ACM, 38*(9), 36-44.

Safire, W. (2002). The Great Unwatched. *New York Times.* Available at http://query.nytimes.com/gst/fullpage.html?res=9A03E7DB1E3FF93BA25751C0A9649C8B63

Safran, C., Goldberg, H. "Electronic patient records and the impact of the internet," Int. Journal of Medical Informatics, vol. 60, pp. 77-83, 2000.

Sahai, A., Durante, A., & Machiraju, V. (2002). Towards Automated SLA Management for Web Services. *Technical report HPL-2001-310 (R.1) on HP Laboratories*

Sahin, F. (2000). Manufacturing Competitiveness: Different Systems to Achieve the Same Results. *Production and Inventory Management Journal, 41*(1), 56-65.

Sahuguet, & Azavant, F. (2001). Building intelligent Web applications using lightweight wrappers. *Data and Knowledge Engineering, 3*(36), 283-316.

Salton, G. (1988). *Automatic Text Processing: The Transformation, Analysis and Retrieval of Information by Computer*: Massachusetts.

Salton, G., & Buckley, C. (1990). Improving retrieval performance by relevance feedback. Journal of the American Society for Information Science, 41(4), 288-97.

Salton, G., & Buckley, C. (1998). Term-Weighting Approaches in Automatic Text Retrieval. *Information Processing and Management, 24*(5), 513–523.

Salton, G., & McGill, M. (1983). Introduction to Modern Information Retrieval. New York, NY: McGraw-Hill Publishing Company.

SAP (2005). *SAP Komponenten und Werkzeuge von SAP NetWeaver: SAP NetWeaver Portal,* 05.01.2005 http://www.sap.com/germany/solutions/netweaver/components/netweaverportal/index.epx/.

Saracevic, T. (1975). Relevance: A review of and framework for the thinking on the notion in information science. Journal of the American Society for Information Science, 26(6), 321-343.

Saracevic, T. (1996). Relevance reconsidered. In Proceedings of the Second Conference on Conceptions of Library and Information Science (CoLIS 2), 201-218.

Scarborough, J. (1998, November). Comparing Chinese and Western Culture Roots. *Business Horizons.*

Schafer, J. B., Konstan, J., & Riedi, J. (1999). Recommender Systems in E-Commerce. In *Proceedings of the ACM Conference on Electronic Commerce.* New York, NY: ACM Press, 158-166.

Schauer, H. (2004). *Knowledge MEMO: Eine Methode zur Planung, Steuerung und Kontrolle ganzheitlichen betrieblichen Wissensmanagements.* Unpublished PhD thesis, University of Koblenz, Koblenz.

Scheer, A.-W. (2001). *ARIS—Modellierungsmethoden, Metamodelle, Anwendungen.*Berlin: Springer.

Schoeman F. (1984). Privacy: Philosophical Dimensions of the Literature. In *Philosophical Dimensions of Privacy: An Anthology,* (F.Schoeman, ed., 1984).

Schonsleben, P. (2000). With Agility and Adequate Partnership Strategies Towards Effective Logistics Networks. *Computers in Industry, 42*(1), 33-42.

Schulze, U. (2000). A Confessional Account of an Ethnography About Knowledge Work. *MIS Quarterly, 24*(1), 3-41.

Schulze, U. (2003). On Knowledge Work. In C. W. Holsapple (Ed.), *Handbook on Knowledge Management—Volume 1: Knowledge Matters* (pp. 43-58). Berlin: Springer.

Scott, J. E. (1999, August). The FoxMeyer Drugs' Bankruptcy: Was it a Failure of ERP?" *Proceedings of the Association for Information Systems Fifth Americas Conference on Information Systems,* Milwaukee, WI, 223-225. Available at http://homepage.cs.uri.edu/courses/fall2007/csc305/Schedule/FoxMeyer1.pdf

Selmi, M. (2006). Privacy for the Working Class: Public Work and Private Lives. *Louisiana Law Review, 66,* 1035-1056.

Senge, P. M. (1990). *The Fifth Discipline: The Art and Practice of the Learning Organization.* New York: Doubleday Currency.

Serkkola, A., Ikävalko, J. Hänninen, S., & Kauranen, I. (2009). Microanalysis in the identification and research of the product and service innovations: A conceptual framework, *International Journal of Entrepreneurial Venturing* (forthcoming).

Shafer, R. (1999). Only the Agile will Survive. *HR Magazine, 44,* 50-51.

Shafer, R. A., Dyer, L., Kilty, J., Amos, J., & Ericksen, J. (2002). Crafting A Human Resource Strategy to Foster Organizational Agility: A Case Study. *Human Resource Management, 40*(3), 197-211.

Shapiro, S. S., & Wilk, M. B. (1965). An analysis of variance test for normality (complete samples). *Biometrika, 52*(3-4), 591-611.

Shardanand, U., & Maes, P. (1995). Social Information Filtering: Algorithms for Automating 'Word of Mouth'. *In Proceedings of CHI'95,* S. 210–217.

Sharifi, H., & Zhang, Z. (1999). A Methodology for Achieving Agility in Manufacturing Organizations: An Introduction. *International Journal of Production Economics, 62*(1), 7-22.

Shaw, S., Foggiato-Bish, L., Garcia, I., Tillman, G., Tryon, D., Wood, W., *et al.* (1993). *Improving Data Quality Via LDL++.* Paper presented at the Workshop on Programming with Logic Databases (Informal Proceedings).

Shepard, R.N.(1987). Towards a Universal Law of Generalisation for Psychological Science. Science, 237,1317-1323.

Shepherd, J. (December 14, 2006). *Infor: The $2B Enterprise Application Company You've Never Heard Of.* AMR Research.

Shin, N. (1999). Does information technology improve coordination? An empirical analysis. *Logistics Information Management, 12*(1/2), 138-44.

Shneiderman, B. (1998). *Designing the User Interface.* Reading, MA: Addison Wesley Longman Publisher.

Shoham, Y. (1993). Agent-oriented programming. Artificial Intelligence, 60(1), 51–92.

Shortliffe, E., Perreault, L, Wiederhold G. and Fagan, L. (2001). *Medical Informatics.* New York, NY: Springer-Verlag Publishers.

Shrivastava, P. (1983). A typology of organizational learning systems. Journal *of Management Studies, 20*(1), 7-28.

Siau, K., & Z. Shen (2003). Building Customer Trust in Mobile Commerce. *Communications of the ACM, 46*(4), 91-94.

Sieger, D. B., Badiru, A. B., & Milatovic, M. (2000). A Metric for Agility Measurement in Product Development. *IIE Transactions, 32*(7), 637-645.

Silverman, D. (1993). Interpreting Qualitative Data: Methods for Analaysing Talk, Text and Interaction. London: Sage.

Singh, N., Zhao, H., & Hu, X. (2003). Cultural Adaptation on the Web. *Journal of Global Information Technology Management, 11*, 3, 63-80.

Sivashanmugam, K., Verma, K., Sheth, A., & Miller, J. (2003). *Adding Semantics to Web Services Standards.* Paper presented at the The 2003 International Conference on Web Services (ICWS'03), Erfurt, Germany.

Skandia (1994). *Intellectual Capital Report, 1994.*

Skandia (1996). *Supplement to the Annual Report. Customer Value, 1996.*

Smith, H. J. (2001). Information Privacy and Marketing: What the U.S Should (and Shouldn't) Learn from Europe. *California Management Review Reprint Series, 43*(2), 8-33.

Snell, S. A., Lepak, D. P., & Youndt, M. A. (1999). Managing the architecture of intellectual capital: Implications for strategic human resource management. In G. R. FERRIS (Ed.), *Research in Personnel and Human Resources Management, S4*, 175-193.

Soh, C., Kien, S. S., & Tay-Yap, J. (2000). Cultural Fits and Misfits: Is ERP a Universal Solution? *Communications of the ACM, 43*(4), 47-51.

Sorensen, H., & McElligot, M. (1995). PSUN: A Profiling System for Usenet News. In *CKIM'95 Workshop on Intelligent Information Agents.*

Spender, J-C (1996). Making knowledge, collective practice and Penrose rents. *International Business Review, 3*, 4.

Spender, J-C. (1996). Organizational knowledge, learning and memory: Three concepts in search of a theory. *Journal of Organizational Change Management, 9*, 63-79.

Spink, A., & Losee, R.M. (1996). Feedback in information retrieval. Review of Information Science and Technology, 31, 33-78.

Spring Framework. http://www.springframework.org/about/, 02.02.2007

Spur, G., Mertins, K., & Jochem, R. (1996). *Integrated Enterprise Modelling.*Berlin: Beuth.

Srinivasan, N., Paolucci, M., & Sycara, K. (2004, 6-9). *Adding OWL-S to UDDI, implementation and throughput.* Paper presented at the First International Workshop on Semantic Web Services and Web Process Composition (SWSWPC 2004), San Diego, California, USA.

Stafford, T., Turan, A., & Raisinghani, M. (2004). International and Cross-Cultural Influences on Online Shopping Behavior. *Journal of Global Information Technology Management, 7*(2), 70-87.

Stanton, J. M. & Weiss, E. M. (2000). Electronic Monitoring in their Own Words: An Exploratory Study of Employees' Experiences with New Types of Surveillance. *Computers in Human Behavior, 16*(4), 423-440.

Stedman, C. (1999, August). What's next for ERP?. *Computerworld, 33*, 48-9.

Stefani, A., & Strappavara, C. (1998). Personalizing Access to Web Wites: The SiteIF Project. In *Proceedings of HYPERTEXT'98.*

Stevenson, J. S., Bruner II, G. C., & Kumar, A. (2000). Web Page Background and Viewer Attitudes", J*ournal of Advertising Research, 20*(1/2), 29-34.

Stewart, D. W., & Pavlou, P.A. (2002). From Consumer Response to Active Consumer: Measuring the Effectiveness of Interactive Media. *Journal of the Academy Marketing Science, 30*(4), 376-396.

Stoddard, D., & Jarvenpaa, S. (1995, July). Reengineering Design Is Radical, Reengineering Change Is Not. *Harvard Business School, case* 196-037.

Stoilos, G., Stamou, G., Tzouvaras, V., Pan, J., & Horrocks, I. (2005). *The Fuzzy Description Logic f-SHIN.* Paper presented at the Proceedings of the ISWC

Workshop on Uncertainty Reasoning for the Semantic Web, Galway, Ireland.

Stojanovic, N., Maedche, A., Staab, S., Studer, R., & Sure, Y. (2001). *SEAL—A Framework for Developing Semantic Portals.* Paper presented at the First International Conference on Knowledge Capture (K-CAP 2001), Victoria, BC, Canada.

Su, Q., & Adams, C. (2005). Will B2C E-commerce developed in one culture be suitable for another culture. *Proceedings of ICEC'05*, X'ian China, August15-17, 236-243.

Subrahmanyam, K., Kraut, R., Greenfield, P. & Gross, E. (2000). The Impact of Home Computer Use on Children's Activities and Development. *The Future of Children*, 10(2), 123-144.

Sullivan, G. (2005). Integrating Business Intelligence and Financial Management. Retrieved October 30, 2005, from http://www.s-ox.com/news/detail.cfm?articleID=1197

Sun Microsystems (2005). *Guidelines Designing Enterprise Applications with the J2EE Platform*, Second Edition. Particularly: J2EE Platform Overview. http://java.sun.com/blueprints/guidelines/designing_enterprise_applications_2e/introduction/introduction3.html#1042891, 18.01.06.

Sun Microsystems (2005). *Guidelines Designing Enterprise Applications with the J2EE Platform*, Second Edition. Particularly: J2EE Platform Overview. http://java.sun.com/blueprints/guidelines/designing_enterprise_applications_2e/client-tier/client-tier.html#1089105, 18.01.06.

Sun Microsystems (2005). *Guidelines Designing Enterprise Applications with the J2EE Platform*, Second Edition. Particularly: The web tier. http://java.sun.com/blueprints/guidelines/designing_enterprise_applications_2e/web-tier/web-tier.html#1094260, 18.01.06.

Sun Microsystems (2005). *Guidelines Designing Enterprise Applications with the J2EE Platform*, Second Edition. Particularly: J2EE Platform Overview. http://java.sun.com/blueprints/guidelines/designing_enterprise_applications_2e/ejb-tier/ejb-tier.html#1055251, 18.01.06.

Sun Microsystems (2005). *Core J2EE Pattern Catalog.* Core J2EE Patterns—Data Access Object. http://java.sun.com/blueprints/corej2eepatterns/Patterns/DataAccessObject.html, 19.01.06.

Swanson, D.R. (1986). Subjective versus objective relevance in bibliographic retrieval systems. Library Quarterly 56(4), 389-398

Sycara, K., J. Lu, M. K., & Widoff, S. (1999). Dynamic service matchmaking among agents in open information environments. *ACM SIGMOD Record (Special Issue on Semantic Interoperability in Global Information Systems),, 28*(No.1), 47-53

Sycara, K., J. Lu, M. K., & Widoff, S. (1999). *Matchmaking among heterogeneous agents on the internet.* Paper presented at the AAAI Spring Symposium on Intelligent Agents in Cyberspace.

Sycara, K., Widoff, S., & M. Klusch, J. L. (2002). *LARKS: Dynamic Matchmaking Among Heterogeneous Software Agents in Cyberspace.* Paper presented at the Autonomous Agents and Multi- Agent Systems.

Systematic (1999). *Intellectual Capital Report 1999.*

Systematic (2000). *Intellectual Capital Report 2000.*

Szekely, G. & Satava, R. (1999). Virtual Reality in Medicine. *British Medical Journal*, 319, 1305-1308.

Tamma, V. A. M., Aart, C., Moyaux, T., Paurobally, S., Lithgow-Smith, B., & Wooldridge, M. (2005). An ontological framework for dynamic coordination. *Proc. 4th International Semantic Web Conference'05, LNCS, 3729,* 638-652.

Tan, P., Madnick, S. E., & Tan, K.-L. (2004). *Context Mediation in the Semantic Web: Handling OWL Ontology and Data Disparity through Context Interchange* (MIT Sloan Working Paper No. 4496-04; CISL Working Paper No. 2004-13).

Tan, Z. and Wu, O. (2002). Globalization and e-commerce: factors affecting e-commerce diffusion in China, *Communications of the AIS, 10,* 4-32.

Tavani, H. T. (1999). Internet Privacy: Some Distinctions between Internet Specific and Internet-Enhanced Privacy Concerns. *The ETHICOMP E-Journal, 1.*

Tavani, H. T. (2004). *Ethics and Technology: Ethical Issues in an Age of Information and Communication Technology.* New Jersey: John Wiley and Sons, Wiley International Edition.

Teece, D. J. (1980). Economies of scope and the scope of the enterprise. *Journal of Economic Behaviour and Organization, 1,* 223-247.

Teece, D. J. (1982). Towards an economic theory of the multiproduct firm. *Journal of Economic Behaviour and Organization, 3,* 39-63.

Tennant, R. (2001, April). Building Agile Organizations. *Library Journal, 126,* 30.

Terveen, L. G. & Hill, W. (2001). Beyond Recommender Systems: Helping people help each other. In Carroll, J. (ed.), *HCI in the New Millennium*. Addison Wesley.

Terziyan V. (2003). Semantic Web Services for Smart Devices in a "Global Understanding Environment", In: *On the Move to Meaningful Internet Systems 2003: OTM 2003 Workshops, LNCS, 2889*, Springer-Verlag, (pp.279-291).

Terziyan V. (2005). Semantic Web Services for Smart Devices Based on Mobile Agents. *International Journal of Intelligent Information Technologies, 1(2)*, 43-55, Idea Group.

Thaden, U., Siberski, W., & Nejdl, W. (2003). *A Semantic Web based Peer-to-Peer Service Registry Network* (Technical Report): Learning Lab Lower Saxony.

Tornatzky, L. G., Eveland, J. D., Boylan, M. G., Hetzner, W. A., Johnson, E. C., Roitman, D., &Schneider, J. (1983). The spread of technology and Government policy and innovation. *The Process of Technological Innovation: Reviewing the Literature, National Science Foundation*, Washington, (pp. 155-216).

Torre I. (2001). Goals, tasks and Application domains as the guidelines for defining a framework for User modelling. In *User Modelling 2001, LNCS*, Springer Verlag, (pp. 260-262).

Trafimow, D., & Fishbein, M. (1994). The importance of risk in determining the extent to which attitudes affect intentions to wear seat belts. *Journal of Applied Social Psychology, 24*, 1-11.

Trafimow, D., Fishbein, M. (1995). Do people really distinguish between behavioural and normative beliefs? *British Journal of Social Psychology, 34*, 257-266.

Trastour, D., Bartolini, C., & Gonzalez-Castillo, J. (2001). *A Semantic Web Approach to Service Description for Matchmaking of Service*. Paper presented at the 1st Semantic Web Working Symposium, CA.

Turban, E., Leidner, D., McClean, E., & Wetherbe, J. (2006). *Information Technology for Management—Transforming Organisations in the Digital Economy*. USA: John Wiley & Sons Inc, 5th Edition.

Ulrich, D. (1991). Using human resources for competitive advantage. In R. Kilmann & Associates (Eds.), *Making Organizations Competitive*. San Francisco: Jossey-Bass. (pp. 129-155).

Ulrich, D., & Lake, D. (1991). Organizational capability: Creating competitive advantage. *Academy of Management Executive, 5(1)*, 77-92.

UNCTAD (2002). *Report on China*.

Unknown. (2002). Comp.realtime: Frequently Asked Questions (FAQs) 3.6. Retrieved 1/1/03, 2002, from http://www.faqs.org/faqs/realtime-computing/faq/

Vakkari, P. & Hakala, N. (2000). Changes in Relevance Criteria and Problem Stages in Task Performance. Journal of Documentation, 56(5), 540-562.

Van der Lee, J., & Zweene, G. J. (2002). Email and Internet Monitoring at Work. *MTA* January/February, 36-37.

Van Ginneken, A. M. (2002) 'the computerized patient record: balancing effort and benefit' International Journal of Medical Informatics, vol. 65, pp. 97-119.

VanRijsbergen, C.J., (1979). Information Retrieval. Butterworth-Heinemann. Newton, MA, USA.

Varelas, G., Voutsakis, E., Raftopoulou, P., Petrakis, E. G., & Milios, E. E. (2005). Semantic similarity methods in WordNet and their application to information retrieval on the web. In Proceedings of the 7th Annual ACM international Workshop on Web information and Data Management—WIDM '05, 10-16.

Vasilash, G. S. (2001). Dedicated Automation to Give Way to Agility. *Automotive Manufacturing and Production, 113*(2), 56-59.

Vastag, G., Kasarda, J. D., & Boone, T. (1994). Logistical Support for Manufacturing Agility in Global Markets. *International Journal of Operations and Production Management, 14*(11), 73-83.

Vázquez-Salceda, J., Dignum, V., & Dignum, F. (2005). Organizing multiagent systems. *Autonomous Agents and Multi-Agent Systems 11*(3), 307-360.

Vernadat, F. B. (1999). Research Agenda for Agile Manufacturing. *International Journal of Agile Management Systems, 1*(1), 37-40.

Vokurka, R. J., & Fliedner, G. (1997). Agility: Competitive Weapon of the 1990s and Beyond? *Production and Inventory Management Journal, 38*(3), 19-24.

Vokurka, R. J., & Fliedner, G. (1998). The Journey Towards Agility. *Industrial Management + Data Systems, 98*(4), 165-171.

Vokurka, R. J., Zank, G. M., & III, C. M. L. (2002). Improving Competitiveness Through Supply Chain Management: A Cumulative Improvement Approach. *Competitiveness Review, 12*(1), 14-25.

Voss, B. (1994). A New Spring for Manufacturing. *Journal of Business Strategy, 15*(1), 54-59.

W3C. (2004). OWL Web Ontology Language Overview. W3C Recommendation. Retrieved April 1, 2005, from http://www.w3.org/TR/2004/REC-owl-features-20040210/

W3C. (2004). Resource Description Framework (RDF): Concepts and Abstract Syntax. W3C Recommendation. Retrieved April 1, 2005, from http://www.w3.org/TR/2004/REC-rdf-concepts-20040210/

Walsh, A. E. (2002). *UDDI, SOAP, and WSDL: The Web Services Specification Reference Book* (1st edition ed.) 0130857262: Pearson Education.

Walsh, J. P., & Ungson, G. R. (1991). Organizational memory. *Academy of Management Review, 16*, 57-91.

Wang, J., Hongwei, D. (2005) 'Setting up a Wireless Local Area Network (WLAN) for a healthcare system', Int. J. Electronic Healthcare Vol. 1, No. 3 pp. 335-348.

Warren, S., & Brandeis, L. D. (1860). The Right to Privacy. *Harvard Law Review, 4*(193).

Weber, G., & Brusilovsky, P. (2001). ELM-ART: An adaptive versatile system for Web-based instruction. In *Proceedings of the International Journal of Artificial Intelligence in Education, 12*(4). Special Issue on Adaptive and Intelligent Web-based Educational Systems, S. 351-384, available at http://www.sis.pitt.edu/~peterb/papers/JAIEDFinal.pdf, 2001.

Wege, C. (2002). Portal Server Technology. *IEEE Internet Computing, 6*(3), 73-77.

Weibel, S., Kunze, J., Lagoze, C., & Wolf, M. (1998). *Dublin Core Metadata for Resource Discovery.* Number 2413 in IETF. The Internet Society, September.

Weick, K. E. (1979). *The Social Psycology of Organizing.* Reading, MA: Addison-Wesley.

Weiss, D., Marmar, C., Fairbank, J., Schlenger, W., Kulka, R., Hough, R. & Jordan, B. (1992). The Prevalence of Lifetime and Partial Post-Traumatic Stress Disorder in Vietnam Veterans. *Journal of Traumatic Stress*, 5, 365-376.

Weiss, R., Vélez, B., & Sheldon, M. A. (1996). HyPursuit: a hierarchical network search engine that exploits content-link hypertext clustering. In Proceedings of the the Seventh ACM Conference on Hypertext, 180-193.

Wen, H. J., Schwieger, D., & Gershuny, P. (2007). Internet Usage Monitoring in the Workplace: Its Legal Challenges and Implementation Strategies. *Information Systems Management, 24*, 185-196.

Wernerfelt, B. (1984). A resource based view of the firm. *Strategic Management Journal, 5*, 171-180.

Westin, A. (1967). *Privacy and Freedom.* New York: Ateneum.

White, J. W. (2002). *Making ERP Work the Way Your Business Works.* Addison, TX: Fuego.

White, R.W., Ruthven, I. & Jose, J.M. (2002). The use of implicit evidence for relevance feedback in web retrieval. In Proceedings of 24th BCS-IRSG European Colloquium on IR Research. Lecture notes in Computer Science 2291, 93-109.

Wickramasinghe, N., Misra, S.K. (2004) 'A wireless trust model for healthcare', Int. J. Electronic Healthcare, Vol. 1, No. 1, pp.60–77.

Wijnia, E. (2005). *Understanding Weblogs: a Communicative Perspective.* Retrieved on April 10th, 2005, from http://elmine.wijnia.com/weblog/

Wiki (2005). *Statistical classification.* http://en.wikipedia.org/wiki/Statistical_classification. 05.01.2005.

Williamson, O. E. (1975). *Markets and Hierarchies.* New York: Free Press.

Wolfe, R. A. (1994). Organizational innovation: Review, critique and suggested research directions. *Journal of Management Studies, 31*(3), 405-31.

Wong, X., Yen, D., & Fang, X. (2004). E-Commerce Development in China and its Implication for Business. *Asian Pacific Journal of Marketing and Logistics, 16*, 3, 68-83.

Woodfield, A. (1995). The Conservation of Endangered Languages. CTLL Seminar of University of Bristol.

Wooldridge, M. (1997). Agent-based software engineering. *IEE Proceedings of Software Engineering, 144*(1), 26-37.

Wooldridge, M., Jennings, N. R., & Kinny, D. (2000). The Gaia Methodology for Agent-Oriented Analysis and Design. *Autonomous Agents and Multi-Agent Systems, 3*(3), 285-312.

Wu, H., Jin, H., Li, Y., & Chen, H. (2005). *An Approach for Service Discovery Based on Semantic Peer-to-Peer.* Paper presented at the Advances in Computer Science—ASIAN 2005: 10th Asian Computing Science Conference, Kunming, China.

Xing, F. (1995). The Chinese Cultural System, in *SAM Advanced Management Journal, 60*(1), 14-20.

Yan, T., & Garcia-Molina, H. (1995). SIFT—A tool for wide-area information dissemination. Proceedings of USENIX Winter 1995 Technical Conference, 177-186

Yang, C. F. (1989). A Conception of Chinese Consumer Behavior, in Hong Kong Marketing Management at the Cross-Roads, Hong Kong: Commercial Press. (pp. 317-342).

Yau, O. H. (1988). Chinese culture values: Their dimensions and marketing implications. *Journal of Marketing, 22*, 44-57.

Yin, R. K. (1994). *Case Study Research*. Thousand Oaks, California, USA: Sage Publications.

Yoffie, D. B., & Kwak, M. (2001). Mastering Strategic Movement at Palm. *Sloan Management Review, 43*(1), 55-63.

Yu, S., Liu, J., & Le, J. (2004a). *Decentralized Web Service Organization Combining Semantic Web and Peer to Peer Computing*. Paper presented at the Web Services: European Conference, ECOWS 2004, Erfurt, Germany.

Yu, S., Liu, J., & Le, J. (2004b). *Intelligent Web Service Discovery in Large Distributed System*. Paper presented at the Intelligent Data Engineering and Automated Learning—IDEAL 2004, Exeter, UK.

Yunos, H. M., Gao, J. Z., Shim S. (2003). Wireless Advertising's Challenges and Opportunities. *IEEE Computer Society, 36*(5), 30-37.

Yusuf, Y. Y., Sarahadi, M., & Gunasekaran, A. (1999). Agile Manufacturing: The Drivers, Concepts, and Attributes. *International Journal of Production Economics, 62*(1, 2), 33-43.

Zamora, E., Pollock, J., & al, e. (1981). The Use of Trigram Analysis for Spelling Error Detection. *Information Processing and Management, 6*(17), 305-316

Zhang, C., Chai, J. Y., & Jin, R. (2005). User term feedback in interactive text-based image retrieval. In Proceedings of the 28th Annual international ACM SIGIR Conference on Research and Development in information Retrieval, 51-58.

Zhou, C., Chia, L.-T., & Lee, B.-S. (2005a). Semantics in Service Discovery and QoS Measurement. *IEEE IT Professional Magazine, 7*(2), 29-34

Zhou, C., Chia, L.-T., & Lee, B.-S. (2005b). Web Services Discovery with DAML-QoS Ontology. *International Journal of Web Services Research(JWSR), 2*(2), 44-67

Zinky, J. A., Bakken, D. E., & Schantz, R. E. (1997). Architectural Support for Quality of Service for CORBA Objects. *Theory and Practice of Object Systems, 3*(1).

About the Contributors

Miltiadis D. Lytras is an assistant professor in the Computer Engineering and Informatics Department-CEID (University of Patras). His research focuses on Semantic Web, knowledge management and e-learning, with more than 100 publications in these areas. He has co-edited / co-edits, 25 special issues in international journals (e.g. *IEEE Transaction on Knowledge and Data Engineering, IEEE Internet Computing, IEEE Transactions on Education, Computers in Human Behaviour,* etc.) and has authored/[co-]edited 12 books [e.g. *Open Source for Knowledge and Learning management, Ubiquitous and Pervasive Knowledge Management, Intelligent Learning Infrastructures for Knowledge Intensive Organizations, Semantic Based Information Systems*]. He is the founder and officer of the Semantic Web and Information Systems Special Interest Group in the Association for Information Systems (http://www.sigsemis.org). He serves as the (Co) Editor in Chief of 12 international journals [e.g. *International Journal of Knowledge and Learning, International Journal of Technology Enhanced Learning, International Journal on Social and Humanistic Computing, International Journal on Semantic Web and Information Systems, International Journal on Digital Culture and Electronic Tourism, International Journal of Electronic Democracy, International Journal of Electronic Banking, International Journal of Electronic Trade*] while he is associate editor or editorial board member in seven more.

Patricia Ordóñez de Pablos is professor in the Department of Business Administration and Accountability, at the Faculty of Economics of The University of Oviedo (Spain). Her teaching and research interests focus on the areas of strategic management, knowledge management, intellectual capital measuring and reporting, organizational learning and human resources management. She is *Executive Editor of the International Journal of Learning and Intellectual, the International Journal of Strategic Change Management* and Co-Executive Editor of *International Journal of Chinese Culture and Management.*

***

Edward T. Chen is a professor of management information systems in the management department at University of Massachusetts Lowell. Dr. Chen has published his research articles in scholarly journals such as *Information & Management, Journal of Computer Information Systems, Project Management, Comparative Technology Transfer and Society, Journal of International Technology and Information Management,* and *International Journal of Innovation and Learning.* Dr. Chen has been serving as vice-president, journal editor, board director, editorial reviewer, track chair, and session chair of many professional associations. Professor Chen has received the Irwin Distinguished Paper Award at the

Southwestern Federation of Administrative Disciplines conference and the Best Paper Award at the International Conference on Accounting and Information Technology.

Regina Connolly is a senior lecturer in management information systems at Dublin City University Business School, Dublin, Ireland and is programme director of the MSC in electronic commerce. In her undergraduate degree she received the Kellogg Award for outstanding dissertation and her MSc degree was awarded with distinction. She was conferred with a PhD in information systems from Trinity College Dublin. Her research interests include electronic commerce, online trust and privacy issues, website service quality, e-government, and strategic information systems. She has served on the expert eCommerce advisory group for Dublin Chamber of Commerce, which has advised national government on eCommerce strategic planning.

Javier De Andrés is an associate professor at the University of Oviedo (Spain). He is also the vice-dean of the Technical Computing School at the same University. He received his PhD in economics in 1998. He has published more than 40 chapters in books and papers in refereed scientific journals such as the *European Journal of Operational Research*, the *Journal of the Royal Statistical Society* (Series C- Applied Statistics), the *International Journal of Technology Management*, and the *International Journal of Digital Accounting Research*, among others. He has received several research grants and research awards.

Jorge Marx Gómez studied computer engineering and industrial engineering at the University of Applied Sciences Berlin (Technische Fachhochschule Berlin). He was a lecturer and researcher at the Otto-von-Guericke-Universität Magdeburg (Germany) where he also obtained a PhD degree in business information systems with the work *Computer-based Approaches to Forecast Returns of Scrapped Products to Recycling*. In 2004 he received his habilitation for the work *Automated Environmental Reporting through Material Flow Networks* at the Otto-von-Guericke-Universität Magdeburg. From 2002 till 2003 he was a visiting professor for business informatics at the Technical University of Clausthal (Germany). In 2005 he became a full professor and chair of business information systems at the Carl von Ossietzky University Oldenburg (Germany). His research interests include very large business applications, business information systems, federated ERP-systems, business intelligence, data warehousing, interoperability and environmental management information systems.

Seppo J. Hänninen is researcher at Helsinki University of Technology Department of Industrial Engineering and Management. He holds a Doctor of Science in technology degree from Helsinki University of Technology with distinction. His research and teaching activities focus on the areas of new product development, commercializing technological inventions, micro-strategy management, entrepreneurship, and networks. He cooperates with several Finnish firms that develop innovations in technology programs. Before joining the research team at Helsinki University of Technology, he worked eight years in the advertising industry and ten years as an entrepreneur in international business. He has extensive teaching experience at the University of Applied Sciences Hame Polytechnic.

Jeffrey Hsu is an associate professor of information systems at the Silberman College of Business, Fairleigh Dickinson University. He is the author of numerous papers, chapters, and books, and has previous business and IT experience in the software, telecommunications, and financial industries. His research interests include e-commerce, global IT management, human-computer interaction, IS education, and business intelligence. Dr. Hsu also serves on the editorial boards of several journals, and has worked on global education, distance learning, and curriculum development initiatives. Professor Hsu received his PhD in information systems from Rutgers University.

Micki Hyde is an associate professor of MIS in the MISDS Department at Indiana University of Pennsylvania, USA. Her PhD is in MIS from Southern Illinois University, USA; MBA from Middle Tennessee State University in Murfreesboro, Tennessee; and her Bachelor of business administration in marketing was earned at the University of Georgia in Athens, Georgia. Her research areas include the development of information systems, the success of information systems, and mobile computing.

Jaakko Ikävalko is Researcher at Helsinki University of Technology. He holds a master of science in economics degree from Helsinki School of Economics. He has research interests in product innovation, entrepreneurship, research networks, and information society.

Artem Katasonov received his BSc degree in 1999 and then his engineer degree in 2000 from Kharkov National University of Radio Electronics, Ukraine. Then, he received his MSc degree in 2001 and finally his PhD degree in 2006 from the University of Jyväskylä, Finland. Currently, he is working as a researcher in the UBIWARE project while teaching several courses as an assistant professor at mathematical information technology department of the University of Jyväskylä. His research interests are in various aspects of software engineering with present focus on agent-oriented software engineering and semantic technologies.

Ilkka Kauranen is visiting professor at the School of Management in the Asian Institute of Technology which is an international university. He has professorship in development and management in industry at Helsinki University of Technology Department of Industrial Engineering and Management. His research and teaching activities focus on the areas of technology-based companies, commercializing technological inventions, research & development management, entrepreneurship, and regional development. In addition to his academic career, Professor Kauranen has vast experience in the top management of companies. He has been a board member in several publicly traded companies and entrepreneurial private companies. He has been a founder of several knowledge-intensive companies. He has worked as a full-time management consultant, acting as the president and one of the senior partners in the company.

Jose Emilio Labra obtained his PhD in computer engineering at the University of Oviedo in 2001. He has been the dean of the School of Computer Science Engineering of Oviedo since 2004. His research interests are Semantic Web technologies and programming languages.

Sylvie Laforet is a lecturer in marketing at The University of Sheffield. She has researched and published in the areas of branding for more than a decade. She has also worked on funded projects in innovation and entrepreneurship and has published in this area. Her other interests include technology-based services and wireless advertising. She has authored over 30 publications and has published in international journals. She has refereed journal articles, books, grants applications, has examined PhD theses and has given talks on a number of issues in branding, packaging and consumer behavior at practitioners' conferences. She is a member of Academy of Marketing Science, British Academy of Management and Institute for Small Business & Entrepreneurship. She has taught marketing at undergraduate, postgraduate levels and has supervised at PhD level.

Hannah Limahelu graduated from the University of Sheffield, Management School with an MA in management in 2005.

Pedro Lorca is an associate professor of accounting and finance at the University of Oviedo (Spain). He received his PhD (2000) in business administration. His research interests include enterprise resource planning and technology management. Dr. Lorca has published over 50 articles in journals and refereed proceedings, that include *International Journal of Management, European Journal of Operational Research, Journal of the Royal Statistical Society* (Series C – Applied Statistics), *International Journal of Digital Accounting Research, International Journal of Technology Management* and *Spanish Journal of Finance and Accounting*. He has received several research awards from economics institutions.

Cliona McParland is currently a PhD student at Dublin City University Business School under the supervision of Dr. Regina Connolly, senior lecturer in management information systems. Her PhD is in the area of technology-related privacy concerns with a particular emphasis on the analysis of dataveillance behavioural outcomes in the computer-mediated work environment. Her research interests include information privacy concerns, ecommerce, dataveillance and ecommerce risk and security management.

Pankaj is currently an Associate Professor of MIS in the MISDS department at Indiana University of Pennsylvania, USA. He holds a PhD in MIS from Southern Illinois University, USA; an MBA from Indian Institute of Management, Ahmedabad, India; and Bachelor of Technology in Computer Science & Engineering from Indian Institute of Technology, Delhi, India. His current research areas include information systems agility, IS infrastructure, IS-centric organizational transformation, and knowledge management.

Arkalgud Ramaprasad is the Associate Vice Chancellor for Academic Affairs at the University of Illinois at Chicago (UIC) and a professor in the Department of Information and Decision Sciences (IDS) in the College of Business Administration. He was the Head of IDS at UIC from 2000-2006 and the Director of the Center for Research in Information Management (CRIM) there. He was the founding director of the Pontikes Center for Management of Information from 1989-2000. His research topics include enterprise eHealth strategy, digital divide in eHealth applications, managing medical knowledge using the internet, patient-physician relationship in the information age, knowledge supply networks, and knowledge management. He has a PhD from the University of Pittsburgh, USA; MBA from the Indian Institute of Management, Ahmedabad, India, 1972; and BE (Electrical), from the University of Mysore, Karnataka, India, 1970.

Ari Serkkola is senior reseacher at Helsinki University of Technology, Lahti Center. He is docent at Turku School of Economics. He has research interests in health and well-being informatics, environmental informatics, information society, and innovation studies. He cooperates with Finnish ICT firms that develop service innovations. Furthermore, Dr Serkkola evaluates Finnish technology and well-being projects and EU development programs.

S. C. Sharma started his career as R & D engineer in 1983 then joined teaching profession in Jan. 1984 in IIT-Roorkee and continuing till date. He has published over eighty research chapters in national and international journals/conferences. He has supervised several PhD in the area of computer networking, wireless networks and continuing supervising PhD in the same area. He has worked as research scientist at FMH, Munchen, Germany in the year 1999. He is the active reviewer of *IEEE Sensor Journal* and chief editor of two reputed international journals. He is the senior member of IEEE, honorary member of NSBE, ISOC, IAENG, (USA). He has also worked as Group leader of Electronics & Instrumentation Engg. Department of BITS-Pilani-Dubai Campus, from Aug. 2003 to Aug. 2005.

Suresh K. Tadisina is currently the associate dean of the College of Business at Southern Illinois University at Carbondale. Suresh holds a BE (Mech.) and an MBA from Osmania University in India and an MBA and PhD in quantitative analysis and operations management from the University of Cincinnati, USA. His current research interests include service operations management, supply chain management, IS agility, decision support/expert systems, and management of technology. His publications have appeared in journals such as *Annals of Operations Research, Computers and Operations Research, Decision Support Systems, European Journal of Operations Research, IIE Transactions, Information and Management, Interfaces, Journal of the Operational Research Society, OMEGA,* and *Project Management Journal,* among others.

Vagan Terziyan received his Engineer-Mathematician Degree from Kharkov National University of Radio Electronics, Ukraine, in 1981. From the same university he received his PhD degree in 1985 and then his Dr. Habil Tech. degree in 1993 along with the title of professor in software engineering. Currently, he is acting as professor (distributed systems) in mathematical information technology department of the University of Jyväskylä, Finland. He is the head of Industrial Ontologies Group and has been the leader of the SmartResource and UBIWARE projects. His research and teaching profile is design of distributed, intelligent Web applications, systems and services, which are: (a) able to automatically discover, compose and integrate heterogeneous components; (b) able to manage heterogeneous data sources; and (c) utilizing for that emerging knowledge-, agent-, machine-learning-, context-aware- and Semantic Web- based technologies and tools.

Duc Thanh Tran studied business informatics and business at Otto-von-Guericke-University of Magdeburg. He is now a member of the research group Knowledge Management within the Institute of Applied Informatics and Formal Description Methods (AIFB) at Karlsruhe University (Germany). His research interests include information retrieval, ontology engineering, knowledge representation and reasoning, ontology-based knowledge management systems, Semantic Web infrastructure and software engineering.

Sandip Vijay is the Member of IEEE, LMISTE, Member of NSBE, ISOC Society and MIAENG (USA). He has more than thirty five international and national journal and proceedings publication in field of wireless communication and networks. He has more than nine years of experience in field of teaching and research. He has supervised twelve M.Tech dissertations. Currently he is pursuing research work in wireless ad hoc network at I.I.T., Roorkee under Ministry of HRD, Government of India fellowship. He is the active reviewer of *IEEE Sensor Journal.*

Giovanni Vincenti is in charge of research and development at Gruppo Vincenti, a family-owned company with interests across several fields. His main areas of research include fuzzy mediation, information fusion, emotionally-aware agent frameworks and robotics. He held several positions at Towson University, including a lecturership with the Department of Computer and Information Sciences. He also taught courses for the Center of Applied Information Technology, also at Towson University. He is the author of many publications, and the father of the concept of fuzzy mediation, as applied to the field of information fusion. He received his Doctorate of Science in applied information technology from Towson University in August 2007.

Index

A

activity modeling 232
ad-hoc networks 115
ad-hoc networks, wireless 115–135
adaptation approaches 137
adaptation approaches, a survey on 136–152
advertising, attitudes toward 166–179
agile information systems 30
agility 23, 42–54
agility, conceptualization of 27
application-level gateway 121
arachnophobia 225
authentication 119
automated monitoring 56

B

Bonfield, Peter 20
Buddhism 93
business process re-engineering (BPR) 105

C

cash on delivery (COD) 96
China, and e-commerce 88–101
China, and Internet users 89
Chinese, e-commerce targeting of the 88–101
Chinese philosophy 93
Chinese Web and regional issues 97
Chinese Web design 92
Chinese Web design, culture and 92
Chinese Web sites 96
Chinese Web usage 94
classification 140

C (continued, right column)

collaborative filtering 137
commercialization 203
communication integrity 119
competitive advantage 3
compulsory technological capital 10
computer supported co-operative work (CSCW) 236
confidentiality 119
Confucianism 93
content-based filtering 137
cosine similarity 140
culture 90
Cuypers engine 139

D

dataveillance 215
DECOR project 236
denial-of-service (DoS) attack 116
diffusion of innovation (DOI) 182
distribution automation 74
dominant agility framework 23
dot-com bubble 211
dynamic semantic network 272

E

e-commerce, and culture 90
e-commerce, and trust 95
electronic medical database system 284
elementary abstract concept (EAC) 138
ERP (enterprise resource planning) system 102–114
ERP, advantages of 104
ERP, and return on investment (ROI) 105

ERP, disadvantages of 104
ERP, history of 103
ERP, total cost of ownership (TCO) and 108
ERP market, vendors and 107
ERP system implementation, reasons to implement 182
ERP systems, Spanish companies and 180–197
ERP vendors 105
ethno-scapes 93
European Union (EU), and privacy concerns 216
extensible authentication protocol (EAP) 119
eXtreme Programming (XP) 21

F

fear 223
fear of flying, and virtual environments 221–230
femininity vs. masculinity 91
fetching 276
filtering 137
finanscapes 93
FLIR systems 110
FoxMeyer Drugs 109
fuzzy logic, and discovery 259

G

gateway 118
gateway, application-level 121
gateway, generic 121
gateway architecture 125
gateway solutions 118
gateway specification requirements 125–126
generic gateway 121
global culture flow, five dimensions of 93
guanxi 95
GUN (global understanding environment) 55–87
GUN, and automation 66
GUN, basic 65–66
GUN, general adaptation framework (GAF) 66
GUN, general networking framework (GNF) 67
GUN, general proactivity framework (GPF) 66
GUN, integration and 66
GUN, interoperability and 66

H

Hera specification framework 141
Hofstede, Geert 91
human-computer interaction (HCI) 222
human capital 7
hypermedia system 136

I

ideo-scapes 93
idiosyncratic technological capital 10
individualism vs. collectivism 91
Infor 108
information systems (IS) agility 19–54
institutionalization 6
intellectual capital 8
intellectual capital report 15
intelligent tutoring 136
Internet of Things 55
Internet of Things, and semantic technologies 58
intuiting, interpreting, integrating, & institutionalizing (4I) framework 5
isolation mechanisms 4

K

knowledge stance 234
knowledge stocks 7
knowledge work 231
knowledge work, modeling of 232

L

Lawson 108
Lehigh University 23
long vs. short term orientation (LTO) 91

M

macro economic cluster analyses 199
mean squared differences 140
mediascapes 93
Microsoft Dynamics 107
mining 276
mobile advertising, and British consumers 165–179
mobile advertising, and consumer belief 171
mobile Internet 169

mobile Internet, and consumer adoption 170
multi-agent system (MAS) 63

O

offshore outsourcing 21
offsourcing 21
Oracle 107
organizational innovativeness (OI) 182
organizational learning 3
organizational learning, a framework 4

P

paper based records 283
patient information system 282–296
Peoplesoft 107
personal digital assistants (PDAs) 282
personalized portal 153–164
personal reader 141
portal implementation 153
Post-Traumatic Stress Disorders (PTSD) 226
power-distance (PD) 91
presentation description (PD) 138
presentation unit (PU) 138
privacy 208–220
privacy, and changing patterns 211
privacy legislation 216
proactive computing 58
process modeling 232

Q

QAD 108

R

relational capital 7
relevance information 271
resource based view (RBV), of a firm 2
reusable atomic behavior (RAB) 72

S

search engines 276
security 291
self-managed computing system 56
Semantic Agent Programming Language (S-APL) 65
semantic gadgets 59

semantic spaces 59
Singapore 98
single-model adaptation 137
smart devices 58
SmartResource project 66
SOCKS 121
statistical matching 139
strategic learning assessment map (SLAM) 5
structural capital 8
syntactic-semantic metric 274

T

Taoism 93
Tata Refractories, India 109
techno-scapes 93
technological capital, in companies 9
technological capital, measuring & reporting 1–18
technological capital matrix 9
technology-related privacy concerns 208–220
technology awareness 180
technology programs 199
telecommunications 200
third generation (3G) device 121
third generation (3G) radio link 121

U

UBIWARE 55, 58
uncertainty avoidance (UA) 91
Universal Description, Discovery and Integration (UDDI) 254
user 270
user relevance feedback 270–281

V

virtual environment, and clinical settings 224
virtual environment, and the fear of flying 221–230
virtual reality 222

W

Web advertising, attitudes toward 166–179
Web retrieval system 276
Web service description languages 256

Web service discovery systems, a survey of
    254–269
Web service model 258
wireless advertising, attitudes toward 167
WLANs (wireless local area networks)
    116, 283
WLAN technology 117
WordNet 272
workplace surveillance 212
workplace surveillance, and productivity 213

Y

Y2K 180

Z

Zhong Guo 92